Political Science Research in the Middle East and North Africa

Political Science Research
in the Middle East
and North Africa

Methodological and Ethical Challenges

EDITED BY JANINE A. CLARK
and
FRANCESCO CAVATORTA

OXFORD
UNIVERSITY PRESS

OXFORD
UNIVERSITY PRESS

Oxford University Press is a department of the University of Oxford. It furthers
the University's objective of excellence in research, scholarship, and education
by publishing worldwide. Oxford is a registered trade mark of Oxford University
Press in the UK and certain other countries.

Published in the United States of America by Oxford University Press
198 Madison Avenue, New York, NY 10016, United States of America.

CIP data is on file at the Library of Congress
ISBN 978–0–19–088296–9 (hbk.)
ISBN 978–0–19–088297–6 (pbk.)

1 3 5 7 9 8 6 4 2

Paperback printed by WebCom, Inc., Canada
Hardback printed by Bridgeport National Bindery, Inc., United States of America

CONTENTS

ACKNOWLEDGMENTS

The idea for this book has been in our heads for some time (and to be fair it was more in Janine's head than Francesco's). In 2013 Francesco moved to Canada, and geographical proximity to Janine was helpful in thinking about this project more concretely. We have been incredibly fortunate that all the contributors to this volume seemed as excited as we were by the prospect of participating in a book project that would speak to the methodological and ethical challenges of doing research in the Middle East and North Africa. Methodological and ethical issues have been prominent in political science for decades, but we felt that genuine, practical advice was missing from the picture, particularly for students and scholars engaged in fieldwork research in a complex region. The murder of the young Italian researcher Giulio Regeni in Egypt, as well as the immense difficulties many local researchers face, convinced us of the validity and necessity of our project. While there is no pretense that this project will ensure safety and security, it offers sufficient "food for thought" on how to think about the challenges of doing research on the Middle East and North Africa.

The editorial team at Oxford University Press has been fantastic to work with from the very first day. The anonymous reviewers deserve special praise because their comments and input genuinely improved the manuscript.

CONTRIBUTORS

Mohamed-Ali Adraoui is a Marie Sklodoska Curie Fellow at Georgetown University's Edmund A. Walsh School of Foreign Service and a Visiting Fellow at Harvard University's Weatherhead Center for International Affairs, United States.

Malika Bouziane is senior key expert at the German Corporation for International Cooperation in Amman, Jordan.

Steven Brooke is an Assistant Professor in the Department of Political Science at the University of Louisville, United States.

Ray Bush is Professor of African Studies and Development Politics at the University of Leeds, United Kingdom.

Francesco Cavatorta is an Associate Professor in Political Science at Laval University, Quebec, Canada.

Benoit Challand is Associate Professor of Sociology at the New School for Social Research, United States.

Janine A. Clark is Professor of Political Science at the University of Guelph, Canada.

Emanuela Dalmasso is postdoctoral researcher in the Department of Politics, University of Amsterdam, Netherlands.

Paul Kingston is Professor of Political Science and International Development Studies and Director of the Centre for Critical Development Studies, University of Toronto Scarborough, Canada.

Geoffrey Martin is a PhD student in political science specializing in comparative politics and development at the University of Toronto, Canada.

Elizabeth Monier is a Leverhulme Early Career Fellow in Middle Eastern Studies at the University of Cambridge, United Kingdom.

Gwenn Okruhlik is an independent scholar and an expert on Saudi Arabia.

Zoltan Pall is a research fellow at the Middle East Institute at the National University of Singapore, Singapore.

Sarah E. Parkinson is the Aronson Assistant Professor of Political Science and International Studies at Johns Hopkins University, United States.

Miquel Pellicer is a Senior Researcher at the Institute of Political Science, University of Duisburg-Essen, Germany.

Massimo Ramaioli is Assistant Professor in the Social Development and Policy Program at Habib University in Karachi, Pakistan.

Paola Rivetti is Assistant Professor at the School of Law and Government at Dublin City University, Ireland.

Shirin Saeidi is an Adjunct Professor of Comparative Politics at George Mason University, United States.

Atef Said is Assistant Professor Department of Sociology, University of Illinois at Chicago, United States.

Jillian Schwedler is Professor of Political Science at Hunter College and the Graduate Centre at the City University of New York, United States.

Lihi Ben Shitrit is an Assistant Professor at the School of Public and International Affairs, University of Georgia, United States.

David Waldner is an Associate Professor in the Department of Politics, University of Virginia, United States.

Eva Wegner is Assistant Professor at the School of Politics and International Relations, University College Dublin, Ireland.

Irene Weipert-Fenner is a senior research fellow and project director at the Peace Research Institute Frankfurt, Germany.

Stacey Philbrick Yadav is an Associate Professor of Political Science at Hobart and William Smith Colleges in Geneva, New York, United States, and a member of the executive board of the American Association of Yemeni Studies.

Mohammad Yaghi is an Adjunct Professor at Queen's University in Kingston, Ontario, Canada.

Political Science Research in the Middle East and North Africa

Introduction

The Methodological and Ethical Challenges of Conducting Research in the Middle East and North Africa

JANINE A. CLARK AND FRANCESCO CAVATORTA

Students and established academics in the broad discipline of area studies devote an increasing amount of time to ensure that sound and appropriate methodologies underpin their research projects. What used to be an almost exclusive concern for researchers interested in formal modeling and quantitative research has over time filtered to subdisciplines in political studies where "fieldwork" credibility used to be what mattered most. Beginning in the mid-1990s with the work of King, Keohane, and Verba (1994), methodological rigor became a central preoccupation for all political science scholars, including the ones conducting qualitative fieldwork. Methodological training is today a central part, if not the most important one, of PhD programs in political science. In addition, ethical considerations have become a much more integral part of what political scientists do, both in terms of the self-awareness of its importance and because of growing institutional requirements, whether one is in agreement with them or not. The proliferation of textbooks, articles, and monographs on research methodology is a testimony to its relevance. Yet, while insisting on methodological rigor and reflecting on ethical issues is necessary, scholars taking to the field need to be aware that there are often significant differences between thinking about their research theoretically and how it is then translated in practice, with gray areas and unexpected challenges or opportunities affecting the process of conducting research. Despite this rather obvious chasm between theory and practice that all scholars experience in the field, there are no specific "guidebooks" on how to go about meeting the methodological and ethical challenges that fieldwork, so crucial for area studies scholars and for empirics-based knowledge more broadly, throws up. This volume begins filling this vacuum, focusing specifically on doing research in the Middle East and North Africa (MENA).

While a guidebook of this kind would be a welcome addition at any time because of the paucity of works dealing with the obstacles and opportunities that doing research in the MENA offers, post-2011 events suggest now more than ever the need for grounded advice on doing fieldwork in the region. There is no doubt that the killing of Giulio Regeni—a Cambridge University PhD candidate doing research in Egypt—in early 2016, most likely at the hands of internal security forces, has had a considerable impact on the academic community, highlighting the dangers of conducting research in the Global South, particularly when politically sensitive topics are scrutinized. What is more, the death of Regeni has brought renewed attention to the problems and ethical dilemmas that affect researchers studying the MENA, as his case is far from unique if we take into account the severe constraints under which many local researchers operate. As Atef Said points out in his chapter, since the Arab Spring, human rights activists and scholars alike have been banned from entering Egypt or put on watch lists at Egyptian airports. Using a European or an American passport to enter Egypt, furthermore, does not guarantee you protection. As he stresses, the situation is much worse with Egyptian researchers and those who live in Egypt and who work in Egyptian universities and academic institutions; these scholars must either avoid politically relevant topics or leave the country. The shifting terrain after the uprisings thus has influenced the ability of scholars to conduct research in MENA countries, some of which have descended into civil war. Sarah Parkinson in her contribution makes an important point on how researchers should behave and reflect on their research when "adjacent" to widespread violence. Other countries have witnessed a retrenchment of authoritarian practices, and others still have maintained the level of control and repression that always characterized them. Most of the contributors to this book highlight different aspects of conducting research in authoritarian settings and argue that there are profound ethical, methodological, and logistical challenges that need to be met. Only Tunisia seems to have become a more welcoming environment for academics, and it is no surprise that studies on the country have proliferated since the fall of the regime in 2011, with scholars flocking to study each and every aspect of its politics and society. Under these changed circumstances, doing research in the MENA has become more challenging, potentially more dangerous, and certainly less predictable.

In addition, it should not be forgotten that Western scholars doing fieldwork in the MENA region also have their own governments with which to contend. The securitization of numerous aspects of life in established democracies did not spare academia, and antiterror legislation such as the Patriot Act in the United States offers ethical and methodological challenges one should be aware of and reflect upon. How does one do research on the Palestinian Hamas, for instance, when this could be construed as aiding and abetting a foreign terrorist group? How does one meet with Hezbollah officials when many of the latter might be on a list of terrorist suspects? Would researchers returning from fieldwork be forced to reveal sources, contacts, or locations to the security agencies of their own countries? Does studying the Iraqi resistance make you a sympathizer in the eyes of US or British or Canadian officials? Equally important, does it make you a sympathizer in the eyes of the administration of the university or research institute to which you belong? These are just some of the questions that researchers have to contend with, as the authoritarian nature of many of the countries that we collectively study in the MENA is far from being the only obstacle we face (Parkinson 2014). While restrictions to academic freedoms in established democracies are not as severe as they are in the region, the very notion of academic freedom is also under greater scrutiny and attack. Few definitive answers can be given in regard to these crucial questions, yet scholars should begin by familiarizing themselves with legal institutions and procedures relevant to their research and by taking data protection, particularly encryption, seriously (Parkinson 2014, 26). Just as importantly, researchers must keep in mind that they cannot promise confidentiality; indeed, not asking, not recording and not photographing may be the most ethical approach to fieldwork in many cases (Parkinson 2014, 26).

Through the contributions of scholars—political scientists and other social scientists asking politically relevant questions and, importantly, using shared methods—who have conducted field research in the region and have first-hand experience of life in MENA countries, this volume offers an important guide to young academics on how to conceive and carry out their research projects. At the same time the topics in the book provide a useful refresher to more established scholars, so that their methodological training and ethical considerations keep pace with novel approaches, changing obstacles, and the institutional constraints of an increasingly neoliberal third-level education.

What sets this volume apart from all others thus is its focus on the methodological "lessons learned" from the contributors' firsthand experiences. Each chapter deals with the challenges of implementing qualitative and quantitative methods in the field, the real-life obstacles encountered, and the possible solutions to overcoming them. While some of the chapters focus on specific countries because of their almost unique set of challenges—Iran, Saudi Arabia, and Israel/Palestine—the volume is not meant to cover countries per se. Rather, it is the themes that are more significant; the country from which the experiences are drawn is, to an extent, incidental. This should not suggest that the country context is irrelevant and that doing research in Jordan rather than Egypt amounts to the same experience, as this is patently not the case. The book, however, deals with crosscutting challenges and opportunities that can then be declined differently according to both time and space. This volume is an important companion book to more standard methods books, which focus on the "how to" of methods but are often devoid of any real discussion of the practicalities, challenges, and common mistakes of fieldwork. The "field" rarely offers ideal conditions for implementing field research techniques, and standard textbooks do not talk about the challenges of working under the possible, if not probable, surveillance of internal security, the various challenges related to gender, or the ethical gray zones not covered by research ethical protocols.

In sharing their lessons learned, the contributors raise issues of concern to all researchers, particularly those of the Global South but also to those researching the Global North. While the MENA may be considered by some as having "extreme" research conditions—ranging from the authoritarian nature of regimes and the sensitivity of political and socioeconomic issues, to the reliability of data and cultural norms and expectations—the contributors in this volume have faced challenges present elsewhere, albeit perhaps in subtler forms. Indeed, collectively, the chapters in this volume help debunk the notion of Middle Eastern exceptionalism. In recent decades, the region has featured prominently in numerous and often interrelated debates regarding issues of governance, political culture, and civil and transnational conflicts. Political science research in particular has witnessed an impressive growth over the last two decades, as the region's political prominence has risen. Despite the considerable output, political science studies on the region struggle to make an impact on policymaking, on the public debate, and, more problematically, on the wider comparative politics academic field. In part, the region has always been treated as exceptional in comparative politics, generating limited linkages to what we know about how politics, broadly understood, works in other contexts.

The methodological challenges political scientists face in studying the MENA play an important role in contributing to this ongoing exclusion. Yet despite the challenges and, in some countries, the presumed uniqueness of "the field," the contributors to this volume do not, on the whole, subscribe to the notion that fieldwork in the region is somehow unique. When discussing their experiences conducting fieldwork in the Islamic Republic of Iran, Paola Rivetti and Shirin Saeidi, for example, note the difficulty in identifying any obstacle to research that is peculiar to it. As they state in their contribution, the difficulties they faced characterize research in Europe as well. Although religious rules to a certain extent constrain a researcher's behavior, namely in terms of veiling, the practicalities of fieldwork remain the same. Other contributors share this point regarding the limited exceptionalism the MENA region presents despite the clearly heightened political tensions that characterize the region. Ray Bush, for instance, notes that the challenges faced in doing fieldwork in rural communities in Egypt are far from unique and can be compared to the ones with which other researchers in the Global South covering rural communities contend. Emanuela Dalmasso argues similarly that issues of sexism are not confined to the MENA. Zoltan Pall and Mohamed Ali Adraoui suggest in their chapter on interviewing Salafis that the obstacles and opportunities in conducting research on Salafi movement are quite similar in the Middle East and Europe.

Researchers of the MENA, the Global South, and the Global North thus share more issues—many of which are the basic practicalities of fieldwork—than those that divide them. Perhaps most common is the universal need, as respectively noted by Janine A. Clark and Paul Kingston as well as other contributors, to forge a rapport based on trust at the beginning and throughout interviews with participants. As

Gwenn Okruhlik relates in reference to her research experiences in Saudi Arabia, she learned early on in her career that her ability to build personal relationships of trust based on her demeanor and character are far more important to her fieldwork than her professional accomplishments or degrees. While issues of trust may be more crucial in an authoritarian setting where interviewees may fear repercussions for facilitating a foreign academic's research, they remain necessary in all interviewing conditions. In a similar vein, Clark and Okruhlik respectively note the importance of "metadata" (Mosley 2015) during interviews. The expression, tone of voice of a person, and the uncomfortable shifts in a chair are all important sources of information. Massimo Ramaioli relates how at the start of an interview with a Jordanian "politico" Salafi, the latter silently showed him his charity's publication, featuring on the first page the picture of King Abdallah II. He then closed it, and the interview began. As Okruhlik states, silences and absences speak volumes about politics and power. Again, while metadata may be more prevalent or important in authoritarian settings, as interviewees are rightfully cautious of internal security apparatuses, it remains an important source of interview information in democracies alike, particularly at times when many issues, as mentioned earlier, have been securitized.

Indeed, in his chapter on conducting research on Salafis in Jordan, Ramaioli raises important ethical questions—questions that would be no different were one to conduct interviews with groups such as the Ku Klux Klan in the United States or neo-Nazis in Germany or paramilitaries in Northern Ireland or anarchists in Greece and Italy. In all these cases, the researcher will face attacks on liberal principles by their interview participants. Thus Ramaioli raises shared dilemmas on how to react when sweeping remarks intended to justify the social exclusion of specific groups are made. As he questions, are we ready to jeopardize our interlocutor's willingness to talk to us by openly contesting his beliefs, often times the very object of our investigation? In these research contexts, speaking truth and gaining trust are one of many tensions discussed, in this chapter and throughout the volume, that researchers commonly face as different research demands appear to be on divergent paths.

Researchers in autocracies and democracies furthermore share similar security concerns. As the respective chapters by Elizabeth Monier and Geoff Martin point out, new technologies have given researchers new tools; yet they also carry with them the shared concern of "digital espionage." In the United States and other established democracies, government agencies are actively involved in monitoring their citizens just like authoritarian states do. Both Martin and Monier underline the new avenues of research that can be generated through the use of social media both as objects of study themselves and as instruments to collect data and information that would substantiate specific research questions. At the same time, both scholars are acutely aware of the "dangers" that social media represent both as a milieu of research and as a research tool. There are thus security concerns for both the researcher and the individuals she or he interacts with virtually. Since 2015, ISIS propaganda has been the focus of extensive research, and online media engagement on the part of the group has been key tool of mobilization. For scholars interested in studying the phenomenon, there are methodological challenges in attempting to explain something they are part of because they have also become "followers." In addition, there are ethical issues because of the fact that by referencing and "redistributing" ISIS material at conferences and in class, one might indirectly extend the propaganda reach of the group and inadvertently glorify its actions. These problems then intersect with the institutional, political, and legal requirements in place to counter ISIS propaganda, suggesting a tension between what might be worthwhile, interesting, and, crucially, independent research and the danger of committing some sort of institutional "crime" or real crime.

While the nonexceptionalism of the region should be highlighted as a starting point, there is no doubt that there are specific themes that run through the different contributions deserving special attention. Such themes are discussed separately in this introduction, but it becomes rapidly clear that they are in fact intertwined to make the fieldwork experience much more complex than one would glean from methodology books. In this book, the chapters are assigned to three separate parts—context, methods, and ethics—and the parts have a considerable degree of internal coherence, with contributions speaking to each other. However, it should be noted that the chapters also tend to overlap across parts, which cannot be and should not be fully separated. While, as noted above, we have highlighted certain contexts that we believed would be of particular interest to readers because of their (at least presumed) uniqueness, the issues raised in the part on context overlap with those in both the methods and the ethics parts. The "ethical dimension" of studying the MENA emerges as a clear concern for scholars and the institutions they work for. It is for this reason that each theme is also explored through the ethical challenges that it gives rise to and how to best contend with them.

Research in Authoritarian Contexts

Certainly, one of the greatest concerns to be raised by the contributors to this volume has to do with the challenges the larger context of authoritarianism presents. The prevalence of semiauthoritarian and authoritarian regimes in the region has meant that researchers must place a premium on the safety of their participants and on their own safety. As Rivetti and Saeidi and as Schwedler and Clark discuss in their respective chapters on doing research in Iran and in Mukhabarat states more generally, activists are particularly vulnerable to surveillance, harassment, and arrest when they have contact with foreigners—particularly when it is believed that those foreigners are seeking to foment unrest and to provide external support for that political unrest. Similarly, Bush illustrates how problematic it might become in the countryside to be in contact with activists and even ordinary citizens because of the ever-present watchful eye of the security services and local notables linked to the regime. Mohammed Yaghi faced similar constraints during his fieldwork as he came into contact with a number of student activists opposed to the regimes in place, underscoring once again the problematic nature that interviewing can have in authoritarian settings. Indeed, early on in her research career in Saudi Arabia, Okruhlik was warned of the prevalence of "mosquitoes," a code for internal security, especially at the universities. Ramaioli's cautionary tale is perhaps the most powerful. He notes that he was more mindful of the watchful eye of the Jordanian government than he was of the Salafis he was interviewing, including those professing their creed in militant jihad. Yet, as discussed by Schwedler and Clark, the red lines regarding the topics and participants that the regimes of the region consider permissible are ever-shifting, particularly so, it appears, since the 2011 Arab uprisings. It can be difficult to know on which side of the red line you stand. Schwedler and Clark describe in detail Clark's encounter with the Mukhabarat as a result of her research on the Muslim Brotherhood's legally registered charities while other researchers, conducting far less benign research or with far less benign participants, were not brought in for questioning. Finally, it should be noted, as Steven Brooke does in his chapter, that the problems related to authoritarianism can affect even methodologies such as survey experiments. Thus, there is no doubt that authoritarian practices influence the way in which research is conducted. There is a methodological aspect to this and an ethical one.

From a methodological perspective, authoritarianism "forces" researchers to make choices on what to study and how. This has the potential of skewing research findings because some topics or sociopolitical actors might be off limits. For example, researchers might prefer to investigate policies or social groups or actors linked to the regime in order to have easier access and demonstrate that the research does not constitute a critique of the political or social order. In this respect, there is greater access for the researcher and acceptance of the sentiment that the work is not potentially dangerous, reducing therefore risks. At the same time, studying voices and groups critical of the regime might not be so easy by virtue of their marginalized—and often illegal—political position. Ensuring the researcher's and the participants' personal safety might mean that the research will miss important insights on how societies and politics genuinely function. In reality, this has not been the case as much as one would have expected, but important dynamics that might have led to at least foreseeing the pre-2011 revolutionary potential were missed because of the considerable focus on elites, authoritarian upgrading, and traditional sociopolitical actors in what were essentially routine interactions within authoritarian structures (Volpi 2017).

From an ethical point of view, operating in an authoritarian environment poses two specific challenges that contributors highlight. The first is how to ensure one's own personal safety and the safety of the participants to the study. Where the rule of law does not exist and the arbitrary nature of power is exercised, considerable care has to be taken in "protecting" the participants and not expose them to risk. All contributors suggest ways in which they have tried to accomplish this. The second challenge is how to meet the institutional ethical criteria contributors have to abide by as part of research institutions. Institutional Review Boards (IRBs) are in place to protect the "objects" of the study from the researcher, but they still seem poorly equipped to deal with the challenges that emerge from doing social science research. On a practical level, researchers in this volume note the ethical challenges of full disclosure of one's research project when it—as political scientists' projects almost invariably do—leads to criticism of the authoritarian regime or its practices. At the core of the concerns is the basic question of whether, given the institutional emphasis on informed consent, political scientists can ethically do research on political issues in authoritarian regimes or not. The chapter by Schwedler and Clark is just one of the chapters in this volume to note the need to stay truthful but to sanitize the presentation of the research project on applications and to interviewees. The need to present less threatening analytical frameworks is paramount in research in authoritarian regimes if any useful finding is expected. As Irene Weipert-Fenner notes, while the leaving out of important conceptual questions or the ambiguous framing of a research project is ethically doubtful, it may be the only way to gain access without distorting the truth. The issue of informed consent raises additional issues for researchers whose methods entail, as Bush states, the proverbial "soaking and poking." While "soaking and poking" is commonly associated with ethnographic fieldwork, in the authoritarian context of the MENA, many scholars engage in intensive fieldwork, often making (intentionally or not) good friends in the field in an effort to navigate their way, secure access, or build the trust needed for an interview. Whether one is using ethnographic research methods or not, research in the MENA raises important additional issues of consent. In her chapter, Malika Bouziane discusses how one interview partner, a female candidate for the municipal elections, trusted her to such an extent over time that she told her in detail about her participation in illegally forging personal identification papers for the parliamentary elections. Should this find its way in published work? If so, how would a researcher ensure replicability of the study without divulging names?

The chapters in this volume thus highlight the numerous tensions prevalent in conducting field research in authoritarian contexts, not least the difficulties of gaining the trust of groups or individuals whose beliefs are a priori considered a security threat, as Pall and Adraoui discuss in their chapter on interviewing Salafis. Thus, researchers struggle with the tensions between regime red lines and the need for entry but also what can be called the participants' red lines and the need for access. The ethical demands of full disclosure are not always compatible with entry to the country of research or with access to the participants themselves. How do we balance out "red lines" with the very interest that crossing such lines generates in terms of research?

The contributors to the volume furthermore highlight another shortcoming to IRBs—IRBs are not intended to protect the researcher, yet in an authoritarian context, the researcher can be just as much at risk as the research participant. As noted above, Schwedler and Clark delineate the type of harassment and questioning that researchers can face. Thus many of the precautions taken to protect research participants are equally important to protect the researcher. This would include the use of code words that make off-limits topics possible to talk about. When discussing incidents of intimidation by internal security in Iran, Rivetti and Saeidi furthermore note an important gendered aspect to harassment: female researchers are more likely than male researchers to face harassment in the form of internal security agents appearing at professional settings and issuing threats. The difficulty of protecting oneself as a researcher is highlighted by the fact that a multiplicity of security organizations are linked to authoritarian states, and coordination among them or, more importantly, control within them is not always clear. Researchers thus must be aware as best they can of shifting and changing red lines they cannot cross. In this context, the ethical requirements of institutional boards do not seem sufficiently thought out and flexible, leading researchers to reassess repeatedly what the limits of their work are. This in turn has potentially negative consequences for research itself—the inability to access what really matters in authoritarian societies—or for individuals involved in the research project—the necessity to have consent from participants no matter what.

Qualitative versus (the Relative Lack of) Quantitative Methods

The second important theme that emerges from the different contributions has to do with the most appropriate methodology in studying MENA politics. In particular, the prevailing authoritarianism in the region has an impact on the type of methods researchers choose. Researchers of the MENA overwhelmingly employ qualitative methods as opposed to quantitative methods; indeed, while the use of quantitative data and techniques is growing among scholars of the region, very little MENA scholarship relies upon it. The contributions to this volume reflect this tendency, and in fact the overwhelming majority of them are concerned with generating insights and advice on how to best take advantage of the opportunities that fieldwork provides as well as how to avoid pitfalls that might endanger the research, the researcher, and the participants. The discipline's emphasis on qualitative methods is not problematic per se, but it has profound implications for the way in which MENA political science literature connects with wider themes in comparative politics because the paucity of quantitative studies makes it difficult to identify trends that might be occurring elsewhere and therefore further challenge the notion of Middle Eastern exceptionalism. This reluctance to engage with quantitative methods, as Miquel Pellicer and Eva Wegner document in their chapter, is largely due to the challenges of data quality and access in the region. As they state, repression commonly has a negative bearing on how freely respondents answer questions and on how freely available administrative data are, a point that Brooke mentions in his contribution as well. While the conducting and the disseminating of opinion surveys have increased substantially in recent years, data quality—predominantly, but not strictly, the representativeness of the sample used—remains an ongoing concern. Engaging directly with participants, as Yaghi shows in his chapter on coding qualitative data, is perceived to be a way to bypass that problem without losing the methodological rigor one has to have in a research design. Another issue is the bias in the responses given—not just, as Pellicer and Wegner point out, because respondents may be reluctant to state their opinions openly but because the bias is most likely to be nonrandom. It is highly possible that the educated may be more likely to be suspicious and refuse to give opinions. As the authors hypothesize, the bias would most likely be more acute the more repressive a country, just as it may be more acute the more sensitive the issue. Again, qualitative work of the kind Yaghi carried out with respect to activism in three Arab countries with its mix of rigorous interviews and access to primary documents is believed to be a better way to reduce the bias, although there is no certainty of it, as other types of biases inherent in the snowballing technique, for instance, might arise. For quantitative researchers, challenges are also significant when it comes to administrative data. Access to administrative data, such as population censuses and election results, is problematic as the data are either incomplete or unavailable (in that information is simply not published because of its sensitive nature) or access is restricted.

All these reasons have prevented scholars from engaging with quantitative research, but an increase in the availability of data and an improvement in quantitative techniques should have seen more scholars employing quantitative methods. Brooke highlights, for instance, the increasing importance of survey experiments, which can provide innovative ways to extract information on new theoretical questions. There is, though, a more fundamental problem in the debate between qualitative and quantitative methods, and it has to do with the still-small purchase and intellectual credibility quantitative techniques have in the field of Middle East political studies. There is certainly a degree of merit in challenging what many see as a mechanical attempt to capture complex social and political dynamics that cannot be condensed to simple numbers. At the same time, it should be acknowledged that speaking the "quantitative" language can improve the conversation with the broader field of comparative politics, where such a language is widely popular. Researchers approaching the MENA for the first time in particular should be aware that they have methodological choices to make that may shape the credibility and relevance of their work. This is even more the case when research institutions and funding agencies employ metrics to allocate material resources, given that such metrics tend to privilege quantitative studies.

Linked to the debate on qualitative and quantitative methods is the rather novel approach of studying important political phenomena through and related to social media. Researching social media or using online media to conduct research presents certain opportunities, as well as solutions to some of the issues discussed above, but it presents a new set of challenges. Particularly for sensitive topics, Monier notes, electronic media provide both an excellent site for fieldwork and a topic for study. They grant the researcher a high degree of safe access to data, and having an online social media presence and profile, such as with Facebook, helps facilitate trust with research participants (although the researcher must be prepared for a loss of privacy). Monier furthermore notes that respondents to her online survey explicitly stated that they regarded the survey as a rare chance to express their opinions about sensitive issues. While purposive sampling is limited with online surveys, using the Internet to distribute questionnaires moreover bypasses a wide range of gatekeepers who would otherwise slow down the research process or inhibit respondents' answers. Thus, as a result of the ease of access, the volume, variety, and originality of the material available and also the opportunity to engage instantly with people and events, Monier notes that she found herself repeatedly being drawn to online media sources for her research. Okruhlik similarly notes that social media provide an effective route around the physical gender segregation present in many countries of the Gulf. Yet, as both Monier and Martin note vis-à-vis their respective research using Facebook and Twitter, the (huge) volume and selection of material present a significant challenge for researchers using online sources. Both scholars similarly point out the problem of accuracy or authenticity—how do you know what information is true, what represents majority opinion, and the degree to which online depictions represent "real world" activities?

In the end, scholars engaging in quantitative methods, including online media, call for the need for a mixed-methods approach. Pellicer and Wegner argue that context knowledge and area expertise remain crucial to developing meaningful questions, working around some of the data's limitations, and interpreting results from quantitative research in a meaningful way. Given the challenges of data access and quality, qualitative data can help researchers assess whether the quantitative data makes sense. What also emerges from this discussion is that researchers face unexpected ethical dilemmas and issues even when dealing with seemingly neutral and apolitical quantitative data. The contributors to this book who have faced such ethical questions outline how they solved them in practice.

Positionality

A third theme to emerge from the chapters in this book is that of positionality—that the complexities of status and power relations as well as identity shape the interactions between the researcher and the participants and ultimately the knowledge that is produced. Positionality is an increasingly important aspect of research because it speaks to the self-awareness that researchers have to display in order to avoid biases that might invalidate their research findings. To a certain extent the discussion on positionality is linked to the debate between those who privilege qualitative methods and those who employ quantitative ones. One of the fiercest critiques against qualitative researchers is their perceived inability to think neutrally and to gather data accordingly, and therefore building significant biases into their research. While this criticism is in certain instances accurate, the self-awareness that an examination of one's positionality brings diminishes the bias and can in fact lead to the discovery and treatment of data that would have been precluded otherwise.

While much of the literature on positionality focuses on the insider/outsider debate, Kingston—as "outsider" to the region and its cultures—discusses how researchers move between outsider and insider through different phases of their research and indeed, at certain points, occupy a position as pseudoinsider. Bouziane, a Sunni Muslim, female, German researcher of Moroccan descent, similarly discusses her status as a "partial insider" while conducting fieldwork in Jordan. Indeed, any rigid division between outsider and insider ignores the multiple and diverse "sets of statuses" that a researcher has. Here is Bouziane when speaking of her own experiences doing research in the region: "Insider status is not an absolute category but intersects with other variables, such as gender, religion, and the biographical background." In her contribution, Dalmasso also discusses positionality in terms of the expectations that participants have when confronted with a Western female researcher working on women's rights and democracy. Local activists have clear assumptions about the supposed beliefs and political positions of researchers, which they infer from their gender or nationality or religion. Great attention has to be paid to such assumptions because they can also be used to the advantage of the researcher to get information that would not otherwise be released.

Along these lines, it follows that the scholars in this volume delineate how these statuses both open and close doors for researchers. Bouziane's position in terms of Arabness and religion meant that interviews commonly turned into informal if not intimate conversations rather than being formal affairs. In this sense, being an insider granted her a privileged position in the field vis-à-vis outsiders. Yet cultural intimacy also posed a challenge for Bouziane: being perceived as an insider meant that, as a result of taken-for-granted assumptions, in-depth discussions on certain so-called realities were dismissed by participants. Similarly, Said notes that aspects of his positionality—an outsider coming from the United States, an insider returning to Egypt, where he grew up and still retains citizenship, a scholar conducting research in pursuit of a PhD at a US institution, a former human rights and leftist prodemocracy activist in Egypt, and a participant in and an observer of the revolution—were a burden, and at other times they were very helpful. His positionality vis-à-vis other activists in Egypt granted him significant access to many insider points of view. Because he knew many of the activists and bloggers personally, he was reluctant to impose on their time or to exploit their friendship. He felt reluctant to ask them to take time away from their political struggle to sit down for an interview with him.

He also was aware of the revolutionaries' disgruntlement with Western researchers who were briefly entering Egypt, allowing just enough time to collect the activists' stories, then disappear and publish their work elsewhere. Moreover, Said found that his connections to the activists made his experiences there and the writing of these experiences for his dissertation later on emotionally intense. It was difficult for him to detach from either the events themselves or his informants. Lihi Shitrit, a Jewish Israeli of North African descent who conducts research in Israel/Palestine, argues that "when doing fieldwork at home, thinking about your own identity, how you fit in, and where exactly you belong is inevitable." The researcher at times is placed in awkward positions with respect to participants who hold specific assumptions about the researcher's beliefs and motives given his or her nationality or physical aspect or name. At the same time, the ethical dimension of such positionality takes center stage because it blurs the lines between the researcher and the participants; it becomes difficult to decide exactly what can be used in the findings of the research and what cannot be as it was said in confidence "to a friend." In a similar vein, Stacey Philbrick-Yadav notes that the researcher's "strangeness" plays an important role in abductive reasoning, helping the researcher to see what for situated knowers is taken for granted, common sense, and tacitly known. Kingston also argues for the necessity of returning to outsider status in the process of academic analysis when re-engaging with abstract thinking after leaving the field.

Yet while Bouziane's insider status as a Muslim and an Arab enabled her to push the boundaries of what could be said and criticized, outsiders have other statuses that can similarly position the researcher as a privileged pseudo- or partial insider. Kingston discusses the normative affinity he had with particular activists, which opened certain doors for him and facilitated an easy trust while closing other doors. Weipert-Fenner similarly notes that presenting herself as a fellow activist inspired implicit trust in the intentions of her research and helped break the ice much faster. Yet these entrées to being a pseudoinsider also have their disadvantages. Weipert-Fenner details how political affinity with certain groups makes it harder to gain the trust of those who do not agree with your political alliances. Kingston found himself "too embedded" when one association representative subtly encouraged him to act as a messenger between rival advocacy networks. There furthermore are important ethical considerations. Certainly the authors in this volume counsel against faking any political affinity in order to gain access, as it can quickly slide into deception, but remaining vague about one's personal opinions might be useful to navigate complex political and social environments.

A further problem implicit in this area is the "eternal" debate about whether one is an activist or a researcher. While it would be mistaken to assume that there is a perfectly neutral way of doing unbiased social science research, scholars have to be mindful of the pressures that exist in academia to conform to a standard, no matter how arbitrary, where the academic work of "activists" does not find the same echo and suffers from diminished legitimacy, no matter how unfair this is. There are thus strategic considerations one has to think about in how one operates in the field, what kind of findings one seeks, and for what purpose one seeks them.

Gender

A fourth dominant theme is this volume is that of the role of gender in conducting fieldwork. Gender is an important issue when conducting research, as patriarchal structures are still very much in place across the globe. Thus, as Dalmasso clearly states in her contribution, this occurs not only in the MENA, but in most research environments and fields. The researchers in this volume speak of gender-specific issues ranging from compulsory veiling and segregation to harassment, but also to the ability to have access where male researchers might not. Conversely, as Ramaioli makes clear, female researchers seem to be absent when the topic of investigation is Salafism, although this should not be necessarily a put-off because some great work from female researchers on Salafi sociopolitical practices exists (Kolman 2016). With respect to the difficulties female researchers encounter, Monier, for example, notes that one of the reasons she is drawn to research using electronic media is that it offers her safe access to multiple and global sites. As she explains, while she has conducted the majority of her face-to-face research interviews without problems, she has also had a negative experience of being harassed by an interviewee who used inappropriate language, insisted on trying to take photographs of her, and, later, subjected her to nuisance calls. As pointed out above, Rivetti and Saeidi note that harassment by internal security agents in Iran has a gendered aspect. According to their and other female researchers' experiences, women are more often approached by individuals who use threats and become abusive. They advise female researchers to be suspicious of individuals who insist on meetings and exchanges that seem unnecessarily prolonged. There are also other less frequently discussed gender challenges, such as a lack of public bathrooms for women in many countries of the region and the fact that many religiously observant men may refuse to shake hands with a woman.

Yet, as mentioned, despite these challenges, female researchers also speak of the opportunities afforded to them as a result of gender—even in, if not especially in, gender-segregated social contexts. As Okruhlik states about Saudi Arabia, there is a common misconception that gender inhibits scholarly research. Yet rather than being a problem, gender is a gift in terms of interview access: a foreign man could not interview a Saudi woman in person without the consent of her guardian. Reflecting on her field research in Yemen, Philbrick-Yadav similarly notes that she was rarely excluded on the basis of gender and was able to attend—often as the only woman—gender-segregated khat chews.

Interestingly, this privileged position—that of a "third gender" (Schwedler 2006)—does not apply to those with "insider status," such as Bouziane, as gender-related norms circumscribed her practices to a certain extent. As she states, non-Arab female researchers enjoy more space for maneuver since their noncompliance to gender norms is ascribed to their different "outsider" values. Bouziane was less able to escape gender-related expectations and norms despite her German upbringing. In this case, her Moroccan descent "played against her" in terms of access because she was expected to follow local norms, as she was not considered entirely foreign. The situation in Israel is rather different for researchers like Shitrit conducting fieldwork "back home" because her status allows her unrestricted access and protection from harassment. The same did not apply to her Arab research assistant.

In Saudi Arabia, you will need a guardian or *mahram*—if not your husband, then a man whom you cannot marry, that is, your father, son, uncle, or brother. A female researcher in Saudi Arabia is dependent on her *mahram* as a source of legitimacy and logistical lubricant. Yet here too there women have some advantages. Echoing Clark, Okruhlik notes the power of two sets of eyes and ears in an interview. She also describes how her guardian—her husband—buys her time during an interview to pause, think, and reframe her questions.

While in Saudi Arabia and Iran female researchers must conform to legally imposed gender-related practices, such as wearing an abaya, in most other research sites in the MENA region, they must find their own balance between being respectful of local customs and, in many cases, being true to their own culture and beliefs. As Clark and Dalmasso respectively discuss, while researchers want to be respectful of local customs, being respectful does not mean belonging. Dalmasso made a choice to fit in but not try to pretend that she shared the morals of others. While respecting the local culture and practices in terms of interactions between genders is paramount if one wants to be taken seriously and be granted access to the participants in the study, it is also incumbent on researchers to remain true to themselves and consequently somewhat aloft from local norms.

Protests, Resistance, and Conflicts

The fifth theme to emerge in this volume is the challenges of conducting research in a region that experiences regular, if not ongoing, turmoil. All contributors touch on issues of safety—their own and participants'. While authoritarian structures might provide an image of outward stability, the reality on the ground is quite different insofar as this perceived stability is often challenged through protests, acts of violence, and all-out conflicts. Provided the spontaneous and unforeseeable nature of such events, it is incumbent on researchers to be flexible and prepared for any eventuality. This preparation ranges from very practical measures, such as having a photocopy of one's passport, to the intellectual ability to change the focus of research in light of an important event. This might not be necessarily in tune with the research design one has spent months on before leaving for the field, but if promising and unexplored areas of potentially fruitful research open up, they should be seized upon. Parkinson describes both how real violence affected her research work on feelings of group belonging among young Palestinians and how the threat of an international war forced her to think about logistics much more than one would have deemed necessary. Okruhlik thus talks about some of the basic precautionary steps she takes in order to protect herself and ensure her safety during crises and war. These steps range from varying her route each day, having emergency luggage always packed and ready at the front door, and, perhaps most important, creating relationships of trust and care so that she has a safe haven. While this might not apply to all contexts in the region, political tensions do play a role in influencing the way in which research is conducted. Indeed, Said points out that research during the Egyptian revolution may have been difficult, but it was not impossible. During the revolution, Egypt was an open society; while there were attacks on protests, people continued to protest and new parties and independent unions organized and mobilized freely. The openness stood in sharp contrast to postrevolutionary Egypt (which is significantly less open than Egypt under Mubarak).

Benoit Challand's chapter presents a special case for fieldwork, that of the occupied Palestinian territory (OPT), in which researchers must struggle with access to the OPT when Israel seals its borders, as well as with the numerous other structures of occupation, including the curtailed freedom of movement and curfews. As he states, these present greater challenges to research than any "internal" hurdles. To avoid the prospect of being denied entry into Israel upon landing at Ben Gurion airport, Challand recommends meticulous preparation—for example, being able to describe clearly the object of the research, the extent of the movements inside historical Palestine, having a visiting card, or, for younger researchers, carrying along an official letter of the university stating the nature and the existence of a supervision mechanism. He furthermore notes that in the past, having an invitation letter from an Israeli research university would have greatly facilitated entry into the country, but, because of the academic boycott (boycott, divestment, sanctions, BDS) enforced by Palestinian universities and research institutes, such letter will probably bar the researcher from speaking with Palestinians for research purposes. The challenges presented by the occupation are most acute for scholars of Palestinian or Arab origins.

As Challand elaborates, it is never an innocent act to study Palestine, let alone reach Palestine. A research trip via Ben Gurion airport or Egypt could be interpreted as acquiescing to the right of Israel to deny Palestinians full sovereignty. A researcher's position on BDS might jeopardize her or his chance to speak with Palestinian counterparts. The topic of the research might also generate troubles. Scholars critical of Israeli policies run the risk of NGO Watch or Campus Watch putting pressure on them in their home countries. Critical Jewish scholars are not immune to these challenges, as they risk being added to web-based lists of Self-Hating Jews (so-called

SHIT lists). Other topics could put researchers in legal trouble. As Challand points out, since the US Supreme Court's 2010 decision to extend its definition of material support to terrorist organizations, American researchers must be particularly wary of certain topics. One example would be studying Islamic charitable associations, some of which have been accused of being terrorist organizations.

While the same strictures and constraints might not apply to, or at least not be as burdensome for, Jewish Israeli researchers, they also play a role because of the politicization of Israel/Palestine as a locus of research. Shitrit examines the challenges of conducting fieldwork with two politically problematic—at least from the normative point of view of the researcher—sides simultaneously (the Israeli religious Right and Palestinian religious Right) and acknowledges her privileged position when doing fieldwork, noting that these privileges do not apply to her Arab Israeli colleagues. When conducting research with her observant Jewish interlocutors, she was perceived as being a Mizrahi Jewish Israeli woman and was clearly more privileged in the field research process than an Arab-Palestinian Israeli scholar who would have to pretend to be Jewish in order to conduct research with the ultra-Orthodox Jewish Shas. Yet Ben Shitrit also found that she was able to work with the Islamic Movement, with Shas, and with the Jewish settlers without having to hide her Jewish identity. Her experiences suggest that positionality acquires even greater significance in conflict situations, no matter how low intensity the violence might be or the actual topic of research.

Ethics

As we have seen, ethical issues cut across the main themes of this volume. There is no doubt that one of the important issues raised here and of concern to researchers everywhere is that of research ethics. Returning, therefore, to the issues of IRBs is necessary to provide a fuller picture of their role and their impact on research in the MENA. While the contributors in this volume take great pains to discuss the role and importance of ethics in fieldwork, several authors raise important concerns regarding formal IRBs. Atef Said, for example, notes the simple fact that the speed of political events in the region may mean that researchers do not have time to obtain IRB approval before leaving for the country of research. Thus, while scholars are aware of the ethical dimension of their work, significant reservations exist as to the institutional instruments that are provided because they are often painfully inadequate to MENA realities. The criticism of IRBs that emerges from a number of contributions has a practical dimension and a philosophical one. In terms of practicalities, it is important to ask how useful formal processes of acquisition of consent are in the social sciences and, particularly, in authoritarian and conflict-ridden contexts, when they have in fact been developed primarily to deal with ethics in the natural or medical sciences. It seems that very few IRBs have given genuine thought to the challenges that exist in simply transferring standardized forms from one discipline to another, particularly when this has taken place, evidently, without much input from those who are primarily concerned, in this case Middle East experts. Weipert-Fenner notes, for instance, the security risk of having a signed consent form in authoritarian and semiauthoritarian states, given the potential harm it can cause to the interviewee should it be confiscated by security officials. In fact, even being seen with individuals—never mind asking for formal consent—under surveillance for their political or social activities might create problems for both the researcher and the participant. In many MENA contexts confidentiality is of paramount importance because the stakes for critics of government policy for instance are quite high, and having them sign forms is dangerous. It is, however, necessary to include their voices if one is to provide genuine, useful insights in the research, and therefore the question arises as to what is the correct balance between satisfying institutional requirements, the validity of the findings, and the safety of participants. Bush's chapter on conducting fieldwork in rural Egypt notes the limited leeway formal IRBs grant to researchers seeking to do research with illiterate populations. Indeed, the scholars in this volume raise important concerns over the impact of IRBs on research agendas and question the extent to which IRBs limit our ability to ask important research questions. While the need for informed consent is rooted in important historical lessons of abuse, the disproportionate focus on IRB ethics makes it impossible for a fieldworker to conduct controversial research on the "bad guys" or the "perpetrators" of abuses. These issues are of concern to all researchers regardless of the field research site.

This widespread criticism about the practicalities surrounding the issue of informed consent of course only holds true if the assumption is that it can be challenged and changed by offering alternative ways of obtaining consent in the field. It is at this juncture that the philosophical dimension of the criticism of IRBs enters the stage. Ray Bush, in particular, emphasizes that the role of IRBs has increased significantly over the past few years in accordance with the construction of the neoliberal university, which is increasingly relying on performance models copied and pasted from the private sector. Thinking of and referring to degrees as commodities, students as a clientele (the all-powerful customer), and publications as indicators of individual performance now characterizes the logic of third-level education. In this context, the formality and rigidity of IRBs are a hindrance to the social critical role that researchers must strive for because this critical role is perceived to have little monetary value. When studying and looking at the MENA—or, for that matter, many other areas of research, both geographic and thematic—it is incumbent on social science researchers to highlight and challenge injustices, speak critically to power, and perform the role of public intellectuals with the aim of raising the quality of the public debate around the crucial issues of our age. The constraints of IRBs, whether intentionally or not, place limits on all of this because their requirements force researchers in the social sciences to deal simply with "safe" spaces and "safe" people.

In the MENA, this means accepting the logic, the ideas, and the actions of the powerful as they are embedded in authoritarian practices that by their very nature point to dissenters as "unsafe" and "dangerous." In many ways, similar constraints on researchers might come, directly or not, from institutes and agencies funding their research. The critical dimension of research runs the risk of being muted or toned down in order to satisfy the guidelines of funding agencies, and it is incumbent therefore on individual scholars to ensure a degree of self-reflection on the autonomy they genuinely have.

When confronted with institutional constraints that have an impact on what is researchable and what is not, individual researchers may find it difficult to resist, and conformity becomes the solution to the dilemma. While we are yet to reach this point as a community of scholars, it is imperative that we remind the institutions we work for that ethical behavior cannot be captured simply with a signature on a piece of paper and that behaving ethically might actually mean challenging the very document we and participants are asked to sign.

Conclusions

Through the insights that this book offers, we hope to tackle the issue of Middle Eastern exceptionalism, to improve field methods, and finally to move the development of new methods forward. While there are aspects of conducting fieldwork in the MENA that are peculiar to region, in particular the intensity of authoritarianism and the threat or use of violence, it should be emphasized that other issues are very similar to the ones that characterize fieldwork elsewhere, including established democracies. How to conduct interviews, the balance between ethical and methodological demands, and the necessity to deal with gender discrimination are just some of them. Okruhlik's chapter has enhanced relevance as a comparative lens through which to evaluate ongoing changes in Saudi Arabia and what they may mean for field researchers in the future. The book aims specifically at ensuring that researchers are aware of all the gray areas that exist between fieldwork and textbooks' methodology. This knowledge also leads us to think about and eventually design new methodologies, as David Waldner explains in his chapter on process tracing. In attempting to deal with causal inference—a perceived weakness in the cross-case comparison he used for his PhD dissertation—Waldner turned to and then progressively refined process tracing, a method that increasing numbers of qualitative researchers are now employing. Brooke's chapter goes in the same direction with his emphasis on groundbreaking survey experiments.

In short, with its focus on methods and ethics, this edited volume hopes to ensure that Middle East studies continue to grow as a discipline and make greater connections with the broader comparative politics literature.

PART I

CONTEXT

2

Encountering the Mukhabarat State

JILLIAN SCHWEDLER AND JANINE A. CLARK

Researchers of Middle East politics have long contended with the challenge of working in a region in which the regimes are not pleased with anyone asking questions about politics, let alone outsiders with notepads and recording devices. Local and international research centers provide tremendous support to help researchers navigate these local contexts, but because every researcher and every project is different, even well-established patterns of accessibility can change. Research challenges are further compounded in contexts of political change, when the boundaries between acceptable and unacceptable topics—or "red lines"—are unstable. In this chapter, we offer a guide to navigating the challenges of doing research in Mukhabarat states—states in which the regime deploys an extensive intelligence apparatus to spy on citizens and foreigners, as well as to intimidate and harass them. Most importantly, we recommend that you do your homework in advance, follow the lead of local sources, secure your data, and be transparent and promote accountability.

Advance Practical Planning

All states gather information on those inside their borders, including democracies, although the degree and type of surveillance can vary dramatically. Before heading to the field, you must determine whether a special visa is required to conduct research. Some states allow you to enter with a tourist visa but then register with a specific agency your intent to conduct research; others require you to enter on a business visa obtained before you travel, or to secure a specific research permit separate from your visa. Some countries do not issue research visas or require registration. You may be required to provide a description of your project and field research plans and a formal letter of affiliation with a local university or research center. In choosing an affiliation, seek input from scholars who have recently worked in that country to identify a center with a good reputation, and one that is on good terms with the government. Begin these steps well in advance, as visas and affiliations can take months to obtain.

If you are working with a local center such as one affiliated with Fulbright or the Council of American Overseas Research Centers (CAORC), or with a European center such as the French Institut français du Proche-Orient or the Council for British Research in the Levant, they can provide guidance as to visa and affiliation requirements, and some states may even delegate research permit application procedures to these organizations. While many maintain information on their websites, we recommend direct contact to convey the specifics of your project and to learn about any recent changes or problems that others might have encountered. Advanced permission is often required for conducting survey research, and some countries explicitly forbid research on certain topics. Research on the royal families, particularly the kings, in the monarchies of the region, for example, is generally forbidden. Under such circumstances, local research centers may also offer useful suggestions about how to explain or phrase your research interests in your application. In one instance with which we are familiar, for example, a scholar was advised that research on Islamist parties would be summarily rejected, but that rephrasing her project in terms of "social conservatives" would increase the chances of approval—and it was approved. Fulbright catalogs can be a useful early resource for all scholars because they identify which states permit researchers in principle and list topics that governments explicitly exclude.

If your home country does not have a research institution in your country of study, determining precise research requirements can be challenging. Countries with bilateral agreements, such as between Jordan and the United States, anticipate scholarly exchange and thus have more routine procedures. In other cases, procedures are not necessarily clear even to officials from the country of study. For example, one might contact the embassy of the country of study and be told that a research permit is not required; upon arrival, however, officials know only how to work with researchers who have obtained a formal affiliation with a known research center. In this sense it is advisable to obtain your visa and arrange an affiliation in advance, which will give you a status with an agency known to the regime.

Sometimes it is even possible to obtain the support of a government official. One scholar known to Schwedler secured the support of the minister of health for a project related to healthcare; the letter opened many doors and conveyed "official approval" for the research. Such affiliations are not always possible, or even desirable. If a formal affiliation is not possible, you may try to obtain a letter from a prominent scholar indicating his or her willingness to supervise your research. Unaffiliated scholars are often viewed with suspicion, so at the very least bring a formal letter of introduction from your university or home institution. Be prepared, as well, to offer documentation of your sources of research funding, especially if you have fellowship funds that are not administered by your university. Unexplained sources of income can be a particular red flag for intelligence agencies. The bottom line is to comply with any formal state requirements. If you are monitored or questioned, you want to demonstrate that you have been transparent and have complied with formal policies. We strongly advise against posing as a tourist when you are on an extended research visit. You may keep a low profile, but do not attempt to mask or hide your project.

In describing your research project for visa applications or when seeking to establish an affiliation, you may wish to articulate a "friendly" version of your project, one that conveys the topic honestly without highlighting aspects that the authorities might find unfavorable. Schwedler accurately described one of her projects as exploring the changing public spaces in Amman, particularly the construction of luxury housing, restaurants, and shopping malls. She did not mention her interest in how these elite spaces exclude certain Jordanians on a class basis and whether Jordanians resented government investment in megaprojects. If she had been questioned by the Mukhabarat, her actual research would have been consistent with her described project. Thus, it may be possible to explore a sensitive topic if you can frame it in a way that will protect yourself as well as those you interview. In all cases, we strongly advise against misrepresenting your project. Do not, for example, say that you are studying parliamentary politics when you intend to research union organizing. You need to have a plausible reason for the people you interview and the documents you collect. Similarly, if you are required to obtain approval for your research, portray your research methods accurately. Do not indicate that you will only conduct archival research, for example, if you plan to do interviews or conduct a survey, even a small one. These practices are both consistent with good ethics and beneficial for your personal safety. Always operate under the assumption that any misrepresentation will be detected and avoid offering any description of your research purposes or methods that you cannot later defend.

In many Mukhabarat states, any political inquiry is akin to political dissent and thus off limits; others are quite open. Some off-limit topics may be self-evident: inquiry into a regime's harassment and poor treatment of its people, or its practice of arbitrary arrests, torture, and surveillance, will likely be unwelcome. Other red lines can be less clear, but there are steps you can take to help you determine what they are and whether you can undertake research on your topic safely.

A first step should be a survey of the existing literature on your topic and your country or countries: what work have others completed successfully, and what topics are absent? There is less literature on the internal workings of security agencies in Mukhabarat states than on parliaments and political parties, for example, because research on the former is implicitly (or explicitly) off limits. Another gauge of the political climate is whether journalists are currently able to conduct interviews and write on subjects related to yours. Acknowledgments in books can also provide important clues. If an author does not thank people by name to protect their safety, she has reason to believe that the state might harass those who facilitated that specific research. Local research centers can be especially useful in learning the (often shifting) contours of red lines. Also contact scholars who have worked in your country recently to get up-to-date information, asking specifically about the feasibility of your intended topic. Most scholars will be happy to discuss field research conditions and help you think through what issues you might face given your research project and circumstances.

Conducting Your Field Research

Once you are certain that your research is feasible, establish a plan for conducting interviews, collecting documents, or engaging in ethnographic study—whatever methods your research requires. If you plan to do interviews, consider a strategy of whom to interview, and in what order. If your topic is uncontroversial, you may wish to speak with prominent individuals first, which can open doors later if others are uncertain as to whether to speak to you. In other instances, having the government aware of your work may make others more nervous. In Schwedler's research on political protests, she opted to interview the most underground activists first, and then move to talk to formal parties, trade unions, government officials, and finally security agencies. Because Jordan does not require that researchers register with a state agency, she was able to begin her work quietly. The logic was that once she spoke to government officials and security agencies, the ability to meet with independent activists could be compromised. However, always expect that news of you and your research will spread once you do your very first interview, if not before.

The prevalence of email has made it much easier to contact potential interviewees prior to arriving in the field, although our experience has been that most will not want to make a firm appointment until after you arrive. In these initial contacts—just as with telephone calls—be aware that everything you write and say may be monitored. If you anticipate that your topic might be sensitive, introduce yourself and outline your general research topic in simple terms, and then wait for the in-person interview to determine how far to take the conversation. For Schwedler's research on political protests, she described research as asking how a quasi-authoritarian state like Jordan legally allows political protests even on contentious issues, such as calls to abolish Jordan's peace treaty with Israel. This positive spin—Jordan's permitting open political protests—did not mask the likelihood that critical material would emerge, but it framed the project in a way that would allow potential interviewees to decide whether they would like to speak. This strategy also works well when making advanced inquiries about access to archival material or documents: state your topic clearly but without highlighting potential critical angles that could emerge. Once the contact is established, follow up with a phone call to establish the logistics of the interview only. Our experience has been that doors only open once people meet you and decide whether or not to trust you, so a transparent but positive first encounter can be critical to obtaining the materials you desire.

It is worth stressing that in semiauthoritarian/authoritarian contexts, even if you successfully secure the interview, interviewees may be reluctant to share their opinions with a foreign researcher they do not know. Much like the framing of your project, you will want to give careful consideration to the wording of your questions. Using well-known euphemisms (for example, using the generic term "authorities" when referring to internal security) will help the interviewee feel comfortable enough to answer your questions. Experienced researchers should be able to help you best formulate questions that deal with sensitive issues.

Securing Your Data

Before you begin collecting research materials, whether interviews, ethnographic data, or documents, you need to consider how to protect it. Data collection and protection has become much easier in recent years with the explosion of smartphones and other portable and wireless computer devices—but those devices can also be vulnerable to hacking and monitoring. When in the past one had to physically carry out written field notes, departing the country was a time of great anxiety. The seizure of physical research material remains a real concern, but you can protect yourself, your interview subjects, and your data by taking precautions.

Most researchers, particularly when working on sensitive topics, avoid keeping research notes on their person, either written or on their computer hard drive. Many will upload their research notes or photographs of original documents to a virtual drive such as iCloud or Dropbox (assuming that cellular and Internet connections are available and reliable). Transmitting data this way is convenient, but keep in mind that transmitted data can be hacked. If you email your notes to an alternate email address, remember to delete and purge the outgoing message as well. In addition, many computers have stored passwords to facilitate easy access to email and other sites. In such a case, remotely stored material will not be secure in the event that your computer or phone is confiscated. For the greatest security, we recommend that you enable password protection for all your devices and enter email and cloud passwords manually for the duration of your time in the field. You will also want to install the latest encryption software. The Mukhabarat may routinely monitor emails and social media, so be aware that such communications may not be secure. Be sure that your security settings for platforms like Facebook are set so that only your "Friends" can see your posts and other online friends. As with other communications, it is best to limit online and texting messages to logistics rather than commentary. And as is true everywhere, Wi-Fi connections are never entirely secure.

In terms of where to conduct interviews, your interviewees will usually suggest a place. It may be at their office, but it could also be after work at a café or bar. Depending on the sensitivity of your subject, your interviewees may or may not want to meet in public, so let them be the guide. Do consider the possibility that anyone you meet could potentially convey information directly to the Mukhabarat. Journalists, government officials, political parties, activists, and union leaders, to give just a few examples, may be monitored by the Mukhabarat, so they may well pass information about meeting you directly to authorities. This may not be to "turn you in," but to win points with the Mukhabarat by "doing their part" in keeping the authorities informed, or else to make sure that the Mukhabarat hears about the meeting directly rather than have someone else report on it. In general, be cautious of people who ask you detailed questions about those you have interviewed or who have provided you with documents or other information.

If the Mukhabarat does begin to monitor you, you may not know for some time. Again, ask other researchers for telltale signs specific to your research location. Take seriously the saying "Just because you are paranoid doesn't mean someone isn't watching you." The challenge is to be aware of potential monitoring and take precautions without becoming paralyzed with anxiety. One strange click during a phone call can easily lead to the worry that your phone is being monitored. Assume that it is. The balance between diligent caution and paranoia can be easy or difficult to achieve, depending on the person. Keep in mind that the vast majority of researchers have a great research experience and are not openly monitored, let alone intimidated, while carrying out research.

A final challenge is that the boundaries of acceptable topics can shift depending on the immediate political climate, with heightened sensitivity in moments of instability. A transition from one monarch or president to a new one, for example, can be a time of increased scrutiny even if the transition is smooth. In 1998, Clark was conducting research in Jordan at just such a moment: King Hussein was terminally ill, the United States was bombing Iraq, and opposition parties had boycotted the recent election and criticized the government in strong terms. Although Clark had been working on her topic for some time, she attracted attention from the Mukhabarat (detailed below) at a time when the agency may have been casting a larger net to identify security threats.

Moments of change also may be particularly risky because they change the resources available to you. One colleague of ours was detained and ultimately deported from Lebanon in 2005 because, as the Syrians departed the country, the US Embassy explained that it no longer had established contacts through whom it could effectively intercede. When conditions stabilized, she was able to return to Lebanon and resume her research.

Even with these precautions, research that you feel is not politically sensitive may still attract Mukhabarat attention. Clark's Mukhabarat encounter came as she was researching the Muslim Brotherhood's charity in Jordan, which has branches throughout the country, including in Palestinian refugee camps. She had conducted numerous interviews inside camps without incident and planned to travel to another soon. Because that particular camp was known for its political activism, Clark asked colleagues and friends whether it was safe to interview there, and no one advised her against visiting. When one suggested she obtain permission first, she made numerous inquiries with various institutions, but none knew that any such permit existed. Researchers who had conducted interviews in that camp told Clark that they had encountered no difficulties. If the Mukhabarat did approach her, one suggested, she could simply explain herself. Clark finally asked the interviewee himself, who assured her that there would be no difficulties.

Yet Clark did encounter difficulties. Upon arrival, she parked her rental car near what seemed the perimeter of the camp, coincidentally in front of a police station. As she looked around to determine if the spot was legal, a man approached to ask if she needed help. She inquired about the parking spot, and he suggested she ask inside the police station. Unbeknownst to her, the man was with the Mukhabarat. An officer confiscated her passport and began what became several days of questioning.

Encountering the Mukhabarat: What to Expect

Most experiences with security agencies are limited to questioning and intimidation; although, as discussed in the introduction to this volume, the case of Giulio Regeni indicates the shifting and somewhat unpredictable post-2011 research terrain. An encounter with the Mukhabarat itself often comes in the form of a request to appear for questioning. If you receive such an "invitation," you should immediately (or as soon as possible) contact your embassy, your research institute or affiliation in the country, anyone you know high in government (if you have good contacts), and your close friends and fellow researchers. You should also contact your dissertation adviser or colleagues at home, so they are aware of what is happening. Set a time to call them again after the questioning, so they will know in the unlikely event that you have been kept overnight or, even less likely, arrested. These varied sources can also provide advice as to the current climate of questioning. You may be tempted to leave the country, but be aware that your name may have been added to a watch list that could prevent you from clearing passport control at the airport or border. Leaving abruptly under such conditions may also heighten suspicion.

When you contact your embassy, ask if a representative can accompany you to your appointment—a policy adopted by many embassies for their citizens. The Mukhabarat may treat you with more respect if you have an embassy representative with you, or even if they are aware that you have contacted your embassy. Be insistent with your embassy if you feel that you are being brushed off, and record the names of everyone to whom you speak. If you have dual citizenship, typically only the embassy of the passport you used to enter the country will be able to assist you, but you should nonetheless contact both and insist on someone taking down your information. Finally, ask for a name and number as your direct embassy contact. You should give that contact to your friends in the country and at home, so they can make inquires if they do not hear back from you. Also provide that contact during your first interview with the Mukhabarat: the more connected you appear to be, the more likely you will receive better treatment. While the Mukhabarat will want to intimidate you, individual officers may not want to make a mistake by treating a "VIP" harshly. Since they probably do not know everything about you, you want to make clear that a lot of people—hopefully in powerful places—are aware that you are there.

Visits to the Mukhabarat can be unpredictable: they could last an hour, a whole day, or stretch over several days. Foreign researchers are seldom detained overnight unless accused of committing a serious crime. Clark's two encounters with the Jordanian Mukhabarat illustrate just how different experiences can be. The first occurred in 1998, the second ten years later. Mukhabarat practices changed significantly during that period: In the first encounter, the primary objective seemed to fear and intimidation; in the second, Clark found the experience far less threatening, even bureaucratized.

The 1998 incident began as Clark entered the police station at the edge of the refugee camp. An officer briefly questioned her and confiscated her passport, instructing her to arrive at a particular entry gate of the Mukhabarat headquarters the following morning. Upon entry into the compound, she was led to a small building with a waiting room where a security check was done. She was asked to surrender her phone, watch, paper, and pens—essentially everything she had with her. Clark later learned that this was a technique designed to make one feel vulnerable, which it did. She was then escorted to a bus, with black curtains covering all the windows, which drove her to her designated building after making numerous turns likely intended to confuse passengers as to their location.

Clark was taken to a large, bare waiting room with rows of benches and large numbers of what appeared to be laborers or agricultural workers of a lower socioeconomic status. She saw no other foreigners. Even more unsettling, most appeared to be visibly frightened, with many crying or pleading with the guards. Eventually, Clark's name was called and she was led up and down stairs and through a maze of hallways until she arrived at an office. This process was repeated for each of the next several days, with the route changing but each time arriving at the same office. Many different people questioned her, punctuating long periods of waiting. Each questioner slowly wrote her responses by hand into a file. Some interviewers clearly played "good cop" or "bad cop" roles: one would be friendly while the next would shout as a bright light shone on her face in a darkened room. In one Kafkaesque example, an interviewer repeatedly asked to see her research permit. When she said that Jordan did not issue research permits, he simply yelled, "Ah hah!" In her file was a photograph of one of her roommates, a foreign researcher. She was not allowed to use the washroom without the escort of a female guard and was released promptly with the end of the workday.

Clark's 2010 encounter was substantially different. Upon arriving at the airport in Amman, she was granted entry but given a slip of paper instructing her to report to the Mukhabarat headquarters two days later, after Jordan's weekend break. The morning of the appointment, Clark took a taxi to the Mukhabarat headquarters. She showed her slip of paper to a guard and climbed aboard a full bus, which appeared to be running on a regular schedule. None of the passengers, who were nicely dressed and looked like professionals, showed signs of being nervous. The windows of the bus were covered with black curtains, as they had been a decade earlier, but they seemed irrelevant. After Clark and the other passengers disembarked, they were led through a quick security check but allowed to keep their possessions. They were then filed into a building with a row of counters. Each had earlier been given a number and was instructed to line up in front of the counter with the corresponding number. A bureaucrat checked Clark's file and directed her to the appropriate floor, where she went unescorted. Each floor appeared to deal with a different issue; those on Clark's floor all seemed to be there for border-related issues.

Unlike during Clark's previous visit, this waiting room was comfortable and segregated by gender. Clark found the women talking in a lively way and sharing stories about border crossings; none seemed the least bit nervous. When a young girl arrived quite upset, the others comforted her and told her not to worry, that this type of questioning was *'adi* (routine or normal), and that the Mukhabarat was just trying to gather information. Anyone could use the washroom as needed, without an escort. And there was no guard inside or outside of the waiting room.

Eventually Clark's number was called over a loudspeaker, and she was asked if she had brought a friend or a translator. She had not, and as she had not known it was even a possibility. She was interviewed by a relatively young agent who spoke fluent English. He was pleasant and told Clark that he was there to help update her "resume," the large file in front of him on the desk. They talked about her trips in and out of Jordan, the general topic for each visit, why she was interested in researching Jordan, and how they both found Cairo to be exhausting. Most of the exchange felt more like a chat than an interrogation, except for one moment when the officer felt that Clark had contradicted herself. She clarified her comments, but for those few moments the officer adopted the harsh facial expression and tone of Clark's interrogations a decade earlier. When the meeting concluded, he offered her some "paternalistic advice." As someone who worried about her being alone in Jordan, he told Clark that it would be best that she stayed at a research institute and not alone in an apartment. In the future she should also apply for her visa in Canada, rather than at the border, and include a letter stating where she would be staying and what type of research she would be doing, even though she would apply for a routine tourist visa. Finally, he suggested that "for her safety" she avoid the cities of Ma'an, Zarqa, and Irbid—politically sensitive places from the perspective of the regime. His voice changed again when he told her that if he found out that she had visited any of them, she would be back in for less pleasant questioning. Thus while the second experience was far different from the first, the message remained one of threat and intimidation, albeit communicated in a velvet glove.

What Do They Know, and What Should I Tell Them?

Part of the Mukhabarat's power is the anxiety created by your not knowing how much they know about you or your research. And as a researcher, you may well have something you prefer to conceal from them. As noted above, take great care with your research materials, including guarding the identity of interviewees for whom you have promised anonymity. Your IRB application should have articulated how to keep identities anonymous, but the Mukhabarat may nonetheless ask you for the names of everyone with whom you have discussed your research. Our advice is to be open and honest about what you are doing, but that does not mean volunteering a full list of names or offer information that can compromise your subjects. Do not share your research notes even if they are coded or seem difficult to read. Here is where providing the name of an embassy contact, if not having an embassy representative with you, can potentially lessen pressure on you to reveal your contacts. If you do feel pressured to reveal names, you may want to let them know as soon as safely possible. You should consider beginning with those who are the most prominent and public—and therefore most likely to be already known to the authorities. This logic is also consistent with the IRB practices guiding "public figure" exemptions.

Finally, in the course of your research or even daily routines you may come into contact with someone under Mukhabarat surveillance, including people who will convey as much to you. Clark once briefly met a Russian man and his daughter living in Amman, only to learn later from friends that the daughter had been the subject of newspaper articles that referred to her as the "Jewish spy." When Clark was later questioned in 1998, she was unsure as to whether she should "come clean" and mention this encounter, in case they already knew about it (she didn't). You do not necessarily need to avoid such people unless they recommend that you do so, but the decision is up to you. If you suspect that you personally may be under surveillance, however, you should avoid exposing others who might become at risk as a result. One colleague we know was conducting an interview with a well-known dissident when he received a phone call from the Mukhabarat outside his home. They revealed the plate number of her car, and she was concerned they were trying to intimidate him for speaking to a foreign researcher. He assured her that the logic was different—they were conveying to him that they knew how to find her, to compel him to limit what he said to her. In other words, because the Mukhabarat could be gathering information anywhere and at any time, and might use that information in any number of ways against any number of subjects, be diligent in considering when to engage (or avoid) certain individuals, either because they may put you at risk or because you do not want to put them at risk.

Resuming Research after an "Interview"

Whether to continue research after an encounter with the Mukhabarat may be a complicated decision. If you are explicitly told that you may not continue your research or that certain topics or locations are off limits, we advise that you adhere to those directives. But if you are simply warned or intimidated, the question of whether to continue your research is both personal and practical. Clark was told in 1998—after being escorted to the airport—that she was on the Mukhabarat's blacklist and was advised that meant she should not return for five years. She took that advice, and when she did return, she was able to conduct her research freely. In 2010, she followed the officer's "suggestions" and was able to successfully complete a new research project; she was even relieved to know exactly what was off limits.

If you choose to continue your research, remain diligent about not crossing those red lines (if they are known to you), and do not under any circumstances engage in any illegal behavior, including drinking alcohol where it is not permitted. In some countries, such behavior may take place quite openly by locals and foreigners and thus appear low risk. But if you are already under surveillance, any illegal behavior can put yourself and others at risk. Embassies and even high government officials may be unable to help if you have engaged in illegal activities.

For others, resuming research might require shifting to a less sensitive topic or even a different country. Remaining in a country in which the Mukhabarat has sought to intimidate you is simply too anxiety-inducing for many researchers. Interrogation and deportation can take a psychological toll. And you will likely be red-flagged permanently. While entering and exiting the country may not always be an ordeal, allow extra time at the airport and other borders, where you will likely be held back for questioning. Only you can decide if you want to continue doing research in a country under such stressful circumstances, so trust your instinct about whether it is a situation you can manage.

Researching Smart, Being Smart

Conducting research in a Mukhabarat state can be unnerving, but the vast majority of researchers have good experiences and are never invited for questioning. Nevertheless, diligence is needed on your part, to protect yourself, those who assist your work, those you interview, and the data you collect. You can increase your chances of having a positive experience by following the advice we articulate in this chapter.

Smart research begins with developing responsible, ethical research practices, guided by your IRB plan but informed by conversations with others who have worked in your country recently. Do your homework and investigate research conditions and potential sensitive subjects ahead of time; not all projects are feasible. Research and obtain any necessary visas or research permits well in advance of your trip. Establish a formal affiliation with a local research institute, think tank, or university department, and follow their advice. Be honest and transparent in your research subject and sources of funding, but without raising critical dimensions unnecessarily. Keep research notes secure, protecting anonymity when necessary. Do not engage in illegal activities or consume illegal substances.

Being smart also means trusting your instincts. If a situation does not feel right, get out of there. If someone is asking what feels like too many questions about your research and interviewees, be cautious about revealing details. If called in for questioning, be your own advocate. Contact your embassy, affiliation, and others prior to the appointment, and follow up afterward. If an embassy representative cannot accompany you, make sure the Mukhabarat knows that others are aware of your situation. Always speak your native language. Try to remain calm and patiently answer questions. If you have a publication record or contribute online material or comments to a blog, Twitter account, or public page on social media, know that the Mukhabarat may be aware if you have written anything critical of the regime. Do not volunteer information about yourself or others, but assume that the interviewers may know much more or much less than they are letting on. If you are called in for multiple days of questioning, provide updates to others about what is going on.

Remember, most researchers are successful in their research, even the few who are called in for questioning. By planning, researching, and being smart in the field, you can increase your chances of having a great experience and producing exciting research.

What Is So Special about Field Research in Iran?

Doing Fieldwork in Religiously Charged Authoritarian Settings

PAOLA RIVETTI AND SHIRIN SAEIDI

Doing field research in the Islamic Republic of Iran is usually considered to be challenging for social scientists. Islamic precepts, security issues, regional political instability, and tight control over the population are elements that constrain the researcher's activities, apparently leaving little room for investigation and critical inquiry. This chapter identifies the factors and the dynamics that make field research in political and social sciences difficult in Iran by challenging the received wisdom that Iran is a difficult field because of Islam. Although religious rules play an important role in Iran's public sphere and constrain the researcher's behavior to some extent (i.e., the compulsory veil for women or limitations to male-female interactions in public), the chapter argues that it is state authoritarian intervention that limits researchers' freedom of inquiry. Such limitations are examined and suggestions are offered as to how to get around them.

The chapter has two objectives. First, we aim to discuss the specific impact of authoritarian interventionism on the field researcher's activities, and, second, we want to engage with the ethical and security challenges we encountered in the field. The latter will help the authors single out what is specific in conducting fieldwork in an authoritarian country. It is rather difficult to identify what obstacles to research are peculiar to our experience of doing research in the Islamic Republic, as colleagues who have conducted research in Europe, for instance, seem to share many of our difficulties. In fact, when facing practical issues in applying research methods, the two "fields" seem to be quite similar, although assessments of the researcher's personal security and others' security may change because of the broader setting. It follows that it is important to refrain from essentializing Iran or the Middle East in order to offer findings for comparative analysis beyond the boundaries of area studies. With this aim, the chapter also elaborates on the relationship between area studies and broader social sciences. We aim to contribute to other disciplines and methodology conversations, as the objective of area studies should be similar to that of other social sciences, namely the development of generalizations that contribute to our understanding of human experience and behavior (Wagley 1948; Mitchell 2004). Area studies of the Middle East should have a bearing on the development of interdisciplinary questions, ideas, and methods (Anderson 1999).

The chapter relies on the two authors' experience with conducting fieldwork in Iran and benefits from the gendered perspective of two young women. One author is a non-Iranian researcher, while the other is a dual-national, Iranian citizen who grew up in the United States. Both lived and worked in Tehran for years. Rivetti has regularly visited Iran for research between 2005 and 2009. She tried to return in 2012 and 2013, but her visa applications were turned down. While a visa was issued for her again in 2014, she could not return to Iran because of security considerations. Since 2015, she has obtained visas and visited the country regularly. Saeidi carried out a several months of fieldwork in Iran during 2007–2008. She moved to Tehran in 2012 and lived there until late 2014. The differences between the authors enrich the understanding of how the dynamics connected to doing fieldwork in Iran un- fold, sometimes in a different way, sometimes in a surprisingly similar fashion, for Iranian and non-Iranian citizens.

An Intersectional Approach to Islam, the State, and Authoritarianism

There are very few states that do not adopt a securitarian approach to research. Although the majority of them are liberal democratic systems, it does not mean that all liberal democracies shy away from securitizing critical inquiry. It follows that it is important to discuss what is specific about the way in which Iran and authoritarian systems in general approach researchers, considering that democratic states too may adopt a securitarian approach. For instance, in many cases on-campus scientific initiatives and events related to the campaign of boycott, divestment, and sanctions against Israeli business and universities have reportedly been censored (Salih 2015), with the case of Steven Salaita, whose offer of a position at the University of Illinois at Urbana-Champaign was withdrawn over criticism of Netanyahu, be- coming the symbol of heavy securitization of research and academic labor (Razazan 2016). James Fitzgerald, a lecturer at Dublin City University, provides testimony on how research is being policed by reporting on his experience of being temporarily detained and questioned at Heathrow airport for possessing some academic books on terrorism (Fitzgerald 2015). Amory Starr, Luis Fernandez, and Christian Scholl offer an analysis of how critical inquiry and activism are discouraged in Western Europe and the United States, and major obstacles stand in the way of researchers who decide to engage in political and social issues independently, especially if those issues are related to protest policing and surveillance of activists (Starr, Fernandez, and Scholl 2011). These testimonies echo Olivier Dabène, Vincent Geisser, and Gilles Massardier's work, which critically reviews Juan Linz's classical distinction between democratic and nondemocratic systems, pivoting around the notion of "limited pluralism" that authoritarianisms allow (Dabène, Geisser, and Massardier 2008). The three authors observe that this kind of pluralism is no longer a distinctive marker, but rather the most diffused type of pluralism in contemporary regimes, with democracies possessing a series of "non-pluralist spaces."

It follows that it is important to acknowledge the existence of a similarity when it comes to conducting fieldwork in authoritarian and democratic countries, which are also present in terms of methodological dilemmas researchers deal with. Obtaining the respondents' trust, the researcher's positionality in the field (Maxey 1999), the reliability and validity of interviews (Berry 2002), and emotional involvement (Woliver 2002) are indeed common challenges that researchers face when engaged in fieldwork. However, although methodological and systemic similarities exist, there is a variation in the way power circulates in an authoritarian political system, and this has an impact on research-related activities.

According to Asef Bayat, while it is true that power is coercive in all types of regimes, what characterizes authoritarian regimes is the "unevenness of power circulation." In some countries, state power is "far weightier, more concentrated, and 'thicker,' so to speak, than in others" (Bayat 2010), thereby increasing the likelihood of a more securitarian approach for researchers. In fact, echoing Bayat, securitization depends on how power is distributed among the institutions that compose the constellation of players that are in a relationship with the researcher in Iran. The ministries of culture (Ershad), information (Etela'at), individual universities and their governance bodies, and security and disciplinary forces are all influential in the research process. Crucially, all these actors can establish a radically different relationship with the researcher. A researcher may be welcome by some institutions, while other organs will be reluctant to cooperate. However, the "uneven" distribution of power among various actors places this structural fragmentation in a distinguishable hierarchy. Additionally, security and disciplinary forces enjoy more substantial and unaccountable power, and, accordingly, the fragmentation of power gains a systemic form and lessens the capacity of political actors to garner personal and collective power. Uneven power circulation and distribution, which benefit security forces, create a research-unfriendly environment, in which researchers, both dual citizens and foreigners, may be the object of securitized measures. Indeed, conducting fieldwork in Iran is also a complicated process for Iranian students based in Iran given the Islamic Republic's general distrust of sociological investigations (Banakar 2016).

This resonates with the findings of other scholars who have pointed out that factors such as Islam are less relevant than state institutions in impeding research activities. Goli Rezai-Rashti tells us about the significant obstacles she encountered, all of which were of a political-bureaucratic nature (Rezai-Rashti 2013) rather than cultural-religious. Research institutions and Iranian universities opposed her research project on women and higher education in Iran because, crucially, they feared that her findings would be used to propagate a negative image of Iran abroad. Rezai-Rashti addresses the bureaucratic permissions she was forced to obtain, and the commissions and committees she had interviews with. She does not, however, mention that the institutions and universities where her research was carried out feared that her findings might undermine religious principles or Islam. This also resonates in Arang Keshavarzian's account (2015) of his fieldwork in Tehran's ba-zaar, where his religious faith was never asked or tested and where, he reports, he never saw any expression of that fanatic religiosity *bazaari* are often accused of displaying. This marginality of religion is consistent with our experience, too. More than Islam, what constrains research is the securitarian approach state institutions have vis-à-vis researchers who, in a hostile geopolitical environment, have often been accused of being spies or plotting against national security.

In most instances, this securitarian approach is activated when researchers are believed to transgress their social categorization. While the way in which the state classifies the Iranian population is not a topic discussed often in Iranian studies, a clear social hierarchy within the public sphere exists. As Arzoo Osanloo (2009) writes, the 1979 revolution and the postrevolutionary state have activated Iranians politically, making them subjects who bear rights and, as such, are involved in a so-cial contract with the state. Both the 1979 revolution and the Iran-Iraq war have had a crucial role in demarcating citizenry categories, with the formation of the notions of belonging to the state and of to whom the state belongs (Saeidi 2010). By virtue of such a mutual recognition, citizens are allocated a specific status within state structures and society, from which they can make demands to the state. Foreign and dual citizens who visit Iran to conduct research are also placed into political categories based on conclusions drawn from national, personal, and local profiling techniques. Generally speaking, their status is quite low on the social and polit-ical ladder, and the category they occupy determines how much access and what "rights" they have as researchers.

In this sense, the role of Islam is "ancillary" to the power of the state because it serves the purpose of concentrating power—whatever form it may take, from re-pressive and military strength to the arrogated right to interpret religious texts—within state structures. Islam is bent to the political necessity of establishing a strong state in the postrevolutionary period. This is also evident in the case of lim-itations to interactions between men and women and in the Islamic garment for women: people are asked to respect the legislation of the state, not Islam, which, according to alternative interpretations that Iranian authorities consider unlawful, neither segregates men and women nor imposes the hijab on women.

Thus, field researchers occupy a specific place in the social hierarchy that various state institutions in Iran collectively create, a place that corresponds to a specific code of conduct. In general, as mentioned above, field researchers coming from abroad, both foreign and dual nationals, occupy a low position on the social and political scale and are required not to interfere with national current and political affairs. It should be noted, though, that exceptions exist if foreign or dual-national researchers are interested in working closely with a particular political faction in Iran. In general, this makes a relatively moderate involvement in local affairs acceptable. Formal structures of power, however, do not explicitly address this categorization; often the information is conveyed to researchers when they arrive in Tehran. For example, during Saeidi's tenure as a volunteer lecturer at the University of Tehran, a PhD student provided "advice" to Saeidi, and openly told her she worked for the Intelligence Ministry, even going as far as to explain the type of "marks" she had seen on her case file. This student would often tell Saeidi indirectly what her boundaries were. For instance, during the 2013 presidential election, this PhD student repeatedly told Saeidi not to attend any rallies or gatherings; if there were any unrest, she would definitely be arrested for inciting it. Saeidi was given the same warning during an interview with officials at the Ministry of Education, so she had reason to think this was an important issue to the state's intelligence apparatus.

There does seem to be overlap between the limits Iranian and non-Iranian researchers face with respect to the state's intention of keeping them out of potentially unstable spaces. This stems from the state's general insecurity in the public sphere. In 2005, a journalist friend invited Rivetti to the annual conference of the Iranian press association. Somehow surprisingly, the wife of a well-known dissident journalist, Akbar Ganji, was invited to speak. She gave a very emotional speech, and, as the public burst into tears, many attendees went closer to the stage in order to take pictures of her. Rivetti did the same, but, as soon as she got close to the stage, where many other photographers also gathered, a security guard caught her and locked her into a room. The episode ended some twenty minutes later, when Rivetti's friend entered the room with the chief of the security service at the conference and freed her. This episode showed how easy it is to stand out as a foreigner, regardless of one's garment and physical appearance, and reminded Rivetti that she was not supposed to mingle too much with local people and involve herself in local affairs.

Limits can be conveyed in an explicit manner, too, to dual-national researchers. In 2012, Saeidi had just arrived in Tehran and went to buy an Islamic hijab at Haft-e Tir shopping area, which is a well-known shopping center for hijabs. Unknown to her at the time, her shopping trip coincided with an anniversary of the 2009 election unrest, and some opposition media outlets had suggested that people protest in the area. When Saeidi entered the area, plainclothes security agents harassed her, followed her closely, and surrounded her at every turn. The message was given that she should go home, and she did. From then on, she understood that she was not welcome in spaces where protests were taking place or sites where the opposition might meet. However, she was allowed to teach and research in the universities of Tehran, and the state permitted and at times facilitated her research, which explores the making of socially embedded forms of citizenship among Hezbollah activists who work on the Islamic Republic's cultural projects. It is best for researchers to pay attention to the personalized limits the state has assigned them, and understand they do not necessarily mean that you are not allowed to carry out research.

However, it would be problematic to "remove" Islam from conducting research in the Islamic Republic. In fact, religion is relevant to the field researcher, beyond garment and behavioral rules, both in positive and in negative ways. A lack of respect for religious practices or moral rules can indeed serve as a reason to target field researchers and their presence in the country. Having extramarital relations, for instance, can be a source of problems for researchers because such behavior makes them visible to authorities as "morally deplorable." By contrast, adherence to morality and shared cultural and religious background can relax securitarian and suspicious attitudes. For example, in the introduction to her book *Marriage on Trial*, Ziba Mir-Hosseini (1993) states that being a sayyid, or descendant of the Prophet, and an Iranian helped her greatly in carrying out research in Special Civil Courts in Tehran during the mid-1980s. Saeidi has also felt that identifying as Muslim allowed her to defend women's rights in the different spaces she was in, including the University of Tehran as a lecturer, as well as a researcher in Hezbollah cultural institutes in Tehran. Her religious beliefs and identity had a central role in helping her build relations with decision-makers. Similarly, Rivetti found the elite members she interviewed sympathetic toward her Catholic background, and this personal information often was remarked with appreciation. The fact that she was familiar with some academics who participated in initiatives of religious dialogue, and the fact that she worked for a period in a Catholic education institution, helped build trust with the elite. Therefore religions, and not exclusively Islam, may be a factor helping the researcher, who, in the eyes of the elite and the decision-makers, may be considered "culturally closer" because of the recognition of his or her religious identity.

Rethinking Security and Research Ethics in Authoritarian Environments

Generalizations can be drawn from the Iranian case as to how the state assigns researchers their "place," a reflection relevant to researchers engaged in various fields. It follows that challenges such as building trust and winning the attention of the respondents are common issues to field researchers when it comes to the practicality of conducting fieldwork. What changes in the case of Iran is what, as noted earlier, Bayat called the "uneven circulation of power," which makes the power the security forces exert much thicker than the power that, for instance, the Ministry of Culture exerts, a condition that securitizes directly and indirectly the work and the presence of the researcher in the field. In such an environment, researchers need to be mentally flexible and ready to change research strategies, reviewing methods as well as decisions. This is valid for research ethics practices too, as broader security concerns can, for example, bring the researcher to obscure local people's contribution or interrupt contacts, although theoretically research ethics posits the opposite. It follows that field researchers have to deal with interconnected security and ethical challenges.

When it comes to security issues, field researchers face two kinds of challenges: the first type is their own personal security, while the second is protecting those who are involved in their research activities. Field researchers, especially if foreign, expose the people they work with. Iranians linked to foreign researchers may be accused of collaborating with dubious foreigners, and can be used to extract information about the foreigners and then accused of being in touch with them.

Researchers of political or social issues who spend a long time in the field are regarded generally as suspicious and, especially if the foreigner, is seen as *fuzul*, nosy or "interfering." They need to be mindful of their own personal security, as a variety of means are used to target their presence and work. Bureaucratized religious morality, meaning state-sanctioned religious morality, is one of those means. Often, suspicions of "immoral behavior," whether real or fabricated, such as having extramarital relations, can be used as a justification to target researchers, weakening their self-confidence, with the ultimate goal of hampering their research. At a conference in Tehran, Rivetti met a young man, a lawyer who studied in Canada and worked for a think tank in the city. Rivetti and this man exchanged their email addresses for professional reasons, and when he invited her out to the cinema, she declined the offer. However, upon his insistence, they went to the cinema with a group of Rivetti's girlfriends. During the following weeks, the man contacted Rivetti several times. She repeatedly tried to stop any contact, being very explicit about her discomfort with his insistence. Some friends suggested that he might be from the security services. He started then to be aggressive, and even when Rivetti asked her male friends to tell the man to stop calling her, he never stopped. When Rivetti left Iran after few months, he called her on her foreign mobile phone, something that shocked Rivetti. It is likely that he was someone from the Information Ministry, although Rivetti was not able to confirm this. However, this is an example of how researchers' personal lives appeal to the security forces, which may use the researcher's personal relationships (real or imagined) to penetrate the researcher's private sphere and target her or his sense of security and comfort. Similarly, Saeidi was approached by a PhD student at the University of Tehran who argued that her ideas and activism inspired him and that he wanted to talk more. Other students, especially female students, warned Saeidi that he was suspected of working with the Information Ministry and was generally a shady character. However, Saeidi did not want to securitize her world and decided to ignore the warnings, concerned that these accusations were made against him because of his lower economic status and rural background. However, after a few meetings she noted that the conversations were mostly about her personal beliefs and practices, so she stopped meeting with him. The male contact then began showing up at her place of work, stating that he suspected she was a spy. He stated that if he made this suspicion public, Saeidi could get into considerable trouble. When Saeidi told him that she would turn him into the university security forces for harassment, she never saw or heard from him again. Although male researchers can also be targeted, there does seem to be a strong trend toward the harassment of female researchers. According to our experiences and those of female colleagues, individuals who become abusive through threats related to professional activities more often approach women. It follows that female researchers should be suspicious of individuals who insist on meetings and exchanges that seem unnecessarily prolonged.

Researchers, both dual nationals and foreigners, can also be exposed to infighting between the regime's factions. An example is the case of F., a dual-national scholar based in Europe, who has contacts with the pragmatic and reformist faction that was instrumental in the achievement of the 2015 nuclear deal. Notorious hard-line media outlets, critical of the nuclear deal, identified F. as an "American spy" with the goal of targeting the opposite political faction, favorable to the deal. This example not only shows that the state is internally fragmented, with factions fighting one against the other, but also that researchers can be at the center of such political fights. The practice of *siaah namaai* (slander), namely when foreign researchers and dual nationals are called spies or accused of being at the service of foreign powers, has the goal of targeting rival factions by exposing a researcher. The "pulse" of international politics is critical to such occurrences. In fact, strained diplomatic relations between Iran and the rest of the international community can affect field researchers, complicating their access to the field or reinforcing securitized approaches to them. In unstable geopolitical conditions, conservative media have depicted foreign and dual-national researchers as part of an international plot to overthrow the Islamic Republic (Therme 2012).

Apart from personal security, field researchers also have to be mindful that local people can be victims of arrest, intimidation, and harassment. For several months during her research stay in 2008, Rivetti was in contact with an activist from a local student group. His role was crucial in helping Rivetti gain a deeper understanding of student politics. One day, he disappeared. Rivetti was worried but did not call him or try to get in touch, to avoid damaging him further. Few days later, Rivetti received a call on her cell phone from an unknown number. A man on the other end told her that he was her friend-activist. He told Rivetti that he had been brought to Rajay-e Shahr prison, drugged, and abused. He insisted that they meet. Rivetti did not recognize his voice and feared that a friendly reaction could be used to find her friend guilty of contacts with a suspicious foreigner. They did not meet, and for the rest of her research stay, Rivetti cut all contacts. He contacted her a few months later, thanking her for not meeting the imposter and not contacting him again. The intelligence and security forces monitor activists regardless of their interactions with others, but connection to a foreigner may provide the justification to target them. It is not in the interest of the researcher or the researched to make an already unstable context more volatile during fieldwork, and these moments should be avoided, for they obstruct the production of knowledge (Nilan 2002).

Approaches to Iranians involved in a field researchers' activity may vary. Security forces approached Saeidi's contacts at times to ask their impression of her. In some instances they were asked to give their thoughts on Saeidi's level of religiosity and even *savad*, or professional knowledge. For instance, a student was asked to comment on Saeidi's scholarship. Intelligence agents asked several contacts if Saeidi wears the Islamic hijab outside of Iran. One interviewee, whom Saeidi spoke with during her PhD research on war martyrs' widows, was asked at her workplace through the *herasat* security forces what Saeidi's questions aimed at revealing. In Saeidi's experience, interviewees the regime trusted were contacted to profile Saeidi, but not harassed for collaborating with her on projects. However, such exposure told the contacts that they were being watched too, reminding them that it is good practice to avoid connections with foreigners and to recognize the boundaries established by the state.

Given these security concerns, ethical practices should be reviewed consequently. Ethical challenges exist for all researchers engaged in fieldwork, as they need to avoid treating people on the ground as "native informants" whose role is to supply them with data for publications. However, it may be problematic to acknowledge the contribution of local people and activists because this might expose them. Rivetti's research project deals with the dynamics of political activism in authoritarian settings, with Iran as a case study. She discussed her research with the activists she was working with, and many asked her to refrain from making it explicit that she had had conversations with them. This request not only came from activists based in Iran, but also from Iranian activists outside of Iran who were concerned for the security of their families and friends back home. This means not only that they asked Rivetti to anonymize their interviews, which Rivetti was going to do anyway, but also that Rivetti's presence was a source of anxiety. In order to respect such exigencies and even discomfort, Rivetti at times did not carry her research through, at others she obscured the existence and contribution of activists, and at others still she suspended interactions during periods of time or terminated them.

However, although field researchers need to be mindful of limitations and stick to the level of freedom the security forces grant them, it is possible to circumnavigate restrictions. Two useful coping strategies can be deployed: one can be labeled the "politics of ambiguity"; the other is the ability to turn to one's advantage the fragmentation of state structures.

While trying to get access to the national archives for research, Rivetti was repeatedly invited for "informal meetings" with management. Given the nature of her research project, focused on contemporary social and political issues, she did not want to provide the details of her work. Furthermore, a foreigner wishing to access archival information could be considered to be "interfering" with national affairs.

However, being a foreigner played out as an advantage in this context. Rivetti's ambiguity when talking about her research was interpreted as incompetence, and therefore not suspicious. Likewise, when policymakers asked about her research, Rivetti could work around those questions by referring to her research interest as *Iranshenasi*, namely Iranian studies, a field often perceived as academically shallow and orientalist in Iran and therefore not worthy of further attention. On the other hand, by engaging in clear and concise conversations with authorities, a foreign researcher becomes more suspicious not only to state agents but also wider society, because no one speaks this way. Indirect, unclear, and evasive forms of talking are often described as *pechundan*, or negotiation. Such nonspecific communication has crucial political functions not only because it grants the researcher room to adapt to unknown circumstances, but also because it leaves space for authorities and listeners to process the researcher's words, to ponder ideas and demands as they wish. State employees value the construction of this space between words, thoughts, and people, for it reinforces their right to remain unresponsive to citizens. During her time teaching in Iran, Saeidi found that this technique also entered the academic writing of students, posing major obstacles for the knowledge production process. It also takes some time getting used to this type of communication, particularly for researchers educated in the West, where explicit self-expression is highly praised. For Saeidi, one of the most difficult aspects of living and working in Tehran for three years was learning this new language. This form of self-censoring, which includes cutting sentences short, avoiding language that clearly places political responsibility on state agents, and maintaining a disengaged demeanor that suggests you are not invested in what is happening, was so debilitating that for the first few months she was speechless or incoherent in the public sphere.

Researchers can cope with constraining pressures and carve out room for investigation by exploiting state fragmentation and infighting. A man we will call "R." participated for years in interreligious dialogue initiatives, reaching out to state institutions in Tehran but also single clerics and clerical institutions in Qom. This allowed him to strengthen relationships with a variety of institutions and individuals who protected him when, in 2010, he traveled to Iran even though the local embassy warned him that he was not welcome because of his Green Movement–friendly declarations. This example illustrates that persons outside constitutional institutions and security forces are part of the constellation of actors involved in the process of knowledge production and transmission. In fact, religious centers and clerical institutions may be much more effective in protecting their contacts than, for instance, the ministers of foreign affairs or education. In such conditions, only well-protected individuals with a diversified network of personal contacts, be they family members, clerics, or even members of the security apparatus, can conduct research in Iran because they can negotiate protection from different sources, regardless of the broader security situation.

Conclusion

The chapter reaches two conclusions. First, we found that, contrary to conventional wisdom about Iran, Islam and religious limitations in everyday life do not constitute an obstacle to the field researcher's activity, even when the researcher is a young woman. The presence of religion in the public sphere does not impede research-related activities, unless state authorities turn it into a control device on the basis of their arrogated right to interpret religion. It follows that it is the state's authoritarian practices that pose major obstacles to the researcher's activities. Researchers need to remain within the political boundaries determined by the regime. They need to be as invisible as possible, and not to mingle in Iran's internal affairs, a condition that de facto may limit the scope of one's research-related activities. Second, we found that our reflections from the field are relevant to researchers engaged in other settings as well, beyond the geographical limitation of the MENA region. In addition, when it comes to applied methods, field researchers deal with common challenges such as winning the trust of respondents and dealing with the latter's expectations and frustrations, regardless of geography and broader political regimes. It follows that area studies should contribute more forcefully to methodological debates in the social sciences.

4

Authoritarianism, Gender, and Sociopolitics in Saudi Arabia

GWENN OKRUHLIK

Why Saudi Arabia?

In the early 1980s, with some notable exceptions,[1] Saudi Arabia was virtual terra incognita for serious social science research that was based on fieldwork. There were two extremes in the literature—either predictions of a revolution that would topple the Al Saud ruling family or glowing accounts of how to become a millionaire overnight in the oil boom. I wanted to grapple with the great gray middle that I thought was surely more real and compelling. As a political scientist, I study power and I am especially interested in sociopolitics, which are salient in Saudi Arabia.

The methodological difficulty of field research in Saudi Arabia means that the rewards are remarkable when you do connect with someone on a human level and uncover new ways of thinking. It is because of these possibilities that I find myself still drawn to the realities of Riyadh, Jeddah, and Qatif. To contextualize the complexity of field research, understand that you cannot easily disentangle social norms, political authoritarianism, and religious privilege as they have been conflated over time by the regime (Okruhlik 2009). One is constantly navigating and negotiating decorum and boundaries to elicit the most meaningful information possible.[2]

Talking Politics in Saudi Arabia

Doing good research under repressive strictures or in crisis is always challenging, and Saudi Arabia is not exceptional. Still, the challenges for political research there are different in degree and in kind. The coupling of social norms and authoritarian political structures keeps life interesting during field research. It is further complicated by a history of limited scholarly exchange. In this chapter, I look at the lessons that I learned in negotiating these differences in kind and in degree.

A researcher must be willing to traverse disciplinary boundaries. Written surveys, tape recorders, and statistical methodologies may not capture the depth and nuance of social and political debates in Saudi Arabia. The most important decision I made before my first trip was to go into the country well-read but without preconceived assumptions. I did not intend to gather data to support an inflexible line of argu-mentation. I had no unchangeable scheme. I listened. I observed. I asked questions. The social and political context in Saudi Arabia requires fluidity in methodology. One cannot be rigidly fixated and expect deep data.

As everywhere, the methods must be appropriate to the research inquiry at hand. In Saudi Arabia, they also often reflect gender, discipline, age, marital status, nationality, and desired sample. My methods reflect all these attributes. Male researchers, single female scholars, scholars on short-term visits, or economists, for example, may utilize diverse methodologies as effectively. My point is that by using creative and fluid methodologies, you can still ask the very hard questions about power and politics. There are ways to do sensitive political research. This was one of the most important lessons that I learned—and I often learned it the hard way. To address how social science research differs in degree and in kind, I pro-ceed in five parts: getting in; interviewing and recording notes; specific challenges for women researchers; field research under authoritarianism; field research in war and jihad, and practical matters. I endeavor to address matters in fieldwork that are common to all researchers and also focus upon concerns specific to women researchers.

Access to Country: Saudi Sponsorship (*Kafalah*) and US Gatekeepers

Academic specialists on Saudi Arabia long lacked regularized networks of support that existed in other countries. For decades, there was a strategic stranglehold on access to Saudi Arabia for US-based scholars, maintained by a handful of key organizations, or gatekeepers, based in Washington, DC (Okruhlik 1999a). These are think tanks, consultancies, and nonprofits that are intimately tied to ruling family members.

It was extraordinarily difficult to get in the first time. For two years, I banged my head against an impenetrable brick wall. Finally, we—my spouse, Patrick Conge, accompanied me—were set to depart the United States only to have our visas rescinded at the last moment. The government makes obtaining official permis-sion a nightmare. I got in with a Fulbright Doctoral Research Grant, I believe, be-cause one individual took a huge risk on me. After months of meetings, letters, and phone calls, he finally trusted me as a human being as he watched me play with his children for hours in a Washington, DC, park. No foreigner—from day laborer to professional—can enter the country without being formally "sponsored" by a Saudi Arabian citizen, company, or institution (your *kafil*). My *kafil* was King Abdulaziz University in Jeddah, and I remain grateful to it. There had been many teachers of English, the hard sciences, and engineering who were sponsored by universities, but not researchers—much less a woman researcher who was studying contemporary politics in a critical light in 1989 under university auspices. That changed everything, and it still affects much of my methodology.[3] It also made daily life difficult. A sponsor is responsible for housing, transportation, research assistance, office space, and, in some sense, your moral behavior. Still today, sponsorship is granted very judiciously, only after a thorough vetting process. In many cases, the printed stipulations that a researcher must agree to have grown more restrictive and vexing.

When university officials discovered that I was not a protégé of the longtime ambassador to the United States, Prince Bandar, and had never even met him, they cut most ties with me out of fear. Colleagues became much more cautious in showing me any support and were wary of my work. This increased my logistical problems but also completely freed me to do my research. This is why my interviews are so rich (Okruhlik 1992, 1999b). Nobody was introducing me to the "right" people, and I could weave my way in and out of Saudi Arabian society.

Perhaps clueless about what to do with me, officials housed me in poor conditions on the outskirts of town. The compound housed several hundred Filipino nurses and was surrounded by a ten-foot-tall cinder block wall topped by barbed wire. Guards were stationed at the single entry and exit point. No landlines existed in the compound. Before cell phones, this meant that there was no communication with the outside world. Nurses were not permitted to leave the premises except on compound buses that took them to work and to a specific grocery store and mall on a set schedule. Often, the drivers confiscated the identity cards of the nurses. The apartments may have been spacious and air-conditioned, but they were beyond filthy. Without understanding what they were doing, my sponsors exposed me to the dirty underbelly of labor-importing countries; for two months, I had to live in the conditions that are usually deep-sixed. I am grateful, in retrospect, as it informed my later thinking on the relationship between dependence on foreign labor and constructs of citizenship (Okruhlik 1999c, 2010).

US-based gatekeepers lost much of their power to control access to Saudi Arabia after September 2001 as their intimate networks became the subject of oversight (Silverstein 2001). Now, the King Faisal Foundation for Islamic Studies and Research in Riyadh is quite good about sponsoring foreign scholars. However, it has become more regularized and has more oversight. Some of the recent "Rules and Regulations" are acceptable. They require participation in an orientation and in all meetings of the Foundation, presentation of a seminar upon completion of the study, and monthly reports. Unfortunately, they also include the stipulations that the Foundation shall organize all the meetings required for research in the kingdom and that visiting fellows must inform the Research Department in writing prior to any formal or informal visit or meeting in the kingdom, inclusive of name and title of person being met, location, and time of meeting. At best, we can hope that these rules are invoked only when the sponsor deems it necessary, not as a blanket procedure on all researchers at all times. Needless to say, such reporting would inhibit deep research.

Interview Techniques: Building Trust

What follows is derived from years of interviews in Saudi Arabia. For me, an early lesson was that people were not impressed by my professional accomplishments or degrees. They were made comfortable by my demeanor and my character. I cannot overemphasize the importance of integrity and of building personal relationships of trust. I establish myself as a scholar and a person of integrity. As a married woman, my husband accompanied me. Today, women do fine fieldwork traveling alone and using methods appropriate to their inquiry (Le Renard 2014; Thiollet 2015).

On the first trip, I was frustrated by a widespread hesitancy to talk with me. Finally, a Saudi Arabian pulled me aside and explained, "We're all afraid that you are a journalist. You must understand that." Apparently, a well-known journalist promised discretion, trust, and scholarship to many old families. People opened their homes and family histories to her only to see their deep family and business secrets published in a nonacademic bestseller. It took me months to overcome this fear. I had to self-consciously separate myself from journalists. Never misrepresent who you are or what you are doing, and distance yourself from those who do misrepresent themselves or you.

Referrals matter. They must be used wisely because *who* the referrer is matters. The nature of the referral may determine how much—or how little—meaningful data you will be able to elicit. At the same time, you must be constantly vigilant to guard against biases inherent in snowballing referrals to gain interviews. You must self-consciously seek diversity (if that is what you want). Periodically, carefully survey your sources. Then, actively seek difference in gender, region, class, status, sect, perspective, sector, or age—whichever attributes matter to your research problem. It can be easier to see sheikhs, ministers, princes, and academics than to see ordinary people in shops or behind clerical desks or pharmacists or students. People sometimes underestimate this and are wowed by the glitz of regal pomp and circumstance, but ordinary working people are the real story. The politics of power and authoritarianism are felt in daily life as it is lived on the ground.

Confidentiality and discretion are primary. I may interview a person who learned beforehand that I spoke with his cousin the previous week, but I never acknowledge that I did so, nor does he. It is unspoken and understood. This confidentiality makes him feel more protected, and he will share with me more data. Never underestimate the continued importance of confidentiality (Jones 2010; Le Renard 2014). There are discrete ways to discuss a controversial subject that allow you to learn while also maintaining a feeling of safety for your interviewee. Code words are a secret language that makes off-limit topics permissible. When people wanted to discuss anarchy and crime in the vast slums of Riyadh and Jeddah that are off the grid, they spoke instead of "Mogadishu," the capital of Somalia. We both understood the real subject, as I heard it several times and connected the dots. Follow the cues that you are given by interlocutors. Think twice or thrice before you mention a member of the ruling family by name—even if you both know about whom you speak by other descriptors.

Finally, deep fieldwork in Saudi Arabia may stress a marriage, but there are also advantages. There is power in two sets of eyes and ears. Though we sit in the same conversation, we sometimes see and hear totally different things. That is valuable. And when we both key in to a particular moment, we know that it mattered. Pat also buys me time in interviews to pause, think, reframe a question to elicit a more thoughtful response, or to record notes. For example, he might ask a question to allow conversation to continue to flow while I gather my thoughts.

Slow and Steady: Observe Carefully

The first 15–20 minutes are crucial and often the most difficult part of an interview. During this time, I establish my integrity, discretion, and the importance of my family. In 1989, Pat would give men permission to talk with me, with a gentle "Please talk with my wife." That explicit permission became subtler over time. In 2003, he would simply say, "Her work is very important." People evaluated me in these opening "social" conversations deciding how much or how little they would give me. If the first 20 minutes were successful, so would be the remaining two hours. Integrity and trust are still key to eliciting deep conversation. I always ask the same basic questions in interviews for purposes of comparability and rigor. But I structure the questions so that they are open-ended. This allows people to answer with a simple yes or no if they are profoundly uncomfortable or to talk for 45 minutes in response to a single question. Both responses are legitimate. Careful construction of your questions allows people to save face. Sometimes, the physical movement of a person reveals an unsaid answer. Perhaps an individual does not want to answer a question—but the uncomfortable shift in his or her seat tells me everything I need to know. That postural change is important. It indicates discomfort with a particular question—and is an answer to my question. Under an extraordinarily repressive security apparatus, even the acknowledgment of a subject can be perilous. Silences and absences speak volumes about politics and power. In a similar vein, interview dynamics can change dramatically by the mere insertion of an extra person in the room. On two occasions, male respondents, unbeknownst to me, invited their wives to our meetings and used them as a foil to avoid hard questions. Instantly, the hoped-for interview became a social gathering with tea and desserts. They counteracted my methodology. In such situations, if you push beyond receptivity, the door might close permanently.

Always end each interview on a positive note no matter how exasperating it might have been. Always seek new lines of inquiry and people with whom to talk. Also, follow up with your contacts to ask for materials or documents they promised you.

Recording Knowledge: Significant Change in Allowable Transcripts

In 1989–1990, each of my 118 interview transcripts was a mere handful of code words. A two-hour interview would be recorded in a dozen scribbled words on a single sheet of paper. To write more words would simply have ended the interview. I would run home and unlock my brain. From each word would pour forth an entire conversation. The key, I learned, was to remember the *transitions* between topics. Transitions were critical to the flow and meaning of the conversation. That was hard. I had to focus to reconstruct the process: "How did we get from that housing contract to that princely land grab to the curriculum to that chamber of commerce election?" Twelve words could become seven pages.

After the events of September 11, 2001, a new generation of scholars began to study Saudi Arabia. And Saudi Arabia, under intense international scrutiny, began to admit scholars to conduct research, in addition to scores of journalists. There is a good deal of valuable work now. The dynamics of field research changed a great deal after 2001. The government felt pressured to open its doors, and people wanted their stories told.

In 2003, I interviewed about 150 people, and, in stark contrast to early research, I took copious pages of notes with few worries about the conversation being abruptly halted.[4] Open discussion of politics was everywhere—in the schools, streets, homes, offices, and shopping malls. People wanted their thoughts included, though they were still anonymous. Fieldwork was still difficult but for different reasons. The concern was not about talking with a woman or a political scientist; it was about the war in Iraq, American aggression, and jihad. Interviews were often painful, like peeling layers of skin off an onion. I often had to work through layers of distrust, anger, and animosity that reflected my American citizenship. Other foreign researchers also encounter suspicion (Le Renard 2014; Menoret 2014). This is not unique to Saudi Arabia; it is part and parcel of conducting research in authoritarian countries where there are prohibitions on open discussion.

Gender and Guardianship

There is a common misconception that gender inhibits scholarly research in Saudi Arabia. This is not exactly the case. Gender indeed is a challenge in terms of logistics and daily practical matters, but it is a gift in terms of interview access. I had access to both genders, and this affords me a powerful position from which to learn about society and politics. Thiollet finds this still the case today (email to the author, 2016). It would be difficult for a Saudi Arabian man to interview a Saudi Arabian woman in person and vice versa. A foreign man could not interview a Saudi Arabian woman in person without the consent of her male guardian. I can do both, but I carefully identify and work within the norms through dress, demeanor, and accompaniment—pushing the edges as far as possible but knowing when to stop. Further, social media have since provided an effective route around physical gender barriers, allowing men and women to interact without accusations of inappropriate behavior.

A *mahram* (guardian), if not your husband, is a man whom you cannot marry—your father, son, uncle or brother. A *mahram* "legitimizes" a woman's behavior. My spouse was my *mahram*. In late spring 2017, King Salman "relaxed" some of the requirements of guardianship so that women can now visit some government offices without the permission of their *mahram*. In September, after decades of women's activism and protest, he issued a decree to grant women the right to drive. As always though, there is a difference in the text of official statements, and how they are enforced in daily life.

Though I had an office in the women's section of the University, all decisions about me were made on the men's side of the University. My spouse was caught in a grip between a university bureaucracy in an authoritarian state and a stubborn wife who was determined to do her research. He was a message bearer between two immovable poles that were at odds. It was an untenable position for him to be in. He occasionally reminds me of the difficulty.[5] I was clearly the main player in the interviews but was utterly dependent on him as *mahram*, driver, and source of legitimacy. We shall see how the new decree that allows women to drive will play out and if it affects foreign women. In the meantime, female researchers can hire a foreign driver to escort them or take allowable taxis.

Gendered Interview Techniques

For most researchers, dress matters. This is especially true for women. Abayas became fuller, longer, and more enveloping over the years. Today, they are often more beautiful and colorful. The old-style wrap abayas had no sleeves or Velcro closures. They were graceful but quite difficult to hold closed while you maneuvered notebooks and greetings. Now, sleeves, snaps, and Velcro make modest movement easy. You must choose your abaya/hijab carefully. They must be appropriate for the work that you are doing and the person whom you are interviewing. They do not always cross class and region. How you dress continues to influence perceptions of you (Le Renard 2014; Thiollet, email to author 2016). Learn the intricacies of modest dress from Saudi Arabian women.

When I interviewed important Sunni Islamist opposition figures in London in 1997 and 1999, one asked me beforehand "to dress as a proper Muslim lady," though he knew I was not Muslim. I wandered down his neighborhood street, covered, accompanied, and non-Muslim. His request keyed me into subsequent interview dynamics and the importance to him of living his ideology outwardly. His ideology and his commitment were reflected in my dress and the accompaniment of my *mahram*. As he began to trust me, his vast and intricate knowledge poured forth. I learned a great deal about the early days of the country and the contemporary grievances against the Al Saud and what he called "the corrupt ulama."

Many Saudi Arabian men prefer to not shake hands with a woman. There is a crucial gesture to ensure that a gender-integrated interview starts well. In lieu of shaking hands, gently place your hand over your heart. This speaks volumes and avoids the discomfort of shaking hands. The restriction on gender interaction is not intellectual; it is only physical. Pat had to be a physical presence in the room but could "disappear" from the conversation. He was sometimes a crucial participant, at other times a silent observer. Rarely but occasionally, I would ask a question to a man and he would answer directly to Pat's eyes, never engaging my own. I would listen to the response and then ask another question to the man. He would answer again to Pat. Everything came to me via passive transmission. I called our unique and effective triangular communication methodology "interview by osmosis." It was unspoken and seamless. We were all at ease and had productive conversations. The point is that you adapt your style to make the person comfortable. A researcher may dance at women's parties, smoke shisha, allow confidantes to sit in on an interview, or attend long social functions without asking any hard questions for weeks in order to nurture familiarity.

Gendered Encounters: Protecting Your Project When Space Is Normative

While gender has not seriously inhibited my research, there are nevertheless many instances of uncomfortable encounters with men when I was perceived to be in a place I did not belong. Always be aware of your surroundings, the people around you, what you might be doing that could be construed as a threat, and what gestures or words make someone uncomfortable. Be aware of other people's discomfort even in a social situation. For example, I was invited to a male majlis (a salon) and was seated on the floor next to my spouse among all the men. Suddenly, there was a quiet and furtive chatter all around. Without being asked, I quietly stood and moved to a corner where I had seen from the corner of my eye that a separate small cloth was being laid for me. I was given a private spatial arrangement. Not a word or apology had to be uttered.

Gendered spatial segregation is enforced by security, by men in authority, and by members of *hay'ah*, the Committee for the Prevention of Vice and the Promotion of Virtue. Informally called the *mutawwa'a*, they have been reined in by the government but are still evident in some areas. In each of several encounters with the *hay'ah*, my spouse's adamant proclamation that we were married was necessary. We also carried our marriage license with us always. I had to use it on two occasions when police stopped my taxi because I traveled alone from women's parties late at night. Today, of course, you can scan everything into your phone, including your sponsor's contact information, so that it is always accessible. Several times, I was told to leave a building because women were not permitted; for example, in the chambers of commerce or government buildings. A rebuttal was necessary, and it needed to be persistent, firm, and polite. Only once was the situation inflammatory and that was when a member of *the hay'ah* challenged a private Saudi businessman whom I was interviewing because he had allowed me to enter his small shop. It was a complex interaction because the person did not challenge me or my husband, but instead angrily confronted the Saudi Arabian shop-owner—in his own establishment. He in turn was livid and embarrassed and argued vociferously with the *mutawwa'a*.

Protect your reputation for integrity and be careful about associating with visiting groups of dignitaries. They may be feted in ways that do not reflect much of society, and they may lack knowledge about local norms such as segregation, decorum, and appropriate subjects. I was asked to accompany a visiting academic delegation from the United States in order to provide context. The untoward escapades of the visitors had important and serious repercussions on my work. After a dinner, some of the American women professors danced repeatedly with Saudi Arabian men. Perhaps this was an effort of the hosts to demonstrate traditional dancing styles and to humor the guests. Though I was cajoled, I refused to participate. This is simply inappropriate behavior, certainly for a researcher. But gossip spread like wildfire across both campuses. Unfortunately, faculty members heard rumors about *me* dancing with men, something I would not do. I was called into the dean's office and asked point blank if I had done so. Though she accepted my answer, our relationship changed, as she now had to protect her own reputation. She could be tarnished by association through accusations that were erroneously leveled at me. She explained this situation to me; our relationship grew more distant and less supportive. Fortunately, we have recovered our friendship over the ensuing years.

In 1989, male academics thought it was prestigious to have a Fulbright scholar visit their campus. So I was greeted with a lavish reception with male university dignitaries. At the time, I was happily ensconced on the women's side of the campus, where I worked at my desk in the large graduate student room for hours each day. The men insisted that I, as a distinguished visitor, be given access to an office on the men's side of campus. It was considered more befitting to a distinguished scholar. It was a profoundly uncomfortable situation, as I did not want the office. I was happy on the women's side, yet it would be a serious affront to them if I refused; arrangements had already been made and they would have to backtrack. I timidly went to the new office, my *mahram* by my side each step. The long story made short is that the arrangement lasted perhaps one and a half days before word came down from the Council of Senior Scholars (*majlis hay'at kibar al-ulama*) Board of Inquiry and Fatawa. Sheikh Abdulaziz ibn Baz relayed that I was to be removed immediately from the men's side of the University. I was told in no uncertain terms, "Do not ever step foot over there again." Of course, that made perfect sense, but it also reflected tense politics and religion playing out at the highest level of the country over my presence. This incident revealed an important lesson to me: "pseudoliberal" academics can be distant from their own society and must have been so to think they could possibly pull off such a stunt. Several later explained that a "conservative" colleague had reported me to the ulama, and they were apologetic and embarrassed about colleagues whom they called "nutcases with beards." I joyfully returned to my prior office. These sociopolitical tensions continue to play out today.

Field Research under Authoritarianism

Omnipresent surveillance and arbitrary arrests are not merely academic subjects. They are part and parcel of life in Saudi Arabia. Indeed, Menoret devotes a chapter, "Repression and Fieldwork," to demonstrating how repression affects fieldwork (2014, 21–60). He describes how interviewees sometimes became absent or less accessible. As the public spaces of Riyadh grew ever more threatening, Saudis retreated "to the protective shell of their homes and their cars." Repression, he writes, "was on the horizon of most activities and everybody, everywhere, was liable to experience it first-hand or inflict it on others" (50). We were warned as soon as we arrived about the pervasiveness of "mosquitoes," that is, informants. "There are mosquitoes everywhere—in the neighbourhoods and classrooms. You must be very careful." A departmental chair cautioned us, "The walls have ears."[6] Universities can be the most difficult place to work and, ironically, to conduct research. There is more freedom of maneuver in the private sector, but still researchers must protect themselves and their interviewees. It is safest to assume that everything you say will be "heard," in some way, by authorities. That is why place, space, subject, demeanor, and interviewee matter so much.

One of the consequences of authoritarianism is that self-censorship is used as a tool for self-protection. During my doctoral research, for example, after weeks of being a quiet, friendly presence in the graduate student room, I began to solicit interviews among the family members of my female colleagues at the University. One day, a young man showed up at my front door in Jeddah, terrified and unexpected. I did not even know who he was. As I opened the door, his eyes darted back and forth. He whispered, "My aunt warned me not to come talk to you. You know, they have lasers now—they can record a conversation from 20 feet away!" I admire this individual for his courage. He came inside and we had a productive exchange even though he had been advised by his aunt to self-censor.

In previous years, in order to travel outside of your home city, you had to carry a signed, dated travel letter from your sponsor that granted you permission to do so. The government did not want mobility and the inevitable comparisons between the regions that might follow. There was much disparity in the country and they knew it. Pat negotiated with the men's side to obtain a travel letter for me. The rector simply refused to grant one even though travel and comparison were written into my original proposal, which had been approved when the University sponsored me. Eventually, after much negotiation, the rector threw up his hands and exclaimed, "Go, see our country! Enjoy your travels! Have fun!" But he refused to give me a letter of permission, leaving me vulnerable. So we amassed a stack of utterly meaningless but official-looking "letters of introduction" and approval. Many were responses from the original two years of my letter-writing campaign. Several were on letterhead and had embossed stamps and fancy golden seals. Some were in Arabic on one side and English on the other side. At the airport, I was asked to produce my travel letter along with my ticket. As I tried to calm my trembling hands, I placed the entire stack of letters on the desk. We simply overwhelmed the clerk. Not one of them was a travel letter from our sponsor. The beleaguered personnel waved us through the gate. I am particularly proud of this accomplishment as I conducted interviews in Jeddah, Riyadh, and up and down the Eastern Province. Indeed, comparison among the regions proved crucial to my arguments. Sometimes, your methods must be creative. Travel letters per se are not required now, but you must always have protective documents readily available.

Do not underestimate the reach of internal security. When I was refused entry to the country in the early 1990s, I tweaked my research focus so that I could pursue my interests in dissent and grievances. Prohibited from in-country field research, I was able to continue my work in another manner, that is, working with opposition in exile in the United States and Europe. These exiles first explained to me the power of 1979 as a watershed moment in Saudi Arabian history and the power of the alternative narratives of social movements.[7] In London, I did not know if the men in black were following us or surveilling the respondents. During a professional conference in 1992, I met with a group of Shia men in a Washington, DC, hotel restaurant. It was a very long, rich interview during a period of intense opposition. Upon exiting the restaurant, a man, presumably from Saudi state security, stood in the entry and said, "I hope you enjoyed your breakfast, Dr. Okruhlik." He knew my name and had watched us the entire time. I replied, "Yes, the omelet was quite nice. Thank you."

You must take advantage of the moment and seize unexpected opportunities. I almost missed such an opportunity when I declined an invitation to serve as the expert study leader on two of the first-ever commercial tours of the country. I thought it was a "gig," not serious scholarship. How wrong I was. I finally relented and am glad I did so. I immersed myself in a unique moment in Saudi Arabian history and interviewed the Saudi Arabian guides nonstop for the duration of both trips and later wrote about the dynamics of tourist encounters with the local contested environment (Okruhlik 2004b).

All in all, political research can be difficult and tiring in Saudi Arabia, but sometimes you must accept and laugh at the absurdity of your challenges.

Field Research in War and Jihad

My methodology has always been to seek protection (or safety) from above and from below simultaneously because you never knew where the danger would come from—an authoritarian crackdown or turmoil in the streets. As the so-called shock and awe campaign rained terror upon Iraqis in 2003, we were given an entry card that provided keyed access to the underground entry of a building should danger arise during the night. But we also purposefully shopped in the old souk and wandered the sweaty alleys every night for hours to build networks of humanity so that we could disappear—vanish into thin air—if necessary. We once were absent for two weeks when Pat contracted a bad eye infection. When we returned to our routine, people were genuinely relieved to see us back. Many had been worried and inquired if we were OK and where we had been. My point is to always build personal relationships of trust and care in various strata and groups in society.

During the war and jihadi campaign, we were cautioned to vary our route each day. Our emergency luggage was packed and kept by the front door at all times. We had to call the airline each week on a certain day to roll over our "escape" flight until the next week in an effort to stay as long as possible. In the buildup to war, I spent much less time doing actual interview work and far more effort on establishing relationships so that I would have safe haven amid rising anti-American fury. It was very frustrating—I wanted to do my research—but it was the wise thing to do.

I briefly met at a young high school student on Women's Day at the *janadriyah*, an annual cultural festival. She enthusiastically invited me to her home, as she wanted me to meet her parents. Her father called me and instructed us to meet him at a particular address on the far outskirts of Riyadh at 10:00 p.m. After a long drive, our taxi arrived at the unlit parking lot of an abandoned wedding hall. Our taxi driver was from Peshawar, Pakistan, then beset by political violence, and he would not drop us off at the place. It was too dangerous even for him. He refused to leave us until her father finally drove up. They exchanged glances, spoke quietly outside the cars, and only after assurances of our safety did the taxi driver wave to us to change cars. We allowed him to make the call on our behalf. Follow your gut instincts and sometimes let others take the lead. It is dangerous to overthink a situation about which you know little. Also, this young girl was so genuine and excited. I did not know her or her family at all but I learned a lot that night about a lower-middle-class perspective on politics.

Sometimes, as a foreign researcher asking about delicate subjects, you must satisfy people's misgivings about you. One older man, a schoolteacher whom I found particularly insightful, expressed exasperation that we never met at my apartment. There was an implicit fear in his voice that I was not who I said I was. I explained that there was only one comfortable chair in our small apartment; there was no room for three people to sit. He did not believe me. We then insisted that he come over. When I opened the door to him, a look of sheer relief flushed his face as he saw exactly one chair in the living room. I asked him to sit. He insisted instead that I take the chair. We both laughed and then, perched on stools, had a great conversation—but he had to see it with his own eyes.

The very week I arrived in Riyadh in 2003, my work was translated into Arabic and posted on Saudi opposition websites—without my prior knowledge. It was a tense time. I was uneasy. Shortly thereafter, I walked into a modest apartment for an interview with a young man whom I did not know. He had somehow contacted me. His dining table was full of papers spread across it. When we sat down, I saw that they were my own publications—the texts highlighted in yellow with notes in red ink in the margins. My heart was pounding. I breathed deeply, ready for devastating criticisms. But, he carefully corrected my mistakes. For example, he said, "You were wrong in this paragraph. Three people were arrested, not four." Expect commentary on your work as a part of the give and take of field research.

As jihadi strikes hit Saudi Arabia domestically in 2003, internal security grew ever more present. When the National Commercial Bank building was threatened, there were antiterror checkpoints with armed military personnel in the streets of Jeddah. We drove cautiously toward the large tanks. Guns were pointed at our faces as we were instructed to roll down the window. Invariably, after a few questions, the soldiers would turn to me and compliment the way I tied my *tarha*. They asked if I were Muslim. I said, "No, my Saudi girlfriends taught me how." Not a single strand of hair was exposed. We were waved through the checkpoint. To this day, I thank the women in Jeddah and Riyadh who taught me how to wear an abaya and wrap a *tarha* with beauty and modesty.

Field research in Saudi Arabia will continue to be challenging with domestic and regional politics so unsettled. Today, there is devastation in Yemen, destruction in the Shia-dominated Eastern Province, and rivalry, real or imagined, with Iran. This affects the choices that researchers must make on a daily basis.

Practical Matters in Fieldwork: Mundane but Important to Your Success

Sometimes, it is the little things that affect the quality of your data and the enjoyment that you derive in compiling it. Thus, know that interviews often begin in homes at 11:00 p.m. (after dinner). This is great except that other interlocutors maintain a nine-to-five office workday and expect you to begin an interview at 9:00 a.m. the next morning. Such back-to-backers are exhausting, but as a researcher, you must go with the(ir) flow.

Your housing matters because it affects how people perceive you. I was fortunate to never live in a gated, luxury, Western compound. That environment would have influenced the knowledge that people would impart to me. In addition to the nurse's quarters and to a private apartment in a quiet neighborhood, one of my favorite homes was in Funduq al Bay'ah on the edge of the old city in Jeddah (*al balad*). Hejazis enjoyed sipping tea on the top floor as I peppered them with questions. From that perch, they could survey the sprawling old souk beneath them—a place of which they had fond childhood memories but had not visited for many years. Several meandered its skinny alleyways after our interviews. That old hotel also enabled me to bear witness to the horrors of a beheading on the square beneath it, for better or worse.

It is wise to be comfortably situated before the adhan, or call to prayer (if you do not pray). Over the years, shops close earlier and earlier. Previously, they would begin closing at the end of the call to prayer. Then, they began closing during the call, and later, at the first word of the call or just beforehand. This changes over time and reflects sociopolitical struggles in the country, but it is not comfortable to be stuck in an awkward locale for the duration. There are reports that prayer is being enforced in private work offices.

There were no bathrooms for women in men's spheres of activity on any of my research trips. This is usually the case still today but must change if the new decree allowing women access to public buildings is enforced. Each time I utilized the facilities, Pat waited outside the bathroom door with his arms crossed in order to protect against mixed encounters. It was an explicitly gendered statement. It was difficult to construct this methodology of protection and it was uncomfortable for everybody, but it also put people at greater ease because they understood the dynamics underway and could avoid any physical interaction. A female colleague could also serve as the guard. The point is that a physical cue that does not require any verbal exchange is useful.

Even though many of us work on the struggles of Saudi Arabian citizens, never forget that a significant percentage of the population is foreign labor. All rentier (oil) countries have a demographic imbalance between citizens and foreign workers to varying degrees. Foreign laborers will impart a radically different interpretation of Saudi Arabian developments, and their insights are valuable. Because many live a precarious, vulnerable existence, they may empathize with your circumstances. Indeed, during the war when we could not leave our small apartment due to the (understandable) anger directed at Americans, foreign workers brought us toilet paper and basic foodstuffs, without us ever asking. That was their way of telling us, "Stay inside for now."

Conclusions: Gaining Access to Knowledge
in Saudi Arabia

I do not argue that Saudi Arabia presents an exceptional case for political science researchers; rather that its challenges are different in degree and in kind. In Saudi Arabia, even for women, the problems of field research are less about gender per se than about the twinning of political authoritarianism with social norms. Negotiating this terrain requires patience, perseverance, and a bit of courage. Needless to say, I did not learn much of this in my graduate school seminars at the University of Texas. Rather, these "lessons learned" came from difficult encounters in the field.[8]

My point is this: using such fluid methods allows you to ask the hard and vital questions of political science. There are verdant research agendas in Saudi Arabia. If people trust your integrity and your word, you can talk about human rights, accountability, opposition, family pressures, Islam, labor and citizenship, feminism, inequalities, and, yes, even corruption.[9] There are ways to do so. What I know to be ethical and effective are these things: Do not misrepresent yourself to interlocutors. Do not whitewash the harsh realities of authoritarianism. Speak what you know to be the truth. Be fluid, creative, and responsive in your methodology, especially in interviews. Build relationships of trust that permeate different social classes. The depth and nuance of the information you elicit is incomparably richer than data obtained in other ways. Aim always for empirical richness and theoretical vibrancy.

There have been many changes over time. There are more scholars in general, more women in particular, and, indeed, women who travel alone to conduct research. A network of institutional support now exists in Saudi Arabia that did not exist before, largely through the efforts of the King Faisal Foundation. This has resulted in a relative wealth of solid scholarship based on fieldwork. There is, however, also more surveillance. What has remained constant is the importance of integrity. For all the difficulties of research in Saudi Arabia, the rewards are many. My empathy and care for the people of Saudi Arabia are deep. The irony in all of this—perhaps to the bemusement or chagrin of this volume's editors—is that this political scientist had to become something of an anthropologist in the field for successful research.

Addendum

In late 2017, as this volume went to press, the dizzying pace of developments in Riyadh left many observers startled. In quick succession—in addition to prior announcements that women would drive and the guardianship system would be relaxed—Crown Prince Mohammed bin Salman jailed many prominent Islamists, rounded up and sequestered eleven senior princes and many businessmen in the

Ritz-Carlton, consolidated his power, and launched a massive anticorruption drive. In parallel fashion, he announced a new Entertainment City, luxury Red Sea resorts, a $500 billion futuristic city called NEOM, and he granted citizenship to a robot. Regionally, the rift with Qatar escalated, the Lebanese prime minister resigned while in Riyadh, and tragically, the brutal war in Yemen continued. Suddenly, there appears to be relatively easy access to Saudi Arabia for foreigners, at least for brief conferences and such. There is reported to be a new social ease in public spaces in the country and, indeed, a plethora of leisure activities.

What does all this mean for field researchers? It is too early to ascertain the breadth or depth of these changes. It is possible that they take hold uniformly across the country. More likely, they will take hold differently across class, region, families, and normative orientations; embraced by some, accepted uneasily or rejected by others. As always, there is a difference between royal decrees and life as it is lived on the ground. It behooves the researcher to listen and observe carefully, to avoid easy assumptions about legality and implementation, and to comprehend the background of the individual being interviewed.

I began this chapter by noting the complexity of field research caused by the conflation of social norms, religious privilege, and political authoritarianism. If the fusion between religion, state, and norms is broken, then indeed, meaningful change is in store. For now, let us be clear—only social norms and religious privilege are being addressed. The irony of reform (*al islah*) is that it serves to protect the centrality of the ruling family. Political authoritarianism is still deeply entrenched.

5

Research in and on the Palestinian Occupied Territories

BENOIT CHALLAND

Palestine as Outlier or Epitome of Difficult North-South Relations?

Palestine is not only at the crossroads of historical trading routes, thus making it a significant place to study the interplay between economy and politics, but also encapsulates so much of the tormented East-West and North-South relations that characterize a post-9/11 world (see Malki 2011; Tamari 1994). It is a place for which discourses abound about the alleged existence of a clash of civilizations, between a self-declared democratic and benevolent Israel and Islamist-led "droves"[1] going after the Western way of life. Such shallow representations of the conflict lead to polarized and highly politicized views, and the difficulty for social researchers is not to reproduce an overdetermination in the study of "Palestine" as *only* the result of these North-South or West-East divides, or occupation by Israel, or as a sui generis conflict. Palestine has a long, complex history that political scientists and sociologists should take as an invitation to disentangle multiple layers and ways to approach "politics" in this part of the Middle East.

This chapter aims to critically engage with the opportunities and challenge that arise from doing fieldwork in Palestine. While presenting important examples of past research on Palestinian politics, broadly construed, it is articulated on the following axes:

- Defining what is Palestine. What are the consequences of a given territorial definition of Palestine?
- What are possible focus or entry points to avoid shallow depictions of politics in Palestine?
- What are practical difficulties that researchers are likely to encounter?

- What are the ethical dilemmas for a researcher working on or in Palestine? What are specific difficulties when working on and in Gaza, a tiny portion of Palestine that is often compared to an open-sky prison because of the Israeli siege and closures?

Defining Palestine and "OPT"

Before offering a reflection on how the particular context of Palestine influences the possibility of doing political research, a word needs to be said about the very term "Palestine," or "occupied Palestinian Territories" (OPT). The phrase "occupied territory" is a legal term, used in international law to refer to a situation in which a belligerent party (i.e., a state) invades a territory that is not recognized as such under international law or the system of state recognitions. Israel has been occupying East Jerusalem,[2] the West Bank (both previously under Jordanian administration), and the Gaza Strip (under Egyptian military administration)[3] since the 1967 Six Day War. There seems to be a de facto consensus that Palestine is congruent with the OPT. UN Security Council Resolution 242, passed after the 1967 war, albeit ambiguous on the extent of the Occupied Territories that need to be returned, and the Geneva Conventions, which the International Committee of the Red Cross protects, have been invoked to speak of the need of a two-state solution based on the line of armistices (the so-called Green Line) reached in 1948–1949 between Israel and its Arab neighbors. Geographically, the OPT represents only 22% of what is referred to as historical Palestine, namely the area between the Mediterranean Sea and the Jordan River bordering Lebanon to the north and the Gulf of Aqaba to the south. Palestinian actors reluctantly acquiesced to a fragmentation of their territories, historical Palestine. For various historical reasons, the sole and legitimate representative of the Palestinians, the PLO, concentrated its efforts on liberating only the OPT (see Hilal 2007). As a result of these compromises made by the PLO, the OPT became the seat of an interim self-governing authority, the Palestinian National Authority (PNA), which was established in July 1994. Since September 2012, after a controversial vote at the General Assembly of the UN, Palestine (as represented by the PNA) has received the status of nonmember observer state in the UN system. It seems that, from an international legal perspective, Palestine has become coterminous with the OPT.

A complication with the terminology of "Palestine" arises when considering human geography. As is well known, a state, to be recognized, needs a territory, a constitution, international recognition, *and* a population. If we look at where Palestinians are based, one discovers that the OPT hosts less than half of the living Palestinians: 4.7 million Palestinians live in the West Bank (including East Jerusalem) and in the Gaza Strip. But many more Palestinians (another 6.8 million, of which 1.7 million are living as citizens of Israel) are scattered around the region and are therefore not represented by the PNA (see Tartir and Challand 2016). In other words, legal territorial definitions of the Palestinian state(-to-be) are not sufficient, since a majority of Palestinians live outside the OPT.

There is therefore a genuine ambiguity in the effort to study "Palestinian politics": is it politics, in a formal sense, of official interactions where a Palestinian (soon-to-be-)state as bureaucracy exercises its limited jurisdiction (it would be improper to speak of its sovereignty)? Or is politics understood in a more Arendtian sense of engagement with the polis, of mutual debates among Palestinians? The first scenario justifies reducing Palestine to the OPT, while the second force us to adopt a larger perspective where Palestinians are mobilizing to defend their right to self-determination in the OPT, inside Israel and in neighboring countries. Even a study of the PLO, the formal organization that has been recognized as the sole representative of the Palestinian people, does not solve the issue. Is it the PLO that has signed the Oslo agreements with Israel, or is it the PLO that negotiate(d) with Israel on what the PNA is allowed to do or not to do inside the OPT? In addition, the PLO is an umbrella organization representing all Palestinians—of the OPT, of the interior (1948 Palestinians), and of the diaspora (in Arabic *shatat*)—but it does not include all political parties, in particular all the Islamist factions (Hamas and Islamic Jihad).[4] No answers can be given as to which are the actual or best contours to adopt for a study of Palestinian politics. It must, however, be underlined that a detour through these definitions can only enrich the questions and material that social scientists will accumulate for and through their research.

How to Avoid Reductive Traps?

The logical consequence of the concentric nature of Palestinian politics (OPT at its core; historical or Mandatory Palestine; then *shatat*; or, in institutional terms, PNA inside the PLO, with a larger pool of Palestinian parties, including the rejectionist camps) is that research in political science faces a difficulty in studying multiple constituencies or multilayered territorialities. And indeed, most of political research replicates the bias of methodological nationalism and concentrates on Palestine as the place where a local self-governing entity, the PNA, has assumed an administrative role since 1994. There has also been a problematic tendency to apprehend Palestine through the tiny, artificially grown city of Ramallah, which functions as one of the de facto capitals (the other being Gaza City, often out of reach for many researchers, let alone journalists or diplomats). This depiction does not do justice to the extreme poverty and harsh closure imposed on the Gaza Strip and on peripheral cities and rural parts of the West Bank (not to mention East Jerusalem, which is often treated as a sui generis case).

Critical scholarship has reacted to this shrinking of Palestine and to the oblivion of a majority of Palestinians living outside of the legal remits of the PNA. Clearly, there is not one unique way to approach "Palestinian politics," but the focal lens should be broad enough to capture surrounding influences and not limit itself to the territories where Palestinians have obtained a form of self-governing under the PNA. In my work on foreign aid for Palestinian civil society, I have approached Palestinians politics at times as limited to the OPT (East Jerusalem included) and, in other cases, as dynamic processes connecting Palestinians of the OPT to those of historical Palestine.[5] But three strands or overarching themes of scholarship can help future researchers in positioning themselves vis-à-vis the difficulty identified above. The first stimulating example is rooted in historical analyses, while the second and third entry points offer complex understanding of spaces and flows that allow researchers to transcend studies limited to the OPT only.

In the vein of historical sociology, Beshara Doumani's study of 19th-century rural economy in and around Nablus is a plea to study the longue durée creation of social and economic spaces, linking Jabal Nablus to trade and social ties with Damascus, Alexandria, and present-day Jordan (Doumani 1996). He thus convincingly demonstrates that historical Palestine is not just a vague equivalent of the Mandatory borders, drawn by Britain, but a rather densely inhabited space connected to what are now other Arab states, a space that was generating an economic surplus, in the form of agricultural commodities, well before the arrival of Zionist migrants. Palestine thus existed well before the first waves of *alyot*, or Jewish migration to the "Promised Land," and is integrated in a larger Arab region.

Space is the second heuristic way to transcend a narrow understanding of Palestine as the OPT, or of Palestine as a reaction to Zionism. Palestine had been at the crossroads of trade and cultural exchanges in the south or southeastern corner of the Mediterranean for centuries. Its strategic location was not lost on British and French colonialists at the end of World War I when they delineated Palestinians' borders. Controlling and limiting spatial connections among Palestinians of historical Palestine (e.g., preventing the return of refugees post-1948), and sealing borders after the 1956 and 1967 wars became a constant political worry for Israel. Thus, authors have noted an attempt at "spaciocide" (Hanafi 2012), that is, an attempt by Israel to deny Palestinians the effective control of social spaces, or added a vertical dimension to Israeli and Zionist obsession with the control of land, often in the name of fluid and land-grabbing notions of "defense" or "security" (Weizman 2007). The study of "Palestinian politics" should therefore also be attuned to non-human factors.

A third stimulating approach in political research on Palestine deals with the question of flows of people, moneys, and ideas. Flows of people have been important during the civil war (at the end of the Mandatory period) and in the *nakba* (or 1948–1949 war, "catastrophe" in Arabic), with more than 700,000 Palestinians forced to leave their dwellings (see Pappe 2011). The 1956 and 1967 wars provoked a renewed share of massive Palestinian uprooting, and the problem of expulsion remains a critical problem for Palestinians. Israel has used new low-profile tactics of microexpulsions (e.g., East Jerusalemites denied renewal of their Jerusalem IDs), combined with the conspicuous building of walls around Gaza since the early 1990s and since 2002 around the West Bank. As a result, Palestinians of the OPT are parked in managed pockets with the recurrent problem of difficult access to mobility. The concentric nature of Palestinian politics is thus connected to this constantly evolving flow of Palestinians, unable to choose their place of residency.

The same can be said about Palestinian ideas and ideals. Take the spread of Islamist ideologies, with the emergence of Islamic Jihad in the early 1980s and the foundation of Hamas in 1988, which have occupied much of political scientists' attention. A focus on the Hamas leadership, some of which lives abroad for fear of direct reprisal by Israel, illustrates how the Palestinian-Israeli conflict is also and still at times an Arab-Israeli conflict. For a long time, the political leadership (Khaled Mesh'al, or Mousa Abu Marzouq) was based in Damascus, but with the 2011 Arab uprisings, they moved to Cairo, and then to Doha. Keeping an eye on their moves informs us of the fate of the Arab uprisings of 2011 and demonstrates, again, that Palestinian politics is deeply entangled with the politics of the entire Middle East and North Africa.

A last relevant flow that political researchers have traced is that of foreign aid. With billions poured every year by the international community to support the creation of a Palestinian state,[6] a study of European, American, Arab, and now increasingly Turkish aid almost allows for the visualization of the battle for influence and power that various regional and international actors have waged with their checkbook diplomacy. The rent economy generated with the flow of foreign aid has created more hurdles to sound participatory and democratic practices than expected or officially declared: be it through credit-facilitated debts (Hanieh 2013), exclusionary results of civil society or peace promotion (Challand 2009), autocratic tendencies of the PA able to steer part of the flow of international funding (Jamal 2007), or an increased securitization of aid (Tartir 2015), official development assistance and foreign direct investments are mixed blessings for Palestinians. Be it with a historical focus, or with a view on spaces and flows, current research on Palestine can generate stimulating answers to the dilemma or multiple ways to define Palestine away from a place of continuous military confrontations. Let us now look at problems of access to Palestine.

The Problem of Access: Practical Issues

One can wonder whether the violent nature of the occupation, and as a consequence of Palestinian resistance, and the recurrent wars on Gaza in the last 10 years may not be a definitive hurdle to doing research in the region. Is access to Palestine a real difficulty? The epistemological nature of these preliminary questions probably matters, in the view of this author, as much as practical difficulties in carrying out research because of limited access.

While access to Palestine is a real potential problem, especially for researchers of local or Arab origin (see infra), doing research in Palestine remains somewhat easier than in neighboring countries. The difficulties encountered by researchers working in many neighboring countries are connected to cases of extreme authoritarianism or of war and violence. Violence and regular wars on the Gaza Strip are certainly important hurdles for research, but domestic politics are less so. The PNA has been criticized at times for its autocratic tendencies, and the PA authorities may have intimidated researchers (local ones in particular), but these have been limited cases.[7] The real difficulty in terms of access arises from Israel's attempt to seal its borders and limit access to certain researchers wishing to reach Palestine. Put differently, the structures of the occupation (curtailed freedom of movement, curfews, hermetic control of external borders) are more likely to generate trouble for researchers on Palestinian politics than are internal hurdles. The best proof is the (apparent, but fluctuating) demand for something akin to a research permit declaring the researcher's intention to go into the OPT, a demand made by Israel, not by the PNA.

Entering the inner circle of "Palestine," the OPT requires transiting, in one way or the other, via Israel, since Palestine is not a sovereign state. Researchers usually reach the West Bank (East Jerusalem included) via Jordan, while to enter Gaza there is slightly more of a chance from the Egyptian border, near Rafah. The crossing from Israel, in Erez, that is, the access point via Israel to the Gaza Strip, has become very difficult to pass since Israel only rarely grants the necessary permit. Palestinian authorities or police forces do not control any of the contact points with neighboring Arab countries. Passing through Eilat, Allenby Bridge, or Sheikh Hussein Bridge from Jordan, or through the Rafah crossing, can easily eat up a day of a researcher's journey, for Israel border authorities often use vexing techniques of closing the border crossings at short notice and with no clear reason. Delayed security clearance is another common problem. The same is true for the Erez crossing, where coordination with an Israeli body, the Coordination of Government Activities in the Territories (COGAT), does not offer any sure guarantee to access Gaza. Researchers should count on a couple of hours to half a day to effectively pass the security hurdles at the Jordanian border. This might be longer, depending on the researcher's place of birth and types of visa or entry stamps from other Middle Eastern countries. Reaching Gaza from Egypt will easily take a day or two, because of the transit to El-'Arish and from there to the Rafah crossing, whose opening and closure are unpredictable. The extremely tense situation in the Sinai due to the presence of Da'esh, increasing since 2014, can make the journey to enter Gaza from Egypt a dangerous one.

The alternative for foreign researchers is to fly through Ben Gurion airport in Tel Aviv, but screening of social researchers entering the country might generate negative surprises. Occasionally, social science researchers, even famous international figures,[8] will be denied entry into Israel, while it is probably a safe bet to say that most requests to enter Gaza via Erez will fail.[9] In the past, having an invitation letter from an Israeli research university could have facilitated entry by the Israeli border authority. But since 2014 and because of the academic boycott vigorously enforced by Palestinian universities and research institutes, such a letter will probably bar the researcher from speaking with Palestinians for research purposes. By and large, denial of entry into Israel has been an occasional nightmare for international researchers and their families, but a much more frequent reality for scholars of Palestinian or Arab origins. A local Palestinian NGO, Right to Entry, provides helpful advice for people, whether researchers or not, who are at risk of being denied entry, an issue that can have broad professional consequences for the individuals incriminated and their family or parents.[10] It is therefore essential to prepare travel to the region meticulously. Concrete preparatory steps can include, but are not limited to, these: carrying a letter describing the object of the research, an official letter, for younger researchers, of the university stating the nature and the existence of a supervision mechanism, providing a business card, and being able to describe one's movements inside historical Palestine. Once inside Israel, it is rather easy to move into the autonomous zones (Zone A or B) under Palestinian control with the exception of Gaza, which is almost out of reach. Before reaching any of the Israeli-manned border crossings, researchers should think about sensitive data posted on their social media, and names or phone numbers on their contact lists. It is not infrequent to discover that, at Ben Gurion airport in particular, your Facebook account has been checked by a third party (border officials). You may also be forced to log in to your social media or to disclose the list of contacts on your smartphone or computer. It might make sense to delete your profile on these or create an alternative profile for social media.

Once the scholar has managed access to Palestine, research can start in full. Distances within Palestine are not great, and when no major military operations are under way, it is rather easy to schedule interviews or visit institutions hosting relevant information, even in two different locations on the same day. Palestinian research centers, such as PASSIA,[11] have useful contact numbers and accommodation advice that will greatly facilitate the stay in the country. Traveling between different Palestinian towns is possible with local public transportation (typically *service*, for collective yellow taxis). Numerous Israeli checkpoints dot the Palestinian territories, but local populations and taxi drivers will tell researchers the best way to reach their destinations. The local population, children included, are eager to speak about their predicament and will easily provide assistance to researchers traveling for the first time in the region. Foreigners might benefit from less stringent moving restrictions[12] than Palestinians, but the behavior of the security staff at Israeli checkpoints (be they military or private subcontractors) is unpredictable. Thus, movements from one town to the other might be denied or might require much longer than normal. For example, a trip from Ramallah to Nablus, which normally takes 45 to 60 minutes, can turn into a four-hour journey, depending on the number of, and decisions made at, Israeli checkpoints. Moving out of the OPT to

Jerusalem will take longer, and researchers should be aware that during major Israeli holidays, checkpoints on the route to Jerusalem (in Qalandiya or Bethlehem) might be closed for a day or two.

Staying tuned to local news is important to find out whether military operations are underway. A high-profile visit in Ramallah or other large Palestinian towns can generate domestic protests, and moving arrangements might have to be rescheduled. In case of flashes of violence or curfews, researchers simply need to stay put and get relevant sources of information through partners (embassy, hosting institutions, etc.) previously identified. Obtaining information about future destinations or likely places of violence is also an important step: clashes with Israeli occupying forces are likely to erupt at usual places, typically near checkpoints, centers of detention, or bypass roads. Such spots should be avoided as much as possible on Fridays, when clashes often occur after the Friday prayers. Moving inside Israel is generally not a problem, and the Palestinian population inside Israel is mostly concentrated in the north, in the coastal town of Haifa, in Galilee, and in the so-called Triangle, namely a region around Umm al-Fahm.

Ethical Issues

Do no harm: The mantra of development workers should also be extended to the community of political scientists. It is never an innocent act to study Palestine, let alone *reach* Palestine. A trip via Ben Gurion or Egypt could be interpreted by some as a form of acquiescence to the right of Israel to deny Palestinians full sovereignty. The movement BDS (boycott, divestment, and sanctions),[13] and the call for academic boycott of Israeli universities and research institutes, are manifestations of the Palestinians' will to defend their own priorities in social research. International researchers must be aware of the meaning of the Israeli boycott and how a researcher's position on the matter might jeopardize her or his chance to speak with Palestinian counterparts. The topic of the research might also generate troubles. Studying Islamic charitable associations, some of which have been accused of being terrorist organizations (Schaeublin 2012), could also get researchers in trouble, and possibly legal battles, in particular after the US Supreme Court's decision of 2010 to extend its definition of material support to terrorist organizations. Other uncomfortable situations, such as public shaming or even difficulties in being confirmed in an academic job, might arise for scholars critical of Israeli policies, with NGO Watch or Campus Watch putting pressure in the United States and in other countries. Critical Jewish scholars are not protected either, as some will end up in web-based lists of self-hating Jews (so-called SHIT lists)

Three last ethical questions arise. One pertains to data protection, and the two are issues of funding and research (one being a general problem in Palestine, and the other specific to Gaza).

First, data collected during research need to be anonymized to protect the sources. At a time of easy electronic storage, storing material and interviews in a digital, online format is probably an elegant way to avoid harassment on the way out of Israel, especially at Ben Gurion airport. Key words: think about your social media when entering Israel and about your contact details (Israeli officials want to know the name of your "Arab" acquaintances) when leaving. On the way out allow for an extra couple of hours for "security" checks at the airport.

Second, large institutions, such as the World Bank and large INGOs (international nongovernmental organizations), have started paying Palestinians to respond to surveys or to participate in focus groups. The overuse of polls and surveys in Palestine has generated a sense of distrust by laypeople against researchers. Such institutions ought to be blamed for a blatant violation of ethical guidelines of research (no research should endanger future research). The sad reality might well be for researchers to be refused answers, especially if they are affiliated with foreign institutions.[14] Being able to communicate clearly to the respondents the nature and scope of the research (e.g., whether the research is funded by a government) might avoid such refusal.

The third issue is connected to the definition of "terrorism." Entering Gaza, under the rule of Hamas since 2006, considered in many countries a terrorist organization and therefore under siege by Israel, might entail the payment of a fee to the government. Since the de facto government in Gaza is Hamas, paying the fee could be considered a form of material support to this political formation. International NGOs willing to work in Gaza have to pay such a tax, but individual researchers normally do not have to pay. Yet researchers should be aware of this possibility and its implications. Furthermore, some form of coordination with a local ministry in Gaza might be requested, depending on the topic of investigation, thereby limiting the possibility of obtaining frank and open answers to questions. Depending on the topic, there might be no way out of this "supervision," and researchers should make clear in the final work whether they have been subject to such pressure.

Alternatives

What can be done when researchers are denied entry or cannot access the field because of flaring episodes of violence in and around Palestine? Instances of denied entry (denied by Israel) must be properly and immediately documented, mostly through the formal diplomatic channel. People who cannot reach Palestine (Gaza in particular) will need to try at another time. Scholars can rely on a dense network of well-trained local Palestinian researchers to carry out portions of the original research. This is especially true for research questions that pertain to development or international cooperation issues. Palestinian civil society is a very rich one, with excellent research centers and local libraries. Often international researchers overlook these resources and thus undermine the possibility of producing fine research taking advantage of local resources. Fortunately for the research community, excellent research centers (Shabaka, MAS, BISAN, Masarat: The Palestinian Center for Policy Research & Strategic Studies, or almarsad.ps), online information and databases (PCBS, BADIL, Mezan Center for Human Rights, ARIJ, Institute for Palestine Studies, Women's Affairs Center–Gaza), and clearing news centers (Maan News, http://www.palestinemonitor.org/, Quds Network, http://www.qudsn. ps/) offer essential information on Palestinian politics. There also exist rich online archives, which can help in preparing research. One such initiative is located in Bir Zeit University (in Arabic).[15]

This author does not subscribe to the view that a sharp distinction can be drawn between theory and practice, or between academic analysis and policy prescription. Rather it must be observed that many scholars seem happy to jump on a fieldwork opportunity to produce policy-oriented knowledge. Palestinians themselves have now excellent research centers, some with clearly applied focus. Scholars working in high-quality Palestinian universities, both in the West Bank and in Gaza, should therefore be on a to-meet list of social scientists working on Palestine. Good social research has feedback loops in the Occupied Territories, so research with explicit policy implications should always include some form of workshops and debates inside Palestine to discuss these implications before the research proceeds.

Conclusion

Tony Judt warned that many studies on the left de facto assume its language and political outlook, thereby enhancing the risk of turning literature on the left into a piece of the militant Left (Judt 1985, 1012). As a consequence, people opposed to a leftist agenda are pushed to refute the arguments because of the lack of "neutrality" or critical distance researchers display. Doing fieldwork in or on Palestine entails, in a way, something akin to this risk of reproducing *political* battles within *academic* inquiry. Indeed, much of the scientific literature produced on Palestine can become an indictment of Israel's settler colonialism or militarized domination, or a defense of Israel's right to survive or continue with the policies originally set in motion with the 1948, 1956, and 1967 wars. As we have seen, the simple use of the terms *Palestine, Palestinian occupied territory*, or *disputed territories* can reveal the political preference of researchers.

This chapter has tried to offer some ways to avoid this trap of politicization or identification with the "cause" (Israeli or Palestinian) through a reflection on the terms used to describe "Palestine," and by pointing to important academic contributions on Palestine to generate critical perspectives, in particular by pointing at the longue durée evolution of population, ideas, and economic flows. Political and material hurdles to access the region have also been discussed, while ethical problems are particularly acute in this part of the Middle East because of its strategic position in many larger Arab-Israeli sources of conflict. Finally, the advice to adopt a well-informed historical perspective can contribute to a larger comparative focus. Palestine is too often seen as a place of exceptions; instead, it needs to be studied in its complexity and with an awareness of the multiple layers of problems that have contributed to keeping the Palestinian predicament intractable for more than 80 years, the time when the idea of a partitioning of historical Palestine was first raised.

Acknowledgments

The author is grateful to Alaa Tartir, Jehad Abu-Salim, Tom Hill, Caroline Abu-Sa'da, Ibrahim Shikaki and the two editors for their comments on a draft of this chapter.

6

Seeing beyond the Spectacle

Research on and Adjacent to Violence

SARAH E. PARKINSON

On January 2, 2014, I gazed out the window as my plane descended into Rafiq Hariri International Airport for a 4:50 p.m. landing. Something looked odd in al-Dahiyya, Beirut's southern suburbs. Bright, multihued lights pulsated from a cluster of concrete apartment blocks. I didn't think much of the visual aberration at the time, focusing instead on clearing customs and collecting my checked bags. Yet when I walked into the arrivals hall shortly thereafter, Raji, a good friend who was supposed to pick me up, was uncharacteristically absent. After wandering the arrivals hall for half an hour, I reluctantly bought an overpriced SIM card from an airport kiosk.

When I dialed, I promptly received a message that Raji's number was unavailable. Looking around, I realized that other travelers were repeating the same motions: trying a number, pulling a confused frown at the prerecorded message, then shifting a smartphone from ear to eyes to check email, WhatsApp, or Facebook again. There was nothing from Raji in my feeds. Instead, I found a note from my friend Chris in Chicago: "Just read the NY Times. You good?" (Email dated January 2, 2014, time stamp 8:54 a.m. CST).[1] Mentally linking the lights in Dahiyya to Raji's unavailable number and Chris's deliberately vague, practiced wording, I apprehensively opened Facebook to scan local friends' statuses. Three people had posted breaking news regarding a suicide bombing in Harat Hurayk, a residential neighborhood in the heart of al-Dahiyya close to one of the Palestinian refugee camps where Raji and I both worked. Four people were dead and dozens were injured.

At 6:26 p.m. Beirut time, after multiple increasingly panicked attempts to call Raji via the overloaded mobile network, it finally occurred to me to message him instead: "Where are you? I am in phone store in airport, your number doesn't work!" He messaged back a minute later: "Crazy traffic, coming, I'm coming," and then, "Big bomb in Dahiyya" (Facebook messenger conversation dated January 2, 2014, time stamp 10:27–10:28 a.m. CST).[2] Knowing that he was alive, I felt my body physically de-tense. Raji's car pulled up half an hour later. The normally 15-minute drive had taken him almost two hours. We sped home through the then-emptying streets to Tariq al-Jadida, a *sh'abī* neighborhood in South Beirut, ordered delivery, and spent the night watching the gruesome news. Commemorative pictures of the victims began appearing in our Facebook feeds.

Our behaviors interacted with a broader set of social routines that activated when violent attacks targeted civilians in Lebanon. When the bombing occurred in the middle of rush hour, people across Beirut shifted from the everyday banalities of the afternoon commute to less frequently deployed routines of postattack protection, comfort, and collective mourning.[3] Like my friends and me, many invoked contextual knowledge (e.g., telling oneself, "The mobile phone network always crashes in a crisis") and practices (e.g., immediately heading home and watching the news on loop with friends and family; reinforcing one's own safety and that of one's friends while sharing photos of the victims on social media). For many, the attack blended with still-raw emotions elicited by a bombing only a few days earlier in Beirut's ostensibly "safe" central shopping district; enacting routines provided a way to practically and emotionally navigate a sociopolitical context that was itself irreducible to a single event.

In this essay, I draw on nearly two years of immersive fieldwork in Lebanon[4] to examine the social knowledge, routines, and practices that people deploy when violence interrupts their everyday lives. Specifically, I develop two further interludes drawn from very different moments: an interpersonal clash that culminated in a stabbing and an international armed dispute between Lebanon and Israel. In doing so, I examine how scale, physical distance, and social proximity to very different events activate different routines, notions of group belonging, and demands on interpersonal relationships. This approach both complements and problematizes scholarship that focuses explicitly on violent *events* such as riots, civil war, or vigilantism. The first interlude, built around a street fight in an amusement park, evokes on-the-ground dynamics of being an immediate bystander to violence, including the physicality of crowd behavior, emotional tensions in how to protect others and oneself, and the centrality of improvisation. It also captures one of the rare moments of visceral, mortal fear I experienced during my research and one of the few times I was present when my interlocutors were actually involved in a violent altercation. The second interlude, constructed around a border skirmish between Israeli and Lebanese militaries, provides a contrast in terms of proximity—the event occurred a three-hour drive away—lack of immediate information and, for most of Lebanon, a waiting game rather than a call to immediate action.

I deploy these specific experiences in tandem with the interlude above in order to achieve two goals. First, I hope to highlight micro-level responses to violence that researchers often leave unconsidered in favor of a focus on violent events, their perpetrators, and their victims. Here, I want to argue that understanding political violence also requires contemplating bystanders' lived experience of it. By taking this tack, I hope to engage readers in contemplating an "ethics of sight" centered on how researchers' views of violence are "mediated—voluntarily or involuntarily—by distance, disguise, concealment, language, and/or technology" (Parkinson 2015; see also Pachirat 2011).[5] Second, I hope to share practical insights regarding research on and adjacent to violence, with an emphasis on both the planning and improvisation it often requires as well as the ethical questions it raises and the emotional demands it presents. Excerpts from my field notes, relevant media reports, and personal correspondence give the reader a feel for how my interlocutors and I experienced things in real time and discussed them with interlocutors and friends.

This approach elicits inevitable tensions. Like many scholars, I worry about the continuous and frequently uncritical construction of Middle Eastern states as "unstable," "violent," or "conflict ridden." Labeling populations and communities in these ways, as other scholars (Khalili 2013; Said 1979) have argued, often produces counterproductive overgeneralizations (e.g., by erasing subnational variation in violence), encourages scholars and policymakers to pathologize entire populations and reify cultures as "violent," and can been used to justify international intervention.

It is also worth noting that my experience of Lebanon has never lined up with what my academic training taught me to expect from a "conflict zone." Lebanon is not in the midst of protracted armed hostilities that produce a thousand battle deaths a year, which is the standard—if sterile and problematic—definition in political science. On a more practical level, while Lebanese Armed Forces (LAF) soldiers or militia members patrol some neighborhoods, they do not engage in anything approaching constant battles with each other. Events that were termed "war"—such as the LAF's 2007 destruction of the Nahr al-Barid refugee camp in northern Lebanon—did not conceptually fit scholarly definitions. Specifically, though casualties were "low" for a war, the LAF functionally destroyed the camp and displaced tens of thousands of Palestinian civilians in the interest of flushing out Fatah al-Islam, a small, radical Islamic militant group not supported by the community. Living and working in proximity to violence, as I will later elaborate, often revealed that life adjacent to conflict often comprises very mundane decisions and routine responses to events as they unfold in real time.

Looking for Blood: Fear and Fragility in a Stampede

One of my most important realizations that I had over the course of my research was the way that relationships in the militant organizations that I studied crossed over into other aspects of life (and vice versa) (Parkinson 2016). "Political" and the "personal" intertwined, coevolved, and clashed as members of political factions socialized, intermarried, or boycotted each other's businesses. As a consequence, I happily accepted an invitation from my friend Layla to join her, her family, and her friends on a day trip up to Faraya, a ski town high in the mountains north of

Beirut. Everyone except for me was both Palestinian and affiliated at least loosely with Fatah; I eagerly anticipated the day as both an ethnographic opportunity and a chance to relax a bit in the mountains. About 40 of us pooled money for a private bus, food, and flavored tobacco, packed up water pipes, and spent the day barbequing and dancing to music blasted from large event speakers. Away from the socially watchful neighborhoods of South Beirut, several teenage couples drifted off to "go for a walk"; older members of the group pretended not to notice.

On the way back into Beirut, someone got the idea to stop at an amusement park by City Mall in Dawra, a semipermanent establishment with carnival rides, games, and a paintball arena. Giggling, the teenage couples headed for the bumper cars as the rest of us trailed behind. There was some discussion of buying tickets for rides; I drifted with Layla's sisters Nur and Salwa along the brightly fenced asphalt pathways. They deciphered the shouting before I did. "Fight," Nur breathed as she grabbed my arm and turned to run ahead of what I quickly realized was a fast-approaching crush of bodies.

The environmental shift in the park was immediately discernible. My mind darkly raced to Bill Buford's description of how soccer riots "go off":

> With that first violent exchange, some kind of threshold had been crossed, some notional boundary: on one side of that boundary had been a sense of limits, an ordinary understanding ... of what you didn't do; we were now someplace where there would be few limits, where the sense that there were things you didn't do had ceased to exist. (Buford 1993, 87)

I had seen it "go off" only weeks before at a Gaza solidarity protest and immediately recognized similar behaviors in the park. However, my conceptual understanding of things going off hadn't accounted for the bystanders.

People *avoiding* fights, riots, or repression may also go off. However, this secondary shedding of limits may be obscured to researchers by a focus on a central, violent incident, rather than on bystanders' behavior. Standing on the main path between the brawl and the exit, we experienced it first-hand. Parents carrying small children, hands protectively cradling toddlers' heads, viciously checked us sideways in order to gain ground. The cheerful, rainbow-painted safety fences created a bottleneck between the carnival rides, meaning that the only way to flee the oncoming crowd was to outrun it. Churning bodies squeezed the air from my lungs as I helplessly realized I was being forced toward the fence. Comprehension of exactly how people die in stampedes—again, my reference was English soccer in the 1980s—flooded my mind. While I had thought through personal security contingencies for situations such as civil war and aerial bombardment, "stampede next to the spinning teacups" had never occurred to me as a possibility. It was not part of my theoretical universe of violent threat.

Then Salwa collapsed. As she fell, I saw her chin jerk forward as she slammed the back of her head on a curb. Adrenaline hit my stomach along with nauseating fear. Nur lunged for her sister, dodging under elbows and breaking through strangers' tightly held hands. Salwa was convulsing violently on the asphalt. Nur worked quickly to shift her onto her side and to shield her body as one of their brothers, Umar, found us and threw himself downward through the crowd at his sisters.

While I had completed an advanced first-aid course before traveling, it had never occurred to me how difficult it might be to properly administer care in the middle of a raging crowd with thousands of colored lights flashing. Now slow-moving bodies squeezed over us and blocked the light; people were packed into the bottleneck. Feeling the crowd persistently press inward toward the protective shell Nur and Umar created with their bodies, I tried to construct some Arabic approximation of "Give her air," failed, and wound up holding my arms straight out and simply screaming into the crowd: "Move!"

The loud, confused setting created coordination and communication challenges. Petrified that Salwa had a spinal injury and realizing that Umar hadn't actually seen her hit her head, I yelled, "No!" when he moved decisively to pick her up. It was the first time I shouted at one of my interlocutors and he looked shocked. Apologetic, I signaled the reason and asked to check her. Gravel scraped my knuckles as I slipped stabilizing hands under her skull and tried to feel for blood. The crush of bodies and the overlapping shadows made it impossible to see the ground, so I tried to sense any wetness on the asphalt. The fight—identifiable as a locus of male voices yelling—escalated somewhere to our right. At this point, more men from our group had sought us out; a ring of family, friends, and gawkers created a protective island in the crowd. Salwa's convulsions eventually subsided, her physical responses seemed normal, and we helped her back toward the parking lot.

The drive to protect had worked in other ways among other members of the Faraya party. The rest of our group materialized from the crowd into the parking lot a few minutes later. Several girls were crying and one of the teenage boys was holding a bleeding stomach. Husayn, a youth in his mid-twenties, ran for the car he had borrowed for the day, while Laila's brother Sa'id looked at us and said grimly: "There was a knife."

If the fight were to be reported in a Western newspaper, it could easily be treated as a case of sectarian violence. Yet the reality was much more banal. A man in his twenties ran over one of the teenage girls' feet with a bumper car. The girl screamed in pain while the boy who'd been courting her got in the driver's face and aggressively demanded an apology. They exchanged curses. The driver's friends then piled in, drew knives, and attacked the unarmed youths from our party, who of course fought back.

At this point, Sa'id noted, they knew the offender and his friends were members of Amal, a predominantly Shiite Lebanese political party/militia. Though I was unsure of how they determined the men's affiliation, I assumed that Sa'id emphasized this point to indicate at least two things. First, Amal is loosely understood as being more "thuggish," less disciplined, and less morally upright than Hezbollah (another predominantly Shiite political party), an estimation that I had absorbed via my interviews and through my volunteer work with Palestinian youths who attended Lebanese schools in South Beirut. The consequent implications were that initial offense and the escalation were deliberate, hostile, and for the offender's amusement. Second, Amal fought Fatah in the 1980s; to be specific, the Lebanese militia besieged and shelled several Palestinian camps during the War of the Camps (1985–1988); it also deployed arson and sexual violence. The girl and her beau could have been identifiable as Palestinians from the camps by their accents, which increased the likelihood of deliberate antagonism. These social facts turned a personal dispute that might have been diffused into a group matter that drew from semidistant politics and proximate collective reputational concerns. The men in our group, the implication was, thus had no choice but to back the youth.

At the time, I fixated intensely on the fact that one side of the fight consisted almost entirely of noncitizens who deeply feared the Lebanese justice system. Apparently, no one called the police, a fact that did not surprise me. It was easy to assume that calling the police would not produce de-escalation, order, or justice. The two most likely outcomes were either the Palestinian men in our group being arrested or the police, upon learning who was involved (Palestinians from the camps and members of Amal), not showing up. I came to remember this moment as one where my interlocutors necessarily became agents of their own defense in the absence of robust state institutions.

However, temporal distance from this particular moment has also made me realize that it would have been difficult—not impossible, but difficult—to determine political affiliations in the midst of a screaming match. While accents and dress can reveal or hint at regional background, social class, nationality, and sect (for instances, through a style of hijab wrapping or an accent associated with the refugee camps), people don't commonly wear "Amal" and "Fatah" T-shirts outside of political events. Stripping back my own emotional reaction, I realized that when Sa'id invoked Amal, he provided deeper justification for an ugly end to a lovely day. Without the Amal factor, we would have been left in the parking lot understanding and possibly supporting, but simultaneously resenting, the lovestruck boy's defense of the girl. Invoking Amal layered additional meaning onto collective action. In a way, it seemed to validate Salwa's scrapes, the men's bruises, and the boy's wounds in a way that chivalry did not. It was a key coping mechanism.

In the next interlude, I explore how many of these microdynamics were inverted during a national crisis in Lebanon. Specifically, I analyze how memory and information interacted in a Palestinian household during a violent border dispute between the LAF and the Israeli military.

Waiting for war: Memories of 2006 and Media Deprivation during a Border Dispute

On August 3, 2010, the Israel[i] Defense Forces (IDF) removed a tree on the Blue Line[6] near the Lebanese village of 'Adayssa. The Lebanese Armed Forces treated this act as a border violation and fired on the IDF in response. The IDF subsequently deployed artillery units and launched limited airborne strikes on 'Adayssa and on LAF positions in the nearby al-Tayba.

News and rumor travel quickly in Lebanon, in part because people tend to rely heavily on personal connections for information rather than news outlets or government announcements.[7] Shortly after the engagement began, Iman, a friend in the Palestine Liberation Organization (PLO), called and anxiously informed me: "Israel bombed two houses in the South. You need to pack a bag and come to my house right now." In a state of vague disbelief, I stupidly responded that there was nothing on the news; she calmly told me that the PLO and Fatah had an emergency phone chain that went into immediate effect when the Palestinian leadership received security information from the Lebanese authorities.

From a practical perspective, and unlike in the amusement park, I had planned for this type of contingency. It seemed as though everyone I knew—whether Palestinian, Lebanese, or foreign—had done so; in the summer of 2010, the July 2006 war between Israel and Hezbollah was still fresh in people's minds. Aerial bombardment by Israel was one of my "red lines": a list of predetermined events that might prompt my early departure from Lebanon. If hostilities escalated, I knew that US citizens might be evacuated by sea, as they had been in 2006.

I methodically ran down a list of things to do before leaving the flat. Packing felt like a morbid riff on the "desert island" game children play at sleepovers; what were the three things I would take? What would I leave behind? It was easy to pack my notebooks, my laptop, and USB backups. Yet I found myself obsessing over how much clean underwear to bring, as if packing four pairs rendered the situation truly serious (and thus implied I should head to the embassy instead). Weighing my friend's concern, I also retrieved the emergency currency I had hidden after a friend warned me that Lebanese banks shut their ATMs during crises in order to avoid cash runs. Pulling out the wads of dollars (one assumed the Lebanese pound would lose value in a war) felt a bit like admitting defeat. Stashing US$1,000 on my body—the potential cost of a taxi to Damascus if the Beirut airport were bombed, also based on 2006 prices—felt deeply uncomfortable. Finally, anticipating undesirable outcomes if people stateside woke up to media reports that read, "Lebanese Army fires on Israel, IDF bombs villages" with no update from me, I sent a quick group email from a preset list of family and three close friends (dated August 3, 5:57 a.m. CST). A US-based friend who was online agreed to call my family; my cell phone couldn't dial out of country.

The news had only just broken on Al Jazeera when I left my flat, but it took me an hour to make the 10-minute trip to South Beirut. The scene in the street revealed facets of Beirut that I had never before witnessed. An email I wrote the following morning described the palpable shifts in mood and behavior that I observed at the time:

> Everyone had left work to head home, so the sheer volume of traffic was astounding. None of the taxis wanted to go even close to the poorer parts of Beirut [where I was heading]—that's where the bombs would drop first. People were flooding out of the city and into mountain and country homes—I saw taxis carrying whole families with bags in their laps (which was seriously premature). People were actually obeying the traffic cops, which never happens—it was as if there was this gentleman's agreement that everyone needed to proceed in an orderly way out of a burning building rather than trampling everyone else (the normal state of affairs). Over the course of my one-hour journey to go about a mile and a half, the taxi driver helpfully told us about how he had fought the Israelis in '82 and sure as hell would do it again.
>
> When I got to the majority-Palestinian neighborhood where I was going, people had already hung Lebanese flags from their balconies.
>
> Afterward, within a two-hour window, the streets were almost clear— this is nearly impossible in Beirut in the summer, when the population swells by several hundred thousand people. In the usually noisy, crowded neighborhood that I ran to, the roads were dead silent. (group email dated August 3, 6:23 p.m. CST)

Compared to my slow race to South Beirut, the rest of the day could be described as boring, sweaty, and exasperating. However, it was also one of the glimpses, albeit very limited, that I got into what life might be during extended but non-geographically proximate armed conflict. At my friend's in Tariq al-Jadida, the power flickered on and off in 10-minute cycles, allowing us to catch limited snippets of news reports and looped video footage. We clung desperately to these bursts at first, hoping for any new information. A clip of an Indonesian peacekeeper leaping into the back of a moving United Nations Interim Force in Lebanon (UNIFIL) truck played on loop for hours. To audiences in Lebanon, the clip not-so-subtly referenced a history of perceived UNIFIL powerlessness in the face of IDF attacks, feeding a sense of shared vulnerability and linking this Israeli incursion to previous engagements in 1978, 1982, 1996, and 2006.[8] The overarching message was that war was imminent.

Given our unpredictable access to information, the situation was maddening. There was absolutely nothing that any of us could do but wait, which was perhaps the most striking lesson I took from the day. It was 90 degrees and more than a dozen people were crammed into the living room, where sliding doors with balcony access offered minimal relief. Without news, conversations alternately descended into rampant speculation or converged on certainty that the situation would de-escalate that day. We spent hours chain smoking, drinking coffee, playing backgammon, and taking turns pacing the balcony. It had never intellectually occurred to me how living in a conflict zone could involve a lot of sitting around and struggling to entertain antsy children. Several of my interlocutors had described living in bomb shelters for weeks in the 1980s. This day helped me to retrospectively realize that I had focused too heavily on the "shelter" aspect of things rather than the "living" aspects.

This particular context—an armed conflict involving Israel—also brought my own positionality to bear on my relationships in new ways. Iman had called out of genuine concern. However, she also saw me as a particular type of connection for the family, just as they had ties to the PLO and the LAF. As Iman's family explained to me, I was their sole link to the United States, which to them meant that I might have "insider" information from the US embassy as far as Israel's coming decisions were concerned. Their understanding of the 2006 evacuation was that the embassy had contacted every American and told them to go to the Port of Beirut to board chartered ships. Throughout the day, they asked casually but repeatedly if I had received a text from the US embassy. I thus became the proverbial canary in the mine; if the embassy were to contact me, they'd know the situation was deteriorating and that they needed to get out of South Beirut. This conversation both underscored and instrumentalized my mobility and privilege as a US passport holder in comparison to their relatively constrained options as holders of Palestinian refugee travel documents.

Concluding Thoughts on Research in and on Violent Contexts

This essay underscores how engaging with an ethics of sight pushes researchers to question existing perspectives of violence by exploring the effects of distance, boundaries, and scale on perceptions of events. I emphasize how evaluating political violence from the point of view of bystanders capitalizes on researchers' own positionality and emotional engagement while allowing them to represent underrecognized facets of political violence. Practicality and the ethics of sight compel researchers to notice the routines and practices that accompany moments of violence and to consider how they relate to conflict processes and politics more generally. Taking this approach allows researchers to develop a fuller representation of their interlocutors' lived experiences and to paint a fuller picture of the political dynamics surrounding violence.

Given the scenarios described above, it is worth noting some practical advice regarding research in fragile states and conflict adjacent environments (Wood 2006; Mazurana, Jacobsen, and Gale 2014; Nordstrom and Robben 1996; Campbell

2017). First, researchers should be proficient in first aid, should pack first-aid kits, and should be familiar with information such as their blood type and how medical evacuation works (Lake and Parkinson 2017). Second, researchers should speak to others who have conducted research in their field site before they depart and ask their interlocutors about their own emergency preparations and protocols. For example, my interlocutors taught me to keep a cash emergency fund in US dollars, nonperishable food, and two weeks' supply of drinking water in my house at all times. I registered with my embassy and preplanned communication protocols—including putting together an emergency email group and giving my family a friend's landline number in Lebanon—in case of political unrest.

Judging whether a specific moment of violence or instability should prompt one's departure from a field site is researcher- and context-specific; everyone has different comfort levels, skill sets, and family and personal obligations. On-the-ground, situated knowledge is of paramount importance when evaluating any situation. Academic mentors and journalist friends impressed upon me that it was important to think through various scenarios in advance and to formulate both "red lines"—events that would force a departure (e.g., aerial bombardment)—and emergency contingencies—what to do in the case of a serious but not "run to the airport" event. Deliberating a departure may elicit feelings of guilt or cowardice. However, scholars should remember that they are not humanitarian workers or journalists; academic research almost never requires us to be on the front lines of a war. While some may treat imminent danger as "exciting" or "sexy," it is essential to ask how staying during a protracted emergency would add value to a project, given the risks and ethical concerns. In addition to exposing the researcher to direct physical threat and potential long-term trauma (Loyle and Simoni 2017), remaining in the field under conditions such as war, purge, or even natural disaster may also imperil one's interlocutors and reduce the resources available to locals. These are serious ethical dilemmas best avoided by rigorous training, careful advance planning, and responsible decision-making.

Doing Research during Times
of Revolution and Counterrevolution

ATEF SAID

On February 4, 2011, I arrived in Egypt to participate in and hopefully to study what seemed to be a popular uprising. My trip to Egypt took two days due to the curfew that had been imposed by the Egyptian regime a few days earlier. When I arrived in Cairo, it seemed almost like a different place. Streets and people were full of anxiety, excitement, and politics. I arrived in the very early morning, and went directly to my parents' home in Cairo. It was Friday, two days after what became known as the camel battle, a confrontation that occurred in Tahrir after Mubarak's supporters and militia attacked protesters in Tahrir Square. I told my parents, "I am going to Tahrir Square." Being apolitical and at the time having no access to information save for propaganda-filled government TV and mainstream newspapers, my parents panicked and got angry at me. They told me something along these lines: we do not understand how and why our son, soon to finish his PhD, and who has a family in the United States, could leave all this in the first place and then come to make trouble in Tahrir. At the time, I had no choice but to make up a story. I told them that for my graduation I had to do research about the uprising and Tahrir.[1] I promised them I was not going to Tahrir—I was only going near downtown to interview some folks for this research. I took a shower, had a light breakfast with them, and left for Tahrir before noon. Soon I started going to Tahrir Square every day. To get there, I had to go through military checkpoints in the streets, something I had never seen in my life, and other checkpoints made by protesters closer to the Square. So-called popular committees were formed in most neighborhoods in Cairo and other urban centers in Egypt to protect people's homes and property due to the lack of security. The committees acted as checkpoints in the streets at night. At these checkpoints, people were stopped and inspected. Because many in the Egyptian public were not initially sympathetic with the revolution or the protesters in Tahrir, committee members were frequently hostile to everyone coming from or going to Tahrir. This was an additional hassle for me as I sought to witness the unfolding events. After a few days, as public sympathy for the uprising grew, things got better with the committees, and my parents and siblings started to ask me about Tahrir and the revolution.

At the time, I had to navigate complex issues in my daily travels to Tahrir. To be precise, I did not have a clear plan about what I was doing. I was excited about the uprising but also anxious and worried and surrounded by the worries of others—my family in Egypt and in the Unites States. For years, I had been put on Mubarak's watch lists and detained at Egypt airports for hours when traveling to and from Egypt. I worked as a human rights attorney and researcher in Egypt for almost 10 years before moving to the United States in 2004. I had also been subjected to extensive police surveillance during many trips to Egypt. Many of my close friends were or are leading prodemocracy activists and bloggers. My phone conversations with them have certainly been tapped. Because of restrictions on my travel to Egypt, I went through the naturalization process and became a US citizen in late November 2010. Some friends advised me to use my American passport while entering Egypt. I used it once on a trip that took place before the uprising and received no harassment at the airport. But my history and associated worries weighed on me when I was going to the uprising. My parents also had a justified history of worrying about me because my activism had caused trouble in Egypt previously.

When I arrived in Egypt on February 4, 2011, I embodied five interwoven layers that shaped my positionality: (1) as an outsider coming from the United States; (2) as an insider returning to a familiar context (I grew up and lived in Egypt until 2004 and still maintain my Egyptian citizenship); (3) as a scholar conducting research in pursuit of a degree at a US institution; (4) as a former human rights and leftist prodemocracy activist in Egypt who still maintains connections with activists and activist networks there; and (5) as simultaneously a participant in and an observer of the revolution. I had to navigate these layers while participating and carrying out my research. When I arrived in Egypt, I was eager to participate in and bear witness to history and yet also eager to do research and be ethical. I stayed in Egypt after the uprising until mid-April 2011. I came back to Egypt for the entire summer of 2012, until early January 2013. I returned again for a short trip in December 2015. After defending my dissertation on the Egyptian uprising in 2014, I have been working on my book. I continue doing research in Egypt. Since 2011, Egypt and the ostensible revolution have gone through many radical changes, from an uprising to a so-called failed transition, before returning to military rule.

In this essay, I will discuss how these interwoven layers of positionality shaped my research in Egypt in two main stages: during the revolution and also during the counterrevolution. I identify the revolution here roughly as the period from the beginning of the uprising until the summer of 2013, when the Al Sisi–led military coup took place. And I identify the period of counterrevolution as the period from July 3, 2013, until writing this essay.[2] The essay is divided into two sections, covering my research during the revolution and counterrevolution respectively.

My aim in this essay is not to compare Egypt under revolution versus counter-revolution, or even to describe how I completed my research. My aim is simple: to discuss how I *experienced* conducting my research in the two periods. I should note here that the research conducted in the first period was completed and culminated in my dissertation. But with respect to the second period, I only recently finished my research and I am still analyzing the data and writing about the results. Thus, while I talk about the process of writing in the first period, I do not cover this in the second period. It should be noted also that I am a sociologist who uses both qualitative and historical research methods. The discussion in this essay is limited to the ways I used these methods in my research during the revolution and counterrevolutionary time.[3]

Researching a Revolution

During the revolution and for my dissertation research, I conducted two major research trips. Both trips entailed extensive ethnographic work, historical research, and interviews. The first trip was from February 4, 2011, to April 16, 2011, which overlapped with the initial 18 days of the uprising; the second trip lasted from July 16, 2012, to January 5, 2013. Before I discuss how my positionality shaped my research and influenced my thinking on ethical issues during my research and writing about the uprising, I would like to emphasize two main lessons I learned from this period. The first is that it is important to be aware of the advantages and the limitations of positionality, especially in such intense research experiences and specifically in the case of complex positionality such as mine. It is important to be reflective and transparent about that. The second lesson is that things change with time. Neither the field nor I have been stagnant entities. Even when doing research about the revolution, my positionality and thinking on ethical issues shifted from the time I was in the field to when I was coding data and writing, and Egypt continued to change while I was finishing my dissertation. In sum, the aforementioned aspects of my positionality shaped my research, but they also shifted over time, with different dimensions becoming more or less relevant in different instances and as circumstances changed.

At times, aspects of my positionality were a burden; at other times, they were very helpful. Specifically, my positionality vis-à-vis other activists in Egypt gave me great access to many "insider" points of view. But at the same time, these connections made my experience of being there and writing about it later emotionally intense. It was difficult to feign any level of detachment from either the events themselves or my informants. In the first round of research, for example, I felt my positionality was a burden preventing me from being fully engaged with the events. Only later did I realize that my anxiety and feeling of being overwhelmed was shared by many of the people I interviewed, as well as other friends and activists, due to the enormous intensity of the time. I was not alone in this. I was perhaps particularly prone to anxiety because I was coming from the United States. At the time, the regime was spreading rumors about foreign spies and agents paying the protesters to destabilize the nation. Progovernment media targeted Tahrir and protesters in Tahrir specifically, labeled them as infiltrators, and emphasized that many foreigners were present. Mubarak's thugs had arrested numerous journalists, especially foreigners, in the first week prior to my arrival. I had to ensure that my wallet contained only an Egyptian ID and Egyptian money; I hid all my American IDs, such as my student ID and driver's license, as well as any American money in a secured place in my parents' home. Of course, I was also concerned that people might not fully trust me because I was now a US citizen and no longer lived in Egypt.[4]

But as noted above, my positionality and being known to many activists over the years assisted me in easily accessing the offices and meetings of political organizations. Of course, many of these offices were also opened to journalists, but I was given access as a friend or as one of the group. So I was able to attend many closed meetings of different groups, including discussions of forming new political parties, for example. It was also easy for me to find young researchers and activists to assist me in conducting interviews or recruiting people for more. At the same time, however, my positionality also became a problem. Precisely because I knew many activists and leading bloggers personally, I was reluctant to impose on their time or seem like I was seeking to exploit our relationship. I understood on a very deep level how intense and tragic some of the events were, and I could not bear to disrespect anyone enduring these horrors by asking them to take time away from their struggle in order to sit down with me for an interview. Also, some of them were being interviewed all the time, especially by Western researchers, and there was already a growing discourse among Egyptian revolutionaries that was critical of the ways that Western researchers were entering and exiting Egypt simply to collect people's stories, only to disappear from the scene and publish their work elsewhere.[5] I was deeply conscious of this dynamic and sometimes found it difficult to request interviews for fear of being perceived as a selfish researcher.

On my second trip, I was more relaxed because I was more prepared. After thinking about the first trip, I also concluded that it was not only positionality that created or formed the emotional intensity I had in the first trip. I was doing research in an exceptional historical moment. When I discussed how I felt during the first trip with activist friends in Egypt, they told me, "We all were overwhelmed." The second trip was also longer. I had also had time to reflect on the emotional intensity of the first round and realize it was not unique to me or my project. I should also say that because the first phase of research was done in a rush, dictated by the speed of the events themselves, I did not have time to obtain IRB approval before leaving for Egypt. I told my informants about this issue, and they simply did not care. I relied on ethnography for the first stage, given the lack of IRB. Despite the difficulty of keeping up with field notes during that time, I was able to sit and write notes later. It was not very difficult given how memorable were the events of the revolution for me. I did, however, obtain IRB approval for the second phase of my research. A few months after conducting archival work, I started to schedule interviews. Because I have many contacts and I was more targeted in doing interviews, things were a bit easier than the first time around. But this time there was the added complication of doing research outside of Cairo, in Suez, Mahala, and Alexandria. I was grateful to a friend of mine, who worked during the revolution as a reporter for Al Jazeera and gave me many contacts in Suez, where she was the main correspondent. A young blogger also shared with me his entire address book.

It was not uncommon for a leading activist to call around to arrange an interview with me; this happened at least three or four times. The success of my research trips in the three cities outside Cairo would not have been possible without the help of activists. In this period, positionality was not a burden at all, but allowed for easy accessibility. It is this positionality that enabled me to meet and interview key people, specifically as previously known human rights and prodemocracy activist. This included being able to interview people as the founders of the Youth Coalition of the Revolution (YCR), an administrator of the "We are All Khaled Said" Facebook page, some of the founders of Kefayya and the National Association for Change, workers who were crucial organizers in the Mahala strikes in 2007 and 2008, and some of the founders of the blogging movement dating back to 2005.

Yet when it came to the fieldwork itself, my positionality created a number of challenges. Information coding, data analysis, and writing have been very difficult given the massive changes that have taken place since 2011 in Egypt, and which continue to twist, turn, and unfold unpredictably. My attachment to some of the interview subjects, who were targeted after the revolution, led me to feel a constant sense of responsibility to keep the research up to date in light of these changes and to avoid leaving out new crises and attacks. Yet, because the main purpose of the research was for my dissertation, I was forced to detach myself from the role of a witness documenting every development, and to focus instead on writing a dissertation that began and ended within a specific historical period. It was very difficult to process intellectually, and emotionally intense as well.

As I began writing my dissertation, for example, two of my informants were serving jail sentences. Both are icons of the revolutionary youth movement and are people I know personally, and whose families and communities I have known for over a decade. Indeed, over the course of writing the dissertation, several of my informants entered or exited jail. And the number now exceeds 10, including activists and young researchers who worked as research assistants during the uprising. The practice of quoting an informant who is at the time of writing in jail was an emotionally terrible experience, especially when my attachment extends to the revolution, which at the time seemed to be going downhill.

One of my dissertation chapters was extremely difficult to write; complex issues of positionality overlapped intensely. It was an intellectually and emotionally exhausting process. In that chapter, I was discussing how most protesters in Tahrir had some reformist vision about the goals of the revolution. Compared to other chapters, where I discussed how Tahrir Square became the central icon and site, and perhaps how occupying Tahrir embodied the main mode of action of the uprising, in this chapter I was discussing how such centralization also limited the uprising. In other words, I was writing critically for the first time about Tahrir and its protesters, myself included, at a time when many activists were in jail. How on earth could I sit in an armchair and blame protesters for the mistakes they made during the uprising after the event took place? Again, the point is not the content of my research or the legitimacy of my analysis, but rather the process of analysis and writing. After very long struggles, I found two solutions. The first is to rely on autoethnography and write reflexively about how I felt at the time. I was overwhelmed and presented with many political and historical decisions. This experience was shared by many of my informants. Their words saved my life, especially when they alluded to the many conflicting historical possibilities and difficulties of making decisions in an enormous event like a revolution. My aim during the time of writing was to reconstruct the moment, not to judge people for their actions. Second, many leading bloggers and activists started writing critically about their experience of the revolution after 2011. This was helpful for my own writing. Maybe it was the troubled transition in Egypt that forced many activists to be reflective and reassess their experiences in the uprising. But sharing these in public was useful and inspiring for me.

Another example is worth mentioning here, for demonstrating how reflexivity and temporality shape the way we look at methodological and ethical issues. Because of my worry about my families (both in the United States and in Egypt) and worries about my own safety, I made the decision not to sleep at the famous sit-in in Tahrir during the revolution. At the time, the decision was difficult: I felt I was giving up a historical opportunity, to be part of history, to witness it. Even if I witnessed it as a researcher, at least I would not *only* be an observer. As an activist, I fostered a deep sense of guilt about not being brave enough to join the Tahrir protesters. I lived with this guilt and shame for several years—that is, until I was writing my dissertation and realized that by not sleeping in Tahrir at night, I had been given another historical opportunity: to participate at night in one of the popular committees in my parents' neighborhood. My point here is that ethically, at the time, I felt that not only was I not a good observer, I was also not really an engaged activist. But a few years later, I realized that it was useful to be able to go around Cairo at night and take part in this rare but important mode of action that took place during the uprising, and to write about it as well. The lesson here is that time matters when we think back about our methods and data. But most importantly reflexivity is a must; we might perceive the benefits and limitations of our methods and decisions differently over time.

Navigating the Impossible: Researching Counterrevolution

Conducting research during the revolution may have been difficult, but it was not impossible. As discussed earlier, I was in Egypt for two and a half months in 2011, and almost six months in the summer of 2012. During this time, Egypt was an open society, or at least that is how I experienced it. There were some attacks on protests, but people continued to protest. New parties and independent unions were free to organize and mobilize. The situation in Egypt at the time of this writing is dramatically different. I am working now on my book about the spatialities of recent protest history in Egypt.[6] I needed to update my doctoral research for the book. After 2013, I tried to continue my research, but Egypt, which was authoritarian before 2011 and experienced some radical opening in 2011 and 2012, has lately become a military/totalitarian state. Security challenges are a hundred times worse than in the time of Mubarak, the uprising, and its aftermath. In Egypt today, journalists, photographers, artists, students, researchers, and many others are jailed just for doing their work. Even political parties and independent unions, whose activities are authorized by Egyptian law, experience surveillance and security threats, for the very fact of doing what they exist to do. Among Egyptians who are currently in jail for doing research is Ismail Alexandrani, who is a most talented young scholar, and who has done very critical research investigating and refuting the regime's narratives about the so-called war on terror in Sinai (Amnesty International 2015). Another example is Hisham Gaafar, a talented researcher and the founder of an important research and media group, the Mada Foundation for Media Development (EIPR et al. 2016). The Middle Eastern Studies Association (MESA) issued a security alert for doing research in Egypt after the murder of Giulio Regeni, an Italian researcher and PhD candidate at Cambridge (MESA 2016; see also Fahmy 2016 and Pyper 2016). Not only rights activists, but some of my close academic friends have been banned from entering Egypt or put on watch lists at Egyptian airports. Using a European or an American passport to enter Egypt does not really carry protection from security hassles or give you any advantages in doing research. But to be fair, the situation is much worse for Egyptian researchers or others who live in Egypt and who work in Egyptian universities and academic institutions. Some of those researchers have chosen to be on the safe side and do not do fieldwork or study politics, or do armchair work, or work with the government.

Simply put, security concerns from the time of the revolution persisted, but the situation worsened radically. It was not a mere issue of safety of researcher or subject, but it is no exaggeration to say that doing research means risking loss of freedom and perhaps life. Suspicion of research has increased. In a hysterical and fascist environment, many ordinary people volunteered to attack researchers or report them to police, especially in an atmosphere that was centered on conspiracy and xenophobia. Also, many key informants who had been critical to the Egypt uprising in 2011 continued to be jailed and their numbers increased dramatically. It is perhaps beyond the scope of this essay to discuss the difference between doing research in an authoritarian context and specifically under authoritarian regimes, which are operating under counterrevolutionary agendas or goals. As scholars of political sociology, we may need to stop discussing authoritarian regimes as if they were generic. In Egypt, in addition to overall repression, there has been specific targeting of revolutionary youth, and it seems that there are systemic efforts to eliminate the 2011 revolution from mainstream media and schoolbooks, or at least in most schoolbooks there is only an emphasis on the role of the military in 2011 and the so-called June 30 revolution of 2013 (Raghavan 2016). As I will show below, I have tried to attend to this radical change, but I am still working through this.

The general picture is that research in Egypt now is almost impossible, and necessarily means risking researchers and their subjects (activists or otherwise). Does this simply mean that we stop doing research in Egypt, or write from a distance? Is it feasible at all to continue doing research in this context, in an ethically and academically rigorous way? Recently I have raised this question with several friends in social media, many of whom are academics who study the Middle East and some of whom are also activists. Some simply told me that the only solution is to do "armchair" writing. Others suggested we cannot stop being creative and must find alternate solutions to good fieldwork. Some experienced colleagues told me this is an important topic and ought to be collectively discussed.[7] These perhaps are important questions. But in a very practical and pragmatic sense I need to finish my book.

I am not the type of researcher who can do armchair writing about Egypt, or at least not for this book. In this section, I will discuss how I continued to do research in Egypt after 2013. I discuss three methods I used to overcome difficulties and again address how my positionality was critical to these methods. While I will discuss the limitations of my approaches and how I tried to address them, I have to admit that some of the strategies below are simply blessings of my positionality, or good luck.

The first approach was seeking trustworthy assistantship. I hired a researcher who happens to be a close friend. He is an experienced activist and a very talented researcher. I acknowledge it is difficult to find someone who is trustworthy, experienced, and committed at the same time, let alone somebody who happens to also be aware of the relevant security issues. Even now, I am not sure if he will be available again to assist me. But in the period from 2013 until the first half of 2016, he did much work for me. We communicated regularly. I gave him lists of materials or data I was looking for. We had long discussions via different communication methods (Skype, Viber, and Facebook messaging, for example). We also had long meetings during my visits to Egypt. In these meetings we laid out a plan for research in the coming year. I am aware that I have been blessed to have such a friend who happened to be in need of extra work. Of course, not every researcher will be so blessed. That said, there were predictable issues of friendship mixed with professional expectations and accountability. I was very fortunate that my friend is a committed and rigorous person. But being aware of power dynamics between us, I sometimes delayed the work when I was not sure of available funding. He was willing to do work without being paid, and he was willing to wait for payment until funding was available. To solve this problem, I established a rule with him that I could ask for any work if I did not have the funds for it.

The second approach was to conduct interviews through emails. I conducted these in the summer and fall of 2015 with the assistance of my friend, as I needed to conduct more interviews to cover the period after 2013, especially dealing with issues of activism, coping with counterrevolutions, and overall political developments in Egypt since 2013. Practically speaking, I was in the United States teaching and was not able to travel as frequently to Egypt, even if it weren't impossible to do in-person interviews there. The targets of these interviews were people who self-identified as belonging to the January revolution. Of course, it may be more difficult to target a wider audience, or other publics, many of which are now against the revolution. I constructed a short list of questions and sent it to a large group of people, aiming to reach a target of at least 50 responses. I succeeded in getting 54 responses. One great advantage of this approach was that I received written responses, eliminating the need for transcription, which is always very costly in terms of money and time, especially when interviews are conducted in a language other than English. It is not easy to find a native speaker who is also an experienced transcriptionist. Another advantage to this approach was to avoid the security hassles of meeting people in public or in their homes, thus putting them at risk. Even if the risk is small, in meetings in public or in private homes under conditions of excessive police surveillance many subjects do not feel at ease to talk freely. Hence, sending written responses was a good solution to sidestep security concerns. Of course, there have been several problems with this approach. To begin with, I had to be satisfied with a short list of questions because I wanted to encourage many people to participate. Longer questions would have deterred them. In addition, many activists are now depressed and exhausted and do not necessarily want to talk. They need emotional support, not a long list of essay questions. I did not have a choice but to make the list very short. The outcome was that I ran into the problem of missing information. I had a number of follow-up questions. As I expected, however, doing a second round was not very successful. Less than half of the informants responded the second time. A related problem was that I also gave the informants the choice not to answer all questions, again to encourage participation. This may have been a good strategy for recruitment, but it had a negative implication for the responses I received. Many informants preferred not to answer some questions. Even though I was very comfortable and confident that I made a wise decision in giving them this option, the outcome was that I did not have a good sense of comparison across interviews, and lacked the full picture of each response. Not knowing the reason for their refusal to answer, I was not able to further explain the questions, or otherwise alleviate their concerns, as might occur during an in-person interview. In addition, some of the answers were written quickly and not as full sentences. I missed the chance to clarify some of the issues the informants raised. I had to make my own judgments as to what they were trying to say. While it is great to be able to communicate with activists in Egypt, and this is better than ignoring their voices entirely, one should be aware of the pros and cons of this approach.

The third approach was what I can only describe as critical and creative ways of doing historical and documentary research. Clearly, I did not plan to be creative; it came spontaneously over the course of my work in Egypt. In a situation where the media was becoming almost entirely controlled by the Egyptian regime's intelligence and security apparatuses and collecting documents was becoming impossible, I had to find solutions to keep up with my research. So I continued to look for news coverage and statements from political parties and other groups. I also continued to look systematically for specific writers in the op-eds of newspapers. But in addition to scouring these traditional sources, I also looked for alternative accounts of the news. Two types of sources proved particularly useful. The first of these involves a number of initiatives for recording and archiving the uprisings and violations that occurred in the last few years. In addition to reports of human rights and civil society groups, these initiatives have been a great source of information. Although it would be impossible to comprehensively list them all, a few examples will suffice. One is Kazeboon (Liars), which was a campaign launched by Egyptian revolutionaries to document and expose the propaganda and lies of the Egyptian military administration that ruled Egypt after ousting Mubarak.[8] Another example is WikkiThawara, which was launched by several Egyptian activists and reporters to document the human rights violations of Egyptian regimes that ruled during the transition periods. WikkiThawara includes many statistics on murder and regime violence, arrests, and other specific events.[9] A third example is the group Democracy Meter (Demometer), which documents and publishes short reports online about protests in Egypt.[10] These and many other campaigns have been incredibly useful sources. These sources are useful especially in the context where there is a specific elimination of records and even news about the revolution.[11]

In addition to this, social media have been especially useful. A discussion of the pros and cons of social media for research are detailed in other chapters in this edited volume. In my case, I have found social media useful for my research in many ways, especially in the last three years. For starters, social media have been very useful for circulating news. I often find critical news in social media first, whether as the source of news (an individual reporting or commenting on something that happened), or the mode of circulation. Beyond mere information sharing, social media have functioned for me as a large site for maintaining a critical and collective intellectual network. Not only do I see great collections of comments and quick thoughts by friends in my network, I also sometimes engage in discussions with those friends about research and political issues in Egypt. In terms of my research, I find important analytical pieces written by academic friends and activists. These have been of great help to my research. In some cases, I have found important analytical posts written by activist friends and writers in Egypt, more sophisticated than much of the academic writing I have seen. I store these posts and ask the writers for permission to cite them. In most if not all cases, they have been happy to comply.[12]

Conclusion

In this essay my goal was to discuss how I navigated the complex and shifting political context in Egypt while completing my research. As I showed throughout the essay, not only has the political context shifted dramatically over time, but these shifts intersected in complex ways with my multilayered positionality, shaping my research in crucial ways. In such tricky interactions (complex context and complex positionality) it is important to be constantly critical and reflexive about the research process. In my case, not only did the changing context cause my positionality to play out differently, but also the subjects of study changed dramatically: from those folks who had high confidence and high hopes and were willing to talk, to those who were exhausted mentally and emotionally and experiencing extreme despair. This has been important for me to remember. While I am writing this essay, I have been I receiving constant news about banning researchers from entering Egypt after detaining them in airports. Some of those are Egyptians and some are foreigners who have families in Egypt. And there are also increasing restrictions on travel for Egyptians who live in Egypt. Several graduate students have told me they will stop doing research in Egypt and find another site for their projects. So again, I am acknowledging that I have been fortunate so far. I am not sure if I will be able to continue research in Egypt in these circumstances.

Researching the Countryside

Farmers, Farming, and Social Transformation in a Time of Economic Liberalization

RAY BUSH

Taking Sides: Fieldwork and Academic Activism

This chapter looks at some of the challenges and rewards in the process of researching the countryside in MENA. There has never been a more important time to discuss rural transformation and agricultural modernization, and yet it is also probably the most difficult time to try to do it. It is the most important because there has now been, in the case of Egypt, 30 years of market liberalization and since 1992 a land reform to privatize and diminish any rural gains that had been part of President Nasser's reforming zeal last century. It is an important time to try to take stock regarding the impacts of market liberalization and how we have and might continue to understand it, and to do this without seeing small farmers, *fellaheen*, as passive recipients of government policy. I am particularly interested in whether rural research can help give a voice to small farmers. Research on the topic is of little importance unless it can be used to help promote justice and equality. My research is not "objective" or value free. That preoccupation of mainstream commentators only reinforces the status quo of inequality and seldom gives voice to the poor. In the period of neoliberalism and its many different crises, an important dimension to rural MENA research is to explore the implications for small farmers of agricultural modernization.

It is the most challenging time for researchers, and the most dangerous. Counterrevolutionary forces not only, but especially, in Egypt have made research of any kind a deadly precarious activity. There is another non-life-threatening challenge to academic researchers based in the United Kingdom or in other higher-education establishments: the restrictions imposed by the neoliberal university.

The chapter goes beyond the methodological wrangles regarding how best to "uncover" the intricacies of rural life, although it raises some questions in this area. The (rural) Middle East is not an exceptional case that needs to be seen and investigated differently from elsewhere. On the contrary, the tools for investigation, the necessary materialist analysis of historical and contemporary social formations, are generalizable. The tools are grounded in the need to explore patterns of capital accumulation and transformation rooted in understanding the dynamics of exploitation and inequality generated by cleavages in social class, gender, and mechanisms for social reproduction. I will demonstrate the analytical heft of rural political economy. While focusing on the ways in which economic reform has worsened rural life chances for small farmers and pastoralists across MENA, I will also refer to two processes that structure the region's countryside: war and conflict, and in the case of Palestine, Israeli settler occupation and environmental crises

I will argue that fieldwork requires the time and space, opportunity, and inventiveness to build trust and direct engagement with farmers and their social interactions. Fieldwork is an important and necessary element in understanding rural MENA. It is a process of investigation that is undermined by the brutality of many MENA regimes and the limits now advanced by the neoliberal university. I defend the importance of fieldwork and of engagement with enquiries that challenge the ways in which power is exercised and inequality is maintained and reproduced in rural MENA. I advocate for the reintroduction of the human subject in politics, international relations, and development studies and challenge the inevitability of, among other things, the hegemony of the neoliberal university's control of its staff (Cliffe 2012).

I also stress, in contrast to the pressures of the "academy" and its flourishing bureaucratic managers, that it is important to recapture and promote "sociological imagination" (Mills 1959) alongside the centrality of political economy. The sociological imagination enables a combination of biography and history in reclaiming grand theory and a project of social transformation. It helps develop an opportunity for individuals to reflect on "the larger historical scene." As C. Wright Mills noted, many years ago, and with continued relevance: "The sociological imagination enables us to grasp history and biography and the relations between the two within society. That is its task and its promise" (1959, 5).

The brutal torture and murder by Egyptian security forces of Cambridge University research student Giulio Regeni has been a shock for researchers and academics in Egypt and possibly the broader MENA region. There has been a lot written about the murder, of the fear that it has spread across all sections of Egyptian society and among Western academics that research in and on Egyptian political and social life (Akl 2016; Pyper 2016; contrast Anderson 2016). For Western researchers it has long been common knowledge that almost all aspects of Egyptian society were researchable—although during the years of Nasser and early Sadat presidencies the rural areas were mostly out of bounds for non-Egyptian researchers. It has always been important to conduct research with care and caution, sensitivity, and a folder full of names of people who can help and offer introductions for fieldwork. Even with a *wasta*, or intermediary and minder, there was never any certainty about being able to do what you might like to do, but that is no different from the anxiety about the realities of conducting fieldwork anywhere in the Global South and the need to be flexible and have time to recast project aims and objectives should that be necessary.

Giulio Regeni's murder eventually raised a limited international outcry. Since the July 3, 2013, military coup d'état, however, Egypt's security state has operated with impunity, kidnapping, torturing, and imprisoning anyone who criticizes the regime, and in March 2016 the interior ministry declared that no research would be possible unless it has been cleared by security.[1] It remained unclear, however, which security agency had control over such "vetting" and whether in fact there was any central control over the multiplicity of security terror organizations linked to the state.

Giulio Regeni's murder fuels the conservative neoliberal university's desire to undermine the importance and significance of fieldwork in general and ethnography in particular. Health and safety is an important issue in research training. The new ethics culture in Western higher education, however, undermines academic autonomy and the possibility of long-term immersion in local culture and the posing of questions that challenge the status quo. The mantra of informed consent and research ethics seems to have cemented a shift in university culture since the 1970s, a move away from "ethnographic fieldwork being an art of being in the world to a growing remoteness from the world and the compensatory emergence of remote methodologies and the simulation of digital alternatives" (Duffield 2014, S75).

The increased remoteness of area studies has been driven by new technology, and fear underpinned by the securitization of development practice. Alongside this has been the recasting of what the academy stands for and how its aims and objectives will be delivered. The university is no longer seen as a "partly protected space" where "the search for deeper and wider understanding takes precedence over all more immediate goals." Instead "universities are coming to be reshaped as centres of applied expertise and vocational training that are subordinate to a society's 'economic strategy'" (Collini 2016, 33). And the mechanisms used by governments to deliver this have been twofold. First, the research and teaching audit culture that has become the yardsticks used by universities to produce a new generation of compliant young academics in an insecure job market. Second, funding councils and government strictures require pathways to research impact to be met. Here research success is defined as providing a "demonstrable contribution that excellent research makes to society and the economy." That is measured by policy and corporate partnerships and correspondence with planners and government wonks confirming policy compliance.[2] In such a context, why bother with spending time in the field or even visiting countries in the MENA when research questionnaires and information can be gleaned online and at a safe(r) geographical distance?

The Rural MENA

There is a paradox at the heart of research on the countryside in the MENA. While it is the world's region most dependent on food imports—more than 50% of its needs—research on the region's food producers—small-scale family farmers—is limited. Indeed, most research on the region's "food security" is tied to time-weary ideas of agricultural modernization that reifies agribusiness and ignores, or more accurately pushes out of focus, any reference to small farmers (Breisinger et al. 2012; World Bank 2010; contrast Bush 2014a). It is a region that is defined by the rhetoric of population growth outstripping both food production and resources of land and water. Yet the states in the region pursue agricultural "strategies" that accelerate decline in sustainability of small-farmer production, preferring instead to incentivize agribusiness and large-scale, capital-intensive agriculture. It might be extraordinary to imagine a series of government policy agendas that exacerbate a food crisis, but that is indeed what has been a regional hallmark in a region where at least 43% of the population is rural, and where there is immense inequality in landholdings. More than 85% of holdings in MENA are less than five hectares, while 6% are in the range 10–50 hectares, equal to 40% of the holding area (Lowder, Skoet, and Singh 2014).

There are two major shortcomings of government policy in MENA that need to be part of researching the countryside. The first is the reluctance to understand how rural inequality is reproduced and the second is to understand the interrelationship between rural social formations and urban social forces. Ethnography is often rich in its examination of "the rural" and the detail of respondents' lives. Several important projects at the Social Research Centre at American University in Cairo from the early 1990s did that, but exploring the detail of the links between respondents and the broader processes of the world food system, and the links between them have been rather limited. To understand rural MENA it is necessary to build from analyses of small-farmer strategies for managing and coping with their livelihoods, in a time of economic crisis, to the processes that link farmers with policymakers at the local, national, and international level (Projects of Rural Egypt, American University Cairo).[3] Three processes weigh heavily in MENA and impact disproportionally the countryside, overlaying the difficulty of conducting rural research.

Conflict, Environmental Transformation, and Economic Reform

MENA has experienced the highest number of wars and conflict of anywhere in the world. Israeli occupation in Palestine and especially military invasions of Gaza in 2008, 2002, and 2014 have killed more than 2,000 and destroyed the livelihoods of 10,000 small farmers and ruined the agricultural sector.[4] In addition to the violence of settler colonialism in Palestine, other regional conflict includes the Western interventions in the Gulf, Iraq, and Yemen and civil wars in Lebanon, Libya, and

Sudan. War kills farmers alongside other noncombatants, displaces agricultural communities, and inhibits farming recovery.

Climate change and environmental transformation is the second and underplayed cause that inhibits family farming and that has influenced research on MENA's countryside. There is of course a link between persistent conflict and environmental degradation. Israel's theft of Palestinian water, dam building in the Greater Horn, and grandiose projects in Egypt, Morocco, and Tunisia restrict rational and equitable use of agricultural assets and intensify struggles over resource capture. More than half of all arable land in the region is rain-fed, and climate variability impacts livelihoods, as does the "oil-fuel-water-agriculture nexus" that has contributed to the dominance of agribusiness and crude definitions of trade-based food security.

The broader context in which farmers in this turbulent region exist is the ongoing impact of economic reform. Economic reform recasts early postcolonial policy of attempts by different states to promote rural development by reducing poverty and promoting state-led agrarian reform. An era of state farms and support for small farmers was destroyed by structural adjustment programs from the early 1980s. Structural adjustment undermined the livelihoods of small farmers, increasing rural indebtedness, accelerating dispossession, raising prices of inputs, and expanding freedom for entrepreneurs and merchants to hold small farmers to ransom in deregulated agricultural markets. Investment in agriculture in MENA plummeted from the 1970s. Privatization driven by donors, notably USAID, promoted the sale of state farms in Tunisia. Law 96 of 1992 in Egypt abrogated Nasserist legislation that had given tenants land rights in perpetuity and rent protection and in Morocco, the "Le Plan Maroc Vert" in 2008 prioritized high-value fruit chains and reduced assistance for small farmers (Ayeb 2012; Bush 2002; Akesbi 2014; Houdret 2012; Sowers 2014; World Bank 2007).

The different and varied types of data production can be discussed in the classroom but they have very different meanings in the field. No textbook can tell you how to conduct fieldwork in MENA's countryside or unravel and distinguish between the differential impacts of violence, environmental change, and economic crisis. Fieldwork, however, can help to highlight, among other things, patterns of dispossession, the extent to which capital penetrates the countryside, what some of the impacts of that have been, and what alternatives to this "modernization" might look like. Fieldwork is more than "a matter of know-how" where the use of intuition, improvisation, and tinkering (bricolage) is crucial (de Sarden 2008). Fieldwork has a starting point, although its conclusions might be more problematic. It is important to start with the farmers themselves: understanding what they produce, where, and how. And what the patterns of social differentiation are in villages and within and between households. It is also important to understand mechanisms for distributing and marketing produce and where and how the surpluses are allocated and appropriated. Crucial too is assessing how the social processes underpinning the findings in these areas may have changed over time.

An important mechanism to try to access this kind of information has been women respondents, whose management of domestic responsibilities and farming and marketing can provide insight and knowledge of local power dynamics. In both Egypt's Delta and in different geographical locations in Tunisia, after the 2010/ 2011 uprisings women respondents described how expectations for rural change were tempered by continued power of landowners and merchants who determined prices and access to farming inputs and market prices.

Accessing data about shifting patterns of land and market access as well as changes in labor hire and relations of production requires time and patience, to listen and to learn from fieldwork experiences that can and often will involve confusion and misunderstandings of what you might experience and hear. Fieldwork may involve a lot of learning by doing, but this is shaped and filtered by the centrality of understanding how production is organized and how households and communities are socially reproduced. How is power maintained and challenged by both formal challenges to authority and informal struggles? Researchers can be helped if they have had an informed and sensitive mentor and supervisor—one who must have the skills of empathy and engagement, understanding of some of the pressures that respondents may be under from within their own communities and outside.

My own mentor had worked throughout sub-Saharan Africa and in MENA only in Sudan and the Greater Horn. His concern was to always hear what farmers had to say, to listen to and engage with all household members and to try to understand the crucial relationship between hands to work and mouths to feed (Bush 2016). In the field this involved for me a knowledge of women's labor in the household, and how this may have changed over time, especially during periods of acute economic transformation like the experiments with market reform that were rolled out in Egypt's countryside after 1987. Women's input in the household, with "domestic" chores of managing social as well as physiological reproduction, shapes the ways in which children are often socialized early into the realm of work. It has also involved women creating or capturing new occupational roles. During several different periods of interviews in Giza and Dakaleya women noted that they took employment opportunities within the village to boost income and also, often without, it seems, knowledge of their husbands, to work in neighboring urban areas to help manage the pressures on daily income needs and provide new livelihood strategies.

Caution is needed in conducting field research to avoid associations with local and village power brokers and landowners. In my early fieldwork, desperate to finally access the countryside, I accepted a recommendation of a young graduate assistant who would help access a village in the Delta. I wanted to understand local patterns of opposition to Egyptian Law 96 of 1992. My delight at leaving Cairo was quickly tempered by two disastrous revelations. The first was that the research assistant's hitherto declared support for small farmers and their conditions of existence showed itself in a most condescending and aggressive distaste for many aspects of rural life: poverty, squalor, "backwardness," "ignorance," "laziness." Second, the assistant was closely related to the landowner who gained significantly from the consequences of the legislation under examination. The advantage of such an assistant was that it did give me access to the large village landowner and confirmation of the ways in which small and nearly landless farmers were disrespected.

Rural data collection that seeks to explore farmer experiences over time and what impacts directly and indirectly on farming households and communities makes most sense when filtered through the prism of the processes linked to agricultural modernization. There is a lot of fun to have in trying to disentangle processes of data generation from interpretation (Van Onselen 1993; Mosse 2015), but the complex interweaving of these processes of knowledge production can be clarified in the way we understand the extent to which capital has penetrated and dominates rural conditions of production and social reproduction. There is a fierce and interesting debate about this but with only very little discussion in MENA.[5]

My own focus in the field, and more generally in my academic-activist engagements, is to explore how socially differentiated family farmers, and the social relations of farming, have been shaped by uneven and combined capitalist development. It has also been to highlight that modernity does not necessarily have to imply or result in the destruction of local conditions of existence. Instead, while the overwhelming pressures in rural MENA are dispossession and commoditization of land and labor that accelerates patterns of inequality and social differentiation, often just dumping landless or near landless families into abject poverty, it remains clear that a persistent feature of rural MENA is the resilience of farmers to resist abjection. This is not an agenda to celebrate resilience and the ingenuity of farmers in coping with poverty.[6] It is instead to identify the strengths and suitability of farming practices and to explore strategies that build on rather than destroy local, often labor-intensive, farming systems. In other words, an important future agenda is to explore how, and why, it is necessary that contemporary farming systems and structures that are often perceived as less modern may actually be the most appropriate for a MENA where small farmers already have some of the highest rates of agricultural productivity.

Conducting interviews, developing life histories and biographies, asking respondents about major turning points in their ability to translate their expectations of life with the realities of it, using semistructured questionnaires of different types and scale as well as focus group discussion and debate, sometimes with the use of film and audio, all this needs time, practice, and enthusiasm but most of all patience and an awareness of when it is as useful to say nothing as it is to continue verbal probing for meaning.

A good time to remain silent, and then to encourage gentle opening of topics, even if they might lead eventually to a cul-de-sac, is in meetings with individual women or by convening female focus groups. These can be particularly instructive in identifying lines of social and economic cleavage in rural communities and in observing the gendered impact of economic reform. While many male respondents debate their access to inputs for farming, labor, and cash restraints in relation to cropping and with regard to land contracts, women respondents in the Delta throughout the 1990s highlighted, on the one hand, their increased labor market participation and, on the other, a dramatic increase in the time that they had to expend managing household budgets, managing changes in diets and souk visits, and managing expenditure on what seemed to be an increased number of crucial health visits for ailing husbands or infant illness (Bush 1999).

Accessing information is not a neutral or passive process, and the relationships with respondents, of whatever quality and robustness, can seldom change the relationships of power that exist between the interviewer and interviewee. While there may always be a tendency to try to confirm what it is that the researcher already knows, (prejudice is difficult to shrug off), critical engagement with respondents is important. This may lead to confrontation and to challenging what respondents say, requiring checking with sources other than interviewees and leading to the researcher possibly modifying the original problematique. "Observation is not simply the colouring of a ready-made drawing." Fieldwork needs to try to develop opportunities to interrogate "preconceived curiosity" (de Sarden 2008, 9).

During the implementation of Law 96 of 1992, fully effective in 1997, interviews with farmers who resisted rent increases, nonrenewal of tenancies, and the fall into greater poverty presented many difficulties. Accessing respondents was the first major hurdle that was facilitated by an NGO that had close and ongoing links with farmers during a period of heightened rural security. One mechanism to help deliver interviews was to meet respondents away from their villages, in a nearby café, even in Cairo itself. Cafés could generate suspicions, but they were also often more relaxed arena's giving the opportunity for farmers to talk more openly. Such meetings could also provide opportunity to triangulate (validate) information with a broader range of respondents than would be possible in the village setting.

Questioning people and their ideas requires consent. But this need not take the form of the much-vaunted research council written consent that can then be scrutinized by university ethics committees in their tick-box complacency to audit researcher compliance. When respondents are illiterate, and in circumstances of conflict, where powerful local officials or landowners may access written consent forms, respondents will be suspicious and worried about their safety if they share information. Security services may view household respondents as collaborators with outside "spies." This tension was well documented recently where the politics of research methods in an Ethiopian town led to a series of "conflictual encounters" for researchers (Cramer et al. 2015). In my own fieldwork in Dakahlia, Egypt's Delta, local dignitaries would often use the disguise of inquisitiveness to probe why a westerner was talking to small and near-landless farmers. Landowners regularly used police and other forces of law and "disorder" to quell dissent, counter small-farmer testimony, and visit farmer organizers at night with security officials to ensure compliance. In contrast, farmer activists told tales of wives and parents being arrested and held until landowner wishes had been met. Local elites do not as a rule enjoy the presence of researchers who seek to explore the ways in which the powerful have benefited from economic reform, caused environmental damage, used labor enforcers to hire indentured labor to farm their land locally, or exercised overt violence and mistreatment of farmers.

Where the presence of researchers is detected, local officials, merchants, and other power holders may need more than a consent form before they cooperate and share how they sustain their positions of privilege. In fact, in many circumstances a written consent is an obstacle to research and no defense of the respondent's needs and interests in sharing knowledge. The police and numerous other security actors in MENA may have more leeway in their ability to intimidate respondents and researchers, as remoteness, exercise of patron-client relations of authority, and historical "respect" for landowners leads to opportunities for bullying and terrorizing. This does not necessarily mean that fieldwork in rural MENA is more difficult or insecure for the researcher or respondents than in urban environments. Geographical remoteness, for example, may also create conditions for a more relaxed security setting and give farmers more time and opportunity to organize politically and collectively. This certainly happened in January 2011 at the time of Egypt's uprisings as farmers occupied or tried to reclaim land from which they had been dispossessed following Law 96 of 1992. And land occupations also took place in Tunisia after uprisings in December 2010 (Ayeb and Bush 2014). It is important for researchers to have time to try to put rural political dissent and direct action into a political context. Investigation of the "field" thus requires time to negotiate a range of important challenges. Researchers need independence and autonomy to explore what they observe and how to put rural politics and social transformation into historical contexts. This complex and intricate series of enquiries requires researchers be trusted and not highly supervised and controlled by, among other things, newly empowered university ethics committees.

Time has been important in the research on the ways in which Egyptian Law 96 of 1992 was implemented that highlighted a systematic and systemic use of violence by many landowners. Defended by appallingly pejorative language of urban superiority and callous descriptions of peasants and rural dwellers (Saad 1999, 2002), landowners would routinely visit rural police units to encourage, and reward the police for, brutalizing small farmers who were reluctant to comply with newly inflated rents or dispossession.

Confrontation with security forces, local informants, powerful merchants, and local power holders may not be pleasant for fieldworkers, but discomfort can be an important emotion to experience. Discomfort can help the researcher understand the feeling of being asked things respondents do not want to answer. Enquiries regarding personal details about assets, income, employment, and relatives are understandably not easily asked or responded to. Yet they are questions if asked sensitively and with vigilance that can help deepen an understanding of what local dynamics

of power and politics are, how individuals and households manage to socially reproduce themselves, and what space exists for transcendence of elite dominance.

Modernity and Farmers' Voices

Policymakers in MENA have advanced agricultural strategies without farmer involvement or understanding of small-farmer practices. In contrast, I have been
concerned with data collection on agricultural modernization that might also facilitate the opportunity for farmers' voices to be heard: voices that might do more
than simply lament a governmental policy of neglect and abjection, although there
have been many of these voices.[7] Creating conditions for farmers to speak of their
anxieties and experiences of being pushed away from rural development has led to
research and fieldwork on three broad sets of institutions and respondents: aid and
international agencies, the state, and farmers. USAID has been linked with and has
helped instigate agricultural reform since the mid-1980s, and for some years in the
1990 sit populated at least a floor of the Ministry of Agriculture in Dokki as well as
having a significant presence in the US embassy. At one level, understanding USAID
policy toward the government of Egypt (GoE) was straightforward. It could be
gleaned from documents increasingly available electronically and online. However,
fieldwork was important to try to understand more clearly what the rationale was
for market liberalization and what influence USAID had on driving Law 96 of 1992.

The International Agencies

It is usually advantageous to have the positionality of a white Western researcher
when interviewing international aid agencies. This was certainly the case before
Google enabled respondents to be forewarned as to the ideological position of the
researcher. I began research on the World Bank in Egypt and mostly on USAID
in the early 1990s before Google highlighted my critiques of neoliberalism. This
meant that I was welcomed and encouraged by a very open USAID (the United
States is more welcoming in my experience than the British) to engage and discuss
and also participate in some of USAID's meetings, including one with the GoE. The
bonhomie of a Western researcher and, as was usually the case, Texan or southern
US policy wonks led to important exchanges that confirmed policy statements, and
what I was reading between the lines of policy documents that stated the intention
of the United States to impose a US farm model on Egypt. Thus strategies of market
liberalization were articulated in terms of efficiency and progress, but grossly unequal access to land, pressures on crop choice and pricing, and marketing structures
undermined small-farmer productivity and livelihoods. USAID promoted a strategy
of high-value, low-nutrition foodstuffs for export rather than consolidation and ex-
pansion of local crops for local consumption (Bush 1999).

Even without the Internet, and as the promises of agricultural reform were un-delivered but farmers were dispossessed and rural indebtedness rose, USAID grew more irritated by criticism. An interview that I had asked for with an economic counselor at the embassy in the late 1990s became an interview of me by three of them. It was clear that they had been trained or at least influenced by the Chicago school of shock doctrine reform. My cover was fully blown when I accepted the invitation to write an essay for *Al Ahram Weekly* (Bush 2001). The head of policy re-form entered USAID's office in the Ministry of Agriculture on Monday after publi-cation, slammed the paper down on a desk, and told workers that the woman whose desk he was standing by was my friend. In fact she had been very wise to the impact of USAID's policy on rural Egypt and had helped me access reports and documents that were in the public domain but not always easily available. The boss had already discovered us in the publications office, and my informant was reminded of the "rule" limiting access to publications weighing no more than two kilograms. My final exposure with USAID came in an embarrassing gathering of staffers before a meeting at the Ministry of Agriculture when the head of agricultural reform in-formed everyone that he knew who I was as he heard me "slag off USAID for a whole afternoon" at a recent AUC seminar: I responded by asking if he was sure it had been me.

Dealing with Governments

Before Sisi's Egyptian regime promoted a rule of terror, accessing government offices may not have been easy, but it was not, at least for a westerner, life threat-ening. The control of data and information and the poverty of government data on the regions rural sector is legendary. The GoE, for example, failed to perform envi-ronmental impact studies on Mubarak's Toskha, and the same state did not know how many tenants or female-headed households there were before implementing Law 96 of 1992. Similar failures of data knowledge and sensitivity in thinking of the need for stronger empirical underpinnings to legislation was evident at the time of Morocco's Green Plan and Tunisia's increased capture of small-farmer water resources.

My own experience has been, among other things, to be interrogated in Egypt's erstwhile Cabinet Information Centre regarding why I wanted innocuous informa-tion on declared rural development strategy and economic liberalization. Accessing senior policymakers was of course dependent upon access to people who may have even a tenuous link with the bureaucracy. And the assumption at an interview with someone who did later become minister of agriculture, that I knew the incumbent (untrue), confirmed the view that I must certainly be sympathetic to the early-2000s strategy for modernization: let agribusiness rip. The same bureaucrat, again prior to his ascension to becoming minister, having forgot I had interviewed him years earlier, did a rain dance at an international food conference in 2012, after the regions uprisings and after I had given a presentation on Egypt's failed strategy of food security. He was unable to contain his rage that I had the temerity to mention the interests of small farmers, criticize the GoE, and fail to see the benefits of market reform.

Small-Farmer Voices

The interests of small farmers refer to understanding what their access to assets was and how their farming activities were shaped by changes driven by economic liberalization, inflated input prices, and monopoly control of merchants who were often guilty of selling out-of-date seeds and overpriced fertilizer. Farmers also and repeatedly announced small-farmer interests across MENA in terms of the need for larger landholdings, secured tenancy, and price guarantees for farming outputs. Small-farmer interests included the need for security and benefits to accrue to female-headed households, which were often prevalent because of either death or desertion of male spouses or labor migration.

Farmers were well aware after the uprisings in Tunisia and Egypt in 2010 and 2011 that the promised results of political liberalization had not been delivered. There was fatalism in that recognition, understanding that it was more difficult than was first thought, to shift the economically powerful from village or nearby-town positions of authority. If local government positions no longer carried the names of erstwhile political parties, the personnel remained the same. This did not prevent the mobilization in Egypt around Tamarod that helped in the toppling of President Morsi in July 2012. Nor did it prevent Tunisian farmers protesting the need for landholdings to be more equitably distributed after struggles for reforms moving away from support for capital and water-intensive farming (Ayeb and Bush 2014).

Research on MENA's countryside is necessary to understand more clearly the pressure and processes linked to modernization in general and agricultural transformation in particular. This is especially important in the contemporary conjuncture when the choice of "progress" seems to be limited to that between capitalism or barbarism: in MENA's rural context, impoverishment and persistent accumulation by dispossession offer little by way of a transition dependent upon noncommodification.

Research on the patterns and consequences of rural underdevelopment in MENA is dependent upon fieldwork. I have indicated that there are a number of radical scholars who are trying to implement a political economy approach that explores the relations between small farmers and the broader social classes with whom they interact. I have indicated what I think the large issues are in this research problematic that seeks to retain the importance of promoting principles of justice, equality, human rights, and environmental sustainability. These are principles that are challenged in the era of neoliberalism and the increased but not yet universal destruction of family farming. Rural mobilizations took place after the uprisings that built on reactions against injustice and acted to channel decades of frustration with rural violence and economic marginalization into agendas for more sympathetic policy toward small farmers. Such has not been delivered, but further research can help provide data and support for a radical transformation of rural MENA. It is the role of political economy, linked to the sociological imagination and importance of biography and history, to defend the interests of small farmers. This is a defense against the ideologically driven universal policy that seeks to fragment rather than to support local patterns of knowledge and farming. This is important, as given help from other rural and urban constituencies, small farmers could be well placed to navigate the increased pressure from the contemporary world food system mediated by national governments. Farmer organizations might then have ammunition with which to promote greater rural equity.

Acknowledgments

Thanks to the editors, Mark Duffield, and Martha Mundy for comments on a draft of this chapter.

PART II

METHODS

9

Interviewing

Lessons Learned

JANINE A. CLARK

Interviewing is interesting, enjoyable, and rewarding. Meeting people, hearing their stories, and pursuing the questions that interest you are some of the joys of being a qualitative researcher. Contrary to the fears of first-time interviewers, political elites in the region often are highly accessible, and the vast majority of people willingly agree to be interviewed. With a little persistence and sometimes ingenuity, researchers generally have little difficulty securing interviews. Interviewees may genuinely be interested in your topic, passionate about their work, or curious about the experience of being interviewed. Commonly they also have a message they want to convey and perceive you, the researcher, as their vehicle. To be sure, it takes courage to make cold calls—particularly in a foreign language. As Goldstein states: "Even the most charming political scientist may find it difficult to pick up the phone and call" (2002, 669). Once at the interview, new researchers also often struggle with their introductions—how personal to be, how much to comment on family photos, and at what point to plunge into a discussion of the research project. And initially your interview questions may not elicit the responses you want. The interviewee may interpret them differently than you intended them or, as is common with first-time interviewers, your questions may be far too broad. It also takes experience to learn how to develop new questions on your feet. All of this is perfectly normal. As Kapiszewski et al. state: "Conducting interviews effectively— and feeling comfortable doing so—involves extensive preparation and practice" (2015, 192). While no chapter can help you practice (other than to suggest doing dry runs of the entire interview), this chapter provides practical advice on preparing for and conducting interviews. The chapter is based on the lessons I have learned, predominantly through trial and error, in conducting open-ended elite interviews based on nonrandom or purposive sampling in Egypt, Jordan, Yemen, Lebanon, Morocco, and Tunisia. It does not deal with integrally related issues such as ethics or positionality or with some of the specific challenges related to some countries in the region, such as dealing with the internal security apparatus, as these are dealt within in other chapters. Rather it provides basic interviewing tips that hopefully will apply to all elite interviewing contexts and topics. Preparation and practice do not mean that every interview will be a success. You will always have interviews that somehow don't "work," but they will be fewer and fewer. And you will usually be able to laugh about them later.

Creating Your Contact List

Before you go to the field, you will want to establish a wish list of preliminary interviewees—ideally, including their telephone numbers and email addresses— that you draw up as a result of your preliminary research and information from your supervisors as well as other scholars. Most researchers are happy to help and provide you with suggestions. Ask if they can recommend someone in your country of research who can help you get your work started. While you cannot expect anyone to hand over a wholesale list of contacts, you will usually soon create a list of names or organizations that will get you going.

Start your field research by contacting local academics and local or locally based journalists regardless of whether you arrive in the field with a comprehensive list of contacts and contact information, merely with a list of names based on articles and newspapers, or with nothing, as I did when I first went to Yemen. Both can be very helpful in terms of their insights into the "big picture," their advice in terms of contacts, and their contact information, as well as other types of advice discussed below (including, if needed, where to find a research assistant or translator).

As Scoggins points out, also consider asking locally based friends and acquaintances about contacts (2014, 394–395). If you meanwhile keep ethical considerations in mind, asking friends for contacts can be surprisingly helpful. On more than one occasion, I have coincidentally discovered that a friend was related to the person I wanted to interview and, as a result, was able to facilitate the interview.

Depending on the sensitivity of your topic, the unwillingness of participants to be interviewed, or the difficulties of identifying your participants, you may be required to adopt a snowball sampling strategy for your interviews. Keeping in mind issues of confidentiality as well as the increase in bias that snowballing entails, in these cases end each interview by asking your interviewee whom she or he thinks you should speak to next. In general, ask for telephone numbers only if you think the interview went well and that you connected. People will usually volunteer telephone numbers, but you don't want to overstep by putting your interviewee on the spot. And be sure to ask if you can mention your interviewee's name when the contacts she or he provided ask you for your source. After all, you only want to use someone's name if it will actually open doors for you.

While it may not seem necessary at first, create a system for keeping track of your contact names and telephone numbers and the sources from which you learned them. You may be surprised to see how long your list will quickly grow, and you will not only want to be able to tell interviewees from where you received their name and telephone number (they usually ask) but be able later to thank your source for helping you by sending you in the contact's direction.

With Whom Do You Start?

Leech writes of starting each interview with "grand tour questions" (2002, 667). I would add that you start the order of your interviews with "grand tour interviews." Start by scoping out the larger context and with interviewees who will help you get the lay of the land. While it will be tempting, never start with the person you think will be your best contact or resource. One thing that has been consistent throughout my interviewing career is that my first few interviews are painfully embarrassing to listen to or reread later and, with hindsight, are often not particularly fruitful. Regardless of how much you read beforehand, the first interviewee often provides a more accurate picture of what is going on than the one you derived from articles and books. If you interview your best contact first, chances are that you will be wasting the person's specialized knowledge on generalities that numerous other people can tell you. And you never know if you will get a second chance to interview someone. For this reason, start by talking to other researchers and journalists about your work first and only later move to the actual people on your wish list.

That being said, the person you think will be the most important interviewee— crucial for your project—usually isn't! The most insightful or useful informants are often in surprising places. In general, it is best to try not to treat one interview as more important than another, because you just never know.

Local academics and journalists also will be able to help you identify whom to contact for the type of knowledge you seek. Knowing whom to go to is especially important in countries such as those in the Middle East where the person with the title may have neither the authority nor the knowledge associated with the title. You may find that the information you need is held by someone behind the scenes. The titleholder may have been hired or appointed for a variety of reasons other than merit or expertise.

Getting the Interview

How does one secure an interview? The answer depends on both the country and whom you are interviewing. When writing about his interviews with political elites, Lilleker states that it is best to locate them via recognized channels and to reach them via a letter (or email) followed up with a phone call (2003, 208–209). This will hold true in some cases in the Middle East, but most emails will simply go unanswered. As Rivera, Kozyreva, and Sarovskii state, outside of the developed world, written or emailed requests have less utility for both technical and cultural reasons, including "a penchant for day-to-day scheduling without much advance notice" (2002, 685). You may be surprised at how many interviewees resist booking appointments far in advance. More than once, an interviewee has suggested that I come immediately or has called back offering an immediate interview. Furthermore, many people in the MENA put substantial weight on the personal touch that, as opposed to an email, a voice over the phone provides.

With more influential interviewees, I commonly do begin with an email; however, overall I have found phoning best. If I am pressed for time, I may ask a local or locally based research assistant (RA) to set up interviews for me—again, I ask him or her to telephone. With some exceptions, I do not email from abroad.

Often you will be given someone's personal telephone number. Depending on the country (or whether you are in an urban or rural area), calling a personal mobile cold may be considered rude. Again you want to ask researchers with experience in your country or locally based friends about the appropriate etiquette. In Jordan, for example, I usually telephone to introduce myself and then text from that point onward. No one appreciates a "cold text." But ask others with experience if follow-up texts are appropriate in a professional context.

Once your interviews are underway, you also may be able to leverage them in order to secure other interviews, particularly those that may be more difficult to get. When interviewing political party leaders, for example, it may help to note when requesting the interview that you have done interviews with the other political parties. Knowing that the "competition" has had an opportunity to present their side of the story often opens new doors.

As one researcher told me, if you are having difficulty getting an interview with people in the political or civil service elite, a final option is to go to their office and sit there! It takes time, but may pay off.

If you are interviewing political elites, it often "helps to have the imprimatur of a major and respected research house" (Aberbach and Rockman 2002, 673–674). This can mean having business cards with your affiliation or including a quick mention of your affiliation when you first introduce yourself. I also have had success securing interviews when an RA calls on my behalf, which may convey a sense of status or importance. Ask a local researcher or journalist if it helps or hurts to have someone book interviews for you and then use your personal judgment. To be sure, I also have contacted many interviewees directly and without the backing of any internationally known research institution and generally have had little difficulty in securing interviews.

In your first interviews with academics and journalists, you will also want to ask about local hierarchies or gatekeepers in regard to the type of interviews you want to do. In an organization, you will want to know if it is best to interview the director first and afterward those beneath him or her or if it is acceptable to interview the person whose knowledge you are seeking directly. It may be important to interview the leader of a movement first, for example, as it will signal to others in the movement that it is acceptable to talk to you. Some political parties, for example, are extremely hierarchical with lower-ranking party members unwilling to do interviews without permission from the top. Furthermore, securing an interview with a high-level political figure or movement leader may be easier if you have already interviewed high-level people. In other instances, however, you might be able to and want to talk to rank-and-file people before talking to top people, since they might be less inclined to fall into the official story if they know you've met "the boss." There is no fixed answer, but put some thought into it given your research topic, and try to get some feedback from others.

Where to Meet

Most interviewees will request that the interview be held in their office, their home, or a café. But interviews can take place in a whole host of locations. As a general rule, interviewees will request to meet you in their offices if the interview concerns their professional position, while they may choose a location outside the office and after regular hours if you are interviewing them about their thoughts on or involvement in other issues.

Of course there are exceptions, and sometimes when you arrive, the interviewee will change the location. I have conducted numerous interviews during car drives. Mayors in Jordan commonly drove me around the municipality, showing me the highlights. I have arrived at an interview only to have the interviewee take me to a social gathering in someone else's home or to a public lecture on a related topic. I have conducted interviews at Quranic study sessions, at khat chews (see below), and in hotel lobbies. This again is some of the fun of interviewing.

My point is that you will want to be prepared (for example, by always bringing a notebook with a hard cover so that you can write in it without a table or desk), and to be flexible. When I conducted interviews in medical clinics in Cairo, the doctors often preferred to do the interviews after the clinic closed. Many were held at eleven at night while we all shared *kushari* for a late dinner in the doctor's office!

If the interviewee seems unsure about where to meet, suggest a place where she or he can speak freely. You will want a location that can ensure privacy, but this does not necessarily mean a private location. A relatively noisy café (provided you can still hear each other) can be the ideal location—the noise provides privacy, as others cannot hear what is being said. Or you might consider a larger café with a quiet back room, where you can talk without being interrupted. Should you be nervous of surveillance of any kind, a public interview can send the signal that nothing suspect is afoot. In any case, be sure to know a location to suggest, ideally one you have visited to assess its suitability for an interview, and give yourself plenty of time to arrive.

How You Present Yourself

When I first started doing interviews, I was surprised how much attention I had to pay to how I dressed. Textbooks offer differing advice as to what to wear and how to behave during an interview. Over the years, I have come to believe in four guiding principles.

The first is to dress appropriately for the country and city in which you are based and to remember that you are a guest. In many capital cities, citizens dress no differently than you do at home. In other cities or in the countryside, they may dress significantly more conservatively. You want to respect these norms and keep in mind that just because some women from the region wear "revealing" clothing (or some men wear shorts) does not mean that it is culturally appropriate for you to do so.

When I did research, many years ago, in Yemen, this meant deciding whether or not to veil. Veiling, including the niqab, is the custom for the majority of women in Yemen; it is not mandatory by law. Many female researchers chose to wear conservative clothing but keep their heads uncovered; others wore the *balto* (the black robe women wear over their clothing). I chose a midway route. I wore conservative clothing and loosely covered my hair with a scarf. Each of these choices was appropriate (at least during that time period). The important issue is that your behavior be appropriate and respectful; Yemenis, like other peoples elsewhere, are well aware that clothing does not automatically make you respectful or respected.

The second is to be cognizant of the professional environment. Are suits appropriate? For example, when I conducted interviews in Jordanian women's associations, I found that the directors dressed relatively formally. This was not the case in Beirut. These considerations are largely so that you set the right tone for your interview. With someone prominent, a suit will show respect; yet the same suit may put others, such as the rank-and-file, ill at ease.

Third, while you want to "fit in," you also want to dress appropriately for your position. You want to dress as is expected of an academic, someone with a high degree of education from an expensive university in an affluent country (relatively speaking). This may mean wearing a suit; it may not. Being an academic can take different forms attire-wise.

Most critical is to be clean, neat, professional looking, and on time. It is a sign of respect, and if you clearly put in effort, you will be more easily forgiven in the event that you don't judge what to wear exactly right.

The fourth issue is that you be yourself. Many texts will give advice on displaying the right balance of professionalism, knowledge, and deference, but in attempting to do this you may be putting on an act, and nobody responds positively to that. In contrast, everyone everywhere responds positively to someone who is respectful and acts naturally.

How to Record Your Data

You also will have to decide if you prefer to take notes or record the interview or do neither. This will depend on the context and the person you are interviewing and whether you wish the interview to have a more formal or casual tone. I have tried all three and find that most interviewees prefer note-taking over recording. But there are many exceptions. In one case, the director of a clinic was thrilled to be recorded, as it clearly gave him a sense of importance (and conveyed the sense of importance that I granted to the interview). In another case, a relatively senior official in Hezbollah brought out his own tape recorder and taped the entire interview.

While many interviewees will forget that they are being recorded, I agree with Scoggins that the best way to make someone uncomfortable is to visually remind them that every word out of their mouth is being recorded (2014, 395). This would apply doubly so to typing notes directly into a laptop during the interview—an option I would not consider. A rule of thumb is that the more sensitive or personalized the information, the less appropriate recording is (Peabody et al. 1990, 454); in the authoritarian states of the Middle East, most topics are politically sensitive.

Moreover, taking notes allows you to write observations in the margins during the interview. These observations or what Mosley calls metadata are your impressions and observations of the interview context including the participant and whether she or he "hesitated in answering some questions more than others, and the context in which the interview took place" (2015). As she states, this "metadata facilitates more-accurate use and interpretation of interview data" (2015, 7). There will be times when these observations will be of little value, but commonly they will be highly useful in informing your data analysis.

The advantage of recording is that it ensures the highest degree of data reliability, as it "yields a complete and accurate transcript of what was said" (Peabody et al. 1990, 454). If your research requires exact quotes, recording will be absolutely necessary. You also can more easily focus on your respondent and formulate questions. Furthermore, as Peabody et al. state, if you are an inexperienced interviewer, recording may alleviate some of the nervousness about taking notes (454).

Note-taking is decidedly challenging. In addition to asking your predetermined questions, listening to the interviewee, reordering your questions, or developing new questions, you have to look down to write while maintaining eye contact or a conversation-like feel to the interview! You also have to write quickly so as not to miss anything. You can take down highlights only, but when I have done so, I typically have found it ineffective—I lose the significance of the highlight once it is out of the context of the rest of the interview.

Over the years, I have managed to learn how to write very quickly and look down relatively infrequently, but my writing is chicken scrawl and with sometimes only a handful of words on each page. I have used up an entire notebooks for one interview! Come prepared to the interview with a notebook (with easy-to-flip pages) and several pens.

"Doing neither" means, as Scoggins states, getting rid of the notebook or recorder and relinquishing control of the interview (2014, 395). Your interview becomes more like a conversation—one that is directed by the interviewee and less by you and your questions. It also means that you have to rely more on memory. Khat chews in Yemen provide an example. Khat chews are informal social gatherings where participants chew on a mildly narcotic leaf; the gatherings last several hours and are relaxed affairs where people share their views in a manner they would not in a formal setting. Note-taking or recording would not only break the atmosphere but give the interviewee a heightened sense of awareness of being interviewed. Of course, you can always excuse yourself, go to the washroom, and take notes if you really must!

If you choose to take minimal notes, as many researchers do, it is a good idea to take time immediately after the interview to sit down and fill out your notes while the information, including the metadata, is fresh in your mind. You may take note of a name or phrase only to forget its significance just days or weeks later. Even if you take detailed notes, you will want to go over the notes as soon as possible and ensure that you can read and understand your chicken scrawl.

Recording your data allows you to store and relisten to your interview repeated times, but type up your notes, including observed metadata, following the interview in order to better interpret the data and prepare for the next interview. Furthermore, you do not want a build-up of tedious hours of recordings to transcribe at a later date.

Using an Interpreter or RA

Another consideration is whether you want to work with an RA or interpreter. You may need an interpreter as a result of your language skills. Whether you choose to work with an RA will depend on both professional and personal reasons. I have worked alone as well as with an RA, depending on the topic. In Egypt, when I conducted interviews in medical clinics attached to mosques, I knew that some of the interviewees would be conservative Muslims. I felt it was important to have a male RA, as he would put male interviewees—some of whom felt it was inappropriate for an unrelated man and woman to be alone in a room—at ease. When doing my interviews with Moroccan municipal councilors, I also decided to work with an RA. I was new to the country and the research entailed driving hundreds of miles from municipality to municipality, making accommodation reservations, establishing contacts, setting up interview appointments, and dealing with language difficulties given that I did not speak the Moroccan dialect of Arabic and that my French was rusty. It seemed too large a task to do alone effectively.

Researchers with experience in your country or based at a local university or research institution can often help you find an RA or a translator. A local language school may also be able to help you find the latter.

If you use an interpreter, you will want to consider how it affects the reliability of your data. Whether you work with an interpreter or RA, you will want to screen and train the person. Even when you do so, you cannot avoid the fact that "every person present, even someone who quietly observes just for a brief moment, can fundamentally shape an interview and the data produced" (Kapiszewski et al. 2015, 194–195). They can reshape it in small and large ways, and you need to understand how their person and their presence does so. This includes how RAs present themselves—how they look and what they say—as they are representing you.

Yet working with an RA has its advantages. Not only are there two of you who are able to pay attention to what the interviewee says during the interview, but after the interview is done, you can benefit from having someone with whom to discuss the interview, put it in context of other interviews or events, and better draw out its significance.

One also should not underestimate how an RA can facilitate an interview, even if by sheer chance. Early in my career, I was interviewing Muslim Brotherhood sympathizers only to discover, during the first few interviews, that my RA's father and uncle had been prominent Brothers in their youth. This connection—many interviewees, upon hearing my RA's name, asked if he was related to them—made the interviews more successful. Granted, this connection could also have worked in reverse.

Cammett found similar advantages when she worked with RAs or "proxy interviewers"—local proxies who were trained and matched with participants with whom they shared various features (sect, for example) to conducted interviews on her behalf (2015). Much like the authors discussing positionality in other chapters in this book, she found this "matching" advantageous, as participants were often more forthcoming with the proxies than they would have been with her as an outsider.

Speaking the Local Language

Do you need to know the local language? The answer is yes, but it is not always necessary to know the local dialect, and, depending on your topic, English or French may suffice. You could conduct interviews with the Muslim Brotherhood, for example, in Classical Arabic as opposed to the local dialect. And more people in the region speak a European language than before. In many countries of the region, one could conceivably conduct interviews with high government officials, business elites, or civil society activists—many of whom went to American or European universities—without knowing the indigenous language of the country.

If your language skills are weak, there are research topics that you can effectively do. But even if you choose a topic that reflects your language limitations, you will still confront some disadvantages; you will, for example, miss the larger political and social context that you would be able to derive from interviews outside the circle that you linguistically can access and from secondary sources.

Don't worry about waiting until you are fluent in Arabic or the indigenous language of your country of research before you start doing interviews. Most people in the region are extremely gracious and patient when they see you working hard to learn the local language, so go ahead and conduct interviews even if your language skills are not flawless (although you do need to be able to get through the interview so that you don't waste anyone's time). But don't be afraid to ask someone to slow down or to repeat something during an interview. Repeating or summarizing will both help you with your language skills and ensure that you get the information correct.

Preparing Your Questions

Know as much as you can about your topic before you go to your interview. As Mosley states, in "the context of an interview, concerns about validity revolve around whether the researcher is asking the right questions, or asking questions in the right way, as well as whether the interview participant is offering truthful answers (and, if she is not, whether the researcher is able to detect this)" (2015, 20–21). This means knowing your topic and using a language with which the participant is familiar. As Leech states: "In an interview, what you already know is as important as what you want to know. What you want to know determines which questions you will ask. What you already know will determine how you ask them" (2002, 665).

Validity also means knowing when the participant is deliberately or inadvertently trying to "play you." Interviewees may tell you what they think you want to hear or frame what they are saying to you as if for a wider, less informed, audience. Decision-makers may strategically recount events in ways that are favorable to them. Others may simply not remember events accurately as a result of time or of trauma. Most people also are (unconsciously) inconsistent in their answers.

For these reasons, do your homework ahead of time and engage with the interviewee so that she or he knows you are aware of the issues. As Mosley states, consider the interview in the context of other information (2015). Ideally, you would go back and interview the same participant more than once in order to ensure consistency in their answers. Since this is often not possible, try also to include cross-checking questions throughout your interview—questions that will clarify and verify your interviewee's answers.

Pilot-testing your questions will help with all these issues.

The Length of Time an Interview Takes

Plan for an interview to take hour but be prepared that it could run far longer or shorter. Few interviews are less than 30 minutes; most run for 45 minutes to an hour. If they are shorter, potentially as short as 15 minutes if the interviewee is called away, you want to be able to use the limited time effectively by asking your most important questions. Before you go to the interview, always prioritize your research questions; if the interview is cut short, you don't want to waste time determining which questions are the most important.

How—and Should You—Keep Your Interviewee on Topic?

Berry appropriately calls open-ended interviewing a high-wire act (2002, 679). It is the "riskiest ... type of elite interviewing ... requir[ing] interviewers to know when to probe and how to formulate questions on the fly" (679). While I have had to use probes (there is nothing more painful than an interviewee who answers open-ended questions with monosyllables), in general, interviewees tend to ramble and frequently can move off topic. In these cases, you will want to wait for a break or pause—try your best not to cut someone off—and then try to redirect the discussion back to your topic.

But while it can tedious or frustrating when an interviewee wanders off into unexpected directions, sometimes these tangents can be very valuable, as they can open up new and important questions and new ways of thinking about your project. So it can be worthwhile to be open and listen in case they are trying to tell you something important. Granted it is not always easy to know when it is worth listening or if you should steer the interviewee back to your topic and your questions. You will have to simply follow your instincts.

Many of my interviewees' tangents have provided the seeds for separate articles for which I have then conducted unplanned and additional interviews. When these interesting and even exciting opportunities happen, keep in mind that this tangent is a side project or a branch that has the potential to lead you too far away from the tree trunk that is your main research project. When it does lead you too far away, pursue the side project in a future research trip.

Of course, there are times when you need to get a story straight or fact-check, and you will want to impose a fairly high degree of directionality to your interview. Fact checking—particularly when it requires acquiring documentation—is notoriously frustrating in the region. A simple fact (an exact date, for example) can require a significant amount of time and persistence. Acquiring documents is not an easy task—commonly it has less to do with its confidentiality than an individual who does not want to share the document (out of sheer suspicion or because of some sense of power). I once had a journalist deny the existence of a newspaper article that he wrote and that had been published one week earlier.

And sometimes you will simply want interviewees to answer a question they are clearly avoiding. While I have successfully asked direct and blunt questions even when the subject was sensitive (and have seen my RA flinch!), in general, a journalistic or combative style of interviewing is neither productive nor appropriate.

In all these cases, building a rapport generally will lead to the desired outcome, although it might take more than one interview. During my research on one of the Hezbollah organizations, the interviewee was reticent to talk, if not hostile. I left the interview knowing that he had essentially said nothing and I had learned nothing. I returned one month later and received a warmer reception and the interviewer was more open. At the third visit, he entered the room with a big smile, demanding that I comment on his significant weight loss! The third was by far the most productive interview.

When it comes to political party leaders who refuse to be interviewed or are adept at talking about nothing, find a "second tier" person to interview. Methodologically, you may want to demonstrate that you have gone to "the source" (and your interview with a leader may open doors) but typically, middle-level members are more forthcoming. They often have insights into party workings but risk little by talking to a researcher (although they may have a grievance with the party, something you will want to be aware of). Former party members also are a good source (with the same caveats as middle-ranking party members).

Concluding your Interview

End your interview with an open question such as whether there is anything important that you missed, at which you should be looking, if you are asking the right questions, or even if there is something more important at which you should be looking. These concluding questions can be highly informative, so plan for them and allot extra time.

Group Interviews

You also want to be ready for the possibility that your planned interview with one individual may rapidly become a group interview. When interviewing mayors, local citizens commonly came in and out of the office. Similarly, when I conducted interviews in medical clinics, neighbors dropped by and offered their opinions. These group interviews can be highly informative, but they may also disrupt the interview or silence the interviewee. Try your best to keep things on track and get the best out of the situation, but don't hesitate to reschedule if you can't. When conducting a group interview (intentionally or not), you will want to strongly consider recording the interview as note-taking is simply too difficult.

How Many Interviews You Should Do in One Day and Other Practicalities

I recommend conducting a maximum of two interviews per day. Many of the capital cities in the region are large and congested with traffic. Consequently, you do not want to book too many interviews per day or too close together in time. You need to allow time for the traffic and for finding the street and building, as street names change with rapid frequency and buildings have duplicate numbers. Interviews may extend much longer than anticipated and there is nothing ruder than cutting someone off to say you have to run to another interview (presumably with someone more important). I also agree with Peabody that "some of the keenest insights may be obtained after the interview is over, and the respondent has relaxed" (1990, 453). Someone can suddenly tell you something of extreme value once the interview is over, even if during the interview your best-planned questions bore no fruit. So be prepared to stay and listen even if your notebook is closed or your recorder off.

And at the end of the day allow time to type up your interview notes. I would agree with Berry, who estimates that it takes him two hours of transcription for every half hour of interview (2002, 680). You also need to allot time both between interviews and at the end of the day for formulating new questions based on the information you learned that day.

Finally, before you even go to the field, take note of any religious holidays and ask experienced researchers whether interviewing during these time periods can be productive. Ramadan, for example, lasts one month and you may find that people more or less willing to be interviewed depending on the country.

And remember, while interviewing in the region can sometimes require determination, doggedness, and even a sense of adventure, it is (almost) always fun.

Acknowledgment

Thanks to Jillian Schwedler for her help in the writing of this chapter.

10

Interviewing Salafis

Negotiating Access and Ethics

MASSIMO RAMAIOLI

My field research experience is in Jordan, where I set out to interviewing Salafis. The yearlong stay was part of my dissertation project. During my training in the PhD program, I perused my good share of readings so as to get acquainted with the challenges of conducting field research (Lieberman et al. 2004; Hsueh et al. 2014; Mosley 2013; Clark 2006), the hardships of a mostly lonely and painstaking enterprise, and the frustration of careful planning that meets repeated failures and obstacles (practical, theoretical, time management). In my case, these challenges may have been heightened given the subject of my investigation: arguably the most uncompromising, and in some ways notorious, Islamist current in contemporary Muslim world.

Whatever the instructions of those general guidelines, I would have appreciated some specific indications in addressing the Salafi community. What follows is therefore a wish list that I would have loved relying on before leaving for the Middle East, particularly as a researcher on a topic that, for better or worse, is likely to attract ever more attention in the future. I will share 10 considerations: orientalism, ethics, risks, context, meetings, approach, language, ivory tower, *muqābala* (encounter/interview), and surprises. Before doing that, I need to describe, however briefly, modern-day Salafism as to allow the reader to make sense of my reflections. As a way to introduce Salafis and their social milieu, I offer a snapshot from an interview I carried out.

"No, It Is Not Possible to Live Like a Good Muslim Here"

'Anis[1] was a 24-year-old sitting in front of me in his spacious house in Saḥab, an impoverished neighborhood in southern Amman. He was living there with his newlywed wife, their infant son, his father, and his two brothers. 'Anis was introduced to me as a new adherent to Salafism. A pious and devoted Muslim, he had recently adopted a way of practicing Islam that he would define as *'ilmiyya*. It is the same adjective Salafi sheikhs[2] use to describe their approach to Islam, and it is widely utilized by Jordanian researchers and journalists when addressing Salafism in its predominant nonviolent, nonjihadi variant.[3] *'Ilmiyya* can be translated as "scientific." What it aims to convey is a proper, rigorous approach to Islam grounded on a direct and literal reading of the Koran and the Sunna.[4] It is not, therefore, how Salafis define a version of Islam that is "their" Islam. It is how they define their approach to Islam itself. By virtue of such an approach, they claim to recover the true Islam, unmarred by a multiplicity of deviant and corrupting "interpretations."

Salafism seeks inspiration for conducting the proper Islamic life in the paradigmatic example of the early Muslim community, usually the first three generations after prophet Muhammad—regarded as *as-salaf as-sālih,* "the pious ancestors," whence Salafis. The proximity to the Prophet and his message granted an unadulterated, pure, and therefore truthful reception of Islam. Three core tenets represent the center of gravity of Salafi discourse. The first is *tawhīd,* the absolute unity of Islam mirroring the monotheistic unity of God. Second, Salafism admits only the Koran and the Sunna as legitimate sources of legislation. Third is the condemnation of any innovation (*bida'*) that contradicts the above principles, usually understood as the sedimentation over time and history of Islamic jurisprudence and scholarship.[5]

'Anis had no religious qualification for venturing into such "scientific" disquisitions about the authentic meaning and practice of Islam, but the local Salafi sheikh reputedly did. He lectured 'Anis about the virtues of a Salafi way of life and suggested books to him. Salafism seemed to provide 'Anis—on and off petty jobs after finishing high school, with a wife and a child to support—with comfort and a sense of righteousness that he could not find elsewhere. I asked him what he thought about Jordan, and how he felt being Muslim there: "Islam is not just a religion, it is life itself," he said, hitting on the main contention of political Islam, "and I need to live in an environment where that life is possible, a place where the only law is sharia." I asked him: "Do you feel Jordan is such a place?" Always calm, he said: "Jordan is a Muslim country. Religion is important here, and that is good." I replied: "They don't uphold sharia here, though, do they? Can you live as a good Muslim here?" "No, it is not possible to live like a good Muslim here. I need to live under the caliphate."[6]

As I was scribbling notes down, I could not but glance over to his father and younger brother, who had been sitting there all along: the former, a pious Muslim himself, following the Sunni Hanafi Islam[7] prevalent in the kingdom, shook his head a bit, showing mixed feelings about his son's devotion. 'Anis's brother, a restless troublemaking teenager, looked at his brother with a big smile on his face while he kept smoking a hand-rolled cigarette. "I am an atheist," he said while escorting me outside the house once the interview with 'Anis was over, "but I know my brother means what he says."

Orientalism

'Anis's desire ("to live under the caliphate") suggests the distance separating the academic researcher from the adherent to Salafism. There are two dimensions to explore in this regard: epistemology and values. While I will deal with the latter in the following section, let me consider here the epistemological difference. The academically trained scholar strives to understand reality with a continuous reassessment of hypotheses in relation to empirical and experimental data. The logical consistency of a theory is located within this space, and honed via discussions on those grounds with his peers. The Salafi bases his assessment of reality on adherence to a text (the Koran) deemed of divine origin and the sayings and practices of the man (Muhammad) who revealed this text to mankind. The logical consistency of his reasoning is thus located within this space. In a sense, a researcher meeting a Salafi might feel as if he were encountering a sort of alter ego. For example, quietist Salafis handed me pamphlets against the Islamic State (IS). Their stern condemnation was predicated upon IS's faulty understanding of the Koranic message:[8] understand the Islamic message correctly, the reasoning went, and by definition a correct assessment of reality will ensue, even for IS. This proposition cannot be contested: different interpretations of the holy texts are either the results of ignorance (jahl) or improper (that is, non-'ilmiyy) methods of inquiry. Both can and should be amended.

By and large, the scholarship dealing with non-Western contexts, especially Middle Eastern ones, has tried to heed what Said submitted in *Orientalism* (Said 1978; Varisco 2012). But the perils of orientalism always lurk beneath the surface. In terms of analytical approach, it is hard, for instance, not to be dismissive, at some level, of proofs represented by a list of Koranic suras,[9] something Salafis tend to do when asked to produce evidence to support their stances and claims. Once, as the subject of Israel and Zionism surfaced, a sheikh expressed views that I perceived as anti-Semitic. I pressed him to explain the reason behind such a stance: impromptu, he quoted a verse from the sura *al-Ma'ida*, where Jews are depicted, together with "those who associate" (*ashraku*, indicating polytheists), as "people with animosity" (*an-nas 'adawa*) toward the Muslim believers.[10] Considerations about Israeli policies came only afterward, within the context of such divinely inspired verses.

Indeed, as scholars we have been first socialized, and then trained, to consider such evidence invalid in backing up causal or normative claims. The divergent methods of inquiry embraced by Salafism may push—unwarily and unwarrantedly—the researcher to question the avowed "scientific" features of Salafis' approach to truth and reality when manifested, as shown above, via a literal reading of a specific *āyā*—the unspoken assumption here being that "their method" is wrong and "ours" correct, a normative (and hierarchical) proposition, not an analytical one.

I am not calling, of course, for a suspension of judgment and critical thinking. But we should be aware that ingrained, wired-in attitudes will likely screen, filter, and deform what our interviewees tell us—and thus possibly negatively affect the entire process. There is, I believe, no way around it. An epistemologically free research is not out there. But we may still strive for an epistemologically conscious one. As Kurzman (2004, 296) argues, "The field holds itself in tension, unable to deny the obvious cultural differences between Islamic activists and Western scholars, yet unwilling to claim irreducible difference for fear of falling into Orientalist patterns." In my research, I strove to approach the interviewee as neutrally as possible: I would resume critical thinking only afterward, pondering over my notes, which I needed to be as much as possible data to work on and not a collection of personal impressions to sort out.

Ethics

As with epistemological differences, the researcher and his interviewees are likely to cherish value systems at odds with each other from an ethical standpoint. Indeed, while Salafism is more appropriately described as a "current" rather than a movement (it lacks, as a whole, a coherent structure, a common program, shared aims, clear membership and leaders), its basic tenets cannot be defined as "moderate," "liberal," or "progressive" as we usually understand these terms.

This stems from the principle of *tawhīd*: in Salafi understanding, it does not admit pluralism or the separation of religion and politics—rather, Islam is deemed a comprehensive and all-encompassing way of life. Questioning and rejecting such basic elements of liberalism, Salafism also jettisons individual rights, freedoms, and democratic values (peaceful alternation of power, ideological and political pluralism, citizenship rights). I managed to have access mostly to quietist Salafis, politicos, and a few individuals who, while not professing allegiance to jihadi Salafism, shared some of its views.

In different ways and tones—from the soft-spoken sheikh, to the articulate Salafi charity manager, to the loud supporter of IS—attacks on liberal principles were consistently forceful and direct.[11] It is worth asking: how are we supposed to react when democratic values—not only procedures—are quickly dismissed with what seem to be a few straw-man arguments? When sweeping remarks about the nature of women intend to provide a rationale for their social exclusion? Or when the IS is glorified as a righteous anti-imperialist force? While of course those kinds of statements are what makes research on Salafism intellectually challenging and exciting, is there a red line where a sense of righteousness should compel us to oppose such statements and (politely) retort? I do not think I have an answer to such a question, but I surely found myself biting my tongue many times: when the late 'Abū Muṣ'ab az-Zarqāwī was described to me as a "compassionate leader" who "will go down in history as a true Arab hero,"[12] I could not help but think about his notorious beheading practices—while keeping quiet to let my interviewee express his views. In this case, I considered that my primary objective was to be exposed and understand specific worldviews, not to enter into a debate about such views, much less to "rectify" them. There is, I believe, the risk that our analytical lenses may be fogged by normative commitments.[13]

Here lies another problem: given how difficult it is to arrange some meetings, are we ready to jeopardize our interlocutor's willingness to talk to us by openly contesting his beliefs, oftentimes the very object of our investigation? Or, again, facing the same dilemma, how are we to answer direct inquiries about our ideological or religious views? Again, I chose, for the sake of putting my interviewee at ease and not fostering any potential suspicion he harbored, to gloss over my stances on religion and politics.[14] Speaking truth and gaining trust seemed to be on diverging paths in those circumstances, and I opted for the latter, sacrificing the former. I do not necessarily recommend this choice. I could indeed change my approach in the future: when asked about my religious affiliation (a standard question you are likely to confront), a defensive and acceptable "Catholic" may become an assertive and very troubling "atheist"—yet more in tune with my personal convictions.

Risks

As I mentioned above, Salafism is a loosely integrated approach, with a few core tenets: it can give rise to vastly different embodiments in social and political life. Thus, when considering personal risks entailed in interviewing Salafis, there is no single answer, as there is no single attitude Salafis display. For instance, with quietist or politico Salafis such personal risks are minimal, if any. Normal precautions apply.

When it comes to jihadi Salafis, different considerations are in order. They embrace an ideology manifesting utter and uncompromising opposition not only to values, but also to policies and countries that the researcher, for better or for worse, may represent. However, as I am about to illustrate, this was hardly a problem I had to face.

In fact, regardless of the specific Salafi strand of my interviewee, I was always met with courtesy if not friendliness. I can only offer guesses as to why that has been the case: are Salafis simply nicer people than assumed? Is there a disconnect between their professed radical ideas (or even violent ones for the jihadis) and their reception of researchers interested in what they have to say? And if I am allowed a crude, culturalist argument, could I say that Arab norms of hospitality (as I met only with Arab Salafis) explain Salafis' attitudes? Joas Wagemakers, a leading expert on Salafi ideology, expresses similar views describing his interaction with 'Abū Muḥammad al-Maqdisī, a prominent jihadi Salafi ideologue:[15] "Not only was Maqdisī a very friendly and hospitable person—his radical beliefs notwithstanding—but meeting the man whose ideas have occupied such a major part of my life over the past few years was quite exciting, and ensured we had a connection that overcame any ideological animosity that I had for him" (Wagemakers 2012, viii).

More than Salafis themselves, even individuals professing a creed of militant jihad, one ought to be mindful of the watchful eye of the government. I found myself receiving instructions about meetings inside cars, as my contact deemed emails and telephone calls too risky. It is true that in Jordan concerns about regime security services (the Mukhabarat; see chapter 2 in this volume) are not as pressing as in other countries; and that researchers, especially if Western, enjoy a degree of protection from police harassment or questioning. But one should not work under that assumption. In terms of red lines that should not be crossed, living in the country for an extended period of time may provide that awareness and know-how which is hard to grasp or attain otherwise. Or, alternatively, your interviewee will notify you about embedded risks in more subtle ways. At a meeting with a politico Salafi, as the interview was about to begin, he showed me his charity's publication, featuring on the first page the picture of a smiling King Abdullah. He then closed it, and the interview began—an implicit reference to the rules of the game. It is important for the researcher to pick up those hints and signs, and understand when a topic is off limits out of consideration for personal safety or potential negative repercussions for the interviewee's social and professional life.

Context—When Politics Hit: Bad Time to Ask about Salafis!

How hard is it meet with Salafis? The answer is—it depends. Let us consider in this section the wider political context in which your research takes place. To begin with, it is relatively easy to get in touch with quietist and politico Salafis. Since they are interested in proselytizing and expanding their societal networks, and since they are at least tolerated by the authorities, nonviolent Salafis are actors operating openly within society. They have offices and research centers, they run mosques, and some prominent leaders have websites with whereabouts and contacts.[16] The real challenge was to set up the actual meeting once I gathered the necessary information. For jihadi Salafis the situation is again different. I managed to arrange far fewer meetings with jihadi than quietist or politico Salafis. This was not only due to the understandable and expected reclusiveness of such individuals. They mostly live under tight government surveillance; at times a minor trespass may be enough to bring questioning from authorities, or even arrest and imprisonment. Jordan may be less of a police state than other countries in the region, but the Mukhabarat is always present in the calculations of Salafis you may be contacting for interviews. Hence, the wider political circumstances factors strongly in their wariness in deciding whether to answer positively your meeting requests.

Let me provide an example. I started contacting Salafis of all stripes in late January 2015. Most of them responded by saying, "Maybe, call me next week and we'll decide—inshallah." Confident that a good number of those "maybes" would become "yes," I waited and called the following week as instructed. Unfortunately, it was exactly when IS released the video showing the brutal execution of Muʿaẓ al-Kasasbah, the Jordanian pilot whose fighter jet had been downed over Syria some 40 days before.[17] Over the next two weeks, the political climate in the kingdom became decidedly tense. Amman was swept by progovernment, proregime demonstrations. Al-Kasasbah was lionized as a national martyr and the king as the emblem of national unity. While episodic pro-IS gatherings were reported before Kasasbah was executed (especially in the poor regions of the south, such as the city of Maʿān), now any such demonstrations would have met the sternest public reprimands, and very likely the heavy hand of the security service. As a consequence, Salafis of a more militant bent became even more reluctant to meet, especially with foreigners: the few individuals who were indicated to me even as loosely affiliated with jihadi Salafism turned down the agreed-upon meetings, claiming most times I could be "Western Mukhabarat." A number of quietist and politico Salafis also retracted their previous commitments: less explicitly so, but presumably the situation was such that it demanded more alertness on their part regarding whom they talked to and about what. In sum: interviewing Salafis, like any other group or movement, but probably even more so given the current situation in the Middle East, is subject to developments and events over which the researcher has no control. Needless to say, one must be ready to deal with a good degree of discouragement and helplessness in such circumstances—as well as keep up the effort and the spirit: while it might sound trite, I found it extremely useful to talk about my research predicaments with colleagues and peers in the field, who are likely to experience or have encountered the same problems.

Setting Up Meetings

I arranged most of the meetings by phone. Local researchers and academics who conduct research on the same subject provided telephone numbers. Before leaving for Jordan, I tried either to get in touch with them or to make sure I would meet them in the country. Other resources to obtain telephone numbers were journalists and activists I encountered over a few weeks of "soaking and poking." These contacts are invaluable in that, even though they may not know any Salafi individual or group, they are very likely to know someone who does. If obtaining numbers is not very challenging, setting up meetings can be. We just discussed the about-face of many potential interviewees given the sudden change in the political climate in the country. But for those who did accept my interview request, I had to face random last-minute cancellations, repeated rescheduling to a later date to be decided, or frustrated assurances along the lines of "I will let you know when I can." In particular, I was three times on the verge of meeting a prominent Salafi ideologue, a possible major break for my data gathering: the meeting was cancelled one time the day before and twice the very same day. With high-profile individuals, this one in particular, I had to accept that the window of opportunity was shut.

This kind of problem, I understand, is hardly a specific feature of researching Salafis: many fellow researchers I met along the way complained about the same issues. However, it might be good to remember how, in interviewing Salafis, government surveillance and the attendant suspicion they may have toward Western researchers could heighten said difficulties.

Approach

When finally approaching an interviewee, I followed what I considered general norms of respectful conduct. I encountered mostly kindness and warm welcomes: without falling into orientalist stereotyping, I believe hospitality and friendliness represent strong social norms to which most will conform. However, one may observe that I am "selecting on the dependent variable," so to speak: a grave sin in establishing causal inference! The ones who did refuse to talk to me might have been examples of more reclusive and less conciliatory attitudes.

Perhaps it is commonsensical, but general familiarity with local customs and etiquette goes a long way: hopefully it is not the first time you visit a non-Western context, it is not the first time in an Arab country, and you have had—albeit limited— previous interactions with self-professed Islamists. In the same vein, addressing and greeting the interviewee in Arabic[18] and possibly introducing yourself too is an excellent way to signal your sincere, genuine interest. I paid a bit of attention when it comes to the attire: in general, modest, unassuming clothing is all that is required. Again, familiarizing yourself with the context will tell you the dos and don'ts: for example, in the torrid summers of Jordan, sandals are not a problem, but short pants are frowned upon (or laughed at). For female researchers, clothing becomes a more sensitive issue: I would advise against wearing pants or shirts that may reveal body shapes, even if modestly so by Western standards; exposing naked forearms is likely not to be welcomed; and covering one's head is a requirement in most places (a mosque, for example) where the meeting may take place. But alas, I can only conjecture about this topic: I have never seen a woman researcher in the places of worship I have visited, nor have Salafis themselves told me about women carrying out similar interviews (while they several times have mentioned male researchers). What

I have stated here is inferred by observing the social milieu where Salafis tend to operate and their averred stance when it comes to gender issues and roles.

As the interview finally begins, your initial introduction may not satiate your interviewee's curiosity. He might then address questions about nationality, political and religious preferences, or general views on the Middle East. As already observed in the section on ethics, since your views are not likely to overlap with his, you are once more confronted with a moral dilemma. Your national background may be a reason for suspicion, although mine—Italian—never was. I do not have a clear an-swer for such attitude. Perhaps Italy is not immediately associated with colonialism or anti-Muslim sentiments.[19] Or, simply, regardless of the nationality, the researcher is only perceived as such, not affiliated with a government held in contempt for its policies. But based on what I saw in Jordan, two nationalities might be more prob-lematic than others: Israeli (for quite obvious reasons) and Iranian.[20] Given both the current climate in the region and Salafism's rigidity in drawing the boundaries of the Muslim community proper, Iranians tend to be associated immediately with Shiism. Both in interviews and in impromptu conversations with conservative Jordanians, Shias were held in particular disdain. I have never felt that Salafis expected me to agree explicitly with their views. That left room for a fine balance between diplo-matic exposure of my opinions and an overtly inquisitive attitude (which is, at the end of the day, part and parcel of the interview process!).

Language

Salafis I encountered did not speak English (or, for that matter, any other major European language).[21] This is not a problem, of course, if you are fluent in Arabic. Educated and learned sheikhs will happily have a conversation in Classical Arabic (*fuṣḥā*). Mosque attendees, participants in Salafi seminars, or study groups (the "rank and files" of the movement) may profess their proficiency in *fuṣḥā* but really be more comfortable with the local dialect (*'ammiyya*), or mixing and switching between the two registers depending on the specific subject of the conversation.

Before going to Jordan, I was aware that my Arabic was good, but not good enough to engage in an in-depth interview possibly featuring complex topics and the need to follow up with specific, unplanned questions about points raised by the in-terviewee. By taking lessons while in Amman and benefiting from daily interactions, I was able to carry out some of my last interviews by myself; but for the most part, I relied on the help of a translator. It was important to find someone who not only could translate properly from Arabic to English, but who was familiar or conversant with the subject at hand. Salafis, as I mentioned, often refer to Koranic passages, examples from Islamic and Arab history, or recent events and developments in local, regional, and world politics. The nuances of such references are likely to be lost if the translator is not ready to pick them up and provide, in a sense, more than a mere translation: explaining what is the meaning, in that specific context, of a particular signifier the interviewee just adopted.

Let me give you an example. I interviewed a scholar with strong Islamist sympathies, appreciation for the "purity" of the Salafi message, and deep aversion to any deployment of violence—whether in the name of religion, politics, class, or ethnicity. The conversation veered toward the current situation in Iraq. He compared Saddam Hussein's rule to ʾAbū Bakr Al-Baghadī, the leader of IS, referring to the former as "sheikh Saddam" and to the latter as "*rafīq* Al- Baghadī." In this way he intended to make fun of and highlight—as my translator immediately pointed out to me—their hypocrisy: "sheikh," a title usually associated with knowledgeable Sunni ulama, cast upon the secular and uncouth Saddam; *rafīq*, the Arabic for "comrade" in Marxist and Communist parlance, attributed to the self-proclaimed caliph, who was thus portrayed as the leader of an atheist and power-grabbing party. I did not catch the nuances of that depiction even though I did understand "sheikh" and "*rafīq*" when uttered by my interviewee. A translator less acquainted than mine with religious titles and Marxist parlance would have not fared much better than me in that instance. Furthermore, the translator is likely to navigate unwritten social norms that the researcher, even after a good amount of soaking and poking, is still just processing. For example, my translator was able to address mosque attendees and persuade them to give me some of their time. While they may have felt a mix of suspicion of and curiosity about an obviously Western man roaming around their prayer hall, a few words from my translator went a long way to soothe their diffidence or to win over their shyness. This is not to say that all such attempts are going to be successful because a local translator is alongside you: we were denied entrance to a social and educational center where we had previously carried out interviews, and rather unceremoniously so despite the valiant efforts from my translator to be let in again.

The Ivory Tower: From Academic Questions to Salafi Answers

Language issues do not pertain solely or even primarily to the linguistic domain. Drafting and formulating questions in order to communicate what we wish to know in a simple, plain fashion is extremely challenging: all the more so to someone who is unfamiliar with the way academia addresses and frames social reality, above and beyond jargon. Too much time in an ivory tower crafting theories and testing hypotheses may hamper our capacity to evaluate how much our academic language is removed from the laymen's, let alone the Salafis'. The result is we could end up asking questions our interviewee does not readily understand: the way we formulate them can be alien, better tailored for an academic conference than for a Salafi preacher. In instances where I made that mistake, the interviewee seemed to assume

I did not know much about Islam at large and Salafism in particular (all the more so if you are speaking to a relatively well educated person: a sheikh or a seminar teacher). Such presumption of ignorance is, of course, true to the extent that you are carrying out a study on Islam and Salafism; but it is also true that you may not need a thorough explanation of the five pillars of Islam or want to delve into the Sykes-Picot agreements. Questions that sounded in my head perfectly clear and focused sometimes elicited a vague and unspecific answer. There is, however, the possibility of recalibrating the next questions, modifying your prepackaged questions to meet the tone of the answers. This problem may in fact occur in any setting. But in the case of Salafis it is perhaps amplified. As I mentioned before, Salafis subscribe to a method of reasoning in which empiricism, rationality, and logic are not the chief coordinates by which to ascertain reality and meaning—rather, revealed truth in a text is. Thus, interacting with Salafis can bring to the fore a system of cultural referents that associates different meanings with the same signifier (word). In academic discourse we attribute a certain range of meaning to such terms as scientific, Muslim, democratic, nation, progress, faith, religion, society, and so on. These areas of meanings are different from the ones our interviewee has in mind, let alone the logical and theoretical connections and implications one may elaborate upon those words.[22]

Let me clarify this: I do not wish to claim that there is inherent and utter incommunicability. Rather, it is possible to bridge this gap with an understanding that, while different, areas of meanings still overlap. In this sense, a word that was particularly problematic was *taqlīd* (tradition; similarly the adjective *taqlīdiyy*, "traditional"). In my project, I wished to understand how the idea of a perfect and exemplar tradition (the paradigm of the "pious ancestors") was articulated in social and political life. *Taqlīd* and *taqlīdiyy* in the answers carried different meanings depending on the context. At times, they referred to social and political conservatism akin to Western usages of the concept (though they did not use the more common Arabic *muhāfaza*) while standing also for "native" and "authentic"; other times, they indicated the jurisprudential body of literature (the four main schools, or *madhdhab*, within Sunni Islam)[23] Salafis reject as a product of innovation (*bida'*). In this case, *taqlīd* stood for the corruption of the pristine and legitimate practice of Islam of the early Muslim community. This different deployment of the concept of "tradition" at first confused me. Practice and reframing questions after each interview eventually made the task of the communicating and understanding easier and smoother.

Muqābala: Interview or Encounter?

The Arabic word *muqābala* stands for a formal interview or a more random encounter. Oftentimes I found myself talking to people—Muslims and non-Muslims,

Salafis and non-Salafis—in unplanned, unscheduled meetings. Paraphrasing John Lennon ("Life is what happens to you while you are busy making other plans"), *muqābala* is what happens to you when you are busy organizing interviews.

Here I am not thinking only about the still extremely valuable experience of "soaking and poking," living for extended periods of times in the field and becoming, to greater or lesser extent, familiar with unspoken rules, common practices, and cultural references. More specifically, I am recalling the encounters with people who were part of the circle around the person I sought to interview: his driver, student, friend, relative, doorman, acquaintance; or just mosque attendees who would spontaneously come and talk to me before or after the scheduled meeting with the Salafi preacher. Informal encounters occurred frequently on my way to scheduled interviews and meetings. Having interviewed also non-Salafis for the purpose of my research (members of the Muslim Brotherhood, politicians, researchers, journalists), these encounters would occur more frequently when interacting with Salafis. However, this fact seems to depend more upon the setting where most of my meetings with Salafis were scheduled than to any specific feature of the Salafi movement itself: as I carried out my interviews around mosques, educational centers, or similar social venues, it was simply easier to encounter people there as opposed to, for example, walking into a researcher's private office.

These interactions were often brief, cursory, and shallow: but they could still be valuable. Other times, they would develop into a full-fledged discussion, almost equivalent to an interview. Technically, they were not interviews: the requirements of the Internal Review Board (IRB) protocol make it clear that, before any interview the researcher intends to collect for her project, a series of steps—caveats, disclaimers, and warnings—need be issued to the interviewee. In the case of some *muqābala* (the formal meetings) that was possible; in the case of other *muqābala* (the informal encounters) that was not. In any case, they did contribute with insights, details, better understanding. Whether the latter kind of *muqābala* makes its way into your final work is not a matter of "if" but "how": perhaps not as a quotation, not as a further observation in your data set, not as an extensive narrative reconstruction; rather, it will inform a more fine-grained and perceptive treatment of the case at hand.

Positive Surprises

Upon embarking in my field research, I had ambivalent feelings. I have tried to illustrate the reasons behind my trepidation, doubts, and, to be honest, anxiety: Salafis do not enjoy good press. Even after reviewing a literature that portrayed a vastly diverse and overwhelmingly peaceful movement, headlines reporting on the crimes of IS, the attacks by al-Qaeda, and massacres by Boko Haram (all Salafi-inspired groups) could not but make a dent in my—hopefully—informed and balanced view on Salafism. As I said, the perils of orientalism are always lurking. But the one of the purposes of this volume is also to explore the "fun"—the excitement, the desire to know, even the naive curiosity—that may enter field research. There can be such a thing as "positive orientalism"![24]

I thus would like to conclude with positive remarks that may soothe fellow students and scholars who experience similar misgivings about this kind of research. Indeed, it was not the reclusiveness or the uncompromising thinking of Salafis that struck me the most. For that, I was somewhat prepared. The surprise was instead discovering positive traits, attitudes and openness. Perhaps a case of orientalist fascination in reverse—an unusual white guy from Europe in a mosque in the outskirts of Amman—nonetheless I experienced welcoming attitudes much more than rejection (which of course did happen, as I mentioned above).

With all the interviewees, I could not but appreciate the amount of time they were willing to spend with me (hardly less than 45 minutes, one interview extending for more than three hours), with a combination of tea, fruits, and sweets regularly offered. On occasions, my interlocutor would give me all sorts of publications (books, articles, reviews, or pamphlets), anticipating my requests. Not all of these were, of course, valuable material (and some were not works I would have gladly opened up at a customs check in Europe or the United States); but the gesture appeared genuine.

Last, I have been asked several times to convert (receiving, that is, a formal call, or *daw'a*). I politely refused. The sheikh would then nod and say: "Look, we have seminars here, the ones I told you about. One week, for free. You'll find it interesting. Anyone can attend, even non-Muslims. Next time, inshallah." While perhaps not for purely religious purposes, in my next trip to Jordan I may consider joining: another venue to explore and make sense of Salafis' practices and discourse—a small contribution, one would hope, to demystifying and better understanding such an important, confounding and fascinating movement.

Interviewing Salafis

Overcoming Fear and Mistrust in Middle Eastern and European Contexts

ZOLTAN PALL AND MOHAMED-ALI ADRAOUI

The academic literature on Salafism has been burgeoning since the 9/11 attacks. The reason is that Salafism is often seen as the chief ideological background of global jihadism, hence the interest in it in Western countries. The majority of scholars who write on Salafism chiefly examine their discourse without actually meeting and interviewing Salafis. The volume of qualitative social science research on the movement is much less available than what for instance mainstream medias tend to show when it comes to Salafism and Jihadism. The main reason behind this is the difficulty of examining the participants of the Salafi movement as subjects of qualitative inquiry. Salafis are difficult to approach and interview, not to say observe during a longer period of fieldwork. Understandably, being characterized in the media as terrorists, and being subject to harassment by security services, they are often reluctant to speak to anyone who intends to get information about them.

Despite these difficulties, we managed to approach Salafis and write books and research papers from a qualitative social science perspective about the movement. Here we share our experiences on successfully overcoming the challenges posed to social scientists when conducting fieldwork on Salafism.

Researcher A, a non-Muslim Hungarian, has done most of his work on Salafi networks in Lebanon and Kuwait. Researcher B, a French scholar with a North African and Muslim background, did his field research chiefly among French Salafi communities. The different contexts of our fieldwork also enable us to highlight the differences and similarities in different approaches to conducting research on Salafism in the Middle East and Europe. Below, we highlight the major challenges we faced while conducting field research, and explain how we managed to resolve them. The chapter contains snapshots of stories to illustrate how to deal with Salafis as subjects of social science inquiry and from which broader lessons can be learned. We focus specifically on the practicalities of fieldwork, and largely avoid theoretical and ethical discussions, which Ramaioli's chapter in this volume discusses in greater detail.

Challenges

Both of us faced difficulties in obtaining data from our interviews when we first tried to engage our research subjects in the field. Salafis, no matter whether in France or in Lebanon or Kuwait, seemed to be very cautious or even unwilling to speak to researchers. One of the main reasons for their unwillingness to engage was the lens of securitization that Salafism is often subjected to. Biased journalism often casts a negative light on Salafism, equating it to extremism and terrorism. In France, for instance, a famous case of purposeful "misunderstanding" between some journalists and a Salafi imam in the city of Vénissieux, near Lyon, took place in 2004.The regional paper *Lyon Mag* interviewed Abdelkader Bouziane, of Algerian origin, and his answers created a huge scandal in the French media and among opinion-makers.[1] Journalists filmed him and requested his opinion on the "stoning of women." The Algerian-born imam did not understand the question and asked for an explanation of the French word *lapidation* ("stoning"). He thought he was being question about "beating up" women (which does represent another way of hurting people, but is significantly different from sentencing women to death by stoning). The press then portrayed the imam as wishing to stone women to death when he was in actuality arguing for the right to physically discipline them when necessary. This was one of Salafism's earliest debuts in media spotlights, and the controversy that followed considerably weakened researchers' attempts to conduct empirically based studies. In addition to being seen as journalists looking for sensationalism, researchers who could convince Salafis that they were principally motivated by serious scientific purposes—namely an in-depth exploration of their beliefs—were criticized for creating material that was likely to be used as a tool to denigrate Muslims. In fact, the term "Salafi" most often appears in media outlets in the context of terrorism and violence, and is used interchangeably with jihadism. Fighters of the Islamic State or the Nusra front in Syria are, for instance, often referred to as "Salafi militants."

It is thus little wonder that Salafis often suspect academic researchers of having the intention of quoting them to prove discourses emphasizing the movement's violent nature. This is also frequently the result of Salafis activists misunderstanding the nature of academic research. Being a research fellow at a major research university does not make the image of the academic scholar different, in the eyes of many Salafis, from that of journalists or researchers at policy-oriented think tanks. It is no surprise that research subjects asked the authors of this chapter on many occasions for the beneficiaries of their research. The obvious question is why would it be in the interest of the researchers' countries to provide funding to conduct extensive travels in order to collect information.

Researcher A once interviewed one of the most prominent Lebanese Salafi scholars in a religious college (*ma'had shara'i*) he founded. The sheikh is well known for his harsh criticism of jihadists and his rejection of any kind of violence against the state in the tradition of purist Salafism (Wiktorowicz 2006). He published dozens of books and fatwas on this issue. Yet when the researcher wanted to interview him about the educational activities and curriculum of his *ma'had*, he refused to provide detailed answers. Instead, the sheikh tried to go back to the issue of terrorism after almost every question, to prove that his college had no involvement in terrorist recruitment. After the interview, researcher A left with dozens of citations in his field notes from scriptures supposed to prove that the modern, jihadist type of violence is not permitted in Islam; yet the sheikh provided little insight into the life of the *ma'had*. Furthermore, he did not give his consent to the researcher to talk to the students and teachers of the college.

Researcher B has also had to deal with questions regarding the motives behind his research. One of the most influential Salafis in the city of Paris, Abdulwaheed, proved to be very helpful when it came to meeting other Salafis, and even to travel to Algeria (the country of descent of his parents). Once, researcher B, Abdulwaheed, and other French Salafis who did the Hegira to Algeria had a discussion in a fellow believer's home. The interviews were exciting and it appeared that their initial doubt about researcher B's intentions had gone away. Yet the Salafis were still very worried about what people (especially those who, according to them, misinterpret Islam and Salafism) would understand from what they had to say. At the end of the meeting, one of the Salafis laid out their concerns: while researchers may have good intentions, society can still misread what their intended messages are. Hence, for them, honest research can still be used to harm Islam. Suspicions about researchers' motives are also due to the fact the authorities and intelligence services in most countries tend to be very wary of Salafis, and regard the whole movement as a security threat. As a Lebanese security officer told us: "Salafis are the same as Fascists in Europe. [Their] ultimate aim is erasing anything that is not in accordance with their worldview." Both young, committed Salafis and sheikhs are often under surveillance, and questioning and arbitrary arrests are not uncommon. For example, in Lebanon, since the end of the country's civil war (1975–1990)—when Salafism began growing in Sunni areas—security crackdowns have been occurring regularly. Both the local Lebanese and the occupying Syrian security apparatuses identified Salafis as a primary challenge to the country's stability and Damascus's dominance over Lebanon. Hundreds of youth have been arrested over the past decades in connection with numerous incidents and conflicts between jihadis and the Lebanese security forces.[2] Many were Salafis, and they were released only after years of detainment without charges. All this places researchers in an awkward position when it comes to engaging Salafis. In Kuwait, the situation is different due to the Salafis' political participation and generally good relations with the ruling family. Therefore, harassment by security forces is much rarer than perhaps anywhere else in the Middle East, though it is not unheard of. Researchers have to be thus aware of the broader context within which they operate.

Europe, and more specifically France, represents a somewhat different case with regards to the intelligence services' strategies to deal with Salafis. At a time of rising Islamophobia in the "old continent," Salafism is regularly mentioned as the most striking illustration that Islam represents a very aggressive religion whose values and norms are antagonistic to Western ones. This has led intelligence services to question all radical forms of Islam today, starting first of all with Salafism, which is often seen as the ideology that generates political violence and terrorism. In the French context the debate is largely focused on the discourses and preaching of a number of imams with a growing online presence. In all places where Salafi imams preach, intelligence services are present. Intelligence agents often collaborate with other Muslims who are requested to warn them should the preaching be aggressive toward French principles. Once a "red line" is crossed, imams who are not French citizens are often deported. Each time this occurs, it becomes more difficult to do fieldwork as researchers are once again seen as collaborating with the state, and more precisely its intelligence apparatuses.

When Western researchers are not believed to be journalists or in the indirect employment of security services, then Salafis associate the image of the "orientalist" (*mustashriq*) with them. Orientalists of the end of the 19th century and beginning of the 20th are often seen in the Middle East as the agents of colonial powers. Many in the region believe that the sole purpose of these scholars was to collect information about the culture and habits of Arabs to make it easier for France and Britain to control them later. Salafis often blame Western academics for harboring purposes similar to those of the *mustashriqs* when they investigate Islamic movements—in particular, Salafism. Leaders and activists frequently express their belief that the increasing interest of researchers in them is because Western countries identify Salafis as their prime enemies. As a prominent Lebanese preacher, Salim al-Rafi'i, put it when researcher A interviewed him, "America, Russia, and Iran are in fact close allies, and they are conspiring against true Islam. They know if [Salafis] manage to erase the Sufi heresy and drive believers back to the true path, the enemies of Islam, especially the West, would have no chance to dominate [the Muslim world]. Even the West itself would be Islamized as millions of youth would utter the shahada if they knew the true face of our religion."[3] In the sheikh's opinion, experts on Salafism seek to identify the weaknesses of the movement so that the intelligence services and policymakers can exploit them.

Given all this, it is no wonder that young and committed Salafis, who are likely to be the most important object of inquiry for researchers, are often reluctant to speak to Western academics. They are often concerned that they might get into trouble with the authorities, or, worse, that they might unwittingly assist the "enemies of Islam" in portraying the religion in negative light, providing information that might help the West oppress Salafis.

Beyond the lens of securitization, doctrinal reasons also make it difficult to approach Salafi individuals. *Al-wala' al-bara'*, or "allegiance and disavowal," set certain limits to contact with non-Salafis and non-Muslims. This principle preserves the purity of the Salafis' belief by distancing them from everything that contradicts their understanding of Islam. For example, all Salafis agree that participating in the religious celebrations of non-Muslims is forbidden. Furthermore, most of them argue that feeling affection for or friendship with a non-Muslim contradicts the doctrine of *al-wala' al-bara'*. Some of them even believe that Salafis should contact non-Salafis only for preaching or business purposes. At the beginning of our research on Salafism it often occurred that our young Salafi interviewees, rather than talk about themselves, preferred to arrange meetings with renowned Salafi scholars, arguing that "Sheikh X will tell you everything you want to know." They believed that religious scholars are best in representing the community, and their knowledge is deep enough to avoid any kind of pollution of the purity of their faith on the part of supposedly Christian westerners or non-Salafi Muslims.

Overcoming Challenges

Conducting successful empirical research on members of the Salafi movement, however, is not an impossible task. Despite the difficulties mentioned in the previous section, during our fieldwork we managed to interview hundreds of Salafis both in Europe and in the Middle East. Dissolving the cloud of suspicion in the eyes of Salafis that the Western researcher works for an intelligence agency or aims to cast negative light on Salafism might be impossible. Yet academics can build some sort of trust with Salafis by clarifying their aims and explaining the difference between scholarly research and journalism or policy work. For us it proved helpful to explain that the data we were collecting would not end up in the media. Instead, our aim was to add to the existing academic debate on the Muslim world to understand rather than undermine it.

Willingness to admit one's own prejudices and biases and asking for clarifications may significantly help the researcher's socialization in a Salafi milieu. In fact, admitting prejudices and "ignorance" often motivated Salafi activists to clarify what they felt were misconceptions. In the beginning of his fieldwork in Tripoli, researcher A once admitted that he had a perception that Salafis were difficult to approach and were not comfortable with coming into contact with those who did not share their beliefs. As a response, two young Salafis invited researcher A for dinner to prove that Salafism is not what westerners might imagine it to be. During the conversation, the two young Salafis explained that the scripture does not forbid interactions with non-Muslims. Quite the opposite is true, as they are obliged to do good to non-Muslims in order to show them the beauty of Islam and convince them to convert. One of them gave the example of the Indonesian archipelago, where, according to him, people became Muslims due to the exemplary behavior of Arab traders whom they met in the 13th century. Researcher A kept in contact with the two Salafis after the dinner and they later proved to be helpful contacts in his research. They intended to challenge "Western perceptions" of Salafism, and were willing to provide further contacts and accompany the researcher to religious lessons both in mosques and in private homes.

Researcher B had a similar experience with French Salafis, suggesting that the milieu of research when it comes to Salafis might not matter much. Many of them wished to learn more about social sciences and how non-Muslims saw Salafis, especially since the attention of politicians and the media was increasingly turned toward the issue of "radical Islam." Some felt flattered to be the subject of an academic work, although they had concerns about being under surveillance from intelligence agencies or being misunderstood. Even if Salafis agreed to speak to the researcher, discussions mostly focused on religious topics, as researcher B initially had to insist that he wanted to learn more about their beliefs. However, nonreligious dimensions had to be highlighted in order to assess the profiles of the people who find appeal in Salafism. This was a huge challenge given that most of the French Salafis, at least initially, wanted to elaborate on why their faith was unique and the true one. When it came to their social and personal background, it became instantly much more difficult to engage them to the same degree.

Interestingly, Salafis almost always try to convince the researcher to convert to Islam and Salafism. It might be beneficial for one's fieldwork if one does not outright reject such attempts, but rather shows interest. This gives Salafis further motivation to engage with the academic in the hope that they might direct him or her to the "right path." In fact Salafis consider preaching their most important task. Thus, to fulfill it by engaging with non-Muslims is not contradictory to the doctrine of *al-wala' wa-l-bara'*. It has to be mentioned, though, that if Salafis see that the individual is still not willing to convert after a certain period, they might lose motivation to maintain contact. This happened to researcher A—he spent almost every day with a group of young Salafis in Kuwait over the course of about two months. They brought him to dozens of religious lessons, and one of them, a young sheikh, allowed him to closely observe his *da'wa* activities. However, toward the end of the second month members of the group asked him when he would become a Muslim. When they realized that the researcher was more interested in understanding the social life of Salafis than in religious conversion, the relationship gradually faded. Researcher B was seen as a Muslim because of his name, which probably made things easier, at least in the beginning. Many of Salafis wanted to gauge the religious current he supposedly favored in his work. Indeed, they knew he was interested in Salafism, but, as expected, comparisons with other conceptions were frequently highlighted (Muslim Brothers, Tabligh, jihadists, Sufis, etc.). As they realized that researcher B was familiar with the different major Islamic movements, they sometimes came to the conclusion that he might belong to one of them. As a result, these Salafis had two types of reactions. First, some thought that the true goal of the investigation was to discredit Salafism by pretending to be carrying out interviews and participant observation, and in doing so, make another strand of Islam appear more appealing. Second, many believed that researcher B was using his doctoral work to get closer to Islam after years of remoteness from religion. The fact that he studied at leading French universities and worked with well-known experts on Islam and the Middle East made researcher B appear to be someone who was misguided and led astray by non-Muslims. Therefore, his Salafi sources believed that talking to him and providing access to other Salafis eventually could lead to his salvation.

We believe that for meaningful research one needs to spend long periods of time in the field. Generally, a one- to two-week visit allows sufficient time to conduct interviews only with religious leaders and public figures, which is inadequate in obtaining a detailed picture on the social dynamics of the movement. A longer period of investigation is necessary to build trust with Salafis. It enables the researcher to become familiar with their larger social milieu. In most Middle Eastern countries Salafis are not socially isolated. They rather constitute a religious vanguard composed of "exemplary Muslims" who intend to follow every aspect of the moral and religious practices of the *sahaba*. Ordinary Muslims often participate in the Salafis' activities,[4] ask them for religious advice, and listen to the Friday sermon in their mosques. Familiarity with these ordinary believers is crucial in understanding the influence of Salafism in a given locality, and discussions with them are often very helpful in getting closer to the Salafis themselves.

When researcher A met one of his most valuable contacts, he did not approach this person directly for an interview. Rather, meeting him happened accidentally. Researcher A was having dinner in a street eatery in Tripoli's traditional Qubba district with a non-Salafi friend (we call him Ahmad here). The conversation revolved around Lebanon's tribal communities living along the eastern border of the country. Ahmad called one of his friends (we call him Abu 'Abdullah here), who belonged to one of these communities, to join them for dinner. Ahmad suggested that this would allow researcher A to better understand the differences between this part of the population and the rest of the Lebanese.

It turned out that Abu 'Abdullah was a committed Salafi, and one of the pioneers of the *da'wa* in Wadi Khalid region. Ahmad suggested that Abu 'Abdullah invite researcher A to his home village. Given his tribal background, refusing to invite researcher A would be a serious violation of tribal traditions that highly value hospitality. During the first visit of the researcher to Wadi Khalid, Abu 'Abdullah felt obliged to spend most of his time with him. That way, researcher A managed to get insights into the Salafi *da'wa* in that region as well. If the researcher had approached Abu 'Abdullah as chiefly a Salafi preacher and not a member of an *'ashira*, his attitude would have been substantially different. Yet researcher A went to Wadi Khalid for a social visit, which initially had nothing to do with his research project. When focusing on Salafism came into the picture, he had already managed to build the necessary trust both with Abu 'Abdullah and with his family and friends.

Having extensive social contacts and friends among local Muslims in France also proved to be extremely useful. Contrary to popular belief, Salafis are not sectarian in the way they conduct and live their daily lives. While their beliefs and religious practices appear to be highly uncompromising, they tend to maintain ties with fellow believers—for instance, to preach to them and engage them in religious debates to highlight the superiority of their views. In this regard, researcher B always benefited from having a good reputation among numerous Muslim communities (articles in the papers, invitations to television shows), which made his requests to meet Salafis sympathizers and imams more readily accepted. Although many of them still believed researcher B was not completely trustworthy, this suspicion diminished over the years. One of the most striking answers that researcher B received when he requested an interview at a Salafi mosque came from a young follower who smiled when researcher B introduced himself. He smiled and said: "I already know you. I know what you do. Do not be afraid. I will talk to you. You have a good reputation. That is OK."

Researcher B has always focused on interviewing religious leaders before approaching their followers. As they are to a large extent the leaders of these communities, gaining their confidence makes their supporters more likely to answer questions and share details of their daily lives. For instance, one of the most influential Salafi preachers in the suburb of Paris is named Abu 'Ishaq and has a popular religious website (www.manhajulhaqq.com). When researcher B contacted him for the first time, he replied instantly, and when researcher B met him at his mosque, he invited researcher B to visit at will. After a couple of weeks, most of the people who frequented the mosque knew researcher B. Among these people were numerous Salafis who agreed to be interviewed. Many of them even took researcher B to weddings and invited him to their homes for discussions. The aforementioned strategy thus turned out to be the most effective in collecting data.

Even when Salafis readily give interviews to researchers, longer stays and socialization remain a useful strategy. For example, in Kuwait, most Salafis are approachable. The reason for this is that in this Gulf monarchy Salafis are an integral part of the political system. Unlike other Gulf States, Kuwait has an influential parliament, where Salafis usually have considerable presence. Nevertheless, a few months' stay and socialization with Salafis provide significantly more data than a one- or two-hour interview. Researcher A, for example, was investigating the fragmentation of Salafi political forces in Kuwait. When he interviewed politicians, they generally dismissed any ideological dimension behind the split and pointed to purely political reasons. Yet, when he started to socialize with Salafis by participating in *diwaniyyas* (traditional Kuwaiti social gatherings), he was presented with a contrasting picture on the role of Salafi ideological debates in the fragmentation of Salafi political parties. In one instance, one of the ex-Salafi MPs, who left the Salafi mother organization, al-Tajammu' al-Salafi al-Islami (Salafi Islamic Gathering—SIG), claimed during a formal interview to share the religious ideas of those who stayed in SIG.

Yet the same person offered a completely different discourse when the researcher went out for a drive with him to the desert. There, the ex-MP complained about the "corrupted" views of some Salafis, who create religious legitimacy to support an obviously inefficient and despotic government. Later, he helped the researcher gain access to others in the secessionist Salafi faction at social events, such as desert camps, and thus obtain a better picture of the ongoing ideological debates.

Notes on the State and Other Sociopolitical Actors

None of the countries where we did our fieldwork are known to be hostile to foreign academics. Yet research on Salafism is sufficiently sensitive to draw the attention of both the authorities and other sociopolitical actors. Researchers who are studying Salafis should expect the state authorities or activists in political parties and movements to approach them with a degree of caution.

Researcher A was once arrested and held for a couple of hours by Lebanese military intelligence when he tried to enter Nahr al-Barid, a Palestinian refugee camp, to interview one of the Salafis there. It turned out that the intelligence agency wanted to prevent both Western converts to Islam (who might be radicalized) and journalists from entering the camp. When the researcher cleared his identity as a non-Muslim, he was released, but the officers did not fully believe his claim that he was not working for the media. Therefore, they blocked him from the camp. In another instance, in the Palestinian camp Mukhayyam al-Baddawi, researcher A was held by a Marxist Palestinian faction, al-Jibha al-Sha'biyya (Popular Front). The militants thought that he was a Western convert who wanted to join one of the Salafi groups active in the camp. Explaining that he was working on his PhD about Salafism in Lebanon proved futile. He was released only when one of his Communist friends cleared him. This example shows that it is a good idea to build as extensive a social network as possible. Local friends, whom the researcher smokes shisha or visits neighborhood cafes with, can be extremely useful when help in security-related matters is needed.

Another concern is ethical. Political actors in Lebanon and Kuwait who were interested in gathering information about local Salafis frequently approached researcher A. In Kuwait, for example, members of Jama'iyyat al-Islah al-Ijtima'i (Social Reform Society—SRS), which is a representative organization of the Muslim Brotherhood, often sought him out. During these meetings the conversation mainly revolved around Kuwaiti Salafi groups, which often competed with the Muslim Brothers for political positions in the country. The activists made it clear that they were interested in hearing the researcher's perspective in order to deal with Salafis more effectively. Researcher A had to maintain a balance between keeping his otherwise very valuable friendship with the Muslim Brothers and harming his Salafi sources. Therefore, he refused to share contacts or personal information on

the latter, while giving inputs on issues such as suggestions for political collaboration between the Muslim Brotherhood and Salafis, or identifying the Salafi groups
that would be potentially open for closer cooperation with the SRS.

Researcher B was frequently invited to give his personal opinion about Salafism as
a religious current, meaning that his expertise had to be interpreted nonacademically
Journalists as well as politicians very often requested researcher B to provide them
with his analysis of Salafism. Whenever a more personal assessment of this ideology
was needed, this created a sort of ethical issue. A personal opinion on Salafism
would have certainly been used to justify a column in a paper or a public discourse
from a politician, which may be framed to argue that even some scholars specialized
in the study of Salafism are warning against its principles. The question here is no
longer "How can we comprehend Salafism?" but "How can we fight it?"—which is a
political question, not an academic one. It means that researcher B was being asked
to suspend his academic role in order to provide consultancy work, which deviates
from the original intention of his work. This is a role radically opposite to that of the
academic, and researcher B has been extremely reluctant to engage in such debates
for both ethical and political reasons. The researcher cannot use material obtained
by doing fieldwork among Salafis to provide advice on how to get rid of the Salafi influence in France. In addition, an academic who is supposed to provide an account,
so far as possible unbiased, on his research should not take a political stand.

Conclusion

We showed in this chapter that the main challenges faced by academics doing research on Salafism stem from the lenses of securitization through which Salafis are
seen. This is combined with certain aspects of Salafi doctrine that discourage unnecessary contacts with non-Salafis. Yet we demonstrated that interviewing and
observing Salafis are not impossible tasks. In order to conduct successful fieldwork
on the movement, researchers must be clear on their intentions, show general interest in the Salafis' religious doctrines, and embed themselves in the subjects'
society.

In conclusion, despite the very different contexts of the Middle East and Europe,
especially pertaining to the interaction between security services and the Salafi
community, field research on the movement can be conducted in a similar manner
in both regions.

12

Interviewing and Gender

EMANUELA DALMASSO

Fieldwork is an intensely personal process (Ortbals and Rincker 2009, 287); it offers the unique opportunity to discover sides of ourselves that we would have never imagined. In my case, the very first time I had to confront a rather different environment was back in 2005 in Egypt. At that time I was an MA student, and I used to live in a neighborhood in Alexandria where my flatmates and I were the only foreign women.[1] Almost on a daily basis somebody took care to remind us that we were different, sometimes in a rather aggressive way. I have a clear memory of my first thoughts in the morning during those days. How can I make myself more compatible with the surrounding environment? What outfit will make me invisible? What really hurt me was the constant feeling of being "discrepant" despite all my efforts to merge with the landscape. I did my best, but nothing worked. Discussing this issue with friends was of great help, and I remember in particular a sobering answer that a non-Caucasian European friend gave me. He said he was very happy that I had this experience so that the next time I used the word *racism* I would know what it really means. According to my friend, the sneakiest form of racism is when you are kindly, but constantly, reminded that you do not fully belong to the country you were born and raised in. In his opinion, my experience in Alexandria could help me to understand many non-Caucasian European citizens' frustration with being asked where they come from. Where do you come from? France, I see, but what are your origins? Indeed, many Europeans do not consider answers such as Italy, France, or Spain satisfying if the person they are talking to is not Caucasian. They may not be racist, but their questions certainly are.

The Alexandria experience worked as self-discovery. There I discovered what it meant to be a foreign woman. A foreign man would probably not have had this experience comparable to racism, and the sexism Egyptian women experience is also different (not necessarily better) than what I experienced. Still, this experience taught me something about my own society and about myself. I could learn how to fit in, even if I would never belong to my fieldwork countries. When, 10 years ago, I started to live and work in countries of the southern shores of the Mediterranean,

I realized that I had to find a way of fitting in. In my personal experience this did not mean that I had to wear a veil or pretend that I shared the surrounding concern about the morals of others. I had made my choice: I want to fit it and I will not try to belong.

This chapter is based on attempts, readjustments, mistakes, and the voracious curiosity that have characterized my journey. My fitting in involved three main processes that will be presented in three following sections. First, I had to learn what gender means to me and how to cope with sexism: with only being recognized as a woman and not as a scholar. In practice I had to learn how to reset, kindly but firmly, the boundaries of the interaction any time research participants were focusing on my gender identity instead of my professional one. Also, I had to accept that something that normally would be unacceptable for me could be rationally understood and, as a consequence, better managed. Second, I had to learn how to recognize respondents' various misperceptions of my identity and how to react to them. According to their political identity and secular or religious orientation, respondents attributed to me different identities. Because I am a Western woman, some of my respondents thought that I would "naturally" be anti-Islamist, others that I could not be anything but an Islamophobic feminist. Finally, I had to understand the intersectionality of my respondents by inquiring into practices, not just discourses.

Before moving to the next sections, I would like to stress to what extent fieldwork has been important for me in the last 10 years. Fieldwork gave new meaning to words such as *trust* and *respect*, especially when these feelings materialized in a context of intellectual disagreement. My work would not have been possible without the generosity and patience of the hundreds of people who agreed to answer my questions. I was privileged to spend time with people who taught me to make the most out of my mistakes. I also met people who shared with me their most private and painful experiences, such as being tortured, while at the same time showing me that humankind can be wonderfully unpredictable.

Madame or Miss? Is This the Question?

Sometimes it is, and I always answer: "Dr. Dalmasso. Very nice to meet you." And I smile. If you do not hold a PhD yet, saying that you are a PhD candidate followed by your name and a smile is a good answer. Over time I have learned to consider myself above sexist comments. Certainly it took me a while, and sometimes this process of learning materialized along with feelings of frustration and shame (Bartky 1990, 83–98). Like any other woman, I could make a pretty long list of the sexist comments I have received during the last 10 years. I would like to emphasize that this occurs all over the world, not only or especially in the MENA region. How to handle sexism?

The first thing I always do when I meet my research participants is to briefly sum up my degrees, my working experience, and the scope of my research. In doing so, I reckon that there is little room for misinterpretation about who I am and the reasons why I want to meet my research participants. If my interlocutor keeps defining me as a young female student after being told that I received my PhD five years ago, I always correct him or her. I do so not because I feel downgraded by my interlocutor's statement, although sometimes this is his or her goal, but for ethical purposes. I want to make sure that my research participants are aware of my professional status, and thus I keep repeating who I am every time my interlocutor blurs the lines between my professional identity and my gender. Sometimes, however, despite my efforts to remind my interlocutors that I am a scholar, they focus on my female identity. In such cases I mentally repeat my personal mantra. When I conduct interviews I am acting and reframing "my behavior as an empowering performance of gender" (Benz 2014). Sometimes this means smiling and carry on with the interview after receiving an untimely comment about my appearance. In other words, it means agreeing with Mügge when she strategically chooses to be more relaxed about being sexualized than she would be in other contexts (Mügge 2013, 544). But why should I allow someone else's verbal lack of self-mastery to undermine my work? I am there to listen to respondents as long as they want to talk, and I am there to ask questions, no matter how unpleasant what they are saying is: as long as there is no attempt to go beyond words. Sexism is their problem all the time; their sexism is my problem only for the duration of an interview.

I have also learned to interact with my research participants by trying to put myself in their shoes and by keeping in mind that gender is much more than a feminine-masculine dichotomy. The majority of men I have conducted interviews with belong to the generation that the Moroccan sociologist Mohamed Sghir Janjar described with the following words: "Have we thought about what we are experiencing? Or we are living so fast that we do not even understand what is happening to us? Our mother taught us to dominate women, and now women want to be equal. Which values [should we adopt]? In which society are we living?"[2] Most of my interview participants, both men and women, are performing the gender roles society has imposed on them, often aggressively. Still, as Nencel correctly pointed out: "Feeling in fieldwork is receiving and perceiving meanings and emotions that are evoked and embodied" (2005, 347). My mere presence in the field challenges some of my research participants' embodied gender rules; their reactions, thus, should be also understood, not excused, as never-questioned gender performances (Butler 1990, 189). In addition, I share Preciado's (2014, starting at minute 6:00) claim that the woman should not be the political subject of feminism:

> The notion of masculinity, femininity, man, woman, heterosexuality, homosexuality, normality, pathology, transsexuality, intersexuality actually are political fictions. ... If we reconstruct the political genealogy that

explains how these political fictions historically materialized and with which kind of political techniques of body control and of subjectivity control they have been associated ... we can rise up against these political shams that made us. [We can do so] by critically unidentifying ourselves and collectively imagining new political fictions that do not produce violence, systematic forms of oppression, and exclusion.

The effects of the above-mentioned political fictions harm those who are still socialized to perform a certain kind of masculinity or femininity despite the fact that the neoliberal socioeconomic context makes it senseless and often unfeasible. When, because of my fieldwork schedule, I deal with somebody who behaves in a sexist way, I try to remind myself that this person is acting according to the gender role he or she has been socialized to embody. Sometimes I manage to do so better than other times, but this understanding allows me to learn from every kind of interaction. This is why in a chapter that deals with fieldwork, I consider theory an essential topic. A clear understanding of what gender means to me (see Preciado 2008) is precisely what constitutes the bulk of my intellectual weaponry in the field, when I confront sexism. A practical example? All over the world and in very different cultural contexts the "'whore" stigma is attached to women on the basis of a unique principle: when they perform their sexuality as individuals (Tabet 2004). That is, as men do. Accordingly, in societies where socially acceptable sexuality is based on economic exchanges or promiscuity, the whore stigma will be attached to every woman who does not ask for economic compensation in exchange for sex or who refuses multiple partners (Tabet 2004, 34–35). Thus, all over the world we can find very different sexual socially acceptable behaviors, but almost everywhere women's agency in the sexual realm is socially unacceptable. Despite the fact that I do not like to be harassed in the street and to be insulted when I ignore aggressors, when I have to confront such occurrences, I understand them through the lens of Tabet's work. It is my agency that bothers others, and not only in the Middle East.

Intersectional Identities

Fieldwork and identity is a topic that has received increasing attention over the last few years. In particular, (mis)perceptions based on one's identity are a widespread concern among scholars, and gender does not constitute an exception. Townsend-Bell describes as unreasonable and naive her assumption that "Afro-Uruguayan women would feel an automatic rapport [with her]" (2009, 312). Nencel (2005, 350) acknowledges her frustration in realizing that the prostitutes she was studying, despite her efforts to build trusting relationships, were more cooperative with her male assistant than with her. Thus, female scholars working on gender issues cannot take for granted the establishment of a privileged relationship with the women about whom they are doing research simply on the basis of gender solidarity. However, during fieldwork I have often witnessed, and to some extent felt uncomfortable with, another kind of misperception of my supposed gender solidarity. When I did research about both women's rights issues and political Islam, my identity became a locus of contestation for my research participants (Henderson 2009, 293) and through their words they "constructed me in different ways" (Henry 2003, 237). Because I am a Western woman, many people assumed that I must share their opinion and consider every Islamist a threat. In other words, they assumed that my gender would play a bigger role than my training as a scholar. As a consequence, they expected me to enthusiastically embrace the stereotyped assumption that Islamism is inconsistent with democracy and inherently against women's rights. I have countless examples of people who define themselves as liberal and democratic, many of them engaged in women's rights struggles, explaining to me that those who want to participate in politics by adopting a religious ethos are "essentially" undemocratic. More recently, I also have examples of liberal democrats who were astonished to find that I did not share their satisfaction over the 2013 Egyptian coup d'état. When listening to such arguments, I usually point out counterexamples of religiously oriented political parties that participate in democracies all the over the world. In doing so, I try to move our discussion toward a broader reflection: the institutional context. Unfortunately, despite my attempt to problematize the issue, my interlocutors often have felt compelled to patronize me. Explanations have varied from "You cannot understand them because they use doublespeak with foreign researchers" to "You cannot compare (religiously oriented Western political parties with MENA ones); it is different in your context." Instead of engaging in a discussion, many of my interlocutors preferred to consider my lack of a priori distrust of Islamists as the result of either my naïveté or my otherness. I doubt that the statement "Islamists are against women's rights" would have be considered final with a male scholar, but the fact that, despite having a womb, I could not feel the Islamist peril really bewildered them. What was at stake during such interviews was not only the uncomfortable position my interlocutors put me in, but also and especially the arguments or, for the sake of accuracy, the stereotypes they used to justify their stance. The first few times I received such comments, questions arose in my mind. Should I pretend that I share their attitude so as to avoid unpleasant comments? Or should I keep on challenging their stereotyped assumptions? I decided for the second option. My choice to continue pointing out that religiously oriented political parties can successfully participate in democratic dynamics and to focus on the institutional context was meant to force my research participants to explain how they built their arguments. If the only way they could do so it was by reducing me to a stereotype, that was not my concern. How research participants build their arguments is what really matters for my work.

The same misinterpretation applies to Islamists, albeit with different results. I got an unreserved blessing and a kiss on my forehead by an Islamist only because, in order to avoid the updated version of what Schwedler defines as the "respect accorded to women by Islam" lecture (2006, 426), I told him that the feminism advocating Islamophobia was not the kind of feminism I support. I also had a very difficult interview with an Islamist woman because she interpreted my questions as the result of my Judeo-Christian identity—she used these words to define me— and the supposed Islamophobic feminism linked to such identity. While I certainly cannot deny my Catholic socialization (which incidentally did not prevent me from becoming someone supporting transgender rights), on that particular occasion I patiently explained to her that my questions were the result of my being a PhD candidate doing her job. I also added that I would be happy to tell her my personal opinion once we finished our interview if she would kindly answer my questions in the meantime. Being a female scholar requires some extra effort in setting the boundaries of the interaction and in resetting them whenever interlocutors, both men and women, begin interacting with you by focusing on your female identity instead of your professional one.

A Different Kind of Power Does Not Mean Powerless

Another important lesson that fieldwork taught me is related to the relation between discourses and practices when it comes to gender issues in the Middle East. In 1935 Malika El Fassi, a leading figure of the Moroccan nationalist movement, wrote: "I am not one of those who say that girls must attain high degrees; I tend rather to favor a high school education that includes every subject, and that makes a girl able to read and write and take care of the house, and to live with her husband and socialize the children. That is enough for her."[3] In noticing that, a few years later, El Fassi was instrumental in opening a women's section of Qaraouine University, Alison Baker remarked that El Fassi had "evolved with the times" (1998, 64). Baker's assumption, however, is inconsistent with what El Fassi told her. When Baker questioned El Fassi about her struggle to give Moroccan women the opportunity to enroll at one of the most prestigious universities in the MENA region, El Fassi went back to her childhood:

> My father was remarkable, and I studied with all the best professors. I remember once in that period I was working at my desk, studying my lessons, when one of my aunts came over to me. She didn't approve of girls studying or getting an education, and so she was always criticizing me for reading books. She said, "What do you think you are going to do with all that? Why are you doing all that studying? I suppose you think you are going to go to the Qaraouine [university]!!" And from that moment—I was about nine years old—I had that idea, the idea: Why shouldn't girls be able to study at the Qaraouine? And I think it was that, from my aunt,

that pushed me to open up education for girls, and to open up a women's section of the Qaraouine. (Baker 1998, 71)

Thus, despite the fact that El Fassi clearly dated to her childhood her desire to open the highest educational opportunities for Moroccan women, Baker did not interpret El Fassi's changing advocacy as a gradual, rational strategy, but rather as an evolution. Reading El Fassi's words I would suppose that, in order to ensure wider support for girls' education, she strategically adopted the least controversial discourses in order to cope with social, cultural, and colonial constraints. I may be wrong, but why should we not at least take this possibility into account? Why should we describe El Fassi's trajectory as an evolution while ignoring the possibility that it could have been the result of a successful political strategy?

To quote a most recent example, Sheikha Moza, the wife of the former emir of Qatar and the mother of the current ruler, is one of the most powerful economic and political actors in Qatar, the richest country in the world by 2015 GDP per capita. While giving the greatest credit to her husband,[4] she founded and oversees the Qatar Foundation. The discourse used to present the Foundation clearly relegates her to a secondary role. However, the Qatar Foundation has been described not only as the institution driving the country toward a "sustainable economy for when the oil runs out—and a more cultured society in the meantime" (Cook 2012) but also as Sheikha Moza's domestic power base (Kerr and Khalaf 2013).

Just because some women's struggles are framed through concepts and stances that a Western audience might perceive as not sufficiently feminist does not make them less effective in empowering at least some women. According to my experience, quite the contrary is true. In interviewing Islamist women, for example, I realized that if I kept on focusing on their discourses I would have missed many important points. Rather than asking what they thought about various topics, I started to ask them concrete questions about their political activities. In doing so I could listen to Islamist women complaining about party meetings being held late in the evening or about the existence of a glass ceiling within their party that prevented them from reaching top positions (Dalmasso and Cavatorta 2014, 296–297). By focusing on what women were actually doing, and less on what they were saying, I became aware of some of those strategic and creative acts. Indeed, as Ramírez's analysis of Moroccan Islamist movements and parties brilliantly demonstrates, Islamists' gender roles should be understood as a dependent variable of their political strategy and not the opposite (Ramírez 2007). As a consequence, for example, Islamists included in the official political sphere display less innovation in gender roles than some Islamists who do not formally participate in the political arena (Ramírez 2006). Focusing on Islamist women's discourses prevents us from understanding their strategies. In other words, as Marsha Giselle Henry points out, we should focus on how other women are "strategically and creatively acting to increase their autonomy and agency while under social, cultural and religious constraints" (2003, 233) instead on how they describe their political activism.

Conclusion

To conclude, I would like to point out two more aspects that are related to fieldwork and gender in my personal experience. First, scholars addressing women's rights in the Middle East confront a dilemma when speaking to Western audiences. In Nadje Al-Ali's words: 'I'm always in a dilemma of whether I should mention the issue of honor killings. ... I have been in situations where I have given a talk for 45 minutes ... and some people went away with the only thing ... Iraqi fathers kill their daughters ... what is more important? Is it important to speak about the abuse of women's rights? Or is it more important to fight against the racism and islamo-phobia?" (Al-Ali 2010, starting at minute 14:07). Second, along with the tension be-tween the need to address women's rights topics while at the same time countering racism, the instrumentalization of women's rights in the Middle East and Europe should also be acknowledged. In recent years women's rights have increasingly been instrumentalized by political agendas that share little with egalitarian and progres-sive feminist struggles. At the beginning of this century, women's liberation in Iraq and Afghanistan was portrayed as a goal worth bombing these countries for, and Morocco and Ben Ali's Tunisia are good examples of authoritarian countries selec-tively promoting women's rights while harshly repressing political and civil society opponents. Nowadays, women's rights are also increasingly used as a litmus test to identify communities deemed not to fully belong to European civilization, de-serving therefore to be controlled and, perhaps, excluded (Mihai 2012). When I do fieldwork research, I deal with all these contradictions; I embody some of them. Working on women's rights in the Middle East requires, along with fieldwork skills, that one be aware of and able to cope with all these contradictions.

Acknowledgments

The author is very grateful to Marlies Glasius and Liza Mugge for their comments. This research was supported by the project 'Authoritarianism in a Global Age' at the University of Amsterdam (http://www.authoritarianism-global.uva.nl/) and received funding from the European Research Council (FP7/2007–2013) [grant number 323899].

Process Tracing and the Political Economy of Development in the Middle East

DAVID WALDNER

Research methods are often seen as preformed and perfected recipes, to be taken off the shelf and applied formulaically to a given research topic. I want to show, in contrast, how a particular research project generated demand for a new method; how that method developed in dialogue with the research; and how, despite some success, the method failed to perform satisfactorily, leading to a new round of methodological innovation. The research context is my doctoral dissertation, finished in the mid-1990s and published in 1999 as *State Building and Late Development* (henceforth SBLD) (Waldner 1999). The dissertation was based on almost three years of field research in Syria and Turkey; my focus in this essay is the procedures used for making causal claims using that data. This chapter details the motivation for developing the approach to case-study analysis I used in SBLD, diagnoses some problems with that approach, and concludes with a summary of more recent refinements of the procedure now widely known as process tracing.

The Research Problem

The project that became SBLD began in the intellectual ferment of the 1980s over the political economy of late development. For the prior three decades, development economists had vocally challenged economic orthodoxies by calling for extensive state intervention to guide development in postcolonial economies. By the 1980s, however, the accumulation of evidence convinced many that state economic intervention was more likely to produce corruption and suboptimal social welfare than to yield self-sustaining growth. In response, economic orthodoxy was making a comeback with widespread calls for structural reforms that would unleash the miracle of the market; these economic critiques would justify the suite of reforms called the Washington Consensus. At the same time, dependency theory was being called into question by the evident success of the East Asian economic miracles of Japan, South Korea, and Taiwan; yet emerging scholarship clearly demonstrated that the success of the East Asian newly industrializing countries (NICs) had virtually nothing to do with the prescriptions of conventional economic analysis.

The large-scale intellectual challenge for critics of orthodox economics was to carve out a third theoretical position, one that neither claimed state intervention as a panacea nor derided state intervention for uniformly producing substandard economic outcomes. This was a period well before economists "discovered" institutions and their role in guiding economic outcomes in terms of constraining policymaking and mediating outcomes of particular policies. The early institutional revival of development came out of two related research strands, one that saw institutions as explaining divergent policy outcomes among advanced industrial economies and the other that looked at East Asian success as a product of a particular set of institutions that Chalmers Johnson called "the developmental state" (Johnson 1982).[1] We can think of these studies as qualitative correlational analysis, first sketching out a set of political-economic institutions, then describing outcomes, and providing relatively informal theoretical models connecting institutions to outcomes.

I was introduced to these debates as a Berkeley undergraduate in the early 1980s. My interests were at the intersection of Middle East politics and the political economy of development. The Middle East was almost entirely absent from debates about the institutional basis of development; at the time, the rentier state paradigm was emerging, and most studies of the political economy of the Middle East focused on the effects of oil.[2] It did not strike me as particularly ambitious to continue the project of qualitatively correlating institutions with outcomes, however. But looking at these debates as an outsider offered a unique vantage point; how could we explain the determinants of the political institutions that in turn shaped developmental outcomes? Put differently, why was there no developmental state in the Middle East? Today, I would know how to pose this question in more respectable terms: given that we know that political institutions are not randomly distributed, how do we account for observed variance in political-economic institutions, and how do we establish that these institutions are exogenous, that is to say, that they are not caused by some prior feature that itself determines economic outcomes? But in those days, my concern that institutions might not be the proper ultimate cause was motivated less by considerations of valid causal inference than by the Marxist theory that political institutions were part of the superstructure, epiphenomenal to the material base, where all the action took place.

With this question in mind, I approached Chalmers Johnson, considered the pioneer of studies of the developmental state, and asked him why MITI—the Japanese Ministry of Trade and Industry that Johnson saw as the central pilot agency of the developmental state—existed in Japan but not in Egypt. His answer was straightforward; why, he asked me, would Japanese technocrats build their pilot agency in Cairo? For Johnson, MITI existed because Japanese bureaucrats understood the requisites of late development. Like many scholars who contributed to the revival of institutional analysis of development, Johnson saw his main objective as challenging neoliberal economists by demonstrating that political institutions and not free markets were responsible for the East Asian miracle; the question of institutional origins was simply not important to him. But for a junior scholar of the Middle East, an approach that ignored the origins of institutions had significant limits; were we to infer that there was no developmental state in the Middle East simply because the idea had not occurred to anyone?

A few years later I entered graduate school determined to tackle the overlooked question of institutional origins. All that remained, as I prepared for my dissertation fieldwork, was to develop an appropriate research design. My first thought was to conduct research in Syria and then to compare Syria to Korea and Taiwan. This sort of cross-regional comparison was still quite uncommon; indeed, at the time there were fewer than a handful of rigorous cross-case comparisons within the Middle East. But a single case study of Syria was a slender reed upon which to base a more general theory of institutional origins. Thanks to the superb serendipity of a semester-long visit to Berkeley by Ilkay Sunar, who had written a fine book about the development of the state in Turkey (Sunar 1974), I decided to combine an intra–Middle East comparison—Syria and Turkey—with a cross-regional comparison—the two Middle East cases compared to the two East Asian cases. The goal was to show how antecedent conditions shaped institutional origins, and how these institutions, in turn, shaped patterns of economic outcomes. Because the argument contained multiple stages, the intellectual challenge was to combine cross-case comparisons with within-case comparisons over time, or what we today call process tracing.

Mill's Methods and Cross-Case Comparisons

Today, qualitative methodology is a thriving field. In the mid-1980s, however, few scholars were actively researching qualitative methods. The most important contribution to case-study methods was Arend Lijphart's article on the comparative method (Lijphart 1971). Lijphart defined the comparative method in large part by what it was not; it was neither an experimental nor a statistical method with formal techniques for controlling for alternative explanations, but neither was it a pure case-study method with observations from only one case. Lijphart saw the method as analyzing at least two cases, maybe more, but fewer than the minimum number of cases required for statistical analysis. For his logic of inference, Lijphart borrowed from John Stuart Mill's method of difference, in which one searched for comparable or carefully matched cases that are as similar as possible along a range of variables reflecting alternative hypotheses, but that differ on the single variable representing the research hypothesis and also differ on the outcome variable. The method of difference, then, mimics experimental designs by trying to isolate the effects of variance in the independent variable, holding all other variables at fixed levels.

The Achilles' heel of this design, however, is that it is highly unlikely that only one factor will differentiate two political systems that also exhibit contrasting outcomes. As Adam Przeworski and Henry Teune observed, "Although the number of differences among similar countries is limited, it will almost invariably be sufficient to 'overdetermine' the dependent phenomenon" (1970, 34). Przeworski and Teune thus recommended a "most different systems" design, one akin to Mill's method of agreement. In their account, one allowed system-level variables to differ as much as possible and then looked for similarities at a lower level, usually among individuals or groups. According to this logic, "To the extent that general statements can be validly formulated without regard to the social systems from which the samples were drawn, systemic factors can be disregarded" (1970, 35).

The two approaches gave conflicting advice: either minimize differences on control variables and maximize differences on hypothesized causes and outcomes, or maximize differences on control variables and minimize differences on hypothesized causes and outcomes. One possible solution to this methodological impasse was to combine the two approaches, to select multiple cases that allowed the simultaneous application of the methods of agreement and difference. This was the design first used by Theda Skocpol in her magisterial *States and Social Revolution* (Skocpol 1979). Cases that were positive for revolution—France, Russia, and China—were matched in a most-different design. Despite huge differences in context, Skocpol was able to identify common sequences of change resulting in social revolution in all three countries. On the other hand, Skocpol included cases of nonrevolution—England, Prussia/Germany, and Japan. These cases represented contrasting outcomes, because despite structural similarities to France, Russia, and China, they did not undergo social revolution.

As many others have pointed out, however, Skocpol was seldom clear which factors were being held constant across which sets of cases. A major step forward in the comparative method was Ruth Berins Collier and David Collier's research design in *Shaping the Political Arena* (1991). Their eight cases of labor incorporation in Latin America were divided into four pairs. Each pair represented a distinct mode of labor incorporation; the four pairs of cases, to a large extent, represented a most-similar research design with different values of the causal variable, different values of the outcome variable, and some potential rival explanations held fixed. Within each pair, on the other hand, differences were maximized, particularly with respect to level of income and degree of ethnic diversity. Within these diverse contexts, similar modes of incorporation produced similar outcomes. The one weakness of this elegant design, however, was that only two variables, income and ethnicity, were allowed to vary within each of the four pairs of cases. The trick was to incorporate a larger set of control variables in the research design.

In SBLD, I treated Syria and Turkey as comprising a matched pair in a method-of-agreement research design. Despite important differences—democracy in Turkey against dictatorship in Syria, private property in Turkey versus socialized property in Syria—I argued that key structural variables were the same in the two cases and produced similar outcomes. These two cases were then paired with Korea and Taiwan to produce a method-of-difference research design. By using four cases, I was able to demonstrate that the East Asian cases shared values of many control variables with either Syria or Turkey. This component of the research design would not have been feasible without incorporating two Middle Eastern cases that exhibited many differences from one another; the method of agreement made the method of difference possible. The full research design is presented in Table 13.1.

It is important to identify the defects of this research design to help motivate the transition to process tracing. The first defect is baked into the design itself; the design allows us to "eliminate" variables that do not systematically vary with the outcome measure only if we conceive of each eliminated cause as deterministic and individually necessary and sufficient.[3] Furthermore, because the entire procedure is based on the logic of elimination, the procedure yields value if and only if there is a single survivor and we are reasonably confident that we have not omitted any critical variables. If, on the other hand, we allow that some causes may be probabilistic, in that they only raise the probability of an outcome without

Table 13.1 **Cross-National Research Design: Mill's Method of Indirect Difference**

Variables	Syria	Turkey	Korea	Taiwan
Political regime	Dictatorship	Democracy	Dictatorship	Dictatorship
Property regime	Public	Public/private	Public/private	Public/private
Political elites	Military/party	Civil society	Military/party	Military/party
Trade orientation	Eastern bloc	West	West	West
Foreign investment	Minimal	Substantial	Substantial	Substantial
Military alliances	USSR	US	US	US
External threat	Severe	Moderate	Severe	Severe
Ethnic heterogeneity	High	Moderate	Low	Low
Majority Islam?	Yes	Yes	No	No
Elite conflict	High	High	Low	Low
Development strategy	ISI	ISI	ELG	ELG
Development state	No	No	Yes	Yes

guaranteeing it, or if we allow that some causes may produce outcomes only as part of a more complex causal package, then the validity of inferences derived from this research design is called into question (Lieberson 1992). These assumptions can be defended; as I explain elsewhere, determinism is a justifiable property to ascribe to causal relations (Waldner 2002). But to justify these assumptions for each and every variable included in the research design would entail a staggeringly complex research design.

In addition to its reliance on a host of untested assumptions, the research design I used in SBLD was too informal, a feature unfortunately shared by too many users of Mill's methods, many of whom have an express aversion to quantitative methods. The informality of the design is expressed in three ways. First, the standard apparatus of measurement has been neglected; there is no discussion of operationalization or of measurement error. Second, by necessity, almost all of the variables have been treated as dichotomous, even though many of them are multichotomous or even continuous. Doing so entails a major loss of information and, insofar as thresholds are semiarbitrary, no doubt entails significant measurement error. Given the ubiquity of problems such as these in much case-study research, Richard Nielsen recommends using statistical matching for case selection, a method that offers the methodological virtues of transparency, replicability, and validity without committing case-study researchers to a "statistical worldview" (Nielsen 2016). Third, more than one variable distinguishes the Middle Eastern cases from the East Asian cases; as Przeworski and Teune had warned us, outcomes will be "overdetermined" because more than one possible cause will covary with the outcome phenomenon.

Finally, the research design is ill-matched to the underlying research problem of exploring sequences of causal relations that unfold over time. At its best, the design demonstrates patterns of association between independent variables and an outcome variable. As such, it excludes two critical elements of within-case analysis: causal mechanisms and sequences of variables constituting an extended causal chain. Consider the last three rows of Table 13.1—"Elite Conflict," "Development Strategy," and "Developmental State." These are not intended as rival hypotheses, but rather as links in a causal chain. It is thus important that all three variables survive the basic cross-national test, but the cross-national research design can take us no further. To make progress, we need to make the transition to within-case analysis, or process tracing.

Toward Process Tracing

In the mid-1980s, there were two basic existing approaches to within-case or historical analysis: Alexander George's early writings on process tracing and Theda Skocpol's advocacy of historical narratives in her *States and Social Revolutions*. It is often not appreciated how distinct these two approaches are from one another. George took experimental methods and quasi-experimental designs as the basic template of causal inference and suggested how within-case analysis, or process tracing, could also yield valid causal inference. Writing with Timothy McKeown, George's basic claim, anticipating the contemporary emphasis on Bayesian reasoning, was that "if observation is somehow informed by a theory or pre-theory, then it is logically possible for the observer to integrate observations with presuppositions in order to arrive at causal inferences" (George and McKeown 1985, 23). For my objectives, however, George and McKeown defined process tracing too narrowly, as a "procedure [that] is intended to investigate and explain the decision process by which various initial conditions are translated into outcomes" (35). This emphasis was proper insofar as George was interested in explaining foreign-policy decision-making, but less appropriate to explaining macrostructural outcomes

For insight into using historical methods for macrostructural theories, one turned to Skocpol's study of social revolutions and the voluminous methodological literature it spawned. Skocpol's explicit methodological reflections stayed very close to her combined use of Mill's methods of agreement and difference and other issues relating to cross-case comparisons; it was her commentators who emphasized the critical role played by the historical analysis in confirming her hypotheses. James Mahoney, for example, conceptualized Skocpol's narrative method as one that "analyzes revolutions as the product of unique, temporally ordered, and sequentially unfolding events that occur within cases" (1999, 1164). As such, narrative analysis relies on a very different standard of causal inference than George's efforts to link within-case analysis to quasi-experimental research designs. As Mahoney summarizes this position, "One criterion for judging a causal argument rests with the ability of an analyst to meaningfully assemble specific information concerning the histories of the cases into coherent processes" (1168). Mahoney then proceeded to present a partial reconstruction of Skocpol's narrative analysis of the French Revolution in a figure that included 37 conditions and about three dozen hypothesized causal linkages between them. Mahoney concluded, as have many readers and admirers of Skocpol's book including myself, that the validity of each link in the causal chain was simply not addressed by Skocpol. It appeared to me, then, that within-case causal analysis must rely on something other than the construction of a "coherent" narrative.

My objective, then, was to synthesize Skocpol's focus on macrostructural variables with George's emphasis on valid causal inference. The results of these efforts are presented, in simplified form, in Figure 13.1. Note that solid lines in Figure 13.1 denote conditions that are necessary and sufficient, while dashed lines denote necessary conditions and dotted lines denote sufficient conditions.

Figure 13.1 represents the critical causal relations constituting the main lines of argument in SBLD. It borrows features from both George and Skocpol, but adds

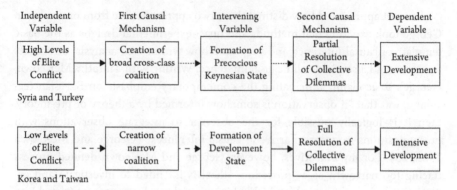

Figure 13.1 Process Tracing in State Building and Late Development.

novel features as well. The entire argument is presented as causal relations between variables; indeed, there is no reference at all to specific events, and at no point in the analysis are any causal claims based upon the ability to marshal extensive detail into coherent historical narratives. Yet, as in Skocpol, the causal account is based upon macrostructural variables; it is not the reconstruction of a single decision-making process.

The largest departure from both George and Skocpol is the explicit reference to causal mechanisms that link together each pair of variables. The main justification for causal inference in SBLD is based on the identification and confirmation of the mechanism-based causal chains. The causal chains of Figure 13.1 imply four causal sequences, each derived deductively from theory and each of which can be confirmed by detailed evidence. The first causal sequence was a micro-level analysis of elite preferences over coalitions, such that only under intense elite conflict did elites pay the high costs of a broad, cross-class coalition. The second causal sequence connects the side-payments with which coalitions are constructed to institutional formats. The third causal sequence linked these institutional formats to the resolution of two types of collective dilemmas, which I called Gerschenkronian and Kaldorian collective dilemmas. The final causal sequence linked the partial or full resolution of collective dilemmas to economic performance and developmental outcomes. The point is that these causal claims could be evaluated along two dimensions: their logical coherence, in terms of the derivation of consequences from first principles, and the degree of their empirical confirmation. Furthermore, and this is a critical point, rival hypotheses that were not eliminated by the cross-country research design discussed above could be eliminated because they could not generate a detailed causal sequence linking independent and dependent variables.

These causal claims make strong claims about necessary and sufficient causal relations that can also be tested using evidence from additional cases. I explicitly stated four such falsifying arguments that would impeach these claims of necessity and sufficiency. The first set of falsifying observations would be that in the absence of intense elite conflict, elites who were otherwise secure in their incumbency voluntarily incorporated lower classes through high levels of side-payments. Second, the argument of SBLD would be falsified by observing that high levels of side-payments created institutional structures distinct from those constituting precocious Keynesian states. A third set of falsifying observations would be that other states with institutional profiles analogous to precocious Keynesian states produced substantially different economic outcomes, especially by resolving the full range of collective dilemmas. A final set of falsifying observations would be that other cases of cross-class coalitions divided between authoritarian and democratic regimes with demonstrably different capacities for resolving the full range of collective dilemmas. Thus, the arguments of SBLD could be disconfirmed by contesting the logical derivation of causal relations, by contending that the available evidence does not sufficiently confirm these causal relations, or by pointing to other cases that contradicted the claims about necessary and sufficient causal relations.

Limitations and a Path Forward

While the articulation of a logic of process tracing in SBLD has multiple virtues, it contains some vices as well. First, while drawing boxes and arrows makes for an accessible presentation, the approach I adopted in SBLD provided neither semantic content to the boxes or arrows nor any rules or guidance for the selection of boxes and the location of arrows. Much more can and must be said about the reconstruction of a causal sequence, and filling in these gaps will retain the heuristic value of the diagrams but will complement it with heightened inferential leverage. Second, the concepts of necessary and sufficient conditions are ambiguous statements about causal relations. There is nothing inherently causal about either a necessary or a sufficient condition. By definition, these two conditions are statements about observed patterns of association. To say that X is a necessary condition for Y is only to claim that one never observes Y without also observing X; symbolically, $P(X|Y) = 1$. Similarly, to say that X is a sufficient condition for Y is only to claim that when one observes X, one will also observe Y; symbolically, $P(Y|X) = 1$. Both statements are about observed associations, and many observed associations are not causal. Much more can and must be said about the nature of causal relations. Third, in reaction to the inadequate defense of narrative analysis advocated by Skocpol and those who followed in her footsteps, this early version of process tracing is unnecessarily hostile to thinking about specific historical events. Much more can and must be said about historical narratives and their relationship to variable-based theorizing. Finally, SBLD relies on an underspecified conception of mechanisms and mechanism-based causal inference. Much more can and must be said about causal mechanisms, especially the integration of mechanism-based inference with existing frameworks of causal inference knows as the potential-outcomes framework or the Rubin-Neyman causal model.[4]

The refined version of process tracing that I have outlined in several recent publications has three major components: causal graphs, event-history maps, and invariant causal mechanisms (Waldner 2012, 2015a, 2015b).

Causal graphs, also known as Bayesian networks, are composed of nodes representing random variables, or probability distributions over a sample space of possible events, and directed edges or arrows representing relations of probabilistic dependence. These graphs are acyclic when no node has a directed edge entering it from one of its descendants. Causal graphs represent the critical feature of exogeneity when there are no omitted nodes with edges leading to the graph's explicit starting nodes and also along another path to the outcome variable—exogeneity is satisfied when there are no backdoor paths to the outcome. Causal graphs must satisfy the Causal Markov Condition; stated informally, each node in the graph is independent of its ancestors conditional on its parents. Causal graphs are compatible with a precise definition of a direct cause: X is a direct cause of Y if and only if an exogenous intervention on X alters Y only by virtue of the pathway from X to Y while holding all other variables not on this path at their fixed values. Note that by the Causal Markov Condition, if we hold the variable M on the path $X \rightarrow M \rightarrow Y$ fixed, intervening on X will not change the value of Y.

Causal graphs serve two critical functions. First, they represent the processes we aim to trace; as such, they are most useful when they are constructed prior to the onset of field or archival research. One must theorize a process before one can claim to trace it. Note that constructing a causal graph requires more than listing a set of random variables each of which, in principle, "matters" for the outcome; the causal graph must satisfy the Causal Markov Condition that places constraints on their construction. Satisfying this requirement, I would suggest, motivates thinking hard about causal relations. Second, causal graphs can easily represent the relevant counterfactual. Assume a binary treatment variable, X: now construct two causal graphs, one each for the two values of X. The two graphs are the relevant counterfactual to the other.

Causal graphs represent what philosophers call "type" causation, in statements such as "Smoking causes cancer." Ultimately we are interested, of course, in specific cases. Specific historical narratives, or "token" causation, are represented by event-history maps. Event-history maps mirror causal graphs; they are the specific realization of the causal graph's random variables within a given historical context. Critical to process tracing is making the full set of descriptive inferences from event-history map to causal graphs, using the standard repertoire of descriptive inferences. The construction and validation of the event-history map makes the critical transition from token to type causation, permitting historical explanations of specific cases. It does so, however, without the nonsystematic, often ad hoc analyses that so many scholars have perceived to invalidate pure narrative analysis.

Finally, valid causal inference requires the identification of invariant causal mechanisms that are not explicitly represented in the causal graphs. Directed edges represent relations of probabilistic dependence, but probabilistic dependence by itself does not equal causation. Invariant causal mechanisms inform us why the relationship of probabilistic dependence is observed, and they assure us that the observed relationship is genuinely causal. To accomplish this goal, we must define mechanisms in terms of their inherent capacity to do work, to alter their environment, including via the transmission of information. To refer to mechanisms as invariant causal principles is to understand their constitutive properties, the relations between parts and wholes such that under given conditions, the mechanism operates reliably to generate an effect.

My claim is that the procedure of process tracing outlined here, albeit in brutally truncated form, provides an adequate response to the "fundamental problem of causal inference" (Waldner 2015c). Philosophers and statisticians working within the potential-outcomes framework argue persuasively that unit-level causal inference (i.e., token causation) is not possible because we cannot observe a unit under treatment and under control simultaneously. In general, when our only observational data pertain to covariation between variables, this is absolutely correct, and the only alternative is to make inferences about average causal effects across populations or samples. Constructing causal graphs and identifying invariant causal mechanisms, however, provides information about what would happen under the relevant counterfactual. This is because causal mechanisms justify invariance assumptions analogous (but not equivalent) to the careful calibration of laboratory equipment to permit careful measurement.

One criticism of this method of process tracing is that it is too demanding a standard (Checkel and Bennett 2015, 265). All standards of causal inference have this demanding quality, however. Consider experiments, long considered the gold standard of causal inference. There is a rich and vital literature about the numerous threats to the internal and external validity of randomized experiments; indeed, there is a growing literature documenting the inability to replicate some experimental effects, suggesting that these demanding standards cannot always be met. But nobody would, I think, recommend that we drop experiments from our methodological toolkits. That standards are high does not mean we learn nothing from work that does not fully meet them; but to lower standards would seem to guarantee unnecessary limits on knowledge.

Perhaps the more interesting question for the author of a methodological autocritique is whether the original research findings would still be justified by the new research methods. I would venture to suggest that most of the original claims are consistent with new norms of process tracing, though looking back I wish I had spent more effort justifying my implicit claim of exogeneity. But I also realize that working hard to adhere to the new methodological norms would have had tremendous heuristic value as well. It is not simply that new methods give us new ways to validate old claims, but that new methods give us opportunities to make new claims as well. This payoff makes the hard work of critiquing and revising old work more than worthwhile, and I encourage others to follow suit.

Ethnography Is an Option

Learning to Learn in/through Practice

STACEY PHILBRICK YADAV

If it is a truism that important life lessons come from our mistakes, this is equally the case for field research, particularly when it is ethnographic in nature. Interpretive methods and ethnography continue to constitute part of a minority postpositivist or interpretivist research tradition among political scientists, but are arguably more popular among scholars working in settings where existing conditions limit many more conventional approaches. While the concept of "political ethnography" has gained traction through the work of some committed interpretivists (Schatz 2009), dedicated courses in ethnographic methods—which range from philosophy of social science to instruction in note-taking technique to the distinctive kinds of ethical questions that arise from sustained participant-observation—are not often a part of a political science student's graduate training. In fact, many of us interested in pursuing training in ethnographic methods before conducting field research have encountered claims that range from dismissal ("Anyone can figure it out by reading a book on fieldwork"), to praise for the instrumental value of "soaking and poking," to outright ridicule.[1]

While graduate programs may praise and promote "mixed method" research and introduce their students to both qualitative and quantitative traditions, graduate training in comparative politics and international relations still remains strongly anchored within a positivist tradition in ways that can strain the ability of ethnographic researchers to make their work intelligible across epistemic communities. Coursework or formal training in ethnographic methods must often be sought out elsewhere, usually in anthropology departments, where political scientists are sometimes seen as interlopers or dabblers, particularly when they have had little exposure to the different epistemologies that underwrite different forms of research. Unless a department offers a course detailing debates in the philosophy of (social) science, students may not be well equipped to describe their postpositivist commitments in ways that can convince others of the validity of their research design, or the work they do in the field.[2]

As Peregrine Schwartz-Shea and Dvora Yanow contend, "when methods that are mixed rest on different and conflicting notions of social realities and their knowability, the mixing can produce research that is not logically consistent or philosophically coherent" (2012, 133). Political science students working in the ethnographic tradition, like other interpretivists, may be tempted to "concede" that their work is not (social) scientific, though thoughtful arguments have been made for an open embrace of ontological and epistemological diversity that underwrites "science" as a concept. As P. T. Jackson has observed, the "only philosophically defensible response to methodological diversity is methodological pluralism" (2011, 209). This ought not be confused with methodological *relativism*, but should instead mean that "different scientific methodologies generate different bodies of knowledge, each of which is internally justified in distinctive ways, but none of which commands unqualified universal assent" (2011, 210). Once the scientific nature of truth claims that rest on different ontological bases is recognized, the issue becomes one of the "ongoing challenge of *translation*," a challenge that is more easily surmounted on the basis of interepistemic recognition (Jackson 2011, 210).

The experience of marginality (within one's own discipline and its research traditions, and in the fields from which we may borrow) should be no deterrent, as ethnographic field research itself may provoke similar feelings of strangeness, an asset explored below. In the context of such dual dislocation, researchers make mistakes (though, arguably, researchers make mistakes in all research contexts and according to all methodologies). When equipped with some of the conceptual tools of ethnographic research, however, at least some of these mistakes may develop into key intellectual lessons that shape research in meaningful ways. In the sections that follow, I reflect on several of the central mistakes I made in the context of my field research in Yemen, in the hope that they can elucidate some of the distinctive advantages of ethnographic field research for students of politics and encourage people to seek out training that will support them in the development of this kind of work.

Learning to Learn from Others: A Cautionary Tale

You're a graduate student in political science, interested in politics (obviously). Specifically, political parties (how boring). And among those, Islamist party discourse (maybe marginally less boring). You are definitely *not* interested in women. Women—and women's politics—is what that professor who passed you in the hall that one time said you *should* be studying because you'd enjoy a comparative advantage. Or because of solidarity. Or something. But you're not interested in all that. You want to study "real" politics, decision-making, and the way it is (or is not) shaped by Islamist speech. So, obviously, you have to talk to decision-makers.

This becomes your mantra. You sit in interviews, as man after man says that he has a sister or a wife or a female acquaintance from his professional syndicate you should really talk to, though they rarely say why. Nor do you ask. *It's because I'm a woman*, you think, and they (like that professor in the hallway) think women must be innately interested in studying gender. So as delicately as you can, you try to direct them back to the "real" story.

You aren't listening.

You're invited to a Friday lunch at the home of a politician whom you've interviewed, a big family lunch with his grown daughters and their families. He's a kind man, a professor, and after four or five interviews, this kind of social invitation seems natural. You accept, relieved at the thought of an afternoon *not* spent chewing khat and taking notes.[3] But on Thursday night, he calls to explain that he has to leave suddenly for a meeting in Cairo. You should come to lunch anyhow, he says—his daughters have been looking forward to meeting you. Fridays can be tough days for doing research, and you have found fieldwork surprisingly lonely thus far, so you buy a tray of sweets and walk through the empty streets, half-heartedly listening to the midday sermons pouring out of the mosques along the way.

His daughters are lovely. At a delicious lunch, they cope with your vegetarianism gracefully. They ask about your work. You give a two-sentence answer and tickle a baby sitting next to you. One of them asks about your research again, more pointedly. Another elaborates on her sister's question. She mentions something that she discovered in her own dissertation research. Before you know it, you're learning about the subjects of *their* dissertations, their own fieldwork, the NGO that one established, the leadership program another is running. You hear from an aunt about her experience running for public office and the reasons she ultimately left this path. One daughter reflects on the campus politics of her undergraduate years, the political campaign (led by those party members that so interest you) to close the gender studies program she was helping to organize. You feel a certain heat rising up your neck, a flush of embarrassment at the narrowness of your own assumptions. You curse yourself for leaving your notebook at home.

An hour or so later, you excuse yourself to find a bathroom, and you see your host in the hallway. He's not in Cairo. You might call his expression a smirk if he weren't always so good-natured. "This was good for you," he says. "You needed to learn for yourself."

Positionality, Relationality, and Space

Learning for yourself in a way that involves flexibility, adaptation, and an ability to incorporate the fruits of your mistakes is essential to ethnographic methods, but what does it mean to "learn for yourself" when you are embodied and relationally bound to others and to your physical environment? In other words, how do you "learn for yourself" when you are, by design, with and among others?

Ethnographic research encourages particular sensitivity to what is called "positional knowledge," or the idea that one's perspective—from the questions one asks (or doesn't) to the categories one uses to describe what is observed to the interpretations one offers—will be shaped by aspects of the scholar's own identity. Moreover, ethnographers are attentive to *relationality*, whereby those identities are performed or articulated in relation to others in a way that precludes an autonomous or "authentic" self. It is particularly important to bear in mind that for ethnographers (or postpositivists, generally) this is not as much problematic as it is inescapable, and the question thus becomes how to manage or account for this in the context of participant-observation.

During the course of my field research in Yemen, for example, I attended many khat chews. These events are a quintessential feature of Yemeni social and political life, and are supremely useful research settings, regardless of how one understands their function.[4] The majority of chews that I attended were held in people's homes, often in a kind of common room known as a *mafraj*. The seating in a *mafraj* is easily modified, with low cushions circling the perimeter of the room and bolster pillows separating participants and allowing for a more comfortable semirecline. The adaptability of the space makes it possible to accommodate newcomers easily, as people come or go over the course of an afternoon.

The spatial dynamics of the khat chew were one way in which I became particularly cognizant of my own positionality and embodiment, and the way in which my identity or identities were being articulated in relation to others. It is uncommon for Yemeni women to chew khat with Yemeni men, but as Jillian Schwedler has argued, many Western women doing field research in Yemen are treated as a "third gender," benefiting from access to both men's and women's spaces, and rarely excluded on the basis of gender (Schwedler 2006). Since I was usually the only woman in the room at a khat chew, and often the only non-Yemeni, the ways in which I (and others) occupied space and moved in the room were at times as significant as what we said. These bodily practices enacted ideas and made claims, were accepted and contested, in ways that parallel other forms of text that can be read and interpreted.

Seating at a khat chew is an important signifier of status and a way in which political alignments are forged and made manifest. My research on the dynamics of cross-ideological alliance building among members of the Joint Meeting Parties began in khat chews, as I observed the way in which overlapping consensus was forged—and tensions expressed—in words but also through embodied practices like seating, performing attentiveness, performing inattentiveness or disregard, leaving the room, greeting a new arrival, not greeting a new arrival, and so on. Attending a chew—sometimes two, once or twice more than two—every afternoon over the course of my fieldwork helped me to build a "visual vocabulary"—a set of cues and symbolic interactions that made it possible to "read" the event as one might another text. My notes often included maps of space, as well as maps of arguments. While I was rarely able to construct these in situ, field notes were also helpful in constructing network maps, showing how (and through what kinds of institutions) subjects were tied to others.

In *Peripheral Visions*, Lisa Wedeen offers an account of the symbolic logic of seating at khat chews, explaining the normative spatial arrangement that she observed, particularly at those at which participants occupied different status positions (2008, 123); against this norm, it became possible to observe experimentation and political signaling that was enacted through the subversion of the norm. When the norm is that the host sits farther from the door, for example, there is significance to his decision to sit next to it, to enact a form of radical equality that is consistent with his stated aims. In some cases, this may be deliberate (and something that we discussed in follow-up interviews); in other cases, perhaps, less intentional but no less effective. This kind of attention to space, embodiment, and relationality is one of the key assets offered by an ethnographic method attentive to everyday practices, guided by the anthropologist's injunction to "make the familiar strange and the strange familiar."

Abductive Reasoning

Another central characteristic of ethnographic and interpretive research is its use of abductive reasoning, an approach influenced by hermeneutics that might best be described as an iterative process of "sense-making." Rather than beginning with a research question and testable hypothesis, abductive inquiry rests on the articulation of a puzzle, where what "makes a puzzle 'anomalous' is a misfit between experience and expectations." As Schwartz-Shea and Yanow argue, "Both induction and deduction are described as following a step-wise linear 'first this, then that' logic, whereas abduction follows a much more circular-spiral pattern, in which the puzzling requires an engagement with multiple pieces at once. Whether one's favorite analogy is a jigsaw puzzle, Rubik's cube, or Sudoku, the non-linear, iterative-recursive play with different possible resolutions that these suggest [is] useful in thinking about abductive inquiry" (2011, 28).

The ethnographer's "strangeness" plays an important role in abductive reasoning. It can help her to "see as explicitly as possible what for situated knowers is taken-for-granted, common sense, and tacitly known," but at the same time, "approximating ever more closely the 'familiarity' with which situated knowers navigate their physical and cognitive settings is important for generating understanding of what is puzzling only to a stranger" (Schwartz-Shea and Yanow 2012, 29).

In my own field research, I often found material objects useful in this process of refinement and reconsideration. Two items, in particular, stand out in this regard. One was a cocktail napkin on which an interlocutor had drawn a rough sketch of a discursive dynamic of particular interest to me. He was trying to explain the effects produced by the widespread circulation of idioms of *takfir*, or what I take as the allegations of apostasy that contribute to a broad "excommunicative discourse."

While he introduced this idea to me and it informed my work on the relationship between language, authority, and power, I did not simply take this as evidence of an existing theory, nor did I use it as inductive observational material with which to shape a testable theory of my own (where either of these would have a role to play in more positivist qualitative research). Instead, I took the napkin with me and asked others to reflect on it, to revise it in ways that made sense to them. Some simply said, "Yes, this is right." Others said, "No, this is not at all how things work," and by far the majority drew sketches of their own to supplement it. This very literal mapping became an important part of my own conceptual mapping of the practice of *takfir* and its operation in a specific social and political context (Yadav 2013).

Another material object that proved useful was a short, photocopied text on *takfir* and the assassination of Jarallah ʻOmar (a prominent socialist figure), stapled together with a copy-shop cover and bearing the logo of the Islamist Islah Party on its back page. The author was a well-known Islahi journalist who published a regular column in the party's official paper, *al-Sahwa*. My first impression was that the text was a sanctioned product of the Islah Party, and could be used to introduce substantive discussions of the politics of *takfir* (allegations of apostasy) as levied against fellow Islahis and directed toward their alliance partners, much as the napkin sketch had been. As I brought it with me to khat chews and interviews, however, what developed was a wide-ranging debate on notions of authority and representation. Some party leaders denied sanctioning the text and characterized it as private speech, while others contended that they could not distance themselves from the effects of *takfir* issued by known party members. I would ultimately be able to see in this echoes of arguments advanced by Pierre Bourdieu about the relationship between "authorized speech" and "legitimate language," but might well have remained inattentive to these dynamics without the unanticipated discussions this item (in its form, not its content) provoked.

In both cases, observing how others reacted to and interacted with these material objects helped to refine my thinking in ways consistent with abductive reasoning. In the dominant positivist traditions, modifications of my initial understandings and expectations would require that I go out and "test" a newly refined hypothesis on "new data." Abductive reasoning does not require this, and in fact requires returning to "old data" in light of these new insights and re-evaluating earlier interpretations. The nonlinear recursivity of abductive reasoning is particularly consistent with ethnographic research as an enterprise, where learning is constant, comparatively unstructured, and often unanticipated.

Ethical Considerations

This volume contains an excellent chapter on fieldwork ethics, so my aim in this closing discussion is to consider ethical questions that are perhaps specific to (or more acute in light of) ethnographic work. In each of the illustrations from my own fieldwork, I responded imperfectly, and while I learned from my mistakes, I undoubtedly passed some of the burden of those mistakes onto others.

Consent, Purpose, and Agency

When a researcher has secured informed consent—when one is "on the record" in an explicit way—the path seems clear and unambiguous. And yet. During the first year of my field research in Yemen, I interviewed—and became quite close to—a number of journalists active in political opposition to the regime of then-president 'Ali 'Abdullah Saleh. Observing their formal exchanges (at events sponsored by the Journalists' Syndicate, and in the pages of their papers) and their informal exchanges (at khat chews, or chatting in the car as we drove to an event) was essential in shaping my own understanding of the quotidian ways in which alliances are forged and sustained through networks between partisan and postpartisan actors (Yadav 2011).

Seeing many of these individuals take real risks and pay personal and professional costs for their opposition was powerful. When I left Yemen and returned to Cairo (where I was living permanently between fieldwork trips), I talked about their courage with some friends who worked in the Egyptian media, and one offered to run an article on the subject in his English-language magazine, thinking it might provide a good way to talk about press freedom in Egypt without talking about press freedom *in* Egypt. This appealed to my own political sensibilities and, I imagined, was fully consistent with the work that these committed Yemenis were undertaking. So I wrote the article and published it, though for reasons that will be clear, I will not cite it here.

The subject of the article related to the role of *takfir* in provoking self-censorship among Yemeni journalists and within the opposition political alliance that was then emerging in Sana'a, a subject to which I would later devote considerable attention in my academic writing. But as a partial consequence of the unanticipated translation and circulation of this article in a local Yemeni paper, one of my central interlocutors was himself subjected to allegations of apostasy. The article contained a number of provocative statements attributed to him—all statements made on the record and with consent, mind you—but his consent was given in the context of a student's dissertation research. I knew I had been well intentioned, and I knew I "had consent" in a formal sense, but I am not convinced that I behaved ethically.

Friendship

This incident also relates to another of the ethical challenges of ethnographic field research: friendship. The work of participant observation is that one spends a considerable amount of one's time engaged in the "everyday" in a way that somewhat naturally leads to the development of bonds of friendship. The interlocutor who faced *takfir* as a consequence of my article, for example, was someone whom I had come to consider a genuine friend, and perhaps the blurring of this boundary contributed to what I regard retrospectively as an ethical failing.

Yet friendship in the field—and after—can have sustaining effects, as well. There is a developed literature on "friendship as method," growing out of feminist and interpretive traditions and tied to participant-action research. This latter approach, PAR, is premised on "a dialogue model, where the subject-object relationship of positivism becomes a subject-subject one," and the validity of its claims is evaluated according to the extent that it "empowers those researched" (Tillman-Healy 2003, 733).

I became very seriously ill during one stint of fieldwork in Yemen, and was unable to leave my house for several weeks. This could easily have undermined my capacity to carry out research, but interlocutors with whom I had developed friendships organized the temporary relocation of some regular khat chews to my home. This generous offer raised a practical challenge: how to address the fact that I, as a married woman living apart from her husband, was sharing a house with a fellow (male) researcher. While friends and interlocutors knew that my housemate and I frequently attended chews together and they seemed happy to know that he escorted me as I moved around the city, I worried that this would be a bridge too far and would undermine my standing, particularly in Islamist circles. In this regard, the bonds of friendship that I had developed over the course of almost two years served me well. The only comment that anyone made as we sat in our *mafraj* and chewed together was that the house was nicely organized by floors, with separate spaces for each of us. *Alhamdilallah.*[5]

Friendship has also enriched my research since leaving Yemen. Colleagues have visited me in Cairo and, later, in New York, and we have met up at workshops and events in London, Istanbul, and Amman. The quickness with which one can "catch up" on key developments is enhanced when bonds of trust are pre-established, and my friends have also been eager to introduce me to others whom they know will be able to speak to research interests that are, by now, familiar to them. The ongoing war in Yemen has made some of these friendships more painful, offering first-hand accounts of the very real costs of the war but few opportunities for action. This is among the costs of entanglement addressed by Owton and Allen-Collinson (2014). Because of the fundamentally intersubjective coproduction of knowledge that characterizes ethnographic work, however, this seems inescapable, and if our bonds of friendship remind of us of the human costs of war, it is hard to imagine that we are worse scholars for it.

A Public Hearing: An Ethic Opportunity

It can be a standard practice for anthropologists to present their research publicly in the communities in which they live and work; this kind of "public hearing" rests on the notion that ethnographic research ought to produce accounts that are at the very least "recognizable" to the communities they represent. Compelled by this logic, I worked with the American Institute of Yemeni Studies (AIYS) to organize a public symposium on my research on *takfir*, in particular, as it was the least conventional aspect of my research and the area where I was most eager to cross-check my interpretations with the people whose experiences I was describing. We drew up an invitation list composed of partisan and associational sector activists, journalists, and some government officials, and booked a hall at a local hotel, since there were concerns that some invitees might decline if it were held at the Institute itself. The event never came to fruition, after the US embassy requested its cancellation for security reasons. As a recipient of grant funds administered by AIYS, governed itself by the rules of the congressionally funded Council of American Overseas Research Centers, I was obligated to comply.

Instead, we organized a far more intimate affair at the AIYS facility, for a group of Yemeni academics and a few others I suspected would be willing to attend. While this audience differed substantially in its composition from the original group of attendees, I nonetheless benefited tremendously from the presentation and critical discussion of my work in this forum. In addition to the practical benefit, however, there is the ethical advantage of recognizing one's interlocutors as coparticipants in the creation of knowledge (Schwartz-Shea and Yanow 2012, 79). To the extent possible, political scientists who engage in ethnographic research ought to consider adopting not only the note-taking or mapmaking strategies associated with ethnography, but its novel ethical practices, as well.

Conclusion: Ethnography in the Age of DA-RT

The current debate among leading journals and professional associations in political science regarding data transparency and research openness (or DA-RT) promises to disincentivize and further marginalize ethnographic work, not because ethnographers oppose the notion of transparency and openness, but because the concepts will have different meanings and different techniques for scholars working in rival traditions (Elman and Kapiszewski 2014).

Qualitative researchers generally, even those whose work is firmly positivist in orientation, have long faced public criticism of their presumed opaqueness, as with the "replication debate" in the mid-1990s (King 1995; Bates 1996). As one scholar quipped in response, anyone wanting to assess a qualitative scholar's claims should "read my footnotes" (Lustick 1996, 6). This concern with transparency has continued to dog qualitative researchers, as ever-more-technical solutions to the "problem" have been developed (Moravcsik 2009). The current DA-RT movement, however, poses an even more distinctive challenge for ethnographers, who participate in the "cogeneration" of data in ways that may be particularly difficult to fit within the dictates of a program built on different epistemological assumptions and commitments.

Advocates of DA-RT define "research transparency" as "a disciplinary norm whereby scholars publicize the process by which they generate empirical data and analysis" (Moravcsik 2015). As Schwartz-Shea and Yanow argue in their supremely useful guide to successfully navigating Institutional Review Boards, fellowship committees, and potential reviewers, it is incumbent upon interpretivists (and, by extension, ethnographers) to learn how to speak about the work they do in a way that is intelligible across epistemological boundaries, yet also true to a scholar's commitments (Schwartz-Shea and Yanow 2012, 136–137). In the current disciplinary context, establishing the social scientific character and value of ethnographic research in political science will remain on those who choose to adopt the practice. Seeking out rigorous interdisciplinary training and drawing upon postpositivist allies within our own field will make such work easier and expand the promise of ethnography's contribution to our discipline.

15

Coding in Qualitative Research

MOHAMMAD YAGHI

The purpose of coding in qualitative research is to support arguments or reveal concepts that are considered to be the building blocks of a theory (Flick 2009). Unlike quantitative methods, according to which coding takes place prior to conducting research, in qualitative methods, the process of coding begins after acquiring the first supporting document, be it an interview, a text, or audiovisual material. In qualitative methods, researchers normally keep refining their codes until the research is saturated, that is until nothing new is generated from collecting more data (O'Reilly and Parker 2012; Guest, Bunce, and Johnson 2006). Many scholars have explained coding methods (Strauss 1987; Charmaz 2006; Glaser 1978; Strauss and Corbin 1990). Accordingly, this chapter has no intention of summarizing these methods; rather it uses the research I have conducted on the protests of 2011 in Tunisia, Egypt, and Jordan to discuss the mistakes I made and the difficulties I encountered in the process of coding qualitative data. I will then suggest how to overcome them. The mistakes were the lack of preparation; the issue of categorization; the question of consistency; and the question of saturation and code refining. After elaborating on them and how I dealt with them, I conclude with lessons learned during my fieldwork that might be helpful to other researchers.

Coding in My Research

My dissertation, entitled "The Structure of Mobilization and Democratization: Youth Activism in Tunisia, Egypt, and Jordan," aimed to answer the following question: under which conditions does youth activism lead to democratization? In order to answer it, I advanced an argument that links what I call the "structure of mobilization" (SOM) with the protests' outcome (democratization or continuation of authoritarianism). The SOM is a concept that describes three variables: the type of the youth movement (YM) that led the protests (autonomous/nonautonomous);

the kind of collective action frames used in the protests (inclusive or exclusive);[1] and the form of the protests' leadership (decentralized/centralized). My assumption was that in the countries where protests succeeded and moved toward democratization (Tunisia and Egypt before the military coup of July 3, 2013), the protests were dominated by autonomous YMs, had an inclusive master frame, and were led by a decentralized leadership; the opposite was the case for one or all of the variables in Jordan.

In my dissertation proposal, I conceptualized the independent variables as follows: autonomous YMs are those youth movements that are independent and/or are the youth branches of political parties that do not participate in elections conducted by authoritarian regimes. I defined an inclusive master frame as one that holds a pluralist ideology, represents the interests of a diverse and wide range of aggrieved social groups, and transcends any identity-related divisions within the country. This criterion was of particular importance to my research, as Tunisia, Egypt, and Jordan are all countries divided along several interrelated identity lines. In addition to the traditional rifts between liberal and religious groups, Tunisia has had regional identity divisions between the people of the interior and coastal regions since independence (Jebnoun 2013), Jordan suffers from a national identity split between Transjordanians and Jordanians of Palestinian origin (Massad 2013), and Egypt historically has had a religious identity division between Muslims and the Copts—the Egyptian Christian community (Iskander 2012).[2] Finally, I defined decentralized leadership as one that involves no umbrella or collective leadership. In this situation, each YM acts independently throughout the protests without any unifying coordinating body.

In order to determine the variation in the protests according to each of the independent variables, I had to code my qualitative data consistently. In the methods section of my dissertation proposal, I defined three sources of data that would inform my research: a representative sample of the YMs with which I planned to conduct a qualitative survey of the activists; documents published by the YMs during the protests; and the protesters' slogans.

Lack of Preparation

The fact that data inform research does not mean that a researcher should approach fieldwork without a plan of how the data should be interpreted. Usually, this plan comes from reading scholarly work on the case study and from gathering data about the research question. Failure to do so may result, among other things, in depriving the researcher of good opportunities to consolidate empirical evidence that supports the arguments of the research. Let me explain this idea through an example from my own research.

In order to show that the master frames of the protests in Tunisia and Egypt were inclusive and that the master frame of Jordan's protests was exclusive, I conducted the survey shown in Table 15.1 in the three countries.

These questions were aimed at revealing whether the master frame transcended identity divisions by drawing on a collective memory (Q2) or a common culture (Q3) in Tunisia, Egypt, and Jordan. In my preparation for interpreting the data, I assumed the following codes: A yes answer to the first question, especially if the symbols and slogans used are divisive, would be considered an indication of the master frame's exclusivity even if the answers were yes to the second and third questions. I basically determined that a yes answer to the first question trumped the potentially contradictory yes answers from the remaining two questions. A no answer to the first question, coupled with an answer of yes to the second and third questions, would be considered indicative of an inclusive master frame. Of course, there was the possibility that I would get an answer of no for the first question and no for the two other questions or to one of them. I planned to interpret this as indicative of an inclusive master frame, as the first question was what mattered more to the argument of whether the master frame transcended the identity division of the protesters.

The answers I received are summarized in Table 15.2

To my surprise, the examples the Egyptian activists provided for question 3 regarding national unity slogans could be further subdivided along two lines: patriotic slogans that focused on the love of Egypt as a homeland; and cross-identity slogans that praised the relationship between Muslims and Copts.

Table 15.1 **Master Frame Inclusive/Exclusive Survey**

Q1	In the protests, did any youth group use its own factional symbols and slogans? If the answer is yes, what were these symbols and slogans?
Q2	Were any of the slogans used in the protests drawn from past protests? If yes, what were these slogans?
Q3	Were any national unity slogans used in the protests? If yes, what were these slogans?

These questions are drawn from a larger survey that also focuses on the reasons of protests.

Table 15.2 **Respondents' Answers of the Survey on Master Frame**

	Q1	Q2	Q3
Tunisia	No	Yes	Yes
Egypt	No	Yes	Yes
Jordan	Yes	No	Yes

An example of patriotism slogans:

S1: All of you say ... Egypt will remain precious for us
(*Qwlwā wrdwā 'inta wā hiyya ... Misr hatifdal ghalīa^2 'līā*).

An example of cross-identity slogans:

S2: Hey Mohammad, hey Boulus ... tomorrow Egypt follows Tunis
(*Yā muḥmad yā bwlus ... bukra Misr tḥsil twnis*).

Because the Copts in Egypt are subjected to a wide range of societal and state discrimination, chanting slogans embracing equal citizenship is a greater proof that Egypt's master frame transcended the country's identity division than provided by those of the patriotic type. I found it especially convincing when the activists chanting cross-identity slogans also responded that they had not raised any factional flags or chanted factional slogans during the protests. Yet, because Egypt was the last of the three countries in which I conducted my fieldwork, I was not able to benefit from my realization that national identity slogans could be further subcategorized into two types (patriotic and cross-identity) in the cases of Tunisia and Jordan. Had I done my homework before going to the field, I would have included the following question in my survey: "Were there slogans that praised the unity of people of different faiths and origins during the protests?" Although I worked around this problem by examining the videos of the protests in Jordan and Tunisia, the inclusion of this question in the survey would have allowed me to triangulate my findings by providing data from both the activists and the videos of the protests.

The Problem of Categorization

The logic behind coding qualitative data is to turn a significant amount of information into categories that can be used to explain a phenomenon, reveal a concept, or to render the data comparable across different case studies. The level of difficulty of categorization depends both on the purpose of coding and on the type of data. The categorization of data, for example, to advance a theoretical concept is more challenging than the categorization of the same data for reasons of comparability. The former involves more abstraction than the latter. Similarly, categorizing a piece of information that can be interpreted in the same way by different researchers as a result of the clarity of its meaning is easier than categorizing data that carries different meanings. I will explain this by giving two examples from my research.

Example 1

In order to study the master frame's inclusivity, namely whether the master frame was pluralist and representative of diverse social groups' interests, I first had to reconstruct the master frame for each of three uprisings. To do so, I decided to rely on the documents of the YMs and on the open-ended interviews that I planned on conducting with the activists. To make sure that the data would be accurate and representative, I included the following question in the qualitative survey: What were the reasons for the protests?

The documents of the protesting groups, the interviews with the activists, and the responses from the qualitative survey showed that there were many reasons for the protests. The qualitative survey alone revealed 21 reasons. They included the suppression of freedom; high rates of unemployment; peasants' debts to banks; the prioritization of members of the ruling party in employment; and the president's family's abuse of power. With this many reasons, the challenge was how to group them into a few independent categories that would succinctly reflect the master frame of the respective protests. One could argue, for example, that all the above-mentioned reasons reflect one category, namely, the degradation of human dignity. While this is true, it is still possible to categorize these reasons into a few distinct categories by posing questions related to each reason. Take, for example, "prioritization of members of the ruling party in employment" as one of the reasons for protests. Now if we ask few questions, such as what this reason means for Tunisians (or Egyptians or Jordanians), who was involved in choosing the employees, and what the implications of this act, it becomes clear that respondents are in fact referring to state corruption. By asking myself these questions, I was able to group the reasons for the protests into three main distinct categories: poverty, corruption, and repression.

Categorization in this case was easy because each piece of information fits into one categorical theme. In other words, if a second researcher wants to replicate my work, he or she will interpret the data in the same way. This, however, might not be the case when the data can be interpreted in different ways. The following example illustrates the level of difficulty involved in some categorization.

Example 2

During the course of my research, I observed that the activists in Tunisia relied in part on incitement— fiery speeches, slogans, and statements that carry almost no demands but simply call for the population to stand against the regime—to spread the protests. With this observation in mind, I categorized the activists' slogans for two purposes: the first was to show that the motivational slogans were based on incitement rather than on political and social demands, and the second was to illustrate the ways in which the activists managed, through incitement, to mobilize Tunisians.

To perform the first task, I isolated the slogans that contained political and social demands. There were in total 39 of them out of a representative sample of 142 slogans. The remaining 103 slogans were motivational; since they did not carry political and social demands, but calls to join protests against the regime, I considered them incitement slogans. In doing so, I showed that incitement slogans occupied an important portion of the activists' strategy to mobilize Tunisians.

For the second goal, showing the impact of these incitement slogans on Tunisians, I had two choices. The first was simply to avoid categorizing these slogans and to make a general argument about them. However, if I did so, I wouldn't be able to say much about how the slogans affected Tunisians. The second was to categorize them and to study the effect of each category on Tunisians. As with the previous example, by asking certain questions about each slogan (for example, its purpose, for whom it was intended, why the name of a city was included in some slogans but not others, and the meaning of the slogan), I was able to delineate four categories.

- Emotional slogans: intended to attract bystanders to join the protests in the name of solidarity and to demobilize the riot police in the name of brotherhood.
- Patriotic slogans: intended to energize individual participants with enthusiasm and confidence of their cause; they constituted a claim on the part of the activists that they love their country and a demand to bystanders to take the moral high ground by joining the protests.
- Anticorruption slogans: they accused the regime—mainly the president's family—of abusing the state's institution for personal gains.
- Regional slogans: similar to the patriotic slogans but referring to a specific region (governorate). Using the name of a specific region (governorate), these slogans intended to restore the collective memory of the people in the specific region regarding the past struggle against French colonization. In other words, the slogans' goal was to equate the regime with French occupation in order to mobilize Tunisians in those regions against it.

Table 15.3 shows an example of each of these four categories of slogan.

While these categories are not perfect and the degree of separation between them is not very clear, they still allowed me to make the argument that the activists spoke to Tunisian emotions, patriotism, and hatred of corruption, and even used regional patriotism to bring people to the streets against Ben Ali.

The preceding discussion suggests that the level of difficulty in categorization is related to the purpose of coding the data. Categorizing the data for the sake of making the argument that motivational slogans were based on inciting Tunisians against the regime is much easier than categorizing them for the purpose of explaining how the motivational slogans attracted more participants to join the uprising. Furthermore,

Table 15.3 **Examples of Coding Incitement Slogans**

Type of incitement slogans	N	Examples
Emotion	56	Hey citizen walk with us ... your silence is treason.
Patriotism	24	There is no fear ... there is no fear ... after Tunis there is no fear
Regionalism	9	Ben Ali ... hey coward ... the men of Kef will not be humiliated.
Anticorruption	14	No, no, to Trabelsi, who looted the state's budget
Total	103	

the example implies that researchers might code and categorize the slogans in dissimilar ways, as the meaning attached to them can be interpreted differently. Replicating the study in this case depends on using the same definitions for the categories of emotion, patriotism, regionalism, and anticorruption.

Inconsistency

Coding qualitative surveys is much easier than coding a text or a slogan. This is because the uniformity of questions in a qualitative survey enforces relative consistency across the collected data. Coding texts and slogans is more difficult because each sentence in a text or a slogan might carry different meaning. Inconsistency in the criteria by which the data are interpreted may result in wrong conclusions vis-à-vis the research question. An example from my work illustrates better this idea.

One of the claims that I made in my dissertation was that, unlike Jordan, where the activists focused on political reforms from the beginning, the activists in Tunisia and Egypt prioritized social demands before the protests reached their respective peaks.[3] It was only after the protests peaked that the activists called for the fall of the two regimes. My argument required two tasks: first, determining the peak of the protest in each country; and second, providing evidence regarding the sequencing mentioned above. Determining the peak of protests is related to the type of protest activities, the societal and geographical spread of the protests, and the number of victims in them. I used the archive of local newspapers, reports of human rights organizations, and official documents in order to determine the protests' peak.

For the second task, showing the sequence of the activists' demands, the data had to be interpreted consistently according to specific criteria. This required a clear definition of what constituted political and social demands. At the same time, the definition had to be flexible enough to account for the different ways the participant movements in the protests expressed these demands. For coding the data according to social and political demands, I defined the former as any statement or slogan that sought social change, including demands for measures to fight unemployment, the reduction of prices, legal changes, and fighting or condemning corruption. I defined the latter as any statement and slogan that sought changes in the state's political institutions, such as changing the political regime, the government, or the parliament, or proposing new laws related to political freedoms.

The flaws in these definitions could not be seen immediately; only through the process of trial and error did I perceive them. Once this happened, I had to readjust the definitions and to reinterpret the data according to new definitions. Again, when their meaning is clear and meets the stated definition, the interpretation (coding) of slogans and statements is very easy; but not all statements and slogans conformed to the definitions stated earlier. Examples 1 and 2 from the protests of Tunisia and Jordan respectively demonstrate this problem.

> *Example 1: A clear summary statement from the Tunisian protests focusing on social demands:*
>> Hamma Hammami, the Communist Workers' Party's (PCOT) secretary general, accused the regime of sending the police to Sidi Bouzid "to suppress the people as it had done in the Mine Basin of Qafsa and Ben Gardane," arguing that the proposal for creating new jobs is "déjà vu propaganda." Hammami challenged the regime to offer "a monthly financial grant and social subsidies to the unemployed"; "a decrease in the retirement age" in order to create working places for the youth; and "the building of new schools" to create new jobs (Hammami 2010).
>
> *Example 2: Clear slogans from the Jordanian protests that focus on political demands:*
>> • The people want an elected government (*3sha'b yuryd ḥukwmh muntakhabah*).
>> • The people want to dissolve the parliament (*3sha'b yuryd ḥal 3barlaman*).

In examples 1 and 2, the definition of what constitutes a social or political demand works perfectly. Thus coding the data in the political or social categories was easy and could be replicated for validation. In other cases, the statements and slogans did not conform to the stated definition without modification. Consider examples 3 and 4 from Jordan and Tunisia.

Example 3: A Summary Statement from Jordan

The statement of the Higher Committee for the Coordination of National Opposition Parties (HCCNOP) on January 16, 2011, attributes the social problems Jordanians face—poverty, unemployment, price increases, erosion of wages, and a diminishing middle class—to the Wadi Araba Peace Agreement with Israel, the privatization of the public sector in accordance with World Bank conditions, the exclusion of Jordan political forces from decision-making, the lack of any process of political reform in which changing "the election law is considered it is entrance and leverage," and rampant corruption and state tyranny. The HCCNOP then offers an "alternative national program" to overcome the crisis. The first four points of that program are political: a democratic election law based on proportional represen- tation; a new election for parliament; the right of parties holding a parliamentarian majority to form the government; and government's acceptance of opposition and civil society forces as partners in the process of decision-making. However, the following four points are related to social demands and include establishing a min- istry of supply, implementing a progressive taxation system, restoring the public sector, and fighting corruption. Furthermore, the last three demands were related to Jordan's foreign policy (HCCNOP 2011).

Example 4: Slogans from the protests in Tunisia:
- Work, freedom, national dignity (*'amal, ḥuriyya, karāmah wataniyyh*)
- Bread and water … But no to Ben Ali (*Khubz wa mā᾽ … Bin 'ly lā*)

How should the above-mentioned statement and slogans be coded? In both examples there were both social and political demands. To remind the reader, my goal was to support the argument that the activists in Tunisia focused on the so- cial demands prior to the peak of the protests, while in Jordan, the focus began as political. To account for this unforeseen problem, I adjusted the definition for the social and political demands to include the word "prioritize." Thus I considered statements and slogans as political or social depending on how the statement or slogan prioritized the demands. Prioritization implies both ordering and meaning. In the above statement by the HCCNOP in Jordan, the list of demands began with political ones and then moved on to social ones. Hence, I coded the statement as prioritizing political demands. In the case of the slogans above, I coded the first slogan as social as it began with a demand for "work." Despite the fact that the second slogan began with "bread and water," I coded it as political based on its meaning—the Tunisians wanted the departure of Ben Ali and were ready to live on bread and water until he left. Once I modified the definitions for political and so- cial demands, I revised the coding of slogans and statements to ensure consistency across data in the three countries.

Of course consistency in coding is not the only problem here. A researcher must also make sure that the data are not selectively chosen to support an argu- ment. Although this problem might seem only tangential to coding, it is vital in qualitative research in order to make sure the findings are conclusive. For the ar- gument I presented above about the social and political demands, I included all the statements issued by the YMs before and after the protests' peaks. As for the protest slogans in Tunisia and Jordan, I confronted two types of problems: how to verify that the protests occurred prior to the protests' respective peaks and how to claim that my sample of protests was inclusive and representative. In the case of Tunisia, I solved the problem by including all the videos found on the two main websites covering the protests, the activists claimed they relied on for information during the protests.[4] The two websites were comprehensive in that they included videos and the dates they were uploaded. In the case of Jordan, I first used the archive of the Jordanian *Aldustour* newspaper[5] to determine when and where the protests happened. Then, I used the search engine on YouTube to locate the videos of the protests. While this method is not perfect, as some protests might not have been recorded and uploaded on YouTube, the method still ensured a high degree of reliability.

Saturation and Code Refining

In qualitative surveys, the assumption is that a researcher poses the same questions in the same order to a number of interviewees. In answering the research question, the researcher codes the interviewees' answers, categorizes them, and compares the answers of several respondents. Accordingly, I assumed that analyzing the data would make more sense if I first conducted a couple dozen of surveys before embarking on analyzing them. This proved to be wrong for two reasons.

First, a researcher will never know how many interviews she will need to conduct until the research is saturated, that is to say, before the researcher knows that any additional interviews will add nothing to the research. Information regarding the number of interviews needed for the research to be saturated can only be obtained if the researcher starts the process of coding data immediately. Let me illustrate this point with an example from my research in Jordan.

To understand why the protests failed in Jordan, I conducted 83 interviews with the activists of both the traditional and the newly emergent opposition over a period of three months. It was clear to me that the new opposition had a Transjordanian social base, while the traditional one was concentrated among the Jordanians of Palestinian origin. Thinking about this after I had completed my research, I wondered whether I needed as many as 83 interviews. Would 50 or 60 interviews have been sufficient? In retrospect, the answer is definitely yes because many interviewers provided the same data. The mistake I committed was related to the fact that I postponed interpreting the data until I had already conducted a substantial portion of the interviews I planned to do. But once I embarked on analyzing the interviews, it was clear that many of them had not been necessary. This was especially true for the interviews with the leaders of the same political party or faction; they just repeated the same information.

Second, analyzing the data immediately gives the researcher the opportunity to modify the qualitative survey by adding, removing, or refining questions to better serve the objectives of the research. While this may result in discarding the first few surveys, the overall outcome of the survey becomes more solid. The example below illustrates this idea.

In my attempt to prove that protests in Tunisia and Egypt had decentralized leaderships, while the one in Jordan had a centralized one, I included the following questions in my survey:

Q1: What were the goals of the protests? (Asked in all three countries.)
Q2: Was there an agreement on who should rule Tunisia? If the answer is "no," why was that?
Q3: When did an agreement between the activists regarding the ousting of the regime in Tunisia appear?
Q4: Was there an agreement on who should rule Egypt? If the answer is "no," why was that?
Q5: When did an agreement between the activists on ousting the regime in Egypt appear?
Q6: Was there an agreement on the type of reforms the activists sought to achieve in Jordan? If the answer is "no," why was that?

While the first five questions for the cases of Tunisia and Egypt provided valuable information that I used to support my argument that the protests had a decentralized leadership, questions 1 and 6 provided me with no help in proving that the protests in Jordan had a centralized leadership. In fact, they had a centralized leadership only for a very short period—during the protests' peak. Had I analyzed the surveys immediately in Jordan, I would have discovered the significance and impact of the March 25, 2011, sit-in on the activists, and, consequently, I would have included questions focusing on this event in my survey. The sit-in of March 25, 2011, was the result of a coordinated agreement between Jordan's activists; it had a centralized leadership. While I used other data, such as the YMs' statements and the open-ended interviews, to support my argument that the leadership was centralized during the peak of Jordan's protests, I could have consolidated my findings far more easily had I had the results from survey questions that focused on the sit-in.

Lessons from Fieldwork

Besides the importance of preparation before starting fieldwork, the need for consistency of coding, and the attention that should be paid to the problems of categorization and saturation, a researcher must keep in mind that every research project has its unique problems in terms of coding. In retrospect, I find the following guidelines very helpful for researchers who need to code their qualitative data and conduct their fieldwork for the first time.

First, be flexible, and open to the process of trial and error. Because coding qualitative data requires both consistency and continuous refining, the researcher must be aware that she might have to recode the data more than once before moving to the final results. This trial-and-error process is normal and should be perceived as part of the coding process. Second, confront your data with questions. The true meaning of data is not always apparent because it is embedded in a text, slogan, or a speech that sometimes uses metaphoric expressions or stresses cultural issues that render interpreting the data difficult. Only by confronting the data with questions can their true meaning be revealed.

Third, do not rush your qualitative surveys. Use your first few interviews to adjust your qualitative surveys to better serve your research question before conducting them. This requires conducting the first few interviews for the sake of gathering information related to your research, but this will put you in a better position to run a qualitative survey that better serves your end goals.

Quantitative Research in MENA Political Science

MIQUEL PELLICER AND EVA WEGNER

In a survey of articles in top-ranked journals in political science from 2010 to 2014, Pellicer, Wegner, and Cavatorta (2015) find that there is still very little MENA research using quantitative data and techniques. While all these journals publish almost exclusively quantitative research, the share of research on the MENA region in such journals ranges from 0% to about 8%. In spite of this, a longer-term perspective paints a more nuanced picture. Fifteen years ago, there was hardly any political science research on the MENA using quantitative data and methods; since then, the share of MENA scholars using quantitative methods has increased, ostensibly forming what is now an exciting field with an active and innovative community.

This chapter looks at recent developments and challenges in the use of quantitative data and methods in MENA research. There has been a substantial increase in the generation and use of a variety of quantitative data, including individual-level surveys (such as the Arab Barometer series and the World Values Survey) and administrative data such as censuses and electoral data. In addition, MENA research is also experiencing an increase in the use of more recent techniques, in particular automated text analysis, allowing researchers to process large numbers of written documents, or survey experiments allowing to address causal relations.[1] The use of quantitative techniques has allowed researchers to challenge preconceived notions about the Middle East, to question assumptions based on qualitative research on elites, and to connect with a much wider political science literature. All these developments are certainly scientifically beneficial and even, sometimes, politically relevant.

At the same time, applying quantitative methods comes with a number of challenges. A first point concerns the problems of data quality and access, often resulting from the authoritarian setting in most MENA countries. Repression has a bearing on how freely respondents answer questions and on how freely available administrative data are. Another point concerns the often lengthy and cumbersome processing of data and the high level of effort and resources required to apply some of these methods. A recurrent theme in the chapter's discussion of different methods is the importance of context knowledge, crucial to develop meaningful questions, work around some of the data's limitations, and interpret results from quantitative research in a meaningful way.

The chapter is organized by data type, discussing the core intuition, findings, and challenges of using opinion surveys, administrative data, automated text analysis, and survey experiments. It concludes with an outlook on the future of quantitative research in the MENA.

Opinion Surveys

The number of MENA countries covered by different *international opinion surveys* has increased dramatically since the early 2000s. The earliest surveys were undertaken within the World Values Survey (WVS) series in the early 2000s, covering Morocco, Egypt, Jordan, Algeria, Iraq, and Saudi Arabia. In the mid-2000s, the MENA region was also included in the Barometer series with a specific "Arab" Barometer, established by scholars in the Arab world and the United States. Since the early 2010s, the "Afro" Barometer additionally covered North African countries.[2] In some countries, namely Egypt, Morocco, Algeria, Jordan, and Iraq, therefore, five or more opinion surveys are currently available over the different years as well as a relatively large "Arab Spring" data set from the different surveys undertaken in the early 2010s.

These opinion surveys focus on different types of attitudes. The WVS looks at a large battery of sociopolitical values, such as attitudes toward democracy, child-rearing, gender, economic redistribution, and the like. The Barometer series, while sharing a number of survey items with the WVS, generally looks at respondents' judgment of the status quo, such as satisfaction with government and political institutions, electoral fairness, or the level of democracy.

Opinion surveys have allowed addressing many important questions where hitherto only limited or anecdotal evidence was available and have served as an important corrective of how findings from qualitative research have often been generalized to the larger population.

The earliest topic addressed via opinion surveys in the MENA is the values and attitudes of citizens in Arab countries relating to democracy (Jamal 2006; Jamal and Tessler 2008; Tessler 2002; Tessler and Gao 2005; Tessler and Jamal 2006; Tessler, Jamal, and Robbins 2012). This research clearly demonstrates that Islam and democracy (or Muslims and favorable democratic attitudes) are not incompatible. Although this might not seem such as surprising finding, it is an important one, given the long-standing debate on this issue, essentially dating back to the Iranian revolution. Until the advent of opinion surveys in MENA countries, evidence presented in this debate was either based on exegesis of the Koran or on the discourses of Islamist thinkers (Wegner 2011). Given these types of sources, it was perhaps not surprising that many researchers had reservations about the compatibility of Islam and democracy, and therefore, it was important to contrast this interpretation with opinions of ordinary citizens in Muslim-majority countries.

Another important topic addressed with the use of opinion data is the profile of voters of Islamist parties. This concern partly stemmed from the same research question as before, namely whether voters of these parties would have particularly antidemocratic attitudes (Garcia-Rivero and Kotze 2007; Robbins 2010). Importantly, this research was able to challenge some established myths. For example, one important assumption about Islamist voters had been that they were poor, uneducated (and therefore easily manipulated by Islamist ideologues), and antidemocratic. As research based on opinion surveys shows, this is not the reality. In fact, Islamist voters are better educated and have more income than the average MENA citizen and have, moreover, more—not less—prodemocratic values (Wegner and Cavatorta 2016). This educated middle-class profile then turned out to be very similar to other activists and beneficiaries of Islamist social movement organizations (Clark 2004) and was a useful complement to the qualitative research.

The importance of these findings notwithstanding, opinion surveys come with a core challenge, namely assessing data quality. Even if it may appear self-evident, it is worth stressing that quantitative analyses can be only as good as the data that undergird them. A first concern regarding data quality is the representativeness of the sample used. All surveys undertaken as part of the WVS or Barometer series aim and claim to be representative. Whether they are or not, however, hinges very strongly on the professionalism and capacity of research centers or universities responsible for sampling, supervising, and implementing these surveys. The relevance of departures from full representativity depends on the question being analyzed. In general, the more descriptive the question, the more important it is that the data used are representative. From our experience, findings from the first surveys that were undertaken in the MENA should be taken with some caution. For example, the first Arab Barometer surveys did not have survey weights—a clear indication that these surveys cannot be truly representative.[3] As another example, the World Values Surveys for Morocco in 2001 and 2007 show dramatic and surprising changes in attitudes that call into question their representativeness. Between the first WVS carried out in the country in 2001 and the second in 2007, Moroccans appeared to have become much less gender conservative *and* much more favorable toward more religion in politics. The magnitude of these changes was truly enormous: in 2001 66% of Moroccans strongly agreed that university education was more important for a boy than for a girl and almost 80% opposed religious leaders' influence in voting decisions; in 2007, the respective figures were 16% and 20%, an unlikely social change in just six years. These types of results strongly suggest problems in the representativity of samples.

Another problem related to survey data quality in the MENA is that survey research in (semi)authoritarian regimes is difficult. It is plausible that respondents in such contexts might be reluctant to state their opinions openly regardless of assurances of anonymity. This applies especially to the Barometer surveys, which do not just probe "abstract" social, economic, or political attitudes but also ask about respondents' judgment of government performance or the extent of actual corruption and government's efforts to crack down on it.[4] Importantly, the bias in these answers is likely to be nonrandom, as some individuals—possibly the more educated or generally more risk averse—are likely to be more suspicious and reluctant to give information. In addition, one could imagine the bias to be more acute the more repressive a country is and the more sensitive an issue is in a particular country.

There are some relatively straightforward approaches to assess the representativeness and in turn the data quality of surveys. One is to compare regional-level basic demographic information from the survey (using the provided survey weights) to information from the census. If the surveys are indeed representative, they should display, subject to sampling error, regional population shares similar to the census (i.e., regions with a high number of inhabitants should have a correspondingly high share of respondents and vice versa), and also broadly similar figures for education and employment levels at the regional level. This approach requires the availability of census data, which is usually not a problem at this high level of aggregation. For example, assessing the data in this way for Morocco suggests that the latest wave of the Arab Barometer is quite accurate, whereas the latest World Values Survey (where only nine of the provinces were included in the survey) is indeed not.

Depending on the research question, there can be additional ways of assessing how much the data are able to say about the topic. For example, Wegner and Cavatorta (2016) use several opinion surveys to study the characteristics of Islamist and left-secular voters by assessing respondents who state that they would vote for a certain party if elections were held tomorrow. The concern here is that the respondents answering such questions might be particularly committed voters. We compare the shares in the survey expressing support for different parties with the share of eligible voters who voted for the respective parties in the latest election. In this case, we find that most recent surveys have a larger share of respondents who identify with parties than eligible voters actually voting for the parties, thus alleviating the concern that we analyze characteristics of a very ideological minority.

Finally, more in-depth context knowledge goes a long way in assessing whether the data make sense. For example, scholars who have studied—qualitatively—Islamist parties can make some reasonably good predictions about what the sensible findings would be about their voters in different countries. It would be certainly surprising to find that voters of the Moroccan PJD, by far the most "moderate" Islamist party in the MENA, are more gender conservative than voters of either the Islamic Action Front in Jordan or the (now outlawed) Freedom and Justice Party in Egypt. This could of course still be "true," but such a finding would require a much deeper check into data quality and robustness across surveys to be convincing. Context knowledge is thus not only required to interpret the findings, but can also be helpful in deciding which type of results require more careful cross-checks.

Administrative Data

The second type of data that has seen an important increase in usage in political science is *administrative data*. This includes population censuses, household surveys (such as labor force surveys), and electoral and government expenditure data. Population censuses, and at times household surveys, have become easily available for a number of countries, such as Egypt, Morocco, Palestine, and Tunisia. Electoral data at the district level are available for some countries, although the publication of these data is restricted to more open countries. Work using government expenditure data is still relatively rare given the restricted access to these data and the considerable efforts related to processing them.

Research into electoral behavior is an important topic addressed through administrative data. A number of studies have looked into MENA voter profiles by creating new data sets through merging electoral data with census data. By determining the socioeconomic characteristics of electoral districts and analyzing which party type is successful there, these studies have generated additional, country-specific insights into electoral behavior.[5]

Other studies making use of such merged data sets have looked into the impact of institutional rules on voting behavior (Buttorff 2015; Pellicer and Wegner 2013, 2014b). For example, Pellicer and Wegner (2013) exploit a quasi-natural experiment in Morocco to study how different voting rules affect support for clientelistic versus programmatic parties. Buttorff (2015) and Pellicer and Wegner (2014b) examine the effect of electoral rules in Jordan and Morocco respectively on the number of candidates and parties and are able to contribute to the broader literature on electoral institutions.

The two key challenges of this approach are data access and data processing. The only data that are quite easy to obtain are census data, although some countries do not publish even this type of data because the information on minorities or service delivery contained in such data is considered sensitive. Useful data sources for socioeconomic data are the Integrated Public Use Microdata Series (IPUMS) at the University of Minnesota, the World Bank, the Economic Research Forum in Cairo, as well as national statistical agencies, such as the HCP in Morocco and the National Institute of Statistics in Tunisia. In addition, a number of geocoded data, such as the freely available satellite data on night lights from the NASA, can be used to proxy for economic development.

Electoral data are less accessible and mostly available at relatively high levels of aggregation (i.e., the electoral district, which in most countries is quite large, there being around 90 in Morocco and around 50 in Egypt). In our own research, for instance, results from local elections in Morocco had to be scraped from an election website of the Ministry of Interior designed to consult results from municipalities one by one. We developed a Python script that automatically went over the different web pages, collecting and processing the relevant information of Morocco's 1,500 municipalities. In other words, obtaining such data might require some extra efforts that would not be necessary in non-MENA countries. Lastly, government expenditure data have proven in our own experience very difficult to obtain. In research that aimed to an-alyze whether Islamist local governments in Morocco were managing local finances differently than other parties, we tried to obtain information on budgets in selected municipalities (Pellicer and Wegner 2015). While this endeavor was successful in some municipalities, in others it stumbled upon political obstacles on the part of the regime administration. Given that except for Tunisia and Jordan, all MENA countries are ranked toward the bottom of the Open Budget Survey, an index that measures the transparency and availability of budget data, we assume that this problem affects most MENA countries. A potential approach to obtaining such data nevertheless, could be via connections to higher regime administration personnel, such as, for example, through well-connected local researchers or international organizations.

The second core challenge in the use of administrative data is the merging of different data sets. Often, a data set merging socioeconomic data with political data can yield particularly interesting insights from a political science perspective. In some cases, the type of political data used is electoral, but other straightforward applications include the use of protest data combined with socioeconomic infor-mation. A relevant problem that occurs in practice when putting data sets together is the multitude of possible spellings of the same name, arising from the various ways in which Arabic spelling can be rendered in Latin script. As an example, a town called al-Qaṣr al-Kabīr can appear as El-Ksar el-Kebir, Ksar Kbir, Ksar al-Kabir, Ksar El Kébir, or any combination of these spellings in different data sets. This requires great attention to detail as well as some basic knowledge of Arabic (and French in case of former French colonies), to decide whether two different town names actually indicate the same one. The main trade-off is then the level at which one conducts the analysis. On the one hand, at a higher level, for instance at the provin-cial level, assembling the data is quite quick, but interesting variation is lost, such as intratown differences between slums and middle-class neighborhoods. On the other hand, at a lower level, such variation can be explored, but assembling the data requires a considerable investment.

Automated Text Coding and Analyses

Recently, MENA studies have also started to engage in the use of automated text analysis. This method is very flexible and allows for digesting vast amounts of texts, such as, for example, Twitter communication, blogs, party platforms, and the complete writings of political thinkers, as long as they are brought into digitized form. In this method, software is "trained" to place documents along certain dimensions or scales. Nielsen (2014), for example, examines whether educational networks contribute to the radicalization of Muslim clerics. This project required the classification of more than 27,000 texts by 101 clerics. Applying a method of statistical machine learning, he was able to compare the frequencies of certain words (e.g., apostasy, jihad, infidel, mujahideen) to a jihadi corpus to calculate each cleric's "jihadi score." Combined with data on the clerics' careers and the number of teachers they had, he was able to generate new insights into how smaller networks correlate with a higher level of radicalization. Compared to qualitative research that can at best get into the writings and political thought of one or two clerics-thinkers, this is a major advantage, given the need to better understand discourse and political thought in the region beyond just a few key, albeit historically relevant, individuals such as Hassan al-Banna and Sayyed Qutb.

Another interesting application of this method is by Jamal et al. (2015), who analyze Arabic-language Twitter traffic between 2012 and 2013 to understand whether the nature of anti-Americanism in the MENA is "political" (i.e., against American policies) or "social" (i.e., against American values). They determine categories to identify whether the traffic was positive or negative, political or social, and analyze the shares of these categories over time and as a reaction to specific events. They find that the volume of traffic with negative comments about American policies is four times higher than traffic condemning American values; they also find a high incidence of negative traffic relating to Iran and conclude that, in fact, what is typically seen as anti-Americanism ought to be considered as anti-interventionism. Again, this finding and strong conclusion would not have been possible with qualitative work on such topic. Had the finding been based on qualitative work, the conclusions would have been vulnerable to criticism for being based on too little, and perhaps selective, data, probably even more so if one considers the political importance of the topic and level of politicization of the debate.

The clearest challenge of this method is the high level of investment in skills and processing. First, for nonnative speakers, it requires the rather unusual combination of mastery of Arabic and mathematical literacy required to understand the method. Second, it requires not only learning the method, but also the development of Arabic-language "dictionaries" for data processing; dictionaries that already exist for many topics are in English.

Survey Experiments

It is important to note that most of the methods discussed thus far are descriptive. Research using automated coding is a good example in this regard. While this type of approach generates vast amounts of data and can be used in statistical analyses, whether causal questions can be addressed with the information depends on whether these data are embedded in an experimental framework. Survey experiments, in contrast, can address causal questions and have recently started to emerge in MENA research. Survey experiments are standard surveys with an embedded experimental component.[6] The core aspect for survey experiments is that respondents are randomly assigned to these different treatment or control groups and that the difference in their attitudes can thus measure the *causal effect* of whatever treatment they received.

To date, topics such as foreign intervention in domestic politics and gender issues have been studied with this method. Bush and Jamal (2015) conducted a survey experiment in Jordan to study whether US endorsements of women's representation harms these type of reforms, considering the high level of anti-Americanism in the region, and whether in contrast imam endorsement helps (for another study about foreign meddling in Lebanon, see Marinov 2013). Although Jordanians have indeed negative views of the United States and positive views about imams, neither endorsement has an effect on support for gender equality reforms. Another experiment looking into the role of women and religiosity is Benstead, Jamal, and Lust (2015), who investigate potential voter bias toward females and explicitly religious candidates in Tunisia. Interestingly, they find overall little evidence of voter bias but that respondents prefer candidates who seem to match their political preferences (e.g., people wanting to decrease gender inequality prefer the female secular candidate).

These examples show how MENA survey experiments have started to tackle important questions, questions that moreover are often difficult to address by asking people directly, because there may be social norms that prevent people from revealing their bias (against women, for example). At the same time, it has to be noted that survey experiments also come with a number of challenges. The first is the cost. With each "treatment" (i.e., experimental branch), the sample size necessary for appropriate statistical power and hence the cost increase. The second is the design of meaningful interventions. From our own experience of using such methods in developing countries, a high level of context knowledge is required to develop treatments that are powerful enough to affect respondents' perceptions and intelligible to survey respondents. Holding focus groups or group discussions about the topic of interest is then an important instrument for designing the survey. Once the questionnaire and treatments are developed, pre-testing extensively with fieldworkers and respondents from the respective country is the core shield against sinking research money into a survey that produces no or strange results. Lastly, context knowledge is again needed to interpret the results of such experiments, especially if they are counterintuitive.

The Future Quantitative Work in MENA Research

Work based on quantitative data and using quantitative methods has increased considerably and contributed to addressing important topics as well as to new insights that sometimes challenge the standard wisdom. At the same time, there are also some challenges to the use of these data and techniques that researchers have to bear in mind.

Some of these challenges such as data access and data quality and possible workarounds have been discussed in this chapter. A recurrent ingredient in all approaches for dealing with challenges is context knowledge. Context knowledge and some level of area expertise is not only crucial for identifying relevant topics for MENA research, developing surveys, processing data, and assessing data quality, it is also key for interpreting findings obtained with quantitative data and techniques. In this regard, the most relevant research is likely to be produced by researchers or research teams who are able to combine qualitative and quantitative perspectives on a topic.

A core challenge for quantitative analysis on the MENA will be data access, and especially the impact of authoritarianism and conflict on access. As countries either remain authoritarian (e.g., Algeria, Jordan, Morocco, Gulf monarchies), revert to authoritarian rule (Egypt), or experience large levels of conflicts or civil war (Libya, Yemen, Syria, Iraq), data access will not only remain a major hurdle but perhaps become increasingly difficult.

In such contexts, implementing surveys or survey experiments remains difficult or has become impossible. The same applies to administrative data being published or accessible on demand. Authoritarian regimes are generally very reluctant to hand over data on voting, spending, or service delivery and prefer to control information themselves. While it was already difficult to obtain some types of administrative data, such as spending and detailed electoral data, before the Arab Spring, the current political climate in the MENA makes the prospects of greater access look bleak. Some countries already show clear signals of regression in this regard. Morocco, for example, published, or at least allowed access to, data on votes and seats for elections in the mid-2000s, but has now adopted a policy of releasing the names only of district winners and moreover has banned parties from bringing mobile devices into polling stations to collect and publish these data themselves.

A result of these developments could be the overresearching of certain countries. It is clear that, currently, Tunisia is the most fruitful country in the MENA in which to conduct opinion surveys or survey experiments or to obtain data on elections, parliamentary actions, or socioeconomic characteristics of the population. However, a Maghreb country with a population of 11 million that is moreover comparatively secular and homogenous can hardly stand in for results that could be generalizable across the Arab world. This overresearching of Tunisia, and perhaps a handful of other countries that are less repressive (e.g., Lebanon, and to some extent Morocco and Jordan, depending on the question), is a clear risk that researchers interested in applying quantitative methods should bear in mind. For the other countries, it would appear that the painstaking, qualitative approaches where the trust of interview partners must be won over several visits remain the only way of conducting research.

Given the comparative dearth of quantitative data and potentially increased difficulties in obtaining such data in many countries, quantitative research will play an important but still limited role in the future. Clearly, innovative approaches such as automated coding of material that is available online (such as social media or perhaps programmatic statements from a variety of sources) will be crucial in pushing ahead with quantitative research in the region.

17

Of Promise and Pitfalls

Population-Based Experimental Research in the Middle East

STEVEN BROOKE

In one of the foundational articles of modern comparative politics, Arend Lijphart noted "the experimental method is the most nearly ideal method for scientific explanation, but unfortunately it can only be rarely used in political science because of practical and ethical impediments" (1971, 683–684). Forty-five years later his observation has been turned on its head: experiments are no longer "rarely used" in political science. Instead, it is a rare issue of a top journal in the field that doesn't contain at least one article based on an experiment. And while this method has only recently reached the Middle East, it has arrived with vigor. In the region, scholars have used population-based experiments to study outcomes as diverse as vote buying and clientelism (Corstange 2016), the effect of gender on elections (Benstead, Jamal, and Lust 2015), anti-Americanism (Bush and Jamal 2015), the link between repression and protest (Lawrence 2017), and Islam and anti-Westernism (Masoud, Jamal, and Nugent 2016).

Population-based experiments hold significant promise for uncovering causal relationships. Yet while there exist a number of excellent introductions to and overviews of the general topic of experimental research, there has to date been no attempt to highlight some of the unique technical, conceptual, and methodological issues that arise when attempting to carry out experimental research in the Middle East (for general overviews, see Mutz 2011; Druckman et al. 2011a; Morton and Williams 2010; Shadish, Cook, and Campbell 2002). This chapter is an attempt to identify some of these specific challenges and offer tangible suggestions as to how to mitigate them, based on my own experiences conducting population-based experiments in Egypt and attempting to publish the results.[1] The ultimate goal is to allow researchers to deploy effectively this powerful method to explore substantively important questions of comparative politics in the Middle East.

Logic and Design

Experiments are "a deliberate test of a causal proposition, typically with random assignment to conditions" (Druckman et al. 2011b, 4). Experiments derive their power for causal inference by the targeted manipulation of key variables. The effects of potential confounding variables on the outcome are neutralized through deliberate randomization of participants; because each participant has an equal chance of being assigned to the treatment or control group, we assume that these two groups do not systematically differ from each other. To the extent that we can claim that the observed difference between the two groups can only be produced by our strategic manipulation of the independent variable, we can claim that the experiment has internal validity.[2]

An experiment is externally valid to the extent that it captures a causal relationship that exists outside the experimental context, that it is generalizable. For example, many experiments are carried out on subsets of the population, such as undergraduate students or Facebook users, which might have only limited ability to speak to a relationship at work for citizens in general. Other methods, such as experimental manipulations embedded in nationally representative population surveys, would suggest broader applicability (Shadish, Cook, and Campbell 2002, 83).

Survey Instrument

Researchers can choose multiple instruments, including an Internet sample (drawn from Facebook or Amazon MTurk, for instance) or by embedding the experimental manipulation in a nationally representative telephone or face-to-face survey. In some cases budget constraints, rather than a careful weighing of trade-offs, will dictate the decision about the specific survey instrument. But the decision may also come down to whether a simple treatment-control version executed face-to-face serves one's research question better than a larger multitreatment or multimanipulation survey carried out over the phone or via an Internet sample. As a general rule, face-to-face surveys will be most expensive, followed by telephone surveys, followed by Internet-based instruments.[3]

There is also an issue of time. Telephone surveys tend to be faster than sending teams of enumerators out into the field, and are usually quicker than Internet-based surveys (which are often left open for a period of time to accumulate respondents). Telephone surveys also allow a higher degree of centralization and thus better monitoring than dispatching multiple teams of enumerators into the field. To the extent that Internet surveys are processed automatically or in-house by the researcher, they offer similar advantages in centralization and monitoring. Particularly where the survey instrument is complicated, or in contexts where experimental research is novel, being able to exercise greater "hands on" control over the process may be a key advantage for the researcher to consider.

Telephone and Internet surveys also reduce the need to randomize across certain interviewer effects, such as physical appearance. For example, based on sample of women from greater Cairo, Lisa Blaydes and Rachel M. Gillum found that Muslim women interviewed by veiled (female Muslim) enumerators *increased* their self-reported religiosity, while Christian women interviewed by veiled enumerators *decreased* their self-reported religiosity. They also found differential effects, as this disproportionately applied to respondents that are younger, lower class, and with less education (2013). And Lindsay Benstead, in a survey experiment in Morocco, found that an enumerator's appearance altered a given respondent's self-reported religiosity: secular-appearing interviewers caused respondents to decrease their self-reported religiosity, while religious-appearing interviewers increased respondents' religiosity (2014). In further research, Benstead has found that men exhibit more progressive views on questions concerning women's political rights when interviewed by women and that *both* men and women were more likely to not answer questions when interviewed by female enumerators (2013). In some cases, researchers also go to great lengths to match respondents and enumerators across key traits, for example, by having Lebanese Christians interview Lebanese Christians, Shia Muslims interview Shia, and so on (Cammett 2014). Particularly in conflict settings, scholars often assign enumerators to interview respondents from their home areas to maximize safety (Lyall, Shiraito, and Imai 2015).

All of the above suggests that variables such as enumerator gender, dress, ethnicity, and potentially factors such as age or regional accent need to be controlled for (randomized) as stringently as more commonly understood potential confounders like age, income, or literacy. To the extent that telephone and Internet surveys lessen the need to account for physical characteristics of the enumerator, this may reduce the list of issues the researcher must control for (and worry about going wrong).

Telephone and Internet surveys may also help cope with the lurking problem of falsification of data. One potential reason why enumerators may fabricate results is to avoid traveling to potentially dangerous areas (Robbins and Kuriakose 2016). Inasmuch as this is a factor, it may disproportionately impact population-based research in the Arab world, where the combination of authoritarian regimes, weak states, and violent subnational actors is particularly acute, as many of the chapters in this volume make clear. Under these conditions—and especially for questions that touch upon potentially sensitive issues—the telephone format can eliminate enumerator concerns over personal safety and thus lower the potential for data falsification.

Telephone and Internet surveys also have drawbacks. Some are purely instrumental. For example, face-to-face surveys are seen as the gold standard in research. So peer reviewers often expect a detailed explanation of why a face-to-face instrument was *not* used, along with a description of how well (or poorly) the sample compares to the general population (especially for Internet surveys). And particularly for Internet surveys, respondents may quickly lose interest and abandon the enterprise (Kosinski et al. 2015). This may heighten problems of differential attrition, where assignment to one of the conditions disproportionately causes a respondent to drop out.

Telephone-based surveys also impose potentially serious cognitive loads on respondents. So while a face-to-face survey in a home may afford the respondent the ability to fully focus on the task at hand, individuals taking a telephone survey—particularly over a mobile phone—will likely be preoccupied with other tasks and unable to devote full attention to the survey (Holbrook, Green, and Crosnick 2003). This is particularly evident with certain techniques used to assess attitudes on sensitive questions. For example, in the list experiment (sometimes called the item count technique) respondents are randomly divided into two groups, and each respondent is given a list of relatively unobjectionable items that they are told "make some people bothered or upset." Respondents in the treatment group are provided one additional item—a sensitive item—and both groups are asked to tell the enumerator not *which items* bother them, only *how many*. This gives respondents in the treatment group protection from selecting the sensitive item because the enumerator cannot tell *which* items the respondent has included in the count (Kuklinski, Cobb, and Gilens 1997; Kuklinski et al. 1997).[4]

Telephone-based surveys magnify the cognitive demands with list experiments—an already complex procedure requiring the respondent to listen to and assess a series of items while compiling a running total of how many they have selected.[5] These demands are especially magnified for low-education respondents (Kramon and Weghorst 2012, 17). List experiments rely on an assumption that the only meaningful difference between, say, a three-item list and a four-item list is the substantive content of that fourth item (thus only the content of that fourth item can be responsible for the observed variation between the two groups). But the addition of the fourth item might affect at least part of the outcome variation not through its substantive content, but simply because a fourth item increases the cognitive demands on the respondent. In some situations this failure would be detectable, for instance, if respondents reacted to being presented with four items by simply refusing to answer or answering "don't know" at a higher rate (e.g., differential attrition). But it may also exercise a more subtle and therefore more pernicious effect: that fourth item may push some portion of respondents over a threshold prior to which they would seriously consider the content of the three items, but past which they would simply satisfice and provide an answer that sounded reasonable.[6] The possibility that cognitive demands may bias certain manipulations depending on survey format should thus be considered alongside topline considerations about which manipulation to use to best capture the "ground truth" (Rosenfeld, Imai, and Shapiro, 2016).

These types of manipulations are a helpful way to give respondents the opportunity to privately provide their opinion on a sensitive topic. But this relies on an underlying assumption of what is taboo: it is usually assumed, for example, that (most) people won't openly proclaim their racism or sexism, so to capture those attitudes respondents must be given plausible anonymity in their answer (i.e., allowed to answer with a technique designed to provide some plausible anonymity, such as a list experiment). But what is, and what is not, taboo changes with the context. For example, some portion of Americans hold anti-Semitic beliefs but do not openly express their opinion for fear of violating the social consensus against anti-Semitism. If given plausible anonymity, however, they might do so (Kane, Craig, and Wald 2004). But in the Middle East the situation could conceivably be reversed: there is some portion of the population who reject anti-Semitism, but do not openly express that belief because of fear of social consequences. So while the experimental manipulation would function the same in both cases, the researcher would have to understand the potential direction and type of social desirability at work to effectively design and interpret the results (Brooke 2017a).

Manipulation

As Becky Morton and David Williams note, "There is no perfect or true experiment" (2010). In my experience this is exactly right—there are certain issues that experiments raise that cannot be satisfactorily resolved. In priming experiments, for example, it can be nigh impossible to craft a truly "clean" control—there is always some potential (although not always plausible) alternate causal mechanism that a particular setup of treatment and control could be seen to activate. In practical terms, this makes it difficult to achieve consensus, for instance from external reviewers, that a particular design precisely tests the proposed theory..

Suppose that we were interested in understanding whether or not social pressures, for example high profile performances of piety around polling stations on election day, help Islamist parties win the support of voters. We might in this case craft an experiment that strategically manipulates enumerator religiosity—a woman in a headscarf/not or a man with a beard/clean shaven—to produce changes in a respondent's self-reported likelihood of voting for Islamist parties. And suppose that the experiment reveals a correlation suggestive of that relationship: individuals interviewed by visibly "religious" enumerators (our treatment) report themselves significantly more likely to vote for Islamist parties than those interviewed by ostensibly "nonreligious" enumerators (our control). The observed difference in means across the treatment and control groups may be the result of, as we theorized, a positive shift in support for Islamist parties caused by the presence of a visibly "religious" enumerator. *Or* it may be the result of a different mechanism, where what we thought was a benign control actually worked to prime respondents *against* Islamist parties. In other words, the presence of a "religious" enumerator had no significant effect on support for Islamist parties. Instead, it was the presence of a "non-religious" enumerator that worked to depress support for Islamist parties.

In an ideal world, we could follow Druckman and his collaborators' observation that "an extensive series of experiments might be required before a researcher can make convincing causal claims about causal pathways" (2011c, 20). This is not always feasible, although the relatively low cost of Internet surveys does open the possibility of running repeated surveys to home in on a mechanism. Instead, one may recognize that a truly clean control can be difficult if not impossible to craft and instead present a "two prime" design (Gaines et al. 2007). Purely as a matter of framing, it is often easier to justify a second prime that renders a marginally tougher test for one's theory than chase a purely innocuous control, although it does require a more extensive discussion of the hypothesized effects actually work.

It can also help to nest the survey experiment in a broader, multimethod research design *and* use in-depth contextual knowledge to mitigate concerns about causal inference. Experiments are generally vulnerable to arguments that their abstract and artificial setup, for instance reducing a complex socio-political interaction in the "real world" to an informational prime in an experimental test, is too stylized to produce useful insight. So any argument resting entirely on a survey experiment has the practical effect of magnifying the importance of the conceptual and technical details of that experiment. In contrast, a survey experiment motivated by different types of evidence can increase confidence in the design and results of the experimental manipulation. If multiple pieces of evidence—drawn from different sources and produced with different methods—point toward a similar causal relationship, then concerns about an unrealistic experimental manipulation should recede.

To return to the above example of support for Islamist parties, one could present evidence about the particular historical and social context of the country case to help identify the causal mechanism. For instance, in countries like Egypt the religious-secular axis might function differently than in a country like Tunisia, with its history of French colonialism and *laïcité* culture. So contextual knowledge would help determine that the downward prime caused by the unveiled woman or clean-shaven man might be more likely in Tunisia than in Egypt. So while there is no perfect experiment, one can use alternative methods and pieces of evidence to produce an experiment that is good enough.

Execution

Through randomization and design, survey experiments allow scholars to make strong inferences about cause and effect. But the same characteristics that make experiments powerful also make them fragile. Basic elements are critical to any experiment's ability to support causal inference—things like random assignment, proper specification of a treatment and control, and exact fidelity to design. And because many of these factors are necessary conditions for the validity of experimental research, potentially small failures of protocol can raise questions about the entire endeavor. Adding to the headache, these failures can often only be discovered *after* the results have come in, leaving the researcher with an expensive jumble of data as the only product of months—if not years—of labor and significant financial expense.

High costs, considerable time investments, and critical issues of design and execution combine to establish very high stakes for experimental research. To minimize and mitigate the risks of failure, I relied on three strategies: closely monitoring the experiment, nesting the study in larger methodological, theoretical, and contextual knowledge, and preparing a backup plan should the experiment fail. I illustrate these in the following sections, drawing on my own experience overseeing a survey experiment of Egyptians in 2012–2014.

Monitoring

Perhaps the largest general problem confronting population-based survey experiments in the Middle East is the relative lack of firms, methodologists, trained pools of enumerators, and established procedures necessary for population-based research. Inchoate survey infrastructures do exist in many countries, thanks in large part to the efforts and commitment of the Arab Barometer and World Values Survey teams to work with local partners to build up a base of expertise. But, as Miquel Pellicer and Eva Wegner note in this volume, the Middle East has generally lagged behind other regions in the production of quantitative research, although recent years suggest that normalization may be occurring.

These gaps in knowledge and implementation are even more acute for survey experiments. So not only should researchers expect a relatively steep learning curve with regard to experiments, they must be vigilant to ensure that critical aspects of the survey experiment are functioning as designed. For example, our survey instrument contained two list experiments designed to measure support for the government and attitudes toward minorities. The pilot finished and the data were furnished to us. In the spreadsheet cells the results appeared as expected; each respondent had apparently specified the number of items on the list that had "bothered or upset" him or her. However, during a review of the paper forms for that pilot, we noticed that specific items on each list were circled. This indicated that the respondent had mentioned to the enumerator *which* of the specific items bothered them, which had been totaled up to produce the number in the cells. This defeated the plausible non-attribution on which the list experiment rests, and thus the point of the experiment. It is unlikely that this would have been uncovered without an in-person review of the raw forms.

Were monitoring necessary in North America or Europe, it would be fairly simple to either accompany the enumerators or conduct random spot-checks with the respondents afterward. In Egypt, however, it is probable that the presence of an obvious westerner arriving with the survey enumerators would systematically influence the respondents (Cilliers, Dube, and Siddiqi 2015).[7] So in subsequent pilots we outsourced this portion of the quality control, and requested that our research assistant—an Egyptian—be allowed to accompany members of the enumeration team to unobtrusively observe the proceedings. We worked to familiarize him with basic survey methodology and provided specific instructions for potential problem areas—for instance, how the addresses were selected, whether or not the enumerators relied on a Kish grid to select respondents at the location, whether the interviews were conducted in private, and whether or not the survey form was faithfully followed. He reported a number of lapses, including interviewing whoever in the dwelling wanted to be interviewed and inconsistent concern for anonymity of the respondent.

Another issue to consider, particularly for PhD candidates and early career (pretenure) scholars, is the often-considerable time investment a proper survey requires. For example, my collaborator and I began writing the survey in May 2012. The survey was deployed in full two full years later, in May 2014, after four pilots. Part of this was due to rapidly evolving events on the ground, as Egypt swung from a military-steered "orderly transition," to political competition dissolving to near-anarchy under Mohammed Morsi, then military coup and renewed repression under Abdelfattah El-Sisi. Each event required a revision, addition, or deletion of questions, which often necessitated new translations and, sometimes, new piloting. It also required renegotiation with the survey company. But the lag between inception and completion was also due to the extensive efforts to monitor quality so that we would have confidence in the results.

Of course, these concerns must be balanced against the realities of executing original research in a difficult region of the world. It is impossible to identify and head off every potential misstep that can occur during an experiment, and especially so if local partners are unfamiliar with experiments or less than careful with the details. Instead, the goal should be to exercise the oversight and quality control necessary to report the results with confidence that as much as possible has been done to ensure that the proper procedures were followed.

Nesting

As noted above, nesting the specific experimental research in larger contexts helped increase confidence in the specific findings of the experiment. My survey experiment was part of a multimethod research design that used different types of interlocking evidence to increase confidence in the experimental results. This reduced my reliance on the results of a single experimental manipulation to test the theory, in effect doubling down on a method that is already difficult to pull off successfully.

My research project began as a dissertation, in which I was interested in the general phenomena of Islamic groups' provision of social services, and specifically medical services. I used a variety of methods to pursue each aspect of the project. For the historical research I scoured Islamist periodicals and memoirs from the 1970s and 1980s. To examine these organizations' relationship to the state, I examined legal registration documents. I conducted extensive interviews with providers and visited multiple enterprises to examine how these facilities functioned. And to explore the geographic distribution of social service networks I mapped out the locations of these facilities and analyzed them within the underlying social, economic, and political contexts.

But when it came to analyzing the effects of this provision on individual attitudes, I was at a loss. I planned to conduct interviews with individuals in the immediate vicinity of the facilities, but I encountered numerous difficulties. Many individuals were reluctant to talk to me, or claimed an ignorance that I found less than convincing.[8] I was also worried about representativeness and, specifically, the possibility that I was missing important sections of the population that Western researchers often struggle to capture. As I thought about how to compensate, the natural course of action was to conduct a standard population survey. One problem, however, was that I was not sure how to isolate causal relationships. For instance, I could not see a satisfactory way to determine whether use of the Muslim Brotherhood's social services preceded or followed political support for the group, which was a key part of my research question.

I eventually judged that a priming experiment would be the best way to simultaneously address these concerns and gather the micro-level data in which I was interested. I used a simple informational prime designed to stimulate respondents to think about the Muslim Brotherhood's medical provision, then measured both respondents' self-reported likelihood to vote for the Muslim Brotherhood in elections and their assessment of specific traits that they associated with the Brotherhood's candidates. The results showed that those exposed to basic information about the Brotherhood's medical services were more likely to vote for the group's candidates, and also more likely to judge the group's candidates as honest, competent, and approachable (Brooke 2017b).

Nesting the experimental evidence within other types of qualitative and quantitative evidence also helped to increase confidence in the ultimate result. For instance, my analysis of historical materials revealed the Brotherhood's deliberate focus on providing compassionate and technically skilled medical care. And I knew from my fieldwork, in particular my site visits and interviews with providers, that the quality of the Muslim Brotherhood's facilities was above average. Thus when the experimental evidence came in, it corresponded with the observational evidence and helped increase confidence that my admittedly artificial experimental manipulation was approximating a relationship that was plausible in the "real world."

Planning for Failure

Even the best-designed, most rigorously tested, and contextually grounded experimental interventions can fail. So while taking steps to ensure this does not happen, one should also design the experimental manipulation so that if a misfire occurs—caused either by a design failure or mishap in execution—it does not junk the entire expensive, time-consuming, and potentially career-critical project.

In my research I found little beyond anecdotal evidence about the depth and breadth of the Brotherhood's social service networks. Most of this evidence suggested that these networks provided generally high quality care to millions of people per year, but I still hoped to obtain more systematic data on the reach and quality of these services. To do so, I used the informational prime to gather these details: those respondents randomly assigned to the treatment group were asked if they had heard about the Muslim Brotherhood's health facilities, if they had been to these facilities, and, if they had, to provide the first five words or phrases that came to mind when they thought about the experience

In experimental terms, this was how I "primed" the treatment group in order to assess the attitudinal effects of this provision—the key piece of the causal mechanism I hoped the survey experiment could uniquely provide. Gathering these data from visitors also allowed me to test two key empirical implications of my argument—that visitors to the facilities will be impressed by the quality of care, and that there would be enough visitors to suggest an on-the-ground effect. I wrote these questions in this manner to also account for the possibility that, if the experimental manipulation failed, the survey would still generate original systematic data that would help me answer important outstanding questions. In the end the questions functioned for both purposes: the experimental manipulation did function as theorized, and I was able to use the non-experimental results to satisfy other important empirical implications of the theory.

The Future of Experimental Research in the Middle East

At first glance population-based experiments seem a quite attractive option—not only are they one of the most powerful tools of causal inference in a social scientist's repertoire, they appear relatively simple to carry out. One theme of this chapter, however, is that this superficial simplicity belies serious complexity, one that certain current characteristics of the Middle East—including authoritarianism, sectarianism, and political violence—exacerbate.

Some of these complexities are technical. For example, the relatively inchoate experimental infrastructure in the region, coupled with the way that procedural questions of randomization and design cast improbably large shadows over the results, speaks to the importance of monitoring the experimental process. Other lessons relate to the conceptualization of the experiment. Perhaps the key takeaway from the previous pages is the importance of having an in-depth understanding of the specific details of the case in which the experiment is being conducted. On the

one hand, this is necessary to ensure that the experimental manipulation is provoking or capturing the intended effect. On the other, grounding an experimental
manipulation in a research design that incorporates different types of evidence
and an in-depth understanding of the particular cases is crucial to meaningfully
interpreting the results of the manipulation.

It remains to be seen how far experiments will travel amid the twin blights of
renewed authoritarianism and violence that currently afflict the Middle East. There
was an unprecedented flowering of opportunities to carry out this type of research
in the region during the Arab Spring, but now the possibilities seem to be in retreat.
As other contributors to this volume note, the flip side of this, of course, is that
this type of research will increasingly cluster in those countries where it tends to
be easier to execute, such as Tunisia or Jordan. But while researchers should take
advantage of these opportunities, they should not lose sight of how these contexts
establish bounds on the type of questions asked, potentially limiting the ability of
these conclusions to venture beyond these borders.

Finally, while the experimental infrastructure in the region is currently relatively
weak, the flood of researchers integrating experiments into their projects means
that local interlocutors are quickly developing an indigenous capacity. This will reduce the demands on researchers to monitor each stage of the process, as well as
raise confidence in our findings, and it is good news. And inasmuch as experiments'
increasing popularity (and feasibility) increases the number of experiments in circulation, it raises the standards of what is expected of authors. This is also a good
thing. But it also suggests that researchers should spend time pondering the theoretical import of their experiments, linking their contributions to key questions of interest to broader comparative politics rather than sequestering them in the narrower
domain of the region.

Online Media as Research Topic and Research Tool

Fact, Fiction, and Facebook

ELIZABETH MONIER

In our ever more connected world it is inevitable that academics will increasingly want, or need, to harness electronic media in order to conduct research and also that the social, political, and cultural phenomena they facilitate will become a popular topic of study in itself. When new media technologies come to the fore, they create new questions; this was clear during the Arab uprisings, when so much attention was placed on understanding the impact of social media on the protest movements (for example, Khamis and Vaughn 2012; Howard and Hussain 2013). As fast as technology develops, then, academics must adapt their research methods and identify the significant implications of it for their field of study.

This fast pace of change offers research material and opportunities that can appear to be virtually limitless by giving instant access to data and contacts. Facilitating networks and connections globally from the comfort of your departmental office also offers access to research subjects and places where it may be difficult or even dangerous to conduct fieldwork. Yet this apparently unlimited aspect can lead to underestimating the drawbacks and overestimating the advantages of such research. On closer examination, researching social media or using online media to conduct research presents new sets of challenges in terms of the research methodology that evolves along with the technology and our application of it. This necessitates the cultivation of a very clear awareness of the limitations and shortcomings of conducting research using social media and online sources. Based on my experiences of studying the use of electronic media and using a variety of research methods adapted to the online environment, this chapter will discuss why I chose to do research in this way. It will examine the advantages of using online media to do fieldwork on the Middle East while highlighting the many pitfalls that you can potentially meet online.

Deciding to Do Fieldwork Online

Between 2005 and 2010 I undertook research that was to form the basis of my doctoral thesis, then of my first monograph, and also several peer-reviewed journal articles. Yet I did not begin my research on the Middle East intending to use or study electronic media in my fieldwork. Three factors emerged in the early days of my doctoral studies that informed my decision to change course and make it central to my work at that time. First, the sensitive nature of the topics I wanted to research motivated me to consider focusing on electronic media, both as a site for fieldwork and as a topic for study. Although work on topics such as sectarianism, Muslim-Christian relations, and state-minority relations has increased in recent years and particularly since the start of the Arab uprisings, they remain highly sensitive (see, for example, Monier 2012; Tadros 2013). In the context of 2005 Egypt, the issue of sectarian strife was highly controversial and often not covered, or covered badly, by Egyptian media (Iskander 2012b). Considering this, and on top of the usual difficulties of conducting fieldwork, I decided that one way to ensure that I could obtain materials for analysis and to make contact with a broad range of Middle Eastern Christians for interviews or questionnaires, was to include online media as a major element of the study and as a central methodological approach. From this, my thesis, entitled "Coptic Media Discourses of Belonging: Negotiating Egyptian Citizenship and Religious Difference in the Press and Online," emerged.

The second factor that attracted me to the topic of electronic media was its originality. Very little was available about the role of electronic media in the literature on the Middle East (exceptions include Alterman 1998; Boyd 1999) and nothing used electronic media as a way to study the social and political aspects of identity and national belonging of Middle East Christians. Electronic media in general were a relatively new topic of study, with many of the related debates being concerned with the value of studying it and which methodologies could be adapted to it (see, for example, Jones 1999; Hine 2000; Mann and Stewart 2000). Social media were not visible at this time. Facebook was only created in 2004 and at first was not in widespread use outside of American universities. Twitter was not created until 2006. Both then quickly rose to prominence and so during the course of my research I accordingly adapted and incorporated material on social media. Facebook in particular caught my attention. The way that it categorizes and organizes users of social media was highly relevant to understanding the social and political implications of media usage among Coptic Christians.

In addition to offering an original angle to the research and helping me to secure sources of information on a sensitive issue, using electronic media offered me safe access to multiple and global sites for research while minimizing the problems that would have traditionally been associated with trying to access such information over such a wide area, such as the financial and time implications and also issues of personal security. I also felt that doing research on and via the Internet would grant me access to data that might not be assured if I were physically in the field due to issues of interviewer effect and interviewer bias, which could have an impact on gathering research data. Further, although I have conducted many research interviews (indeed the majority) without problems, I have also had a negative experience of being harassed by an interviewee who used inappropriate language with me, insisted on trying to take photographs of me on his phone and later subjecting me to nuisance calls.

Issues of safety are of course a consideration regardless of gender. In 2003, I drafted a research proposal that focused on Iraq, shortly after the United States launched the war on Iraq. Later on, I still hoped to research Iraq, but the only way I could realistically think to do so was to use the electronic media route. I did in fact obtain questionnaire data from Iraq, as well as many other regions of the Middle East and Eastern Christian diasporas across the globe. Although eventually my thesis came to focus on Egypt alone and the Iraqi data have not (yet) been utilized, electronic media had made Iraq a potentially viable option for inclusion in my research despite a volatile security situation and the improbability that I could have carried out fieldwork there in person. Finally, there might be issues of academic freedom to consider depending on the country and subject on which you are conducting research. It is necessary to consider all these aspects when designing a research methodology both for your personal safety and for the integrity of the research.

Addressing Methodological Pitfalls Online: Knowing Your Limits as a "Virtual" Researcher

Despite the positive aspects outlined, I did meet skepticism and resistance with regard to my plans to use online methods. I agree that online media alone are insufficient as a research site, unless your aim is to simply investigate what online media "do" and not to use them to say something more broadly about a particular community or phenomenon. I was doing both. One aim was to analyze the way in which Coptic Christians use print and electronic media and what the content revealed about this practice. However, I also wanted to analyze their relationship with the national sociopolitical culture. In my case then I needed to combine methods and demonstrate my awareness of the advantages and disadvantages of each approach so that the research data I collected could be used appropriately.

Eventually I decided to use several different approaches to online research and I also combined my work on electronic media with print media for a comparative element and conducted interviews, along with a small number of focus groups in the field in Egypt. One main approach was to incorporate participant-observation methods both online (Miller and Slater 2000) and in the field so that I could employ triangulation to evaluate and confirm my findings. Kendall (1999, 57) particularly recommends the use of participant-observation in researching interactive online forums since it contributes to an understanding of the meaning given to participation in the media. Finally, I distributed questionnaires online. The questionnaires were produced in both Arabic and English to reduce barriers to participation and contained a mixture of open and closed questions. As a result they provided me with both material for quantitative analysis and authentic subjective responses for qualitative interpretation (Silverman 2001, 87). Distributing questionnaires via the Internet enabled me to incorporate data from multiple geographical locations. I posted the link to the questionnaire on Coptic forums, websites, and message groups and relevant Facebook groups. I also sent the link directly via email to contacts, asking them to forward it to their contacts. This was extremely time consuming but eventually contributed to good return rate of almost 500 completed questionnaires.

The questionnaires that I distributed online were central in gathering information from a large group of people in order to establish patterns of belief and social processes. They provided information on media usage and wider issues affecting the Coptic community from which I established if and how media are used to discuss the concerns of the Coptic community. I left space for free comment and a significant number of respondents used this space to elaborate their views and to give their opinions regarding the questionnaire and the research topic. The large number of positive and appreciative comments on the research topic indicated to me that focusing on the way media are used was important to the community I was studying. Some respondents explicitly indicated that this was a rare chance to express their opinions about the issues facing Copts, reinforcing the need for research exploring whether and how media give Copts a voice they otherwise might not have. Based on the information I received, especially from the open questions and the space for free expression of opinions, I believe that most of those answering the questionnaires were doing so as a means to express their genuine opinions. This is supported by Wallace (1999), who found evidence that online self-presentation (apart from imaginary platforms or virtual worlds, which did not inform my research) is less divergent than expected. Furthermore, as Mann and Stewart (2000, 209) argue, there is no guarantee that people answer more truthfully in questionnaires distributed in hard copy through the mail or in person.

Access issues inevitably limit purposive sampling in online research, and studies comparing response rates to web and mail surveys have shown variable results (Kaplowitz, Hadlock, and Levine 2004), suggesting that more work is needed to improve electronic survey methods. On the other hand, using the Internet to distribute questionnaires bypasses some gatekeepers. For example, to be able to distribute questionnaires among the congregation of a church, I would have needed to negotiate access through the priest of the church and possibly to have obtained permission from the church authorities. The recipients would have been limited to those who attend a specific church. Both methods of survey distribution, then, are likely to have resulted in shaping the demographic of the respondents, so as my questionnaires aimed to obtain information on who uses Coptic electronic media and how, I decided that web-based surveys were more appropriate for my purpose. However, I did have to be careful to use the data obtained within these limits and not to draw my conclusions about Copts more broadly. For example, on the surveys I included a question about ethnic identification and found that a number of respondents referred to a separate Coptic ethnic identity (Iskander 2012a, 16–17). However, the issue of Copts defining themselves as ethnically different is controversial (McCallum 2010, 74) and not echoed in public discourses of the Coptic Church, for example (Iskander 2012a, 107). In fact, I had to bear in mind both that most of those responding to the questionnaires were under 30 and also that a significant proportion were from the Coptic diaspora.

It was while working to distribute and promote these questionnaires that I became most aware of my role as a "virtual researcher" (Kendall 1999) and on several occasions, I was required to defend myself and my research. Some respondents first asked for guarantees on confidentiality and asked me to disclose my motives and funding for this research. I often posted these responses online so they were available to all and I gave a dedicated email address for people to contact me with any questions. A number of people did contact me directly to check my identity, and on several occasions I was even asked if I was being "funded by the CIA," to which I was tempted to say (but didn't) "Unfortunately not!" People were clearly concerned to determine my motives and whether I was trustworthy, but those who contacted me directly were usually quickly satisfied by my answers and then completed the questionnaire, often offering to forward the link to other Copts. Some also asked for the results to be posted online or forwarded to them so that the Coptic community could benefit from the research directly. Yet I found when posting on forums about my research and the questionnaire, some comments warned people not to respond to me. I later found out that one forum moderator had sent a message to all members advising them not to answer my questionnaire for reasons of security. After I eventually met and interviewed him face-to-face, he told me he had sent the message, and he apologized for his earlier reaction, which was based on the fact that I was an unknown person and, given the anonymity of the Internet, could have been anyone.

Confidentiality is crucial in encouraging respondents, particularly when the topic is sensitive. In order to ensure confidentiality, the questionnaires were anonymous, although comprehensive demographic data were requested to aid with the coding of the results. To reassure respondents of confidentiality, I used an anonymous web-based survey rather than an email-based survey that would have collected information in email replies and thereby compromised anonymity (Mann and Stewart 2000, 74). Clearly, though, the breadth of access afforded by using online media methods must always be tempered by an awareness of the different kind of limitations produced by the methods. It is therefore crucial to be aware of the restrictions on the type of conclusions that you can draw from the material, as well as the impact on the role and position of oneself as a researcher and the impact this has both on how you conduct the research and how you and your research are perceived.

Facebook: Friend or Foe?

Although I did feel the need to turn to more traditional fieldwork methods to complement my research and supplement my data, I found myself being drawn back again and again to online media sources: partly because of ease of access—the volume, variety, and originality of material available—but also because of the opportunity to engage instantly with people and events. Since I was interested in the narratives being expressed by Egyptian Christians as they engaged with media, the Internet seemed to offer me unlimited material. However it was this very fact of "unlimitedness" that caused me my first major delay in my research. Each day I woke up to countless new posts, articles, and comments. Placing a limit on this limitless source of information became a challenge for fear of missing something vitally interesting. The amount of data was simply impossible to collate. It took me some time to accept this and to cut off the data-gathering process in order to begin the analysis. Learning to select data was one part of the process, but adapting to the new patterns of online media usage and technology was the other because I found that types of online media were always changing and developing. As social media developed rapidly, this quickly became important in a way that it had not been at the start of the research process, and I had to adjust my focus to adapt to this.

Facebook, rather than Twitter, turned out to be of particular interest to my work because of the networking aspect that enabled me to make contacts and to examine how people make links and interact with information and different networks to which they link themselves. Through using Facebook myself and observing its use (participant-observation methods) I noticed the powerful tendency to join networks that reflect an individual's place in the real "offline" world. Facebook is a way to represent yourself (not necessarily objectively, but that is another topic), your likes and interests, and where and in which networks you belong (Iskander 2011). I found that it was being used in this way by Copts (Iskander 2009; 2012a, 53) At the time of my research, I found that Facebook had over 500 groups that identified themselves as Coptic, the larger of which had over 10,000 members each. Being part of this gave me access to spontaneous exchanges and discussion that I don't believe many other research sites could have facilitated. In one such debate observed in June 2010, a status update quoting an extract from the Coptic vespers service on one friend's profile elicited 189 comments from Facebook friends debating church doctrine and Pope Shenouda's statements. The owner of the profile did not comment except to indicate surprise at the strong reactions and the polarized comments dividing comments questioning some of Pope Shenouda's teachings from those rejecting Copts' right to discuss his teachings at all.

For my qualitative approach, such exchanges were fascinating and vital in providing me with textual "objects" for analysis (Talbot 2007, 9–10), although it again proved difficult to limit the amount of information I was gathering. To some extent there was also an element of luck in being online at the right time to pick up such an exchange, which would have soon become lost on my news feed if I had not checked in shortly after the event. Again this introduced the challenge of managing large amounts of continually updated interactions. However, the volume and selection of material was just one problem. Another consideration was the ethical aspect of how I gathered and used the material (see King 1996; Reid 1996). I wanted to demonstrate the qualitative richness of the material and illustrate my discussion with direct quotes, but this had to be balanced with confidentiality and upholding trust. My answer to this dilemma was to use online participant observation to inform general discussion on the way Facebook was being used and the kind of topics that were prominent, which I ensured was anonymized. However, for obtaining specific answers that I could cite I contacted individuals directly, disclosing my full identity (for those who did not know me personally) and purpose. Even though I had sought information direct from individuals and gained their permission. I still anonymized their data when citing in order to maintain confidentiality and maintain my networks and profile on Facebook among my contacts. This strategy formed the basis for an article on the use of Facebook during Egypt's uprising in 2011 (Iskander 2011).

A third issue that became clear to me as I participated in, thought about, researched, and wrote about social media was the problem of accuracy or authenticity. How do you know what information is true? What represents the majority opinion and what is the accuracy of Facebook depictions? It was significant for my research into the Coptic community and its relationship with communal and national authority that social media provide a space for expressing controversial opinions. Yet I had to acknowledge that Facebook is closed except to a circle of acquaintances. Therefore, the researchers' access is limited to friends, whether preexisting or made online. As with a normal circle of friends there will be a bias toward certain interests, viewpoints, and information that you share. While I had priviledged access to discussions, as described above, I did not have access to discussions outside of my network. This can lead to a skewed perspective. For example, in my case the majority of my Egyptian Facebook friends are Coptic and on the liberal side of the political spectrum. This affects my perspective on events taking place in Egypt as a whole by giving more weight to certain perspectives and interests, thereby obscuring the breadth and diversity of interpretations and implications of an event and of the key concerns of the society as a whole. For work on social media the researcher must always be aware that Facebook is not representative of anything other than the Facebook users in your network.

Not only is the information accessible via Facebook defined by your network of friends, but the content also is shaped by the platform on which it is shared. Although I have found that real-life identities, interests, and relations shape our online interactions (Iskander 2011; 2012a, 54–55) research on electronic media also indicates that our behavior can be influenced by the online platform. One example I found was the "flaming" strategy that members of an electronic group used to protect it. Group owners and other members would post critical messages about other users who were deemed to have published comments and opinions inappropriate to the group. This flaming reaction is often seen on electronic groups because they are not set in a physical location, so the virtual "boundaries" are reinforced through strictly upholding norms and group identity, thereby appearing to create extreme polarization and the expression of views that might not be help in reality (Iskander 2012a, 138–40; Philips 1996). However, while it is interesting to examine such behavior in terms of understanding media usage, the researcher must be careful to interpret the information on social media and online behavior within its context and with an awareness that behavior online might not reflect the reality on the ground because it is a different environment. As the network-style platform of Facebook can give a sense of bias in terms of information and opinions, online behavior of groups might lead to an apparent polarization of views as particular Facebook users dominate a group with their opinions, making it appear as if there is a consensus where in fact there is not.

A final issue regarding content that researchers using Facebook will meet is that of the accuracy of the information shared. The ease of posting or sharing a link or a comment means that rumors and hoaxes are easily spread, and many users share a story without checking if it is true. This behavior is interesting in itself but makes life difficult if you are using Facebook for the purpose of obtaining objective data on phenomena outside of Facebook. This is why Facebook is *one* source of (mainly subjective) data that must be combined with other sources and with rigorous analysis before drawing conclusions.

How 'Sociable' Should a Researcher Be?

Social media are inherently social and therefore raise another issue: privacy and the researcher's online identity. Having a social media presence and a profile, such as on Facebook, facilitates the building of trust. In my experience, people on Facebook were much more willing to trust me and participate in my research than those on the forums in which I posted. On Facebook I am an identifiable person with perhaps some common friends or common interests, with a face attached to the name. The compromise is, of course, that I had to reveal my identity to people who might be unknown to me and this caused me anxiety with regard to my privacy. It was especially difficult because along with people I added (and who added me) for the purpose of my research, I also had family and friends in my network for whom Facebook was a means of keeping in touch, sharing pictures and posting updates on life events and so on.

At first I didn't think too much about this. Facebook was new and my friends and family were largely yet to discover it. I didn't post very much personal information or photographs, and most of my posts and interactions on Facebook were related to my research interests. However, as Facebook became more widespread, my use of it changed and it became more personal. I wanted to be able to post pictures of my family but didn't feel comfortable giving access to private images to all the friends on my profile. I began to introduce security settings and stopped adding or accepting people unless I knew them or had a common connection with them.

I could have set up a second profile and separated private and work networks, but I found that the two had blurred somewhat. This likely would have been an option if I had continued to research Facebook, but as my research project came to an end I gradually left some of the Facebook groups and even deleted some of the contacts I had not interacted with for some time. Some contacts had become good friends over the years through our interactions on Facebook and I eventually even met a few of them in person. So they became "real" friends and part of my permanent social world. Had I continued to focus on online media in general and Facebook in particular, I would have had to have taken a different approach, keeping in mind the objectivity of my research and addressing the issue of my own privacy.

Conclusion

Social media are a fact of life now, and academic research cannot overlook them as a research site and an additional tool for research methods. Its appropriateness depends very much on the research subject being pursued and also the realities of the field being studied. As with all methodologies, careful consideration must be given to the advantages and disadvantages of using it, and efforts must be maintained throughout the research process to ensure, as far as possible, that ethical and confidentiality standards are maintained and that biases are minimized and taken into account in the analysis of the data. My approach was a qualitative one incorporating social science and ethnographic methods, and I extended this to my thinking about researching online in order to guide the process and support the integrity of my data collection. This experience illustrated that many of the same issues that are problematic for traditional methodologies also apply online. However, there are inevitably new challenges that the researcher must address. Due to the continual developments of online technology and platforms, the researcher must be creative and adaptable in identifying and addressing these challenges. The researcher must also remain conscious that social media tend to represent a certain section of people, both in terms of creating a network based on an individual's social connections and also in terms of the demographics, such as age, of those who tend to use social media more.

With Facebook, in particular, the relationship between myself as the researcher and my research subjects was one of which I was constantly aware and one that required adjustments in my approach and behavior in order to ensure best practice. The main challenge was to identify and remain aware of those aspects of Facebook that enriched my research and those that could undermine it. Its value, in my experience, was as a source of contacts and for observing social practices online. It is an interesting additional site for the performance of participant-observation methods and for gaining access to data and insights that would otherwise elude many researchers. For me, Facebook was the site that offered most in terms of contacts and in understanding social interactions online among my research group. Trust issues were less of a problem than with other online sites, such as forums and message groups, because I had a visible online identity. The compromise was that my own privacy was weakened, and that the selection bias in my network reduced the breadth of conclusions I could draw. Eventually I concluded that online media and Facebook in particular were both friend and foe to me and my research, but I believe the balance is tipped in favor of it being a friend, as long as checks and balances are carefully maintained.

19

Researching Twitter

GEOFFREY MARTIN

"Tweet, tweet, tweet," I lamented. "They will not stop talking about Twitter," I thought as I listened to young Kuwaiti activists talk about their protest plans in one of many interviews during my fieldwork. What I soon realized is that I had found a hypothesis explaining the initial success of protests in the small Gulf state: the notion that the social media tool Twitter significantly contributed to mobilization efforts.[1] This is an interesting puzzle to decipher, but how does a researcher realistically test and compare Internet technology use to offline events such as protests? Investigating this type of variable in collective action processes has substantial methodological challenges. Fortunately (for me), I am not alone, as few social science studies have explicitly grappled with how and under what conditions protest participants and Internet technology have changed participation dynamics at the micro level.

In this chapter, I will discuss some of the major issues in studying the use of Internet technology—focusing on Twitter—in protest mobilization. I found that the core constraint is assigning causality to online organizing for offline events. Comparing qualitative interviews with activists to their online activities can be para-doxical and forced me to construct a strict metric to achieve representative sampling and coding rigor. The content analysis I constructed can validate within the limited scope of the cases some sampling techniques and compare offline and online events effectively. This type of framework is especially relevant for those studying social forces and Internet technology in specific authoritarian environments, where evaluation criteria and challenges to validating interview data are symbiotic concerns. But at the core, this chapter offers a simple lesson: when you have limited resources and are constrained by different factors, be creative and honest about what you can accomplish.

"Inducting" the Puzzle

My fieldwork project in Kuwait began in 2012 after the initial phase of the Arab Spring. Social groups in Kuwait, like those in other countries in the region, seemed to have substantively improved in terms of the quality of their collective action efforts (Kareem 2013a, 2013b). The escalating tensions between defiant Kuwaiti groups and state security forces led to the November 17, 2011, storming of the parliament by activists, unprecedented public criticism of the royal family, and mass rallies where approximately 30,000 to 150,000 people marched.[2]

This diffusion of protests, simultaneously across different social divides and in locales entirely unused to the scale of such demonstrations, challenged my assumptions about the agency of social forces in the small Gulf state. Structural obstacles to collective action processes in Kuwait—where patron-client relations, repression, and tribal or sectarian identity cleavages seem to stifle social mobilization—no longer seemed as durable (Crystal 1989; Ghabra 1997; Al Najjar 2000; Longva 2006; Yom and Gause 2012; Al-Nakib 2014).

My first set of exploratory interviews—concerning the mobilization and the overcoming of these obstacles—raised this structure-versus-agency issue. Activists told me that they had multiple concerns in the early stages of mobilization. It was very difficult to recruit people to join their movement. Different groups had little connection to each other and were generally working in isolation due to divisions in ideology and identity and a lack of information about each other.[3] Each social movement organization (SMO), as one campaigner mournfully explained, was a "movement of a small finger" with little resources or capacities to mobilize people or bridge the various groups.[4] What overcame this? How were they able to connect and disseminate demands or tactical information?

After the initial interviews, I took a look online to see if the hypothesis about Twitter would bear empirical fruit. From this cursory probing of the macro level, the answer clearly was Twitter. This is interesting in and of itself as Kuwait has a larger than average number of people who use the Internet and social media devices. In fact, Kuwait ranks third in the level of Internet penetration in the MENA, behind Qatar and Bahrain. Furthermore, in contrast with other Arab Spring countries, the level of Twitter use is proportionally higher in Kuwait than average (see Figure 19.1).

At this point it was clear to me that a macro-level analysis supported the tentative hypothesis that two-way communication through Twitter may have reduced collective action costs and helped activists organize protests between 2011 and 2013. But all I had was very general and anecdotal information on the subject. So I needed to dig deeper to try to solve the puzzle.

"Deducting" the Truth

While the interviews seemed to point to the Twitter "revolution" so commonly talked about in the media, proving such a claim provided significant challenges. My first obstacle was theoretical. Research that focuses on the use of social media tools

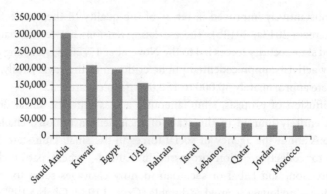

Figure 19.1 Twitter Users in Top 10 MENA Countries in 2011. Source: Salem and Mourtada 2011.

(such as Twitter, Facebook, and blogs) as direct channels for tactics, frames, or solidarity to diffuse is collective action processes are almost nonexistent. In scholarly journals such as *Mobilization, Social Movement Studies,* and *Journal of Democracy,* where aspects of social movements and mobilization tools are most commonly dissected, the digital dimensions of activism are overwhelmingly absent (Plattner 2012; della Porta 2012, 51).[5] Generally, writers only reference the uses of social media as part of a list of factors, not as a potential agent of change in their own right (Snow 2004; Gamson 2004; Lim 2008).

Yet I gained some important insights from several literatures that became vital to the construction of my methodology. At the macro level, the social movement theory literature examines mobilization by analyzing a triad of independent variables: political opportunity structures, resource mobilization, and framing. Theorists argue that these variables provide the necessary conditions under which a social movement can emerge (Tarrow 1998, 41–42; McCarthy and Zald 1977; Snow and Benford 1988; McAdam 1995; Soule 2004; Tilly 2004). For example, the political opportunity structure approach analyzes how structures—such as international structures, regime type, or transformation within a group—impact the "acceleration or deceleration" of episodes of collective action (Wiktorowicz 2004, 116). Resource mobilization theory examines the mobilizing structures for groups, which are used to recruit, socialize, and mobilize contention. These structures vary from formal "meso-level" organizations, like mosques, to informal groups, such as familial networks (Wiktorowicz 2004, 135). The third variable, framing, takes culture and the perceptions of participants seriously as an ideological-tactical tool to mobilize contention and support collective action under a united banner (Wiktorowicz 2004, 116; Beinin and Vairel 2013, 5–7).

Another literature I investigated, network theory, examines the micro-level connections between activists and theorizes how different groups of people and groups connect with each other, thus leading to collective action (Granovetter

1973; Burt 1995; Borgatti and Halgin 2011). In the simplest terms, this literature argues that collective action occurs in two ways. First, people form ties that only incidentally prove useful such as meeting in an Internet chatroom or on Facebook. The second way is when activists strategically and instrumentally access previously developed networks of people such as friends, families, or co-workers.

Despite the differing perspectives in these literatures, all authors tacitly accept that a necessary condition for the emergence of a social movement is direct channels of communication (person to person) for strategies, frames, or opportunities to spread between activists and the larger movement. So as it concerns the study of Twitter, direct connections seem to be a necessary condition for periods of collective action.

The last literature I reviewed, on "digital politics," has two main groups of scholars, "cyber optimists" and "cyber pessimists." Cyber optimists argue that social media are a revolutionary organizing tool for activists to communicate with one another in order to organize collective action (McFaul 2007). They can also be used as a digital alternative to a free press for the diffusion of mobilization information (Diamond 2010). Lastly, social media are a potential site for a virtual public sphere (Everett 2006; Rheingold 2003).

The pessimists, on the other hand, argue that social media cannot overcome obstacles or impediments that hinder activism in real life. Disparities in social, cultural, and economic capital—the structure of social forces and their relation to the state—are replicated between voices online (Dahlberg 2007; Morozov 2011).

This review of the literature made it clear to me that activists needed direct connections, through familial or incidental networks, and that there were potential instrumental advantages to using Internet technology.

The second challenge was dealing with the paradox of offline/online activism in terms of making a causal argument. During the early interviews, activists in numerous groups stated that they heavily used Twitter in their mobilization activities to spread information and connect with each other. Activists genuinely believed this microblogging site was a place for social solidarity, bridging communities, and drawing supporters from across all divides. One commented that, in Twitter, "the mighty power really is not reactionary, but in the hands of the people."[6] Another mentioned that Twitter is "good as a tool because it can't be blocked or stopped by the government and is easy to use for whatever purposes one desires."[7] This person continued, "That's the beauty of Twitter; you will only be as rigidly boxed into a 'pattern of use' as you allow yourself to be."[8] Some selective "tweets" echoed this sentiment:

I do not belong to any policy or ideological movement.
Our movement is not about ideology that closes doors but about making politics in Kuwait free and fair.
The beauty of Twitter is the discovery that we are all not the sons of tribe, the sons of Shia, and the sons of urban thieves.

But just because someone says that Twitter is important doesn't make it so. Aside from the anecdotal evidence "cherry-picked" from a few Twitter accounts and interviews, there was not enough empirical information to make a causal argument with which I was comfortable. To overcome these challenges I constructed a metric to compare online activity with the development of offline events, focusing on a breakdown of how activists use the medium.

The first step in gathering data was conducting qualitative interviews. While other authors in this book discuss the challenges of interviewing in more detail (see chapters 9–12), the physical, psychological, and ethical constraints due to the political (and nondemocratic) environment of Kuwait did have a major impact on my research. The nature of authoritarian rule forced me to conduct nonstructured interviews with open-ended questions. In many ways the interview method picks you and not the other way around. Learn to deal with this and go with the flow.

I conducted two layers of interviews that focused on seeking information concerning Twitter usage. The first layer focused on the nature of the protests (particularly their development, activities, and the sociohistorical context),[9] the physical setting, and the material resources available to activists and civil society groups. It also took account of the online and offline interactions between activists involved in organizing protests, and activists' understanding and use of social media technologies.[10] After these initial interviews, the second layer targeted notable activists in SMOs who were involved in protests from late 2010. I also picked from a wide variety of ideological, sectarian, and urban/rural backgrounds. I borrow this method from Van Laer (2010), who uses individual-level data in studying nine different protest demonstrations in Belgium to compare activists using the Internet as an information channel. I focus on SMOs as intervening variables (at the meso level) in studying the processes of collective action as it concerns the use of social media. Without knowing the structure and character of the social organizations participating in protests, there is little real evidence that what people are saying on the Internet has any real bearing on offline events. This being said, selecting specific SMOs was a difficult process due to constraints on my knowledge of the social terrain as well as the fast-moving nature of mobilization. In the end I selected activists in 12 SMOs in Kuwait that I was most confident could be studied comprehensively.[11]

Case selection should always be on your mind. While I was in the midst of planning this metric I had several concerns about the validity of interviewees' claims about online and offline events. I wanted to make certain that these activists not only represented a specific subset of Kuwaiti society but were also representative of the larger social movement and its online presence. For example, one group that initially presented itself as "the vanguard" of the protest movement turned out to be a disaffected group of youth who were too afraid to actually participate in protests, even though they wanted to. I conducted numerous interviews to ensure the importance of the person and the organization as a key part of the greater protest movement. At the very least, the study was designed to be internally generalizable and representative of these groups and their use of Twitter in the protests.

In the second methodological step, I collected and conducted a content analysis of tweets from Twitter, which gave me access to potential online mobilization efforts.[12] The measurement and analysis of collecting tweet output present researchers with a formidable challenge: the sheer volume and diversity of tweets make them impractical to analyze comprehensively with the tools that I had during fieldwork. Furthermore, while in the field, the Internet connections to which I had access were of poor quality. In addition, I had to deal with the ethical implications of collecting tweets under the surveillance of the state. The security services are always watching life in both the real and the digital world. But more than ever before, they are watching the Internet and everything that is produced on it. Protecting the brave individuals I interviewed and watched online was extremely important. Sometimes this involved protecting them from themselves in what they want to share online. Always remember that you can be held and deported for your research, but these people can lose their livelihoods, families, and lives. Don't ever get too caught up in the excitement, because, as researchers, we are generally protected and our subjects are not. I would suggest never contacting someone online in these situations. You don't want to get caught in a situation where you implicate others in an activity that contravenes the law. Assume that everything on your computer is public information no matter how good you think an encryption program is. Leave as little of an electronic trail as possible. Use a network of contacts and friends to meet people. Word of mouth is always the best safety precaution.

The next major task was how to collect tweets. The best place to go is to Twitter's own data mine or Google Analytics, but due to limited resources I had to find imperfect substitutes. They were Twitter archive sites, snapbird.org and topsy.com, which are free websites that you can collect tweets from. Using their search engines, you can search for hashtags, specific accounts, and dates on which to look for tweets. With minimal resources, collect what you can when you can. Cast a wide "net" (pun only partially intended) and think outside the box. If you spend too much time trying to be perfect, you'll get nothing.

One way to sample tweets is to examine the most influential Twitter users who self-identify as activists and members of SMOs. The sample of tweets I analyzed was drawn from Twitter accounts of the 15 influential activists interviewed. From these activists' accounts, I collected a random sample of 30,000 tweets (2,000 from each) dating from December 8, 2010, to October 1, 2012.

The second sampling method I used examined tweets with relevant hashtags from the random sample.[13] I selected hashtags (i.e., "#kuwait, #bedoon, #kafi, #Dec8 2010") in order to provide a contextual base for studying the online organizing. Following hashtags was important to place my project in a context, even though the sample was largely anecdotal.

The third sampling method was a comprehensive content analysis of tweets. I constructed a four-layer analytical framework to ascertain how activists used Twitter. These layers examined Twitter as a means of organizing collective action, as a tool for spreading information, as public space, and as a place to overcome offline obstacles (see Table 19.1).

After reading each tweet I categorized it using the simple content analysis metric to determine the intention of Twitter posts and their relevance to mobilization efforts. I looked at users' daily chatter, conversations, news reporting, information sources, friends, and information.[14] For this content analysis, 5,000 tweets were randomly selected from the larger random sample collected in order to be analyzed in closer detail.

This method, I argue, provides a balance between depth and breadth in the examination of Twitter. Much of my methodological framework was designed through trial and error. Be flexible and focus on quality over quantity and how activists actually use the medium. Without being flexible in these types of fieldwork situations, one can fall prey to the "anecdotal trap": relying only on the opinions of a handful of contacts and secondary sources to make a causal argument. On the opposite side of the spectrum, it is easy to become ensnared in the "numbers game." To provide a statistically significant sampling methodology would have been more methodologically sound, but I think would have also been shortsighted. Fieldwork is messy and you work with what you have. I suggest you build something that makes sense and is simple to collect. Be realistic about what you can accomplish and don't worry about sample size. Couching our studies in empirical language is important, but we need to be realistic and honest about the conditions under which we construct our studies. The type of study I created is largely foundational and ideographic. Admitting its

Table 19.1 **Testing Twitter's Organizing Capacity**

Logistical Tool	Public Sphere	Alternative Free Press	Mobilization Obstacles
General protest information such as location, time, character, numbers, general trends	Discussions about critical protest issues.	Ground-level narratives, including direct, firsthand observations	Negative references to tribal, religious, ideological affiliations
Tactics or strategies for coordinated action, resistance	Rhetorical expressions of solidarity, demands, metaphors	Links to news or blogs	Negative references to government repression or co-optation
Links to the aforementioned	Links to the aforementioned	Choice of news/ blog site	Negative references to participation among civil society group

limitations early on helped liberate me from any delusions of grandeur and helped me focus on experimenting with a method that worked.

The results of this metric illustrate that this methodological approach has, at least, some merits. As Figure 19.2 and the subsequent explanation illustrate, Twitter remains largely ineffective as an organizing tool. In the coordinated action category, which made up only 9% (450 tweets) of the 5,000-tweet sample, a marginal number of tweets directed coordinated action or resistance tactics. Links to sites that post general protest information, resistance tactics, or forums used to coordinate action were also rare, making up only 4% of the sample.

As the sample in Figure 19.3 outlines, Twitter's use as an alternative free press is not as influential as some might assume.

Postings were too infrequent in number (no greater than 8%) to be considered representative of a larger trend of spreading collective action frames or protest advice through various news media. The most important media among these links were blogging sites, followed by online newspapers and YouTube videos. Most tweets were retweets (62%) as opposed to a conversation or statement. In Kuwait there are also a disproportionate number of automated Twitter accounts, which are programmed to retweet other accounts' tweets, as opposed to actual individuals (Arab Social Media Report 2011; Takhteyev, Gruzd, and Wellman 2012; Shuai et al. 2012). This means that there was not a lot of different information being provided to a wide audience—it was generally the same information regurgitated over and over. Overall, this means that there are not enough examples in my sample to make Twitter an important impetus for mobilization efforts through information diffusion.

Furthermore, given that it is common to use Twitter in a conversational fashion with commentary under tweets, it is surprising that only a few users employ the medium to engage in debates about protests, political issues, or underlying ideals. Less than 1% of activists used Twitter for this purpose (see Figure 19.4).

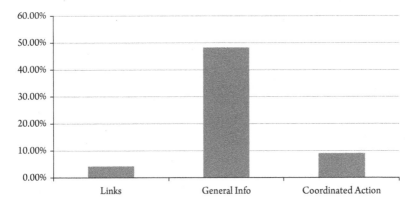

Figure 19.2 Twitter as a Logistical Tool.

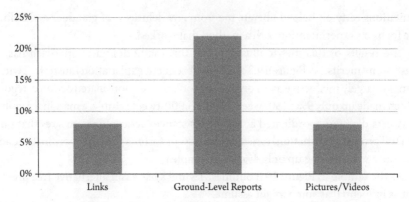

Figure 19.3 Twitter as a Digital Alternative Free Press.

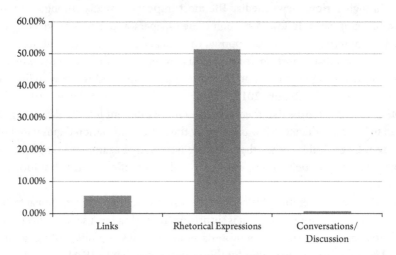

Figure 19.4 Twitter as Virtual Public Sphere.

Instead, the majority of tweets are broad rhetorical slogans and statements—making up 51% of the sample.

What factors explain why Twitter might be less than helpful in mobilization efforts? Tarrow wrote that overcoming collective action problems requires "shared understandings and identities" because they are the foundation of trust and cooperation (1998, 21). Negative references to obstacles reveal (see Figure 19.5) that social and political cleavages play a key role on Twitter. When investigated closely, many tweets had divisive connotations that emphasized the cultural, ideological, and political differences between users.[15] My second set of interviews with specific activists was vital to corroborating this. I talked to interviewees about tweets and asked for specific examples of obstacles to communication. Follow-up interviews

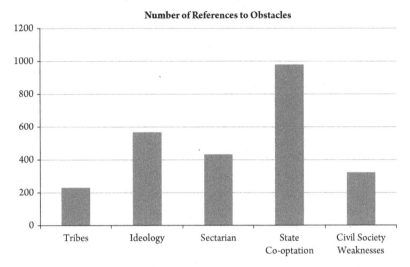

Figure 19.5 Obstacles on Twitter.

are the most difficult and most important factor for learning about obstacles. Try to ensure that your first interview is not too long, and politely ask for a second. This seems simple, but in many authoritarian environments building trust with interviewees is a monumental task so plan this ahead of time and hope you are lucky. This being said, ask the uncomfortable questions about activists' rivals as carefully as you can; the payoff is worth the cost.

Obstacles references were broken down as follows: Tribal Identity (231), Ideology (567), Sectarianism (432), State Co-optation (979), and Civil Society Weaknesses (322).

Over 50% of the sample (2,531) tweets were coded as containing references to obstacles of some kind. Several examples illustrate the divisions between activists along sectarian, urban-rural, and ideological lines. Some of these cleavages are sectarian. This tweet by members of a conservative group framed protests of stateless Kuwaitis as Shia backed, which is factually inaccurate:

A large number of protesters from the Shiite community demonstrating in the Square [Taima] will insult the faith.

A second example illustrates a leftist group criticizing a tribal conservative group for sectarian polarization:

To all sectarian idiots: My religion is my personal business. Put ur religion at home, in the closet. Keep it between u & ur God—Malcolm X.

Criticisms of the policies of other groups were also rife on the Twittersphere:

> The storming of the parliament by them is no less dangerous than what the government is doing.
>
> Shame on you @Kuwaithr! You belong nowhere in human rights activism definitely, it is the most difficulty I have ever had getting support ... No NGOs, nobody.
>
> It is not morally justified to force me to choose between the authoritarian regime and the [formal] opposition, the two sides are the death of each.

While the results of the study largely refuted Twitter's effectiveness, the potential negative effects go further when compared with the offline context of mobilization. In the early conversations activists stated that their use of Twitter was a sign of their status, rank, and importance in Kuwaiti society. In time it became apparent to me that many interviewees seemed to be more interested in their online status than in organizing protests. Status politics significantly impacted how members of organizations used their accounts. Khaled in particular felt this way about the number of followers he had:

> Khaled achieves record in less than 24 hours God bless ... #Worthy.

Another interviewee stated that as a new recruit his job was to retweet the leaders' tweets, not to provide his own information or views. He commented that this results in a "groupthink" mentality that reinforced activists' beliefs and made them less easily adaptable to changing situations.[16]

There also seemed to be gap between information acquisition and collective action. Many activists from different organizations indicated that they were unlikely to attend seminars, rallies, or protest events of other SMOs they found out about on Twitter. As one activist stated, "It is not that I directly participate in the event, it is enough that I know about it."[17] If an individual's private action cannot be transformed into collective action aimed at public political participation; mobilization is unlikely to occur. I decided to investigate this further to expand my empirical support for my observation.

I looked at each activist's account to see whom they were "following" (whom they see on their Twitter feed) and who "followed" them (who follows their feed). I found that all but two of the activists were not connected to other activists from different groups on Twitter, as shown in Figure 19.6.[18]

An offline example illustrates these findings. One activist stated that during a major protest many of the members of her group were arrested.[19] During another protest the next day, this activist couldn't find any information on Twitter; she did not know anyone else on Twitter who had been at the protest.[20] The activist commented that their group was poorly equipped to handle offline and online

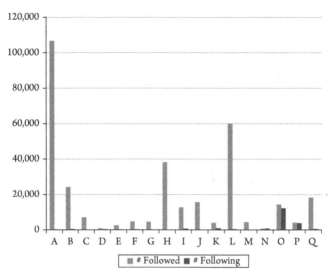

Figure 19.6 Twitter Audiences for Activists.

communication with other groups in tandem. There was little time for them to monitor what other groups were doing offline—much less online—without jeopardizing their own activities and planning. [21]

Overall, the evidence strongly suggested that there are few credible grounds for believing that, in and of itself, social media offered activists any special advantage or "edge" in their attempts to influence the public's choice to go to the streets.

Concluding Thoughts

The narrative I discovered in my interviews with activists about Twitter led to a project that looked at how activists spread information and connect with each other. In my attempts to assess the validity of their claims, I confronted numerous theoretical and methodological issues. There were many important things I learned that I hope to pass on to the reader. Most importantly, realize the limitations of your work. Don't always trust the macro evidence when caught up in exciting events. Make sure to look at different dimension of politics; don't get stuck at looking at one level of analysis or get bogged down by simple anecdotal arguments or methodological purism. Cast a wide net. Lack of funds and constraints on collecting data can lead to novel metrics that, while imperfect, shed light on issues not before studied. Triangulating interviews with activists and their social media accounts is a paradoxical process because the interviews can initially upset the empirical evidence you find. Follow-up interviews are key to learning about obstacles; don't forget them or take them for granted.

The main constraint—assigning the causality of offline events to online activism—was partially addressed through the development of a metric for analyzing tweets. I argue that I found some interesting solutions to the challenges of gathering solid empirical data that can back up, falsify, or at least raise questions about what activists think is possible online and what they actually do. Be innovative in your fieldwork, and something positive will come from it.

PART III

ETHICS

Blurred Lines of Inclusion and Exclusion

Research Ethics for Political Sympathizers

IRENE WEIPERT-FENNER

Positionality is frequently discussed in the context of research methods. It is concerned with the need to reflect on how the researcher's prior knowledge and normative standards might influence the conduct and results of field research. Who we are and how this affects access to the field, however, is also relevant to research ethics. In this contribution I thus explore the broader ethical repercussions and dilemmas of positionality by focusing on the specific case when a researcher's political affinity with the subject under study is so close that the line between the insider (the research subject)[1] and the outsider (the researcher) may become blurred. Including the contrasting case of being extremely distant from the research subject's political actions and beliefs helps bring out the specific challenges of political affinity. The aim is to contribute to a wider debate on research ethics in the study of politics in the Middle East and North Africa (MENA) (Clark 2006; POMEPS 2014) by describing specific challenges and possible solutions for one important subcase and thereby gathering experience on best (possible) practice.

Having carried out research in North Africa both on topics and with actors I feel politically close to as well as very distant from, I will discuss my experiences in relation to the general norms of research ethics. Being mostly critical of suggestions concerning the implementation of the norms made by research ethics committees, I will try to offer some solutions to the dilemmas identified; these include making compromises, being aware of the need for ongoing reflection and exchange, and keeping in mind the impossibility of eliminating biases completely due to the inevitability of positionality. Taking the normative foundation of *any* political science research into account (cf. Schwedler 2014, 22–23), being an activist or sympathizer oneself might even be an advantage in making one more aware of one's own position, including its assumptions and the potential for positive discrimination. The aim is therefore not to argue against researchers being activists themselves but to encourage the use of caution when switching between the two roles. Although I will focus on my own position as a scholar born and raised in Germany with experiences in left-wing activism, party politics, and election campaigns, parts of my reflections can also be of relevance for scholars from the region who are or were politically active in their home countries (although they will most probably face different challenges to access than I do). I believe that the dual experience can be turned into a fruitful, mutual exchange. However, this requires awareness of the tensions this specific position can create with regard to the major ethical norms: respect for the person, beneficence, and the "justice" of research.

Which Benchmarks for Research Ethics? General Norms and Limitations to Their Implementation

Research ethics committees try to uphold three major overarching norms, respect for persons, beneficence, and justice, by formularizing their implementation (cf. Clark and Cavatorta in this volume). These checklists, however, originate from abuses in experiments in biomedical research, and their appropriateness for the social sciences has recurrently been questioned (Fujii 2012; Yanow and Schwartz-Shea 2008, 2014; Guillemin and Gillam 2004, 267). Yanow and Schwartz-Shea draw attention to one fundamental difference: in biomedical experiments the participant is in many ways less powerful than the researcher: the location of the study is usually the researcher's natural environment (clinic, laboratory); the process of the study is planned in advance and under the control of the researcher. This stands in stark contrast to any field research experience. The research subjects usually decide on the setting, which is often unfamiliar to the researcher. The research process itself is not a process of recruitment of participants but of trying to get access to the subjects' world (Yanow and Schwartz-Shea 2008, 489–491). This does not mean that there are no power asymmetries in favor of the political scientist in the field, but I would like to problematize *ethical dilemmas resulting from the attempt to get access* to actors or situations of interest.

There are *practical limitations to fulfilling the general requirements of research ethics committees* in any kind of field research (except surveys and field experiments that are similar to natural science experiments), but social scientists might also struggle with the *limitations resulting from these requirements on fulfilling self-set norms*, that is, ensuring respect of the person, minimization of potential harm, and maximization of research benefits, as well as a "just" selection of research subjects. This means we might need to develop new best practices in order to solve the problems identified.

There are several dilemmas with regard to personal relationships resulting from this fundamental research logic faced by researchers across all fields of the social sciences that employ qualitative methods. The topic of how to find the right balance between being close enough to gain access but not so close as to lose analytical capacities is much discussed (Maier and Monahan 2010). Being in the field, especially over a longer period of time, leads to emotional ties. "Friendliness" can turn into friendship, with researchers developing the need to give something back to their research subjects (Maier and Monahan 2010). But there is another relevant dimension, that of political affinity. I will argue that being politically close to the actors under study can facilitate access to their social world. However, it creates specific problems in terms of transparency, protection of the research subject, knowledge production, and reciprocity, including the question of advocacy.

Respect for the Person and Informed Consent

Informed consent is a benchmark that is often belittled by social scientists working with qualitative methods. Indeed, it is difficult to picture how a researcher—as a participant observer—could obtain a signed consent form from everyone he or she talked to during a march or a mass demonstration (Brown 2014, 13). The practical impossibility is one thing; distorting effects on spontaneous, informal conversations (by suddenly pulling out an official consent form) are another. Even more important, a signed form of consent can cause harm to the interview partner if it is confiscated by security officials in an authoritarian regime and would violate the research subject's right to confidentiality (Dolnik 2013, 230).[2]

The norm—to treat persons respectfully and therefore to enable them to make a conscious and informed decision whether to participate in the research—is certainly appropriate. The question is rather how to balance the obligation to explain research with the major challenge of field research: gaining access to persons and situations in which the researcher is interested. I argue that there are different ways to present research that responds to varying degrees of political proximity to the research subject. When I wanted to conduct interviews with parliamentarians of the ruling party in Egypt under Mubarak, it was obviously difficult to put my research interest in the forefront: power relations and legitimacy beliefs among the ruling elite, including insights into patronage and clientelist networks. I first framed my research as being "on the Egyptian parliament" in general. This evoked the impression of a naive Western (young, female … you name it) scholar, looking for a democratic institution in an obviously authoritarian regime. It made it more difficult to gain access in the first place, as middlemen did not take my research very seriously. Stubbornness as well as references to Egypt's long parliamentary history (evoking national pride) finally got me into a position to conduct interviews with parliamentarians. Sitting with them, I explained that I was interested in the practices and beliefs of the MPs, such as their motivation for becoming a member of parliament or if and how they cooperated with fellow delegates of the same governorate. Instead of offering a vague and abstract description of my research (the Egyptian parliament as such) I switched to the micro level of my research, the reconstruction of beliefs and actions. I clearly left out my mid-level conceptual questions. This omission was possibly ethically doubtful, but as a genuine outsider (and opponent of the regime the MPs participated in) I thought it was the only way to gain access without distorting the truth. In addition, thinking about the way I would present my research agenda helped a great deal in becoming aware of the negative stereotypes I had in mind before approaching the field—and being surprised by a much more ambivalent and mixed picture.

How informed should the research subject be about my research when I am very close to his or her cause? The challenge here is the other way around: by being more candid, I would probably gain more access. Presenting myself as a fellow activist would inspire implicit trust in the intentions of my research and help break the ice much faster. It would foster access to broader networks of interesting people and increase willingness to put time and effort into the support of my research, which can be perceived as rallying for the same cause. However, I think this is ethically questionable, not because it breaks with the ideal of an objective, neutral researcher (something that I do not believe exists, as explained later), but because it creates an illusion of how far the relationship between researcher and the specific person will go and suggests that the logic of actions will be identical (which they are not). This raises the immediate danger of sacrificing respect for the person in order to gain access. It is important to keep a certain distance that maintains different roles for researchers and activists (in the joint fight for a better world if the researcher does not want to give up lofty ambitions). In the interview situation it is relatively easy to keep a certain distance within the framework of the research project, its immediate goals, and relevance, because these shape the encounter. However, it is much more difficult to maintain distance during participant observation, especially of everyday practices. The researcher becomes part of a conversation. People will ask how certain things work in the researcher's home country, and here, honesty will lead to political statements that will make the overlapping consensus visible. I think it is the researcher's responsibility to find a balance between showing conviction and insisting on the line of demarcation. This is not always easy, especially when access seems to fade away, as the following example illustrates.

I once arranged an interview in Cairo with a labor activist in post-Mubarak Egypt. On the phone I clearly stated that I was a researcher from university X and that I had received the activist's contact details via a friend who worked for the international organization Z. The head of the union arrived an hour late, under great stress and sorry for his delay. He explained that he had had to come all the way from Alexandria, but this meeting meant a lot to him. I started to feel that something was wrong. He then declared that cooperation with organization Z was of utmost importance to him. I remembered that when I had set up the meeting the phone reception had been bad, so that he must have misunderstood me. Of course, I clarified the situation, but while talking I could tell that he had become furious. (I understood perfectly—for a researcher from a university he had never heard of he had traveled all the way from Alexandria on a packed train and through Cairo's rush hour traffic.) I felt that access was almost gone. This was when I described many of the nonacademic contacts I had gained from being an activist myself that could be relevant to him (without portraying myself as an activist) and suggested that I could do something for him, too, even if it was only to report about his cause (which I did). It was a razor's edge, on which I balanced truth and possible positive outcomes of a conversation with me. I am still not sure whether I overdid this when, after three hours during which I collected fascinating interview material, he personally accompanied me to the taxi and asked me to come back any time.

Beneficence I: Minimizing Harm in an Authoritarian Context

Regarding the second norm, beneficence, it is highly doubtful that a researcher, particularly in a foreign country, is able to assess all potential harm that his or her research might cause for the participant in terms of social pressure and political repression, especially in an authoritarian regime, and in particular before the actual field research visit (Fujii 2012). On the contrary, a researcher who believes that he or she has thought through *all* potential risks *at home* is very dangerous, as there are many possible perils that are discovered only in the field, and the researcher needs to be alert and willing to learn all the time.

This is specifically important for the MENA region, as the shaky transformation processes in many countries require keeping the degree of protection high, even when political freedom has increased at a given time. For instance, this might require keeping the identity of sources anonymous even if they give permission to quote them by name. One Egyptian interview partner—after 2011—once told me: "Of course you can quote me. If they [the security forces] want to arrest me, they can find so many other reasons to do it." I struggled over the decision but kept the interviewee's identity anonymous in the end—and in view of developments in Egypt in recent years I am very happy that I did. But to be honest, this resulted more from a research habit I had developed in the Mubarak era. Thinking about it now, several dilemmas were involved in this question. The first one is how much information needs to be covered up to protect the informant but revealed to prove there was a credible source for the information and the interpretation offered. This constitutes a balancing act between "mindful ethics" and professional incentives (Fujii 2012, 721). But it also needs to be weighed against the push to give something back: mentioning actors or organizations by name in publications, especially when they are portrayed in a positive light, enhances their international visibility and perceived credibility, and this can raise their chances of international cooperation and funding. Sympathizing with the specific actor probably increases the urge for tangible returns.

Regarding research subjects' privacy and confidentiality, the extent to which these rights can be ensured is questionable, particularly in times of digital espionage that even the most powerful countries cannot fully protect themselves against. Still, researchers have to look for technical ways to do the best they can: How can I get my data out of the country? Can I rely on any cloud or email provider? What is a safe way to communicate confidentially with my research subjects and local colleagues? There may be technically adept political scientists to whom these questions sound trivial, but for a large proportion of researchers (to which I belong), regularly updated best-practices guidelines would be of great help.[3] Things become fuzzier in regard to social media. Should I accept invitations to networks and platforms? I never got into this position when I conducted interviews with parliamentarians of the ruling party under Mubarak, but immediately faced the question when I was carrying out research on labor and left-wing activists in Egypt and Tunisia after 2011. I am fairly sure I would have declined an invitation from a member of the autocratic ruling elite, but I never did with left-wing activists. I automatically accepted them. Though my intentions were good, did I consider potential repercussions resulting from my doing so? This seems to be a problem uniquely tied up with political closeness and blurred lines of inclusion when private and professional lives overlap. Of course, Facebook and the like are the easiest ways to keep in touch over a longer period of time when phone numbers and email addresses change. These also allow following up on activities and recent developments. On the other hand, they make it easy for security forces to detect links between activists and foreigners—especially when local activists can be prosecuted for being "foreign agents." It is difficult to find the right balance, and a little too much caution might be better than too relaxed an attitude. However, if researchers believe that their research subjects' activism and the subject they are researching are of vital importance, they may be more willing to take a risk in order to stay in touch and ensure long-term access. And if the activists do not want to surrender completely to security concerns, neither do we as researchers—do we?

To me, the best way to avoid this dilemma seems to be constant deliberation. First and foremost, the solutions to challenges should be elaborated according to the logic and needs of the relevant disciplines and contexts (as is done in this edited volume). To establish guidelines and checklists based on the specific field can be of great use, but the actual assessment of risks needs to be done in collaboration with colleagues, in particular local ones. This is also necessary in order to find alternative ways and loopholes for conducting research if these are needed.

Beneficence II: Maximizing the Benefits of Research: (Over)identification and Advocacy

Although the fact is not always stated clearly, most research in political science is motivated by some kind of expected benefit, in terms of scientific results, of course, but often also for "the real world." The "so what" question may be easily answered when the researcher identifies with the cause of the subject. But there are two extreme cases that result from overidentification with the research subject.

The first one seems to involve portraying a specific group as *good* and its adversaries as *bad*. Basic information is completely missing, such as the aims of the groups, their relations with other players in the field, or how they have developed over time, not to mention any critical view (such as gender questions or socioeconomic cleavages) that might question the group's supposed normative superiority. It is apparent that this kind of knowledge reproduction based on a romanticized idea of the actor being studied that basically reframes an activist discourse as a scientific result is not desirable. This is of course nothing specific to the MENA region, but with the events of 2011 this phenomenon was intensified by the Arab Spring revolutions and became more widespread. Suddenly researchers had an offer of many "good" key actors with which they could easily identify such as "labor" for left-wing sympathizers or "the Facebook youth" for political liberals. Taking sides with the weak in ethnic and confessional conflicts also seems inviting for blurring the lines and for the researcher to become the mouthpiece of a movement, rather than its analyst.

The other extreme case is when the researcher is an activist in the same field and feels that he or she knows "how to do it right." Carapico (2006) describes the patronizing behavior that is based on the researcher feeling his or her own values are superior, which is turned into advocacy in the field itself. This may cause rejection and closure on the part of the actors, and, most importantly, it turns a blind eye to the research subjects themselves. Just because a researcher thinks the cause being lobbied for is a good one and may relate to it because of his or her personal background as an activist does not necessarily mean that he or she truly knows what the activists under study are rallying for. However, I think this situation can be turned into a productive clash between the researcher's own expectations (based on personal experiences) and the observed perspective of the actors being studied. Any surprise or tension will lead to new questions and consequently to new empirical and theoretical insights. This is one way of implementing a technique of interpretive methods based on the research strategy of abduction (Friedrichs and Kratochwil 2009; Schwartz-Shea and Yanow 2012, 33).

Beside these extreme cases of a high level of identification leading to relatively unfiltered advocacy of either the research subjects' or the researcher's point of view, even "sober" analyses will lead to a point where the benefits of the research can be expanded beyond academic publications—or not. Being politically close to the topic or group might increase the perceived urge to do more, also as a way to give something back to the activists. There are different ways and degrees to pursue this: awareness of overlooked issues can be raised in public lectures and media contributions, or strategically planned use can be made of specific events (like elections) or anniversaries (five years after the Arab Spring) that will encourage public debate of the topic in general. Influence on policymakers can be sought by playing the role of an "expert." Most of us will know how quickly it is possible to be perceived as an expert on a specific country or topic when demand is created by crises, revolutions, and the like. But knowing more than the general public does not necessarily mean knowing better. There is a critical debate on the role of experts in policymaking that cannot be summarized here. However, the crucial questions put forward in Philip Tetlock's book *Expert Political Judgement: How Good Is It? And How Can We Know?* (2005) are not easily discounted. There are more pitfalls than potentially being one-sided as a researcher, but of course this is one recurrent problem. Being sensitive to the biased results being advocated is crucial, and greater awareness may also be achieved by actively examining the possibilities for "justice" in the field research process.

"Justice" in the Research Process

I use the term "justice" in reference to general guidelines on research ethics, but I write it in quotation marks, as it sounds misplaced in a political science discourse. The idea, however, is relevant: the selection of the group of research subjects should not be motivated by personal preferences or convenience but based on a systematic assessment of the field. In the language of social sciences, the aim is to avoid selection bias and thus to gain generalizable results. This leads to the question whether this is feasible or whether instead one should continually bear in mind why the topic was initially selected—and how conditions in the field shape the specific part of the social word one gains access to. The initial decision on researching a topic is to some degree always motivated by personal interest or assessment of "what matters" (Schwedler 2014). Concerning the research process in the field, Yanow and Schwartz-Shea point out how differently recruitment of participants for a biomedical test works than, for instance, recruiting interview partners (2008, 489–490). Some doors will close; new ones will open up. The biases created by the "snowball system" need to be kept in mind during and after field trips.

A further need, and this is especially important for most of the MENA countries, is the need to deal with a high degree of political and social polarization: between Islamist and secular actors, between different confessions and ethnics, between "remnants of the old regime" and "revolutionary forces." A thorough study of any group would need to include relations and interactions with other relevant groups (including their perspectives), but it is often very difficult to gain equal access to the other side, especially when methods other than semistructured interviews are employed. As soon as the researcher decides to delve more deeply into the social world of one group, doing the same with "the other side" often becomes unfeasible, particularly when the researcher's investigation becomes publicly visible. Demonstrations, marches, and sit-ins can lead to clashes between these groups. There is no best solution on how to deal with this issue: the researcher can adopt the position of one side and neglect the other, or stand in between and therefore distant from both camps, or even switch sides, jeopardizing previously established trust and personal relations. Furthermore, the researcher may even be associated beforehand with one side based on his or her personal appearance, attitudes, and so on. It needs to be made clear that the neutral, "objective," noninteracting researcher is a myth and not an ideal. Carapico criticizes the "fly on the wall" idea because it ignores the normative statements the researcher emits in simple everyday practices such as selection of clothes, beverages, or means of transportation (2006, 430). In polarized settings, the effect is even stronger, as, intentionally or not, the researcher's own position simultaneously closes and opens certain doors. This can never be totally avoided, but an attempt can be made to balance it by trying to get at least some access to the others, cross-checking with other sources, and involving colleagues whose work is concerned with the relevant "other" to discuss results—but always reflecting on the imbalances left in their research. This is what "doing justice" to one's research could mean when applied to political science field research.

Preliminary Conclusions

In this contribution I reflected on the ethical challenges to field research by political scientists in the Middle East, for instances when political affinity between researcher and research subject is very high or extremely low. Several dilemmas were identified in each of three general norms of research ethics. Most of the solutions offered entailed some kind of ongoing reflection and open exchange with colleagues. The author's own experiences highlighted difficulties, temptations, and debatable compromises that indicate further debate about research ethics is necessary. In order to establish a set of related best practices, this chapter pursues a specific strategy for addressing research ethics more deeply by describing specific cases (here in regard to positionality) and the ethical challenges they pose. The need to constantly rethink and revise best practices is stressed by ongoing developments in the MENA region, such as nonlinear and ambivalent political transformations featuring a high degree of polarization, as well as new means of communication and surveillance. All in all, an open debate about the challenges faced and mistakes made by political science scholars in the field is indispensable so that difficulties can be avoided or dealt with skillfully in the future.

21

Playing with Positionality?

Reflections on "Outsider"/"Insider" Status
in the Context of Fieldwork in Lebanon's
Deeply Divided Polity

PAUL KINGSTON

All academic field researchers take on a variety of roles and "positionalities" in the research sites they live and work in and with the research subjects with whom they interact. It is impossible not to. From the moment we arrive, we begin the process of transforming our status from that of an "outsider" laden with externalized theoretical assumptions and having few contacts with and knowledge of our research site to, to varying degrees, that of a "pseudo-insider" (Herod 1999, 323). Indeed, the argument here is that we make choices when moving from outsider to insider roles (and between them), contingently adapting our positionality in the hope that it will help us better understand the political dynamics that underlie our research projects.

What follows is an attempt to portray my own fieldwork experiences and my own recollections of how I thought about—and adjusted back and forth between—my outsider and insider positionality as a field researcher in postwar Lebanon. Before arriving in Lebanon in 1995, for example, I was the quintessential outsider. I am a Canadian with no family roots in the Middle East at all, let alone Lebanon; I am both male and able-bodied, two traits that would place me on the outside of two of my three areas of policy research—women's and disability advocacy politics; and my Arabic was (at best!) at an advanced-intermediate level—leaving me ill-equipped to carry out interviews without the use of a translator and needing copious amounts of time to work through documentation in the language. I had been briefly to Lebanon before as part of my responsibilities as a program officer with the United Nations Development Programme in Syria, and I had dabbled in the study of Lebanon during course work as both an undergraduate and a graduate student. But, even here, given the dearth of scholarship on Lebanon as a result of its 15 years of civil war, the academic lens through which I knew contemporary Lebanon was limited and dated. Finally, I was also coming to Lebanon as a young scholar eager to prove himself within the academy. I had received my tenure, but my work up until that point had been historical in nature and mostly focused on archival research with limited and selective elite interviewing. My new Lebanese research project—designed to be a general, empirically rich critical study of the dynamics of civil society and advocacy in this deeply divided and war-torn society—was to be my first foray into contemporary social science field research. Hence, there existed a desire to establish a stronger professional positionality that I brought into my fieldwork, which intermingled uncomfortably with my parallel desire to be an empathetic researcher, eager to let my research subjects speak for themselves as much as possible.

This outsider status, however, would quickly dissipate, whatever its perceived advantages. I was deeply interested on a personal and conceptual level in Lebanon—the result of a variety of factors that I will describe below—and this enthusiasm alone would bring me into the fold. Moreover, in coming to Lebanon, I also brought along my normative values as a liberal-minded Middle East and development studies scholar, eager to understand both the challenging context and the agency of associational actors working to overcome the marginalizing structures of domination in the country; a normative position that would connect me inevitably with some of my research subjects while potentially alienating me from others. Finally, as all who write on fieldwork positionality recognize, the lines between being an insider and an outsider are blurred, characterized more by shifting degrees of one or the other. Andrew Herod writes, for example, that "the issue of positionality was, in fact, quite messy on the ground. Specifically, it is apparent that the positionality of the researcher can shift depending upon a number of considerations, in the process disrupting the supposedly stable dualism of 'insider'/'outsider'" (1999, 320).

What follows is an account of my field research experience in postwar Lebanon relating to this debate about insider/outsider status. I have divided up my field research experience into three phases. In the first, during the early days of my field-work, I was clearly on the outside looking in and desperately trying to acquire a rudimentary knowledge of the players and scope of politics in the field site. The second phase emerged when my local knowledge had reached a certain threshold level, one that allowed me to make strategic choices as to how I would position myself within the inside/outside binary. The third was the writing phase—one in which I "retreated" from the field yet continued to engage and mold it through the ways in which I chose to represent it. It is during this phase that these insider/outsider debates intersect most clearly with epistemological questions about the degree to which researchers "represent" versus "construct" social and political life in the research sites within which they work.

Phase One: Entering the Field—the Advantages
of Openly Acknowledging One's Outsider Status

I set out to Lebanon in the summer of 1995 eager to investigate the possibilities of starting a new research project on the politics of civil society in this fragile country, just a few years removed from its debilitating and prolonged civil conflict. I had chosen to focus on Lebanon for a variety of personal and academic reasons. Personally, as mentioned above, I had already been to the country in early 1991 as a representative of the UNDP in Syria.[1] That interest resurfaced at a donor conference that I attended in Ottawa in the early 1990s sponsored by the then Canadian International Development Agency (CIDA) and the International Development Research Centre (IDRC) designed to forge partnerships between Canadian NGOs and local NGOs from the Middle East region. While NGO interests in most countries of the region were represented by one unified national "civil society" committee, Lebanese NGO representation was split into two[2]—an anomaly that generated questions about the political dynamics behind this associational split and sparked my interest in returning to the country to investigate further. Finally, I also surmised that Lebanon would be a country in which I could carry out a research project of this nature, despite my linguistic limitations. In spite of the presence of Syrian troops and security forces that added a centralized authoritarian dynamic to Lebanon's deeply divided sectarian democracy, for example, the power of Lebanon's state remained highly circumscribed, constrained by the underlying power of the various sectarian movements jockeying for power within the parliament, the cabinet, and the state's executive offices (Leenders 2012). This not only left considerable if contingent space within which local associational life could continue to flourish (as I was quickly to verify upon arriving in the country), it also left academic researchers, local or foreign, with considerable space to carry out research projects, especially if they didn't seemingly touch on "high" political issues and sensitivities. As a result, I was free to come and go in the country as a researcher as I pleased. Moreover, because my project targeted politics at the elite rather than popular level (middle-class, educated professionals involved in associational life, civil servants, and some politicians), I judged it possible (while limiting) to conduct most of my interviews in either English or French.

That being said, for all the reasons listed in my introduction to this chapter, I was the quintessential outsider, not only because of my personal background and training but also because of the complete lack of any academic, let alone policy, sources on politics and society in postwar Lebanon. While there was an excellent body of academic literature on Lebanese history and politics mostly written before the civil war, there was virtually no research narrative at all on the dynamics, past or present, of Lebanon's civil society, and this was accentuated by the fact that the start of my research project predated the Internet. Complicating this further was the methodological nature of my emerging project, predicated on the desire to dive deeply into the micropolitics of civil society in the country in order to discover its own internal dynamics. It was also a period when emerging scholarship on civil society was predominantly normative, expecting and hoping that civil society would contribute to democratic transitions in the region. I wanted to test these normative claims through an in-depth study of the politics of Lebanese civil society.

To overcome these barriers relating to positionality and the lack of scholarship on civil society and politics in Lebanon after the civil war, my initial strategy was to target those who might be able to provide me with a bird's-eye, if not a detached, view of the civil society field in which I was interested—those who could put on the hat of an outsider while also claiming to have insider knowledge. These first contacts—primarily Lebanese academics and representatives of foreign donors that had been active in Lebanon for much of the civil war period—turned out to be crucial starting points in my efforts to construct a basic "analytical map" of the field, helping me answer such basic questions as (1) who were the main associational players, (2) what were the most active sectors of associational life, and (3) what were the most prevalent political challenges facing associational life in the postwar period. Given the scope of my research project as it ultimately unfolded, I had to repeat this preliminary process for each of the four "policy domains" in which I chose to do field research: social welfare NGOs at the national level, environmental NGOs, women's NGOs, and NGOs in the field of disability advocacy.

What led many of these representatives—most of whom were Lebanese—to open up to this young Western researcher who had little understanding of postwar Lebanese political dynamics is unclear to me. Perhaps my deep interest in the topic, my excitement to be in Lebanon, and my friendly and enthusiastic personality all proved helpful in establishing a quick rapport. Perhaps my status as a Canadian (as opposed to an American) and as a researcher from a well-known university also lessened suspicions and gave me some kind of credibility—especially given that I had been a "first mover," descending onto Lebanon in advance of the wave of researchers and doctoral students from the West that was to come.[3] Perhaps these representatives also saw some potential benefit in having a Western researcher raise the profile of their work at a time when donor interest in Lebanon was beginning to recede. Or perhaps, combined with all of the above, was a shared sense of empathy for an outsider trying to come to grips with the complex dynamics of associational life in this complicated political arena.

Whatever the case, these initial interviews were crucial, giving me those first insights into Lebanon's associational field—its main actors, scope, and dynamics. That being said, I couldn't stay in this safe place on the periphery of my research project for long. Still a complete outsider myself, I had no capacity to question the analytical narratives relayed to me by donor informants. In order to move beyond the boundaries set by these preliminary interviews and formulate my own organizing principles for my research project, it was time to enter the field itself and start the exciting yet messy and uncertain process of interviewing associational players.

I was immediately surprised at how fluidly these initial fact-finding interviews unfolded. I was in a position of utter dependence; without the cooperation of these informants, I would not have been able to get my research project off the ground. This "power differential" looked particularly daunting with respect to my initial interviews with representatives of Lebanon's national social welfare NGOs—many of whom had direct connections and dealings with Lebanon's elite political class. Why would they choose to cooperate with a "meddling" foreign researcher with seemingly nothing to give back to them and whose knowledge of the field was rudimentary at best? I had even greater concerns about my positionality as an able-bodied male researcher when trying to enter the fields of disability and women's advocacy. Indeed, to overcome—or perhaps to avoid facing—these initial anxieties in the latter field, I hired a female research assistant to carry out my initial fact-finding interviews.[4] Yet, despite these anxieties and seeming positionality disadvantages, these initial fact-finding forays into each of my policy fields—social welfare, environment, women, and disability advocacy—proved extremely fruitful. I had little difficulty in getting interviews, my interviewees would often spend considerable time elaborating on their work and challenges, they would usually be open to multiple repeat interviews if requested, and they were more than willing to provide additional contact information, allowing the process of "snowballing" to quickly take off. There rarely was a day when I did not have an interview to conduct and, as the process unfolded, multiple interview days became the norm.

I attribute this initial success to two main factors. The first relates to the advantages of being open about one's status as a relatively powerless outsider; the second revolves around contextual factors related to what was, at the time, Lebanon's recent emergence from its position of relative isolation during the civil war and to the competitive nature of associational life more generally in the country. When introducing myself and my research goals, for example, I was open about my lack of knowledge about the particular associational field in which my interviewee was involved, hoping that this would set a relaxed tone to the interview. I followed this introduction with a set pattern of very open-ended questions, the first about the interviewee's personal story of how he or she become involved in the association, the second about the history of the association itself and its network allies. My overall hope was that my interviewees would join me in mapping the particular "policy domain" of the field I was researching—akin to "participatory" exercises that I know had been employed in community-level research in the field of development studies (with the large exception that I carried this out on an individual rather than on a community-level basis). In the process of these initial interviews, I also worked hard to maintain a strict political neutrality about the viewpoints being expressed, recognizing that it was too early to translate these individual empirical narratives into more-grounded analytical ones and to prevent any personal normative biases from affecting the eventual analysis.

At times, this approach was time-consuming, "meandering," and not always of immediate benefit. Yet there were also moments when my interviewees would choose to express in pointed fashion their challenges and their frustrations, hinting at the broader and hidden political dynamics at play. I would like to think that this happened in part because of my ability to create a momentary sense of trust between interviewer and interviewee or, as Mullings phrases it, "a space where researchers and their subjects can view each other as ... equals" (Mullings 1999, 340). But it is also clear to me that contextual factors were just as important in producing these rich initial field research rewards. My interviewees—whatever the policy domain in which they were situated—were all embedded within highly competitive associational fields, in contention with not only segments of the Lebanese state or their associational rivals but also with their associational allies. Underlying these contentious dynamics were several factors: heightened postwar sectarian tensions that emanated from such factors as wartime legacies of mistrust, maneuverings associated with the spoils of the postwar reconstruction process in the 1990s (Leenders 2012), and the struggles over Lebanon's geopolitical orientation in the wake of the assassination of Rafik Hariri and the ensuing "Independence Intifada" in 2005.[5] These were further accentuated by more immediate associational dynamics—competition for limited donor funding and the interplay between personalities and ambition among associational rivals that are often endemic to associational life. Whatever the explanation, these contentious and competitive dynamics were readily apparent in many of my preliminary interviews; their revelation proving crucial in helping me plot out the membership of, and various fault lines between, the rival networks that made up the various "policy domains" about which I hoped to write.

In short, in this initial information-gathering fieldwork stage, repeated for each of my four policy areas of associational life in Lebanon, my outsider positionality as a researcher was clear. Without the kind of knowledge needed to anchor more challenging and pointed questions, I really had no choice but to acknowledge this reality with my interviewees with the hope that they would help me in the initial stage of my project. For the most part, all did, responding generously with their time and situated knowledge in ways that allowed me to begin to build up basic "analytical maps" of the associational policy domains that I was examining. However, as a picture of those "maps" began to develop, a parallel move also occurred, shifting my positionality away from that of an outsider toward that of a pseudo-insider. What follows are my reflections on the increased options this shift gave me as a field researcher—requiring me to make choices as to how best to position myself with respect to my various research subjects.

Phase Two: Shifting Positionality—Moving beyond Outsider Status

What does it mean to cross some kind of threshold into pseudo-insider status? How and when does one know? For me, that realization came slowly, variably, but was evident when I could begin to make analytical and normative judgements about the information being relayed to me. Analytically, I became more aware of fault lines dividing my various policy domains, ones that indicated which associational actors and networks were implicated in the workings of power and which ones were on the outside. In terms of the normative values I brought into my field research, it also became clearer which associational networks I had greater affinity for (those pushing for progressive reform from outside of the workings of power)— although, given the penetration of political sectarianism into the very heart of Lebanese civil and political society, these distinctions were never unambiguous. Nonetheless, all this produced a significant shift in the nature of the interview process from being one characterized by seemingly harmless information-gathering sessions to one characterized by more challenging exchanges between me and my research subjects aimed at discovering the hidden political dynamics and alliances at work behind the scenes; exchanges sparked by pointed questions around such issues as political orientations, political connections, political pressures, and political payoffs.

This new stage of interviewing raised questions about what I would reveal to my research subjects and to whom—in short, which positionality I would adopt with whom. If I were to explicitly lay out a rationale for the calculations through which I made my decisions about positionality, it would look something like this: the more associational actors and networks seemed to be implicated in the workings of power—in other words, those whose politicking contributed to the reproduction of sectarianism in the country—the more I would adopt the position of a neutral, "fly-on-the-wall" researcher (Carapico 2006, 429–431), seeking to understand how these actors had come to adopt this particular strategic approach to their associational advocacy while keeping hidden my own analytical and normative judgements. My research into the postwar politics of environmental advocacy, for example, led to an intense series of interviews with the leading members of the main coalition of environmental associations in the country—one that had effectively been clientelized by Lebanon's elite political classes in order to prevent it from emerging as a platform for more rigorous environmental oversight of the postwar reconstruction process. Not wanting to alienate these crucial research subjects, I had to straddle a fine line, asking probing questions about the political networks within which these associations were connected while withholding my own judgments about the degree to which these political connections represented forms of political opportunism and personal self-aggrandizement (which many of them clearly did) as opposed to genuine efforts at working the system to promote more rigorous environmental policymaking.

This created some awkward—but admittedly very exciting—fieldwork experiences when certain interviewees, seemingly oblivious of how their statements would be interpreted by me, proceeded to answer my questions in ways that analytically "dug their own graves" in terms of the compromised normative values that informed their discourses and their activities. These experiences were numerous but included a representative from a leading political family describing how their promotion of environmentalism had proven incredibly useful in re-establishing their family's hegemony—indeed, the word "sovereignty" was used—over villages in their area that had been weakened as a result of the long civil war; or the representatives—all elite women—of a traditional and long-standing women's organization located within an old quarter of central Beirut expounding upon the work of their association in trying to maintain the lifestyle of old middle- and upper-class families of the quarter—through charitable activities—in the face of the growing incursion of Sunni fundamentalist elements and "the Shia."

On the other side of the normative equation were representatives of associations and associational networks whose values I shared and whose approaches to advocacy work I respected. In the Lebanese context, these were the representatives of associations that, by and large, faced difficult obstacles in being heard within Lebanese political society. These interviews were, by and large, much easier. I was clearly excited to be able to study and understand the work of those struggling to promote the kind of progressive social change that I valued. I was at ease revealing to them my own agreement with the goals of their associations—both because I wanted to show my respect to them for their work and also because I hoped that this might help in establishing an ongoing working relationship with them. Indeed, while I would not call my work ethnographic in a strict sense, it was nonetheless the case that, through the course of my fieldwork, I literally spent hours and hours in multiple interviews with these research subjects, ones that persisted for close to a 10-year period of repeated return visits.

This level of engagement was certainly a privilege and raised one of those underlying ethical questions that most Western researchers face—what could I do to minimize the "extractive" nature of my work. While I did, at one point, accept the invitation of one of my associational collaborators to give a public, media-attended talk about my work, an event that was, in part, designed to raise the public profile of the work of this particular NGO, I did not adopt what Carapico calls "the activist approach" to my field research (2006, 430). Rather, my fieldwork edged closer to what she called the "reciprocity approach"—one that recognized the difficulty of mitigating the unequal nature of exchange between researcher and research subjects but which, nonetheless, sought to find ways of reciprocating using our own academic strengths—such as writing a serious book that might raise awareness of their struggles for social justice within the policy circles that they work (Kingston 2013), or contributing funds after my research was complete to help support the library of one of my NGO collaborators that I had utilized on many, many occasions.

That being said, these interviews with progressive organizations also posed some challenging dilemmas for me as a researcher. Within the various policy domains that I was researching, not only were there conflicts between more progressive and sectarian organizations, but I also consistently encountered friction and divisions within the ranks of the progressive advocacy networks themselves—sometimes over questions of strategic approach and at other times over questions of personalities and ambition. On the one hand, this competitive dynamic within progressive associational networks proved invaluable for my research, clarifying the varying perceptions of the obstacles being faced by progressive advocacy organizations and of the varying strategies they adopted to achieve success. Perhaps responding to my status as a pseudo-insider, associational representatives felt the need to tell me "their side of the story." This allowed me to begin to deepen the process of uncovering the various conflicting narratives and perceptions, sometimes after long, difficult, and repeated interviews in which I would push for as much empirical evidence as possible.

At other times, however, the intensity of these interviews put me in an awkward position, catapulting me into the role of a messenger (though certainly not mediator) between advocacy rivals. I can remember moments when the representative from a leading association in one policy network that preferred an advocacy approach based upon "quiet" and "insider" diplomacy hinted to me that it might be useful if I could suggest to progressive network rivals that they hold back on their more vocal, public, and antagonistic advocacy approach for fear that it might slow down, if not stop, potential movements in a nascent reform process. It was only a hint, and, as a researcher, I did not think it appropriate to speak on behalf of one sub-network to another, so I did not act on the suggestion. However, the experience indicated to me just how embedded researchers can become in the dynamics of their research field sites and how much this embeddedness (read pseudo-insider status), however crucial it is in order to derive insights about the underlying dynamics at work, can complicate questions of a researcher's positionality.

Phase Three: The Retreat—Returning to the Safety of an Outsider

Once the fieldwork is completed, researchers face the challenging task of writing up their dissertations or books. To do so, we usually leave our field research sites and return to the "safety" of our university setting, usually (but not necessarily) somewhere outside of the Middle East region and often in the West. Why do most of us leave our field research sites to write? And what effect does this departure have on our positionality as analysts?

Of course, there are practical answers to these questions that revolve around the expense of doing extended field research, the need to reconnect with family and friends, and the obligations to return to the responsibilities associated with being a graduate student or professor in terms of teaching or administration. But there are also important issues of positionality when we leave the field and write up our analysis—issues that revolve around the advantages of creating, once again, distance between researcher and research subjects. After having worked so hard to embed ourselves in our research sites and cultivate some of kind of pseudo-insider status with our research subjects, it now seems that an important part of the field research dynamics is to work to re-establish our positionality as a pseudo-outsider.

Although I did not carry out ethnographic research in a strict sense, I have been struck by the usefulness of the discussion among political ethnographers to these questions. On the one hand are those that practice ethnography for its own sake as a way of understanding the "insider meaning and perspectives" of communities in which they have been embedded (Schatz 2009, 9). Their particular challenge, emanating from an understanding that all knowledge is "coproduced," is to acquire enough distance from the research site to decipher as best they can "the researcher effects" (Schatz 2009, 15). On the other hand are those political ethnographers (or those, such as myself, who try to approach their work with an ethnographic sensibility) who work under the assumption that some degree of "decontextualized knowledge" can be revealed through the course of field research. Schatz, for example, writes of "the careful and incremental search for small-t-truths," of close attention to detail being useful in uncovering theoretical complexities and generating "middle range theories" (2009, 10–14); and Allina-Pisano similarly argues that it is possible for ethnographic analysis to have "some purchase on causality" and for researchers to acquire "an informed outside view" (2009, 55). Creating distance from the microdynamics of the field can aid in this process of producing "qualified neo-positivist" analysis, not only by facilitating the identification of the "researcher effects" so crucial to the constructivist ethnographic approach noted above, but also by allowing the researcher to refocus the analytical lens on larger abstract perspectives. Geertz writes of this as a continuous process for the field researcher, "tacking between the most local of local detail and the most global of global structure in such a way as to bring them into simultaneous view" (1983, 69). But there is also a more definitive or permanent process of distancing ourselves from the field at the end of the field research itself—of returning to the positionality of being an outsider—when writing up. This allows field researchers to refocus their gaze on the broader analytical framework of the research project needed to formulate broader theoretical implications of the project as a whole. As Katz describes, the result of this is a shift in positionality, moving the researcher away from having conversations "with the field" toward speaking "to the field" (Katz 1994, 68).

This dynamic certainly resonates with my own experiences. Upon completion of my first extended fieldwork stint in Lebanon, for example, a six-month stay in 1999 in which I mostly carried out research in the field of environmental advocacy politics, I came home still unsure of what the overarching analytical framework of my research project would be. I essentially spent the next few months rereading my field notes and placing them in tension with the more abstract literatures on civil society and political clientelism. It was only out of this experience of struggling to make sense of my research material by leaving the field and re-engaging with the abstract literature that a more precise analytic framework for my fieldwork experiences began to unfold. Certainly, what I produced was not how my research subjects articulated their own experiences. That is the very nature of academic analysis—that it often employs language and concepts not used in everyday practice and discourse. In that sense, the product of the academic exercise and of writing analytically is bound to end up producing something that is an imposition on the field of study in question by an outsider—however embedded a researcher has been when collecting research material "on the inside." In short, this retreat to the positionality of an outsider seems to be an inherent and beneficial part of the academic exercise.

The hope is, of course, that the analysis produced will resonate within the field, provide former research subjects with new understandings of the questions and challenges they face, and contribute to new, more abstract theoretical understandings, if only of a "middle range" variety. In my case, for example, this initial process seemed to turn out quite well, at least in terms of capturing some "small-t-truths" about the dynamics in the field itself. In my discussions with former research subjects after having published my first article on my environmental research in Lebanon (Kingston 2001), for example, I was told that the person who was minister of the environment during much of the time period about which I wrote, after having caught wind of my published article, asked for a copy and, after having read it, remarked that it seemed to capture quite well the political dynamics at play during that time—a rare and, I must admit, quite satisfying moment of affirmation for a field researcher who had definitely struggled with being such an outsider! I can only hope that my subsequent book has garnered similar reactions from those of my former research subjects who have read it.

Conclusion

There appear to be interesting ironies emanating from my fieldwork experiences. When an outsider, I strove to become more of an insider; when the status of a pseudo-insider was achieved, it was time to remove myself from my fieldwork site and return to the safe confines of being an outsider again. Yet, in the end, each form of positionality offered several advantages. Outsider status at the outset of research did not prove to be the kind of disadvantage that I had feared it might be, at least with respect to the research subjects that I encountered within Lebanon's NGO world. Being a "first mover" certainly helped, with many of the NGO representatives that I interviewed responding helpfully to the attention that their associations were struggling to achieve. But so did honesty about my lack of knowledge about my field of research and my more open-ended approach to my initial interviews. This seemed to put the interviewees at ease, allowing them to steer the interview in directions they desired. While not all initial interviews proved fruitful, the sum total during this initial outsider phase resulted in my ability to begin the process of establishing more nuanced analytical maps of my fieldwork terrain.

Paradoxically, once this status of a pseudo-insider began to emerge, the interview processes became more dynamic but also more challenging. Certainly, greater familiarity with my research site allowed me to probe more deeply into its political dynamics. It also presented me with an opportunity to adjust my positionality in ways that would enhance my access to research material, establishing closer ties with those research subjects whose work I admired, while maintaining a more neutral positionality with those research subjects whose work I surmised was tied up with the workings of power. At the same time, however, this also raised important questions about "researcher effect," evident in my case when finding myself caught in the middle of competitive dynamics between associations with whom I had established especially close research ties. All this points to the need for researchers to manage carefully the inevitable transitions in the field research process between outsider and insider status—to be mindful of one's changing positionality, to take advantage of the variable opportunities that these different positionalities present to the field researcher, all with an eye to either reflecting or informing in the most useful fashion possible the research field within which one has conducted field research.

Intersectionality Theory
and Working with "Both Sides"

LIHI BEN SHITRIT

Intersectionality theory aims to make visible the experience of people whose identities encompass intersecting categories that often make them invisible in political analyses resting on simple binary categories. A self-reflexive examination of the researcher's own identity will often reveal the unsatisfactory nature of binary categories employed in discourses about various conflicts in the Middle East (Sunni vs. Shia, Muslim vs. Jewish, religious vs. secular, etc.). Such reflection can help scholars avoid reification of reductive dichotomies in their research and writing. But more importantly, intersectionality theory also seeks to examine how categories of difference are conceptually related to each other. Rather than assuming we know the nature of that relationship before starting our fieldwork, we should let it remain an open question for investigation. Drawing on my family's North African Arab/Berber/Jewish history and my experience doing research in Israel with Mizrahi and Palestinian-Israeli women activists on the Jewish and Muslim religious right, respectively, this chapter points to the importance of thinking about intersectionality before, during, and after conducting fieldwork.

The Challenge of Binary Categories in the History
of the "Arab-Israeli" Conflict

I work on religion and politics in the Middle East, and much of my research to date has been about the Israeli and Palestinian religious Right.[1] Within this broader subject, I focus on gender politics, and I work in a feminist tradition. The intersection of multiple identity categories and forms of oppression that disturb simple binaries is something that I cannot escape in my research. That gender intersects with class, race, ethnicity, nationality, sexuality, and various other categories is an empirical reality that presents itself in the field, and this makes intersectionality theories and methods very useful tools. But this is true not only for feminist researchers who ask questions about gender in the Middle East. I think that any Middle Eastern scholar becomes uncomfortable with reductive, dichotomous narratives if she reflexively considers, even briefly, the history of her own identity. Talk of binary ethnic and sectarian cleavages of Sunni-Shia, Arab-Persian, or Muslim-Jewish kinds, to name a few, quickly break down when confronted with real people and personal histories.

The modern narrative of an "Arab-Israeli conflict" is one such overarching theme or cleavage that often obscures more than it reveals and reifies more than it clarifies. This is nothing new and yet it still requires stating. That most Israeli Jews are of Arab, or Middle Eastern (Mizrahi) descent, and that Palestinian-Arab Muslims and Christians make up more than 20% of Israel's citizens, is not news to anyone. And yet these two populations receive little attention in the scholarly literature on the Israeli and Palestinian religious Right, which constitutes the tradition I was hoping to contribute to with my work. Moreover, the literature has been all but silent about pious Mizrahi women and religious Palestinian-Israeli women who are active on the Jewish and Muslim religious right, respectively. The intersections of nationality, ethnicity, religion, class, and gender have made them close to invisible.

My interest in these women activists was, I think, a result of both an intuitive and a self-reflexive understanding of my own place in the landscape of the so-called Arab-Israeli conflict. When doing fieldwork at home, thinking about your own identity, how you fit in, and where exactly you belong is inevitable, as several of this volume's chapters highlight. Like many others, my family's histories fall outside or on the edges of mainstream Zionism and Arab nationalism, the two grand narratives that constituted the central dichotomy of the Arab-Israeli conflict in the twentieth century. My parental great-grandparents, who were Moroccan, were thrilled by the establishment of Israel, not because of a secular-nationalist Zionist ethos, but out of religious longing to live their last years in the Holy Land, which the establishment of the state made possible. Their son, my grandfather, was less enthusiastic. He had little interest in religion or in Israel. And yet he was required to accompany his parents who wanted to immigrate because in the 1950s the new state would not take an elderly couple from an Arab country without a family member who was "fit for hard labor" (as the doctor conducting my grandfather's medical exam prior to immigration noted). My paternal grandmother and her family, on the other hand, fled their native Egypt following the rise of Gamal Abdel Nasser and the bitter clash between Arab nationalism and Zionism. The Egyptian authorities stamped her Egyptian passport with the words "exit without re-entry," severing her ties with her birthplace.

But even the other side of my family, of European descent, did not exactly fit the bill of early twentieth-century European Zionism or later Holocaust survival narratives. My maternal grandmother was born in Mandatory Palestine but grew up in India, where her father took the family because he was inspired by Mahatma Gandhi's nonviolent anticolonial methods. He went to meet and study with the

Mahatma and stayed in India for eight years—from 1940 to 1948—with the naive objective of modeling a nonviolent Jewish nationalism against the British Mandate after the Indian example. Needless to say, that didn't work out quite the way he had hoped. But one of the outcomes of his failed attempt is that some of my grandmother's formative memories were from the partition of India, rather than that of Palestine.

These personal histories meant that the given dichotomous categories of the conflict, or of any conflict for that matter, were always unsatisfactory to me and to many others because they left out large populations that did not neatly belong. In the Arab-Israeli context countless articles and books by Mizrahis and Arab-Palestinian citizens of Israel have been written about these two "in-between" segments of the population. Some have written in the hope that these communities could be an intersectional bridge to peace, others as a way to reconfigure who fell within native and settler categories. Some served as more poignant critiques of Zionism, others as critiques of Arab nationalism. Many of these works, particularly feminist ones, have also paid attention to the politics of gender, class, and sexuality as these intersected with such subgroups within the overarching dichotomous categories of Israeli-Jew and Palestinian-Arab.

Yet scholarly writings about the growing religious Right in Israel and Palestine have tended to largely ignore both gender in general and in particular women activists on the Jewish right who are "Arab-Jews" (Mizrahi) and women activists on the Muslim right who are "Israeli-Arabs" (Palestinian citizens of Israel).[2] Women are often ignored in studies of social movements on the religious right in this conflict because they are not seen as important actors in the severely socially conservative, patriarchal movements that constitute the Jewish and Muslim religious Right. But even more so, Mizrahi women and Arab Muslim women citizens of Israel who are on the religious right are almost never addressed in this literature. My book *Righteous Transgressions: Women's Activism on the Israeli and Palestinian Religious Right* tries to fill some of this gap by studying women activists not only in the religious movements that are the usual suspects in the conflict—the settler movement and the Palestinian Hamas—but also in the largely Mizrahi ultra-Orthodox Shas movement and in the Israeli Islamic Movement (Ben Shitrit 2015).

Two Projects: Making Intersectional Categories Visible or Reconfiguring the Relationship between Categories?

Ange-Marie Hancock succinctly explains that intersectionality theory encompasses two intellectual projects. The first is "an inclusionary project designed to remedy specific intersectional stigma or invisibility." The second is "an analytical project designed to reshape how categories of difference are conceptually related to each other" (Hancock 2016, 34). As I mentioned, it was the former task of inclusion and of making visible that came almost intuitively to me as a feminist scholar with Mizrahi heritage. Not seeing pious Mizrahi women or pious Palestinian-Israeli women as important political actors on the Jewish and Muslim religious right was not an option, because I knew they were there. It was also easier for me to reach these activists because of my performed identity.

My unmistakably Moroccan-Berber Jewish family name and the fact that I grew up in 1990s Beit Shemesh, a town on the Jerusalem periphery whose inhabitants at the time were mainly Mizrahis and new immigrants from Russia and Ethiopia, facilitated access and relationship with the women activists. With Shas activists, these identity markers opened doors, with some women telling me that I could see things from their point of view, and others asking to hear about my family history and sharing their own North African family stories. In my research with Islamic Movement women activists, some remarked to me that Mizrahis were basically Arab (overlooking ethnic diversity within this group). Others turned the ethnographic lens on me, asking me to explain why these basically Arab Mizrahis seem to predominantly vote for anti-Arab parties, and where my own family stood politically. Others were curious, again, to hear about my family history and connection to Arab culture and heritage.

With the second, analytical project of intersectionality that looks to reconfigure how categories of difference conceptually relate to each other, I struggled. Because I am a political scientist I saw different identity markers such as gender, class, ethnicity, religion, and nationality as something akin to separate control variables. They allowed me to construct a KKV-style qualitative research design[3] to isolate the effect of the main variable of interest for me in my research (political ideology) on forms of women's activism in the movements I studied. For example, when comparing women activists in Shas and in the Islamic Movement, I had something akin to a "most similar" design. Except for the fact that one movement was Jewish and the other was Muslim, gender, class, and Arab ethnicity were markers that activists in both movements shared, so I thought, in a way, I was holding those "variables" constant. But as Hancock (2016, 21) points out, this sort of fusion "of intersectional premises with positivistic social science conceptualizations of relationships between 'variables' like race and gender is a popular yet incorrect operationalization of intersectionality's core insight." This mistaken application relies on an additive or multiplicative logic that ends up inadvertently producing "competitions among differently situated activists for the role of 'most oppressed' based on a high number of identities or experiences of multiple oppressions" (Hancock 2016, 62). The problem here is that intersectionality doesn't work as a clear formula for measuring oppression to simply determine who is more oppressed than whom. Rather, the ways different intersecting categories intersect with each other to produce an effect is an open empirical question.

Yet as a scholar doing fieldwork I personally often experienced intersectionality as additive or multiplicative. Here are a few examples. Because research interlocutors perceived me as a Mizrahi Jewish Israeli woman (due to my name rather than my appearance) I was clearly more privileged in the field research process than, say, an Arab-Palestinian Israeli scholar. Dr. Nuhad Ali, for instance, who has also studied the Islamic Movement and Shas, had to pretend to be Jewish in order to conduct his research with the ultra-Orthodox Jewish Shas.[4] I on the other hand was able to work with the Islamic Movement, with Shas, and with the Jewish settlers without having to hide my Jewish identity.[5] The only problem I faced was the occasional short-lived initial suspicion among certain Jewish and Muslim interlocutors that I might be an intelligence agent (i.e., that I might have *more power* than I let show).[6] For Dr. Ali it was racism and the potential denial of access to the field that forced him to hide his religion (i.e., it was the perceived *lack of power* associated with a particular identity).

Furthermore, it seemed to me that Dr. Ali nevertheless was more privileged than Jumana,[7] a Bedouin, Palestinian-Israeli, female university student who volunteered with me at a women's rights organization in a Bedouin town in the Negev Desert. When I asked for her help with my work. it required a lot of convincing for her family to let her accompany me on a research trip to the north. Such types of family restrictions were not hurdles that a male Bedouin student, or a non-Bedouin Arab-Israeli female student, or a Mizrahi Jewish female student would face.

When we reached the train station in Tel Aviv, I quickly passed the metal detector and security guards at the entrance. Jumana, walking just behind me, was stopped by the guards, who wanted to search her backpack again and ask her where she came from and where she was headed. Outraged by the blatant profiling (it was clearly her hijab that elicited their attention), I started to loudly argue with the security personnel, accusing them of racism and profiling and making a scene. Jumana remained composed and asked me to calm down and to just let it go. She appeared to have a certain defeated acceptance that came from repetitive experience. It looked to me like a survival mechanism that allowed her to go on with her life despite constant indignities.

As a Jewish Israeli the prospect of the security guards calling the police on me was not daunting due to the privilege I have that allows me to not fear the police or the guards. I know I will hardly be arrested or physically harmed by them. Even my sister, who has brown skin unlike my white skin, and who performs a certain delinquent Mizrahi teenage identity and socializes with Mizrahi youth who are constantly in trouble with the police, has little to fear from law enforcers. Jumana does not have the same privilege that a Mizrahi Jewish woman has in this regard, and both probably don't have the same privilege in this interaction as an Ashkenazi woman or an Ashkenazi-looking woman. Moreover, unlike a secular Palestinian-Israeli man or woman, being *muhajjaba* meant that Jumana didn't even have the option of "passing"; her hijab was a visible mark of difference.

Adding to that, when we arrived for the interviews I planned to conduct in an Arab town in the Triangle region of Israel, Jumana faced another indignity. The Islamist women activists spoke mostly to me and largely ignored her. They also pontificated on "backward Bedouin mentality" and their own work to uplift and educate Bedouins. We left with Jumana furious at the condescension from fellow Muslims who were not Bedouin, and exhausted with the thought of the rest of our trip that would invariably involve more security guards in bus and train stations.

This account does sound a little like an "oppression Olympics" (Hancock 2007). At the least oppressed spot would be an Ashkenazi man, then an Ashkenazi woman, then perhaps a Mizrahi man, followed by a Mizrahi woman. As we move up the levels of oppression (or down the levels of privilege) there will be an Arab-Israeli man, then an Arab-Israeli woman, then a Bedouin man, and then a Bedouin woman. And that is before we considered Ethiopian Jews, Asian guest workers, African asylum seekers, Palestinians in the Occupied Territories, and sexual minority identity, disability, and socioeconomic class within each of the categories.

However, this approach misapplies intersectional insight. Reconsidering the relationship between identity categories means that a simple additive or multiplicative logic is often misleading. Sometimes it is indeed the case that intersectional categories add up in a predictable way, but at other times this logic breaks down. The "oppression Olympics" leads us to believe that each category operates by itself in a knowable, consistent, unitary, and independent way, so we can know a priori the contours of a person's experience (particularly of oppression) and subsequently explain her behavior by simply adding the independent effect of each identity marker or category.

When I understood the ambiguous and shifting nature of the way intersecting markers are experienced and subsequently shape people's responses, I began to question my positivist framework that applied identity markers as a sort of "control variable." The actual experiences of my various research interlocutors at times confirmed but at other times complicated and disturbed my neat, parsimonious framework. Yet I also saw an overarching compatibility between my positivist design and intersectional insight. For example, I found that difference in forms of activism *within* an intersectional category (for instance, Palestinian-Israeli women activists in the Islamic Movement's northern and southern branches) was greater than difference *between* intersectional categories (for example, between Mizrahi-Jewish Shas women activists and southern branch Islamic Movement activists). I also found almost identical patterns of discourse and forms of activism among the most politically privileged group in my study—Jewish women settlers—and the most politically oppressed group—pious Palestinian Hamas women activists in the Occupied Territories. The intersecting identity categories activists inhabited interacted with each other in ways that did not fully determine the contours of their experience or their political response to it.

My main advice for others doing this kind of work, therefore, is to challenge their thinking about how categories interact with each other, and to conduct extensive fieldwork *before* settling on a research design. At times a positivist framework might work, but often interpretive tools would need to supplant, modify, or replace it for a more accurate account of political phenomena. This is something that I understand in retrospect. To make place for this understanding, I ended up including in my book a tremendous amount of my interlocutors' own words, their interpretive accounts of their experiences, and extensive descriptions of their actions taken from my field notes. This meant that sometimes their words and actions confirmed my book's main arguments, but it also meant that sometimes they challenged my conclusions and my authority, showing that categories don't always spell out realities, experiences, and behaviors in the way we expect them to.

Working with "Both Sides"

While intersectional thinking shatters a dichotomous view of the world, it still operates in a world that many, including some of my research interlocutors, might see in strict binary terms. Another challenge for me, then, was doing fieldwork with various movements on the Israeli and Palestinian religious right that see themselves as positioned in a fairly clear binary opposition to each other, within the context of the Israeli-Palestinian conflict. I did not see them as being on "opposite sides" for several reasons. First, in some of them the presence of intersecting identity axes, such as ethnicity and class, defy strict dichotomous differences (for example, between Shas and the two branches of the Islamic Movement). Second, all four movements in my research share overwhelming family resemblances in terms of their religious-political commitments. They are all ultimately devoted to affording a particular interpretation of religion a greater place in the lives of individuals, in regulating social affairs, and in formal politics. And finally, all four uphold permutations of a similar gender ideology. They all advocate what they consider a conservative, religiously based, heterosexual gender complementary model (with women and men having different, complementary, divinely sanctioned roles) as the key to the well-ordered, moral, and pious society they wish to create.

In their religious-political visions, the movements had more in common with each other than any of them had with me—a secular, feminist, postnationalist, pluralist, liberal democrat.[8] I faced the challenge of working with interlocutors who were in some ways my political antagonists.In other ways, though, the challenge was made even more acute by the fact that these movements also saw each other as political antagonists. Navigating a fieldwork landscape in which the researcher may be in profound political disagreement with research interlocutors, and in which interlocutors themselves have profound enmity toward the researcher's other interlocutors, was an emotional and ethical minefield. The method I employed for addressing the first challenge of political antagonism between self and research participants, I think, might be a useful strategy for other researchers in other contexts to contemplate. My bumbling attempts to address the second challenge, that of working with or on groups who see themselves as political "enemies" (especially the settlers on one side, and the Islamic Movement and Hamas on the other side) might be considered a tentative failure. But even accounts of failure can be useful for other researchers as a cautionary tale or a tool for devising better methods and approaches.

There are indeed ethical pitfalls entailed in doing fieldwork with groups whose politics are abhorrent to the researcher. In particular, when one's research goal is in direct conflict with the goal of research participants, the use of deception about the purpose of the research for the sake of the researcher's political commitment can be all too seductive. For me, the problem of my disagreement with my interlocutors entailed two different issues. The goal of my research did not stand in opposition to research participants' life-projects. On the contrary, because they were my political competitors, my research objective was to arrive at a better understanding of these women activists' perspectives and lifeworlds, about which I felt we knew very little. The purpose of this knowledge, however, is not to devise ways to undermine their objectives, but rather to find ways by which a potential pluralist, liberal, democratic framework could include illiberal, socially ultraconservative, so-called religious fundamentalist actors, and engage them in conversation. In addition, by merit of my being a native Israeli, my particular coded language and idiom betrayed my political identity to such an extent that there was little room for mistake about my political leanings. It was clear to my interlocutors that I was not a political "insider" in the groups or an ally of their religious and political agenda.[9] But the question that presented itself was, Was I a person who could really listen to them? Was I a person who could potentially open herself up and truly hear what they had to say? To me it was clear I was not. And yet I wanted to be. One of the motivations for the project was to try to understand my political "others" in order to make room for them in what I knew was currently an exclusionary liberal framework that had no place for what some problematically call "religious fundamentalists."

My inelegant method to address this challenge, which I elaborate on in my book, is what I ended up calling "acting as if." What if you acted as if you could listen and open yourself up to the lifeworld of someone you saw as your political adversary? Would that open up the possibility that you might actually hear something that you couldn't before, when acting "authentically?" Let me give you some examples. When I sit in a lecture by a prominent sheikh who trades in the most ubiquitous anti-Semitic tropes, about Jews historically being of a devious nature, about their proclivity for prophet killing, what should I do? Should I disrupt the lesson to express my disagreement, a reaction that will foreclose further conversation, or should I try to listen to all of what he has to say? Or in a synagogue lesson where the rabbi explains that Arabs are both the progenitors and progeny of "evil inclination" (*yetzer hara'*), should I start to lecture him back on the profound racism of what he is saying? Or what about the countless times I heard in lessons and lectures by sheikhs, *da'iyat*, rabbis, and *rabbaniyot* that a woman is a jewel that must be kept in a safe, while the secular woman who rolls in the street is treated like garbage because she doesn't guard her modesty?

In each of these instances, acting "authentically" would mean foreclosing the continuation of the interaction. Once when I brought my sister with me to a famous rabbi's lecture, her reaction expressed how I would have conducted myself authentically. When the rabbi said something particularly racist, she got up from her chair at the back of the women's section in the audience and said, "I am going to slap this bastard!" to the shocked gasps of the women around us, for whom the rabbi was a revered authority. Needless to say, that kind of authenticity, while righteous and satisfying and expressing exactly what I myself felt, could not facilitate further engagement. "Acting as if" I can listen allows me to continue my engagement and brings me closer to the possibility of really seeing my interlocutors' worlds. For me "acting as if" was an embodied, physical exercise in trying to cultivate an openness that I lacked on the inside, in the hope that the external effort would have an effect on my interiority. A clear example of this embodiment is going to West Bank settlements. It is something that for political reasons I do not do, and yet in the research I had to physically take my body across the Green Line and into settlements, "acting as if" I could go there, even though "authentically" I could not.

Whether or not this exercise was successful is for the readers of my work, my research interlocutors, and others in their movements to judge. I struggled with the sense of inauthenticity. I have presented a few of the people who participated in my research with chapters or articles addressing their movement, and their reaction has been positive. However, the fact that in my book I have placed side by side movements on the Jewish-Israeli religious right and the Muslim-Palestinian religious right has been upsetting to some. In all cases the objection focused on the fact that Hamas and the settlers are both included in my comparative framework. The focus on Hamas and the settlers, of course, continues to ignore the presence of Shas and the Israeli Islamic Movement, again erasing intersectional complexity for the sake of binary clarity. For example, a positive review of my book in *Haaretz*, an Israeli newspaper, carried the unnecessarily provocative title, "What Do Settler Women and Female Suicide Bombers Have in Common?" The title (but not the body of the review) really missed what my work was about—the dynamic, complicated, and varied gender politics of conservative religious-political movements and the mechanisms that shape women's activism in them. The title's aim was perhaps to make both settler sympathizers upset about a comparison between pious settlers and "terrorists," and Hamas sympathizers outraged by the comparison of martyrs for the cause of liberation with colonialist usurpers. Even though any sort of judgment of moral equivalency was really not the point of my work (I even say so quite explicitly, that the point is not about symmetry in the context of the Israeli-Palestinian conflict—since there is none, there's clearly an occupier and an occupied), it has been hard for either side to see it any other way.

And indeed, in a review of the book in the most popular settler newspaper *Besheva*, the author admits to not having read the book, and to the fact that from the *Haaretz* description it seems that I have actually captured a great deal of what settler women activists hold dear and how they see themselves. Yet, because the research covers settler activists and Hamas activists in its framework, it is an unworthy exercise and, the author concludes, "If book-burning was considered to be a valid cultural experience, this book would certainly be a preferred candidate for the flames." The mere treatment of settler "women of valour" alongside Hamas "terrorists" was an immoral transgression, in the reviewer's view. On the other hand, on Arabic-language websites sympathetic to Hamas, I had been deemed "the Zionist scholar Dr. Lihi Ben Shitrit," even though I have never been affiliated with any Israeli university or state institution and even though I am hardly a Zionist. Some fellow scholars who are committed to the Palestinian cause have also, somewhat like the reviewer in *Besheva* but from the opposite direction, appreciated the research's rich and unique ethnography, but also deemed the fact of the comparative framework morally questionable.

I tend to agree with the critics from both sides. Placing all four groups in one book together and trying to offer fair representations in which activists from each movement can see themselves in my descriptions, and which allows me to try to go beyond my and the reader's aversion to their political projects, is politically challenging and morally hazardous. It also does not serve my own clear antioccupation agenda, which would have been perhaps better served (symbolically more than concretely, of course) by singly producing a scathing critique of the settler-colonial project. But I felt that that type of work, as well as its ideological counterpart in the plethora of "terrorism" studies that see Hamas strictly through a terrorism prism, has been done and continues to be done by many other scholars who are much more adept at it than I am. What I wanted to add by working with "both sides" was to first understand, rather than condemn, my political adversaries, and second to use this understanding not to fight these adversaries but to open up a conversation with them by adequately and fairly representing their worlds. I think I succeeded in creating fair accounts, but I don't think I succeeded in creating the conversation I had hoped for. Yet I hope that at least I provided a meaningful attempt that others can build on and execute better.

23

The (Ambiguous) Fieldwork Experiences of a German Moroccan in Jordan

MALIKA BOUZIANE

Over the course of the last five years, I have conducted more than 20 months of field research, seeking to examine how informality shapes state-society relations in Jordan. In order to understand the complexity of political dynamics in Jordan and the negotiated boundaries between formality and informality, I opted for qualitative, field-based, and ethnographic research methods. While doing so, I engaged in debates on critical ethnography on reflexivity, power relations, and the researcher's positionality in the process of knowledge production.

Based on personal experiences gained during field research in the south of Jordan, this account illustrates how the perception of me as a Muslim German woman of Moroccan descent influenced the process of knowledge production. I explore how different facets of my identity—Arab descent, religious denomination, German socialization, and gender—structured my access to the field and the process of data generation. In doing so, this chapter takes the insider/outsider debate as a starting point. This debate considers the question of how the researcher's status as an insider shapes ethnographic field research (Narayan 1993). Insiders—researchers who have background ties to the culture being studied—are often ascribed a privileged position in the field. It is claimed that they have a comprehensive view of their culture and society and a good understanding of the daily routines, symbols, and value systems (Van Ginkel 1998, 256). Thus, they can "offer new angles of vision and depths of understanding" (Clifford and Marcus 1986, 9).

The rigid division of the insider-versus-outsider debate not only neglects the position of being in-between the insider and outsider, the partial insider. It also ignores that researchers can "belong to different communities simultaneously" and have a multiple subjectivity incorporating diverse identifications (Narayan 1993, 676). Thus, researchers do not have one status, but a "set of statuses" (Merton 1972, 22). With this chapter I seek to reflect on the implications that these statuses have for doing field research in a context that is culturally familiar but is not one's own society or culture. Integrating these statuses into the debate on insider researchers' positioning enriches the discussion about endogenous ethnography as it draws our attention to another layer of complexity with regard to the already varied positioning of the insider researcher (Kempny 2012, 43).

This chapter starts by laying out a theoretical perspective on the researcher's positionality in the field, relating it to intricacies of insider/outsider status and illustrating why it is important to integrate reflexivity in field research. Drawing on this, I subsequently examine how the perception of me as a partial insider shaped my access to the field, as well as the complexities inherent in the relations between the researcher and the interlocutors. I then specifically elaborate on how the two attributes of Arabness and religion played out in my ethnographic fieldwork in the Jordanian South, and explore my gendered experiences and the relevance of my Germanness for gendered norms and interactions. Finally, I discuss some ethical considerations that occurred during the field research and how I dealt with them.

Positionality, Reflexivity, and the Status of (Partial) Insider

In line with the postmodern turn, my own field research has been based on the con- viction that my subjectivity is relevant for ethnographic field research and that it shapes the process of data collection. Researchers are not "empty baskets." Rather they bring in their own interpretative systems and enter the field with assumptions, hopes, and expectations (Cerwonka 2007, 26; Kanaaneh 1997, 7). Reflecting on and acknowledging the researcher's role and interactions with the researched is a constitutive moment of knowledge production (Abels 1993, 8). "Facts are made," argues the anthropologist Paul Rabinow (1977, 150). Therefore, he continues, they cannot be collected as if they were stones, lifted and packed in a carton and shipped home to be analyzed in a laboratory. Rather, knowledge is historically situated and embedded in power relations (Wedeen 2010, 719). Thus, researchers should be conceived as positioned writers (Okely 1996). In their quest to highlight the sig- nificance of positionality and reflexivity for knowledge claims, feminist researchers developed the concept of "situated knowledge" (Harding 1991; Hartsock 1999). Knowledge is situated since it is always partial and "situated in the relation to people we study" (Narayan 1993, 678). Thus, the reflexivity of the research should include reflecting the process and in particular the self and the power relations shaping interactions between researcher and informants in the field (Kempny 2012, 41).

This chapter addresses a kind of reflexivity that is discussed in anthropological literature as "endogenous ethnography"—an epistemological debate on "native" researchers and the complexities between identity and the process of knowledge production (Abu-Lughod 1988; Karim 1993; Narayan 1993; Van Ginkel 1998). The specific positionality of the native researcher for knowledge construction and

the situatedness of epistemological claims have become core elements of ethnographic debates on field research, insights that have been almost completely neglected in mainstream political science. Indeed, reflexivity in general has been
disparaged by positivist political scientists as "navel gazing" (Wedeen 2010, 258).
Recently, however, a growing, though still limited, number of political scientists
have started to grapple with ethnographic method(ology) and the question of (self-
)reflexivity in the research process (Bayard de Volo and Schatz 2004; Cerwonka
2007; Harders 2002; Lenner 2014; Wedeen 2010). As indicated earlier, I refer to
the insider/outsider debate in order to examine how my subjectivity influenced my
field research and with this the process of knowledge production. Given that insider status is usually ascribed to researchers who have cultural ties to the society
being studied, what makes me an insider? As a daughter of Moroccan parents who
grew up and was socialized in Germany, I was in a privileged position to become
acquainted with both cultures and both languages. Though living in Germany, my
parents were keen to teach my brothers and me the language of our origin and religion (Sunni Islam). To this end, we took classes in Classical Arabic and Islamic theology at a private school. I spent more than 10 years learning Arabic and grappling
with Islam. Being well versed in Moroccan culture, having Arabic-language skills,
and knowledge in Islamic theology were competences that made me—from the
perspective of my informants—eligible for insider status. However, having background ties to the culture and language of the society being studied does not imply
that cultural identity is the decisive factor influencing field research. Such assumptions have been criticized for their underlying essentialism. They neglect not only
the complex background of native researchers but also the possibility that "factors
such as education, gender, sexual orientation, class, race, ... may at different times
outweigh the cultural identity" associated with insider status (Narayan 1993, 672).

For the purpose of this chapter the question of how the category of gender shapes
research is of particular interest (Altorki and El-Solh 1988; Karim 1993; Robbins
and Bamford 1997). Feminist research has sensitized the debate on methods and
methodology to the role of gender as a structuring category with regard to access
to informants, data generation, ethics, and the interpretation of field results (Abels
1993; Coffey 1999; Harders 2002). While some accounts highlight the limiting
effects of gender, others have convincingly argued that gender does not constitute
an absolute category. In the field, the gender category encounters other variables as
well that tend to minimize the potentially constraining impact of gender (Altorki
and El-Solh 1988, 6). With regard to the Arab world, there is only a limited academic methodology literature examining how the intertwining of the gender category and insider status shapes fieldwork experiences (Al-Ali and El-Kholy 1999;
Joseph 1988; Sherif 2001). One exception is the unique anthology *Arab Women
in the Field: Studying Your Own Society*, in which Arab researchers discuss the ways
in which their (actual or ascribed) status as Arab women affects fieldwork in their
own societies (Altorki and El-Solh 1988). In this volume, the researchers fit into

two groups: those who were socialized in the Arab world (Altorki 1988; Shami 1988), and those who grew up in Europe or North America (Abu-Lughod 1988; Joseph 1988). While my personal biography places me in the second group, the fact that my research is based in a different Arab country (Jordan) than my parents' place of origin (Morocco) has implications for the insider/outsider debate and its dichotomous perspective. I have not studied my own societies (neither Morocco nor Germany), but I have conducted research in a country, Jordan, that is culturally not foreign to me. Therefore, I describe myself as a partial insider. Given the cultural proximity of both countries (Jordan and Morocco) the perception of me is usually that of a "fellow Arab." The implications of researching a foreign country in a culturally familiar area have only rarely been discussed (Al-Ali and El-Kholy 1999). This account aims to contribute to filling this gap in the methodology literature by elaborating on questions regarding the status of a partial insider in the Arab world, emerging from the researcher's positioning within an intricate mesh of cultural and social fields.

Research Experiences of a German Moroccan Women

From 2009 to 2014 I conducted field research in Ma'an, a city almost 300 kilometers south of the Jordanian capital. My field research in Ma'an included interviews with experts and ordinary people but also informal discussions and participatory observation. I began my field research by doing what I thought a political scientist is supposed to do; I conducted expert interviews. During this first explorative period I noticed that my interview partners paid particular attention to my Arab descent— my Arabness, as I call it. Although I spent my entire life in Germany, interlocutors perceived me as a woman who belonged to the same cultural, linguistic, and religious community as they did, who came from a country (Morocco) that suffered from societal, political, and economic inequalities similar to theirs. Thus, many interviews began with discussions about the familial relationships between the Moroccan and Jordanian monarchs, or about the political system of the two countries. Particularly in the Jordanian South my personal life was, from the beginning, a subject of great interest to my interlocutors. Indeed, the majority of my interviews usually began with questions about my German-Moroccan background and religious denomination. Once my interview partners could position me within their own scripts—a Sunni Muslim female German of Moroccan origin—the following discussions would usually take the shape of an intimate conversation rather than a formal interview. Informal discussions created a situation of trust in which informants did not see the necessity to present more positive narratives; I usually would receive the nonresearcher, non-European stories that usually were more (self-)critical. These experiences confirm assumptions of the insider/outsider debate that insiders often adopt a privileged position in the field. However, this does not mean that all facets of my subjectivity have been equally relevant for all interview partners. Depending on the context, the relevance ascribed to the different facets of my identity could differ significantly.

The perception of "our" sharing the attribute of Arabness and religion put me in the unique position of having instant access to the rather closed local community of Ma'an, which is generally reluctant to open up to foreigners. My partial insider status accelerated the process of building social networks, as my interlocutors were supportive and gave me easy access to their networks. I started my field research in Ma'an with an interview with the director of a local nongovernmental organization. In the course of this interaction, and once my interlocutor had insights into my research, he arranged five other interviews for me and was willing to provide me with further contacts. Though I did not experience the foreign researcher's usual struggle securing access to the researched site, I was dependent on those I sought to research. Thus, at the beginning of my field research it was "they" who defined who was relevant for my research and to which scripts and perspectives I would be exposed. However, as Harders (2002, 61) notes, interview partners and researchers are in a process of continuous and often indirect negotiations about status and power relations within the research situation. As status changes in the course of time, power relations do as well. I was gradually able to broaden my social networks in Ma'an and to generate knowledge about local social and political dynamics. This in turn allowed me to free myself from the often-paternalistic behavior of my interlocutors and to decide independently about the people I wanted to interview. Acquiring social capital and knowledge changed the relationship between me and those people who supported my research project as gatekeepers.

Arabness and Religion

People in Ma'an did not have much experience with foreign researchers. The concept of being interviewed for a research project was relatively new to the majority of my interview partners. They were as curious and keen to learn from me as I was interested in learning from them. During one of my first interviews, one informant interrupted the interview to call several relatives after having learned about my Moroccan heritage, telling them to come over to meet the Moroccan woman in his living room. The interest of my interview partner in presenting me as an "attraction" resulted from his claim of having Moroccan roots and the circumstance that I was the first Moroccan he had met. So we spent the first hour of the interview trying to contextualize the roots of his tribe within Moroccan history. Encounters like this created moments that let me become aware of the relevance of my Moroccan-Arab descent for my field research. The perception of me as an insider due to my religious and cultural background created a sense of familiarity and proximity that not only made access to the field easier and conversations intimate, but also made it possible to address and go beyond power asymmetries between me and my informants. Furthermore, my status significantly contributed to the ways in which I could push the boundaries of what could be said and what could be criticized, without causing my interviewees to close off. As an insider, I was entrusted with information that an outsider would not be able to access. In some situations, informants responded to questions but asked me not to translate their answers to my non-Arab colleagues who joined the interview. I found it particularly revealing to see this happening even in interview situations in which I accompanied other European colleagues to *their* interviews. Sometimes interlocutors would focus on me and completely forget that it was my colleague who was supposed to conduct the interview. The perception of "our" sharing the attribute of Arabness made me an accomplice of the interlocutor, with whom she was willing to share knowledge on the condition that this knowledge was not transmitted to non-Arab participants. Over the course of many visits to Ma'an, mutual trust increased and some interview partners came to see me as a confidante whom they could trust with their secrets. One female candidate for the municipal election, for example, told me in detail about her participation in (illegally) forging personal IDs for the parliamentary elections.

Beside the Arab origin, it was people's perception of me as a Muslim that ascribed to me the status of an insider, as mentioned earlier. Knowing that I am originally from Morocco, many of my interlocutors assumed that I am a Sunni Muslim. Sometimes, when interviewees would directly ask about my religious beliefs, I would confirm their assumption that I am a Sunni Muslim. Though I did not correspond to the(ir) idea of a "proper" Muslim woman because I was not wearing a veil, my belonging to the "Sunni community" seemed to be sufficient to receive their approval and acceptance. The majority of my interlocutors acknowledged my limited ostentatious religiousness by ascribing this to my socialization in a European (non-Muslim) country. Indeed, many of my interview partners would articulate their astonishment about my good Arabic language skills and my knowledge about Islamic history and theology in expressions such as *masha' allah*. Being a Muslim living in Europe, my interview partners expected me to share with them my knowledge about the living conditions of Muslims in Germany. In these moments it was I who was ascribed the position of the expert. Experiences like these ones exemplify how ambivalent and negotiable social relations are. As Lenner (2014) rightly argues, power asymmetries are not static in the sense that the researcher or interview partners completely control the situation. Rather, researcher and the researched negotiate indirectly their respective status depending on the knowledge required in the respective situation and power positions within the research situation. The perception of my person as a Muslim became especially apparent when interviewees, as a matter of course, cited verses from the Koran or sayings by the Prophet and his caliphs in order to substantiate their arguments or to justify behavioral practices. For example, the head of a local NGO cited the famous quotation from ʿUmar ʾibn al-Ḥaṭāb (the second caliph), "If poverty were a man, I would have killed him," as a "leitmotiv" for his own fight against poverty.

Gender and "Germanness"

However, the familiarity and proximity to interlocutors due to my Arabness and religious beliefs could not entirely counterbalance the gender component. In the end, I was an Arab woman, and as such I had—to a certain extent—to abide by gender related rules. Non-Arab female researchers enjoy in this regard more space for maneuver since their noncompliance is ascribed to their different (Western) culture. However, this does not imply that interviewees approve practices that do not conform to gender-related rules. But interviewees will be more indulgent to non-Arab female researchers. Being a German of Moroccan descent who could have been a Jordanian woman according to my external appearance, I was not always able to escape gender-related expectations and strict social norms when in public spaces. In practice this meant that I was not able to spend time in a café, for example between two interviews, or meet interview partners in public places. In these moments I struggled with conflicting identities: the German graduate student who was doing research for her PhD, the Moroccan woman, and the feminist who was annoyed by patriarchal dominance. Practically the constraining environment meant organizing a place where I could spend my spare time. It also meant dressing appropriately if I did not want my reputation to suffer and wanted interlocutors to take me seriously. Ultimately, not abiding by these rules would have compromised my access to the field, in addition to spoiling my gatekeeper's reputation. However, in contrast to Jordanian women, my German socialization allowed me to assume the role of an "Arab foreigner," meaning that during research situations I was still perceived as a Moroccan woman, but because I was also a German I could—to a certain extent—distance myself from the gender roles ascribed to Jordanian women. Interlocutors' knowledge about my German background helped me to manipulate the traditional societal barriers between the genders in Jordan, which ultimately provided flexibility and mobility. Thus, I was able to enter social arenas dominated by men, as well as the private spaces mostly reserved for women; I conversed with dignitaries in their divans and women in their own living rooms.

However, as my experiences illustrate, insider status is a two-edged sword. On the one hand, as described earlier, the perception of me as a partial insider with whom informants shared a religious and cultural background made my field research definitely easier. On the other hand, cultural intimacy can be a disadvantage for the researcher. Being perceived as an insider can impede in-depth discussions on certain social and political "realities" due to taken-for-granted assumptions. For my field research, this meant that detailed information and interpretive knowledge were seldom explicit, since implicit normative and practical assumptions were presumed from the beginning to be shared. While the majority of interlocutors demonstrated goodwill and answered my questions, others would express their astonishment about my inquiring about the "obvious." Once, I asked an interview partner about the role imams play in Ma'an society. My interlocutor answered by pinpointing my Moroccan origin, suggesting that I should know that. Pointing out the differences between sociopolitical structures and dynamics in Morocco and Jordan, I tried to counter his expectations and encourage my interview partner to provide explanations for what he considered evident, without discrediting my position as a partial insider.

Though my Arabness and religious denomination were the predominant lenses through which the majority of my interview partners perceived me, in certain contexts my Germanness was the most important attribute to which interlocutors would refer. In 2011 I accompanied a female candidate who intended to run for office in the upcoming municipal elections. Um Ali and I visited several women in their homes to ask for their support for her candidacy. During these encounters Um Ali continuously introduced me as her friend from Germany who was doing research for her PhD. Introducing me to third parties as a German researcher, I realized, was a narrative that allowed Um Ali to demonstrate to others her broad social network—which included people from Europe—and to promote this as an argument for her candidacy. In this context, my Germanness—more than my Arabness—was advantageous for the purposes of Um Ali. In a paternalistic manner she decided which facet of my subjectivity was relevant and forced me to accept it. My intention to be a silent observer was undermined by Um Ali's behavior since people became curious and wanted to know more about the "German friend" who did not correspond to their image of a German women.

Ethical Considerations

Although other foreign researchers may envy my easy access to Ma'an society, it was also linked with ethical considerations. As my field visits to Ma'an and rapport with several informants increased, I rapidly became part of different local community circles. This included invitations to social events such as weddings or other informal social occasions. Though I was an integral part of these interactions, social events to which I was invited as a guest—and was not addressed as a researcher—were an excellent opportunity to observe and experience social normality. These encounters turned out to be revealing experiences, as people would completely forget about my presence and continue to chat, exchange stories, and tell each other the latest news and gossip. However, these encounters were also very revealing with regard to political dynamics on the ground. They were particularly revealing during elections, as they gave me another perspective on local political dynamics and helped me to position the different narratives I received during interviews. During the parliamentary elections of 2010, I had the opportunity to accompany one of my interlocutors to the polling station and afterward to a family gathering. During this get-together women discussed the ballot and the coalitions between different tribes, exchanged rumors on candidates, and predicted who would win the elections. Being part of these encounters allowed me to generate in-depth ethnographic knowledge.

However, these less formalized settings confronted me with ethical concerns. During these social occasions, participants were usually not asked if they consented to my participation. Sometimes participants did not even know that I was doing field research or the purpose of my project because I was introduced as a friend of the family. They also did not have the choice to end their participation in these interactions. The question I was concerned with was if and how I could use the ethnographic knowledge I generated during such encounters for my research. Is it ethical to make use of data I generated during social events though their producers did not know? Similar questions arose with regard to data I collected during intimate conversations with interlocutors to whom I developed a friendship-like relationship. These people would usually offer me, the nonresearcher, critical narratives.

To deal with these ethical concerns I decided to use information gathered in informal settings as background information, and to only quote people indirectly. When citing people in my writings I completely anonymize names and in most of the cases also functions of the informants to ensure that personal identities could not be easily deduced. If I used data generated in the course of informal gatherings during formal interview situations, I would be extremely cautious not to mention the persons from whom or the circumstances through which I received the respective information. This was in particular important in interviews with officials. Though I did not promise confidentiality to people I met in the frame of informal settings, in my writings I make sure that I have disguised any material used so that the identity of informants is concealed from their community and from anyone who might know of them or come to know of them. Yet giving priority to protecting informants and maintaining confidentiality brought up other ethical questions, most of all the lack of credit to my respondents. The presumption of anonymity protects informants against being harmed, but on the other hand anonymity enforces power asymmetries in the research relationship, as the researcher appears as the author while the researched remains anonymous (Alcadipani and Hodgson 2009; Floyd and Arthur 2012).

Conclusion

Based on personal field research experiences in the Jordanian South, this account illustrates that the social, historical, and cultural background of the researcher shapes the process of knowledge production. Informants' perception of me as a "fellow Arab" has certainly provided me with a privileged position in and facilitated my access to the field. However, as the chapter demonstrates, insider status is not an absolute category but intersects with other variables, such as gender, religion, and the biographical background. Being perceived as an insider does not imply that "native" researchers do not struggle with ambiguities, ambivalences, uncertainties, and intellectual irritation inherent to each research process. My personal experiences confirm that subjectivity shapes and affects knowledge production. Acknowledging this, in turn, means admitting that the researched phenomena can only be understood from a particular situated position of the researcher. Therefore, reflexivity in the research process must include a critical reflection on the positioning of the researcher, and in particular the ambiguous power relations that characterize interactions between the researcher and researched. The new interest of political scientists in ethnographical method(ology) offers the discipline an opportunity to elaborate theoretically and methodologically on this question and to rethink the epistemological claims of political science.

NOTES

Chapter 4

1. An early exception of research that was based on fieldwork was Motoko Katakura (1977). She was followed by Soraya Altorki (1986) and Sadeka Arebi (1994). Altorki discusses her methodological challenges at length.
2. I conducted fieldwork in Saudi Arabia on five different occasions, two of which were for almost a year, three of which were for two to three weeks. Outside the country, I conducted extensive interviews with Saudi Arabian political activists, both Sunni and Shia, over a span of eight years.
3. Kiren Aziz Chauhdry is a female political scientist who conducted early and important field research in Saudi Arabia and Yemen. Her personal networks were more developed beforehand and her sponsor other than a university.
4. I conducted 153 interviews about how people wanted to renegotiate the social contract that was hotly contested. I was on a Fulbright Scholar Grant and sponsored by the King Faisal Foundation. See Okruhlik 2004a, 2005.
5. He even lost his name. Saudi women keep their family name after marriage, yet they are sensitive to the US custom of a woman adopting the last name of her spouse. They assumed that I took Pat's last name. For the duration, he was referred to as Dr. Okruhlik.
6. As do the ceiling lights. When we walked into our apartment, we would flip the light switch on and greet the light fixtures in a loud voice, "Hi Prince Naif! How are you? What did you think of the interview today? I thought it was a really complicated but good meeting." Naif was the longtime, notorious minister of information.
7. I conducted extensive, in-depth interviews in Washington and London over the course of eight years. See Okruhlik 2002, 2004a.
8. It was trial by error. Several Saudi Arabians remarked, "It is good that you came early. If it were someone else here now, there would be no more researchers." An economist whispered, "If you play your cards right, you can be a very rich and powerful woman." Apparently, I misplayed my hand.
9. More difficult subjects might include succession and intra-Saud rivalries as well as studies about sexuality.

Chapter 5

1. These are the controversial words of Israeli Prime Minister Benjamin Netanyahu on the day of the 2015 elections. See http://972mag.com/netanyahus-race-baiting-was-long-planned-not-a-lapse-in-judgement/116313/.

2. Despite attempts by Israel to declare Jerusalem its unified capital, East Jerusalem is part of the Occupied Territories.

3. It also occupies Syrian territories on the Golan Heights. The Sinai was returned to Egypt in the 1970s.

4. Not to mention the additional complication that the PLO still has its official seat in Tunis.

5. For the first approach, see Challand 2009. For an example of research comparing Palestinian civil society from the "inside" (i.e., Israel) with that of the OPT, see Challand 2011.

6. Anne Le More would add also to pay their feeling of guilt towards Israeli. See Le More 2008.

7. E.g. the so-called Petition of the Twenty in 1999 calling for a stop of Palestinian corruption. See: "Editorial: Petition of the 20," *News from Within*, XV, 11, 2–4, 1999.

8. For ex, see Falk, Richard, "My expulsion from Israel," *The Guardian*, December 18, 2008. At http://www.theguardian.com/commentisfree/2008/dec/19/israel-palestinian-territories-united-nations.

9. Even journalists or diplomats are regularly denied entry.

10. http://www.righttoenter.ps/. It also lists very helpful points for any researchers traveling to Palestine: inform family and colleagues of your travel; leave copy of passport with them; inform your embassy or consulate of your intention to travel, with phone number; be familiar with the Israeli regulations and polices.

11. Located in East Jerusalem, with an office in Ramallah, PASSIA is the Palestinian Academic Society for the Study of International Affairs. It publishes a yearly diary with list of hotels, and contacts to Ministries, parliamentary members, NGOs, etc. See www.passia.org. They have now an app where all this information can be located online.

12. Providing that the person has the necessary documents, typically a valid passport and visa. Researchers usually come on a tourist visa, which lasts 90 days. The main potential trouble is getting into Israel and Palestine. Once there, movement should not be an issue.

13. https://bdsmovement.net/. The movement was created in 2005.

14. See Mohamed Bamyeh's (2015, 12) report on the state of social sciences in the Arab world where the author relays a critical view on the use of quantitative surveys in Arab societies. See http://www.theacss.org/uploads/English-ASSR-2016.pdf. I have never had this problem.

15. http://awraq.birzeit.edu/.

Chapter 6

1. Video posted on the *New York Times'* website shows rescue workers on the scene by 4:42 p.m. Beirut time, meaning that I probably witnessed the immediate aftermath of the attack during the descent. See Hubbard and Barnard 2014.

2. For clarity, I have edited messages and emails for typos, spacing, and different phonetic spellings of Arabic words and locations.

3. See, for example, Moughnieh 2012 on routine discussions of "the bomb" as a political actor.

4. During seven trips between 2007 and 2014, I conducted research on the evolution of Palestinian militant organizations in Beirut and southern Lebanon. During two trips in 2014, I also studied interactions between Palestinian and Syrian refugees in South Beirut.

5. The term "ethics of sight" is a riff on Timothy Pachirat's concept of a "politics of sight" (Pachirat 2011). For brief introductions to fieldwork in the Middle East and to research ethics see Fujii 2012; Clark 2006; Schwedler 2006.

6. The Blue Line demarcated Israel's full withdrawal from Lebanon in 2000. However, it is not technically an international border; it is possible to be on Lebanese territory south of the Blue

Line. The Blue Line is also distinct from the 1949 Green Line, which follows the Mandate-era border between French and English zones of control.

7. Most news outlets are owned by political parties and are understood as reporting through a specific ideological lens.

8. For example, in June 1982, UNIFIL soldiers watched from the side of the road as long lines of IDF tanks crossed the border at Naqura (Fisk 2002, 199); in April 1996, 120 Lebanese civilians were killed and several hundred, including four peacekeepers, were wounded while sheltering at the Fijian UNIFIL contingent's base in Qana. UNIFIL was established in 1978 to confirm the IDF withdrawal from southern Lebanon, to help the Lebanese government re-establish sovereignty in light of Palestinian guerrilla activity in the region, and to generally keep the peace ("UNIFIL Background" 2016).

Chapter 7

1. At the time, I was a fifth-year PhD student. I had a different PhD project, and when the uprising started, I simply decided to jump in and go to Egypt. I wrote a short proposal quickly and received permission and endorsement from my adviser to study the emerging event.

2. I am finishing this essay in mid-May 2016. I should clarify here that since the focus of this essay is mainly methodological, I will not go into detailed theoretical discussion about the definition or the use of "revolution" and "counterrevolution" as analytical categories. Analysts of Egypt and many activists in Egypt are in disagreement about when a so-called counterrevolution started. I also will not go into detail about the nature and the problems of Egypt's "failed" transition to democracy. These discussions are beyond the scope of this essay. I chose the temporal markers in this essay (the revolutionary phase from January 25, 2011, until July 2, 2013, and the counterrevolution from July 3, 2013, until the time of writing this essay) for two reasons. First, there is a strong agreement among activists and critics about a radical closure of political space and doing research in Egypt after the events of July 2013 (see Said, forthcoming); (2) I also experienced this radical difference between the opening of the revolution for doing research compared to the difficulties in the aftermath of July 2013; and (3) these temporal markers are justified and also useful for analytical purposes.

3. Discussing which methods worked better than others and in which times, if this is a viable question in the first place, goes beyond the scope of this essay.

4. Not many people in the activist scene even knew that I had become a naturalized US citizen; only close friends knew. But I still worried, given the context of distrust regarding foreigners, and my own internal sense of responsibility and positionality. I should note that my immigration and naturalization processes were not easy either, not least because they took place after September 11, 2001. I cannot say with certainty that my history as an activist in Egypt caused the various delays and harassments in these processes, but I do know for certain that my research has been always been shaped by my positionality and political choices.

5. Sociologist Mona Abaza (2011) described this phenomenon as "academic tourists sight-seeing the Arab Spring"; see also El-Mahdi 2011.

6. The tentative title of the book is *Revolution Squared: The Politics of Space and Time in the Egyptian Revolution*.

7. I believe this volume may be a great step along this path.

8. See, for example, YouTube channel of Kazeboon https://www.youtube.com/watch?v=_1VQ4Gqcqhg.

9. See their website https://wikithawra.wordpress.com/author/wikithawra/.

10. See their page at http://demometer.blogspot.com/.

11. On the fifth anniversary of the revolution, there was an important report published about organized efforts by mainstream news sources to erase information about the revolution from their web archives (see Al-Sayad 2016).

12. Even though many times the posts are public and meant to be shared, I feel obligated to ask their permission.

Chapter 8

1. See, among other things, the harrowing accounts in Stevenson 2015, and for an illustration of the systemic and systematic use of torture Human Rights Watch 2011.
2. Research Councils UK, http://www.rcuk.ac.uk/innovation/impacts/, accessed March 4, 2016.
3. The most exceptional work that makes the links and reveals the interconnectedness between producers and the world food system is McMichael 2013.
4. This section draws on my research on family farming in MENA, forthcoming; summary available Bush 2014b. On humanitarian disaster for Palestinian framers see, among other things, Zurayk et al. 2012; FAO 2009.
5. On the general literature see Bernstein 2010 and van der Ploeg 2010, 2013; and on the MENA see Bush 2016.
6. On the general critique of "resilience" see Evans and Reid 2014.
7. See the documentary film by Habib Ayeb and Ray Bush, *Fellahin* (2015), available from https://www.youtube.com/watch?v=U5wyOycrzaA.

Chapter 10

1. I will use only fictitious names in my account. I always offered to record the interviews under a fake name, and some of the Salafis preferred that option.
2. "Sheikh" is a title I usually employed whenever with an educated Salafi (an *alim*). The title is also used to indicate authority figures within the community at large, even when not based on religious prestige or scholarship.
3. In a foundational study about modern Salafism, Wiktorowicz (2006) proposed three categories: "quietist," largely apolitical, interested in praying, studying, and proselytizing; "politicos," bent on peaceful political activism via pressure groups or via institutional channels and party politics; and "jihadi," the loud minority calling for violent religious-political militancy. While these distinctions have been criticized in some quarters (Wagemakers 2009), they remain widely in use within academia and policymaking circles as well.
4. The Sunna represents the collection of the deeds and sayings of Muhammad aside from his pronouncements and revelations as God's messenger.
5. For Salafism in Jordan see Wiktorowicz 2000.
6. Interview with 'Anis, Sasab, Amman, June 10, 2015.
7. Hanafi is one of the four major schools of jurisprudence within Sunni Islam. It is considered the most flexible and diverse in terms of the sources of jurisprudence admitted. For an overview of all the schools see Vikør 2005.
8. IS was specifically linked to the radical splinter current of the *khawarij* of the early days of Islam.
9. The chapters or sections in which the holy book is divided. An *ayah* is a line within a sura.
10. I asked the exact reference of the sura (5:82) and checked it after the interview. Unless you have a deep knowledge of the Koran, whenever exposed to direct quotations of its suras make sure to ask for its coordinates.
11. By way of comparison and clarification, member of the Muslim Brotherhood that I met showed vastly different attitudes—as to be expected, for sure, but again singling out adherents to Salafism in their uncompromising stance within the Islamist galaxy.
12. Interview with Muhammad al-Tamimi, Amman, November 25, 2015.
13. For an elaboration on the subject, see Mahmood 2011, in particular chapter 1 ("The Subject of Freedom") and the concept of "normativity of freedom."

14. Atheism in the Arab world, as far as I have experienced it, is still a thorny subject among certain sectors of society—and definitely within the Salafi community. I have had mixed reactions when revealing my (lack of) belief. For an unproblematic answer, I have at times chosen to profess myself as Catholic, a stance accepted and recognized easily. I am never happy, though, whenever I lie for the sake of expediency.

15. Abu Muhammad al-Maqdisi was reportedly the chief jihadist ideologue according to the *Militant Ideology Atlas* edited by William McCants. The report is available at https://www.ctc.usma.edu/wp-content/uploads/2012/04/Atlas-ExecutiveReport.pdf.

16. For example, prominent quietist Salafi scholar Ali Al-Halabi has his own website: http://alhalaby.com/.

17. http://www.bbc.com/news/world-middle-east-31121160.

18. See the following section for the issue of language.

19. I have never visited Libya, though, the only Arab country Italy colonized.

20. Israeli citizens can enter Jordan relatively easily, although during my sojourn there I met only one Jewish Israeli. In tourist sites such as Petra and Wadi Rum, Israeli visitors are more frequent, although most of them seem to be Arab Israeli.

21. There was only one exception: a recent convert to Salafism from Lyon, France, whom I talked to during a visit in a Salafi mosque in Rusayfa, northeast of Amman—a good opportunity to use my rusty French.

22. For an important work addressing the issue of different meanings attributed to the same signifier in different contexts, see Schaffer 2000.

23. Interview with ʾAnis, Sasab, southern Amman, June 10, 2015.

24. I am thankful to Prof. Ling for discussing this concept with me (Ling 2015).

Chapter 11

1. "L'imam Bouziane relaxé pour ses propos sur le châtiment des femmes infidèles," *Le Monde*, June 22, 2005.

2. The most important among these security incidents were the 1999–2000 clashes in the Dinniya region and the 2007 battle in the Nahr al-Barid Palestinian refugee camp. In the first incident dozens, in the second hundreds, died on both sides. Clashes between infiltrating jihadis and Lebanese soldiers have happened regularly since the start of the Syrian civil war.

3. Interview, Tripoli, Lebanon, August 2, 2011.

4. "Ordinary Muslims" refers to those who are not affiliated with any religious movement, living their lives in ways that are comparable to the majority of Lebanese. Some of them might be explicitly sympathetic to Salafism, for example, yet this does not mean sharing the latter's lifestyle.

Chapter 12

1. I use the adjective *foreign* because it is the only one that could define us all in that particular context. We were not all North Africans or Europeans. We were not all atheist or Catholic or Muslim. We were all young, unveiled women living together.

2. Interview with the author, July 28, 2009, Casablanca.

3. Excerpts of Malika El Fassi's article "About Girls' Education" published in March 1935 in *Al Maghrib*, quoted in Baker 1998, 64.

4. See http://www.qf.org.qa/about/about.

Chapter 13

1. For a recent survey of this voluminous literature, see Haggard 2015.

2. For an overview, see Cammett 2017.

3. In the framework of contemporary causal inference, we would express the underlying logic of inference more formally in terms of the conditional independence of assignment and treatment, such that across matched units, assignment to treatment is "as good as" random.
4. For an overview of the Rubin Causal Model, see Holland 1986.

Chapter 14

1. The "soak and poke" reference is to Fenno (1986), in which the author advances the case for immersive field research as a precursor to the development of testable hypotheses and rational choice models. It has been invoked as an instrumental justification for field research, but is still firmly positivist in its orientation. For an example of full-throated ridicule of participant observation that not only reduces ethnography to this instrumental logic but also openly mocks it, see Doug Rathbun's 2011 post to the Duck of Minerva, "Stuff Political Scientists Like #6: Soaking and Poking."
2. Peregrine Schwartz-Shea and Dvora Yanow offer an excellent critique of mixed-methods approaches that do not attend to the need to speak "across epistemic communities," and do not recognize the distinctive "abilities and training required to conduct interpretive research" (2012, 131). In their discussion, they find Ahmed and Sil (2009) particularly useful in elucidating the limits of promoting mixed methods (within a single research study), though they share the latter's openness to the notion that a researcher may wish "to explore a research *topic* that encompasses several research *questions*, each of which necessitates adopting a different approach" (134).
3. The leaves of the *Catha edulis* shrub are chewed to release a mild narcotic stimulant. This is a well-established local practice whose significations are interpreted differently in the academic literature. See note 4.
4. Interpretations of what khat-chews are, what they do, and for whom, vary widely, but no scholar of Yemen avoids them entirely. Sheila Carapico argues that "for research purposes a qat-chew amounts to a 'focus group,' for people to speak openly and the guest is invited to introduce a discussion topic, listen in on other business, and to take discreet notes" (1998, xi). Lisa Wedeen suggests that "it is the very equality-inducing openness of many qat chews that also reproduces status distinctions by generating occasions on which social classes mix, although hierarchically (2008, 123). Reflecting on his experience chewing khat as a component of his field research, Paul Dresch contends that the experience "was not well described as simply 'dialogue.' Nor was it 'data collection,'" but instead "the more mundane and empirical the published facts ... the more collecting them resembled clandestine intrigue" or "a trade in secrets" (2000, 109–110), while Dan Varisco argues that for Yemenis, "chewing is an act with symbolic references that any Yemeni can follow to reinforce and in some cases to create a cultural identity" (1986, 3).
5. Expression praising God, functionally equivalent in this instance to "Thank goodness!"

Chapter 15

1. In social movement theory, collective action frames are the frames that link a movement's activists with one another. They are a set of understandings shared by the movement's adherents about some problematic condition or a situation they define as being in need of change, about which they make attributions regarding who or what is to blame, articulate an alternative set of arrangements, and urge others to act in concert to affect change. Master frames do the same tasks, but they refer to the frames that link several movements with each other (see Snow and Benford 1992).
2. Identity division involves a set of discriminatory practices against a particular group, leading an individual to acquire a feeling of solidarity that translates into a salient identity.
3. The peak of protests is period of time in which the protests reach their utmost level in terms of public participation, activists' use of disruptive actions, and the state's use of repression. In

Tunisia, this period started on January 12, 2011, and lasted until Ben Ali fled the country two days after. In Egypt, this period began on January 28, 2011, and lasted until Mubarak's resignation on February 11, 2011. In Jordan, the protests reached their peak on March 24, 2011, when the protesters organized a sit-in at the Interior Ministry Circle and lasted one day, after which the protests became weaker.

4. The two websites are *The Tunisian People Are Burning Themselves, Mr. President* (*Sha'eb Tunis Yihriq fi rouho ya siadat alra'is*); and *The Tunisian Street Agency* (*Wikalat Anba' al-Shar' al-Tunisie*).
5. A daily printed newspaper with a website: http://www.addustour.com/.

Chapter 16

1. The survey of this literature is not intended to be exhaustive; rather the intention is to illustrate it with a number of examples of quantitative MENA research. Explicitly excluded is research in economics that obviously has a much longer tradition in analyzing quantitative data, as well as research in which MENA data are used but that does not deal specifically with the region such as the substantial literature on the resource curse. Other examples of such work would include the research based on existing indices relating, for example, to regime characteristics (e.g., Polity IV) or gender equality.
2. The Pew research center also ran a number of polls in the region.
3. Nationally representative surveys based on small samples usually assign stronger weights to undersampled individuals, usually the rural population that is more expensive to survey. The opinions of these individuals then carry more weight when looking into national level averages.
4. An example of such a question is the following: Here are some statements that describe how widespread corruption and bribe taking are in all sectors in [country name]. Which of the following statements reflects your own opinion the best?" The possible answers range from "Hardly anyone is involved in corruption" to "Most officials are corrupt" to "Almost everyone is corrupt."
5. For example, a study on Islamist voters in Morocco and Tunisia confirmed the educated middle-class type of profile from the opinion surveys (Pellicer and Wegner 2014a), but a study on Egypt argued that in this case it was indeed poorer voters who were supportive of Islamists (Elsayyad and Hanafy 2014). A study on Tunisia remained inconclusive; it did find a positive correlation of Ennahda support and socioeconomic development but to a lesser extent than for some other parties (Gana, Hamme, and Rebah 2012). Compared to studies based on survey data, they have the advantage that they look into real voting, not just expressions of support in a survey; their major disadvantage is they typically have to use highly aggregated data because electoral outcomes are not available at the polling station level but only at the district level. High abstention rates in MENA elections make these studies vulnerable to "ecological fallacy," because it is unknown whether, from a socioeconomic point of view, the "average voter" went to vote, or a particular subgroup voted that is, in fact, not representative of the district. Therefore, the number of electoral districts in a country on which these findings are based is crucial. The study on Morocco is based on the country's 91 districts, the study on Egypt on 46 districts, on Tunisia on 264 districts.
6. The component may be, for example, information that is given only to a treatment group, or questions that are framed differently for respondent groups. An important subtype of this are list experiments that allow probing attitudes where social desirability bias can be expected to be strong, such as, for example, attitudes related to race or gender.

Chapter 17

1. The survey was conducted in collaboration with Jason Brownlee of the University of Texas at Austin, hence I will use "we" in the remainder of this paper when providing examples from that survey. I alone am responsible for this chapter.

2. Natural experiments, in which individuals are assigned to the treatment or control by some natural or bureaucratic process rather than the deliberate intervention of the researcher (e.g., a housing lottery or the arbitrary drawing of a border) are not considered here, nor do I discuss randomized control trials, in which the researcher designs and applies the treatment in real-world situations (e.g., randomly digging water wells across a sample of villages, or assigning certain schools in a country to teach a program on interfaith tolerance).

3. Another consideration, which proved a happy accident for us, was that while we set out to conduct a face-to-face survey, repeated piloting was unable to provide us confidence in the results of the survey. We used the remainder of the money to transition to a telephone-based survey because the cost of a new face-to-face survey was prohibitive.

4. List experiments rely on two general assumptions. First, adding the fourth item does not impact how respondents feel about the other three items ("no design effects"). This would mean, for instance, that the fourth item is so outlandish that it suddenly makes the other three items seem inconsequential by comparison. Second, there are "no liars"; individuals *want* to provide their true opinion but are held back by concerns that they would be subject to sanction if they answered truthfully (see also Glynn 2013).

5. Other sensitive question techniques which may stress cognitive thresholds, particularly over the phone, are types of randomized response techniques.

6. Kramon and Weghorst suggest potential fixes for these issues in face-to-face administration of list experiments, such as using cartoons to communicate concepts and use of whiteboards to keep track of items. Some of these have analogues that are worth considering for telephone-based list experiments (e.g., keeping track of items on one's fingers), while others are not applicable.

7. While it was not an issue of overwhelming concern in Egypt at that time, in other contexts there may be a security—in addition to a technical—risk that is triggered by the in-person involvement of a Western researcher.

8. I made a conscious decision not to interview or approach patients inside the facilities themselves because I was not sure I could obtain informed consent (I did not want to risk respondents thinking that their continued access to the facility rested on their decision whether or not to talk to me, let alone the content of our conversation).

Chapter 19

1. Parts of this book chapter are in my MA thesis (Martin 2013).
2. In effect, mobilization efforts redefined Kuwait's state-civil society relations. These events fit with Tarrow's concept of protest cycles. Tarrow 1998; Hagagy 2012.
3. Interview, February 12, 2012 Bayan, Kuwait.
4. Interview, February 23, 2012, Hawalli, Kuwait. Social movement theorists generally conceptualize social movement emergence as occurring through the collective action of nonstate actors in "civil society" via SMOs (Tarrow 1998). These groups of SMOs—which are civil-society groups comprised of activists—foster the solidarity, collective identity, common purpose, and sustained contention necessary for emergence. Authors perceive SMOs as the main agents of mobilization efforts in state-civil society relations—mobilization being recruitment, dissemination of information, or public debates that lead to protests, rallies, or other efforts that contest state powers (McAdam, McCarthy, and Zald 1996).
5. A notable exception is Honari 2013.
6. Interview, April 11, 2012 Jahra, Kuwait.
7. Interview, March 4, 2012 Mangef, Kuwait.
8. Interview, April 29, 2012 Sharq, Kuwait.
9. I borrow themes from Oliver, Cadena-Roa, and Strawn 2003 to analyze the cultural narratives, identities, and logistical capabilities of interviewees who were participating and organizing the protests.

10. This metric was borrowed from Eltantawy and Weist 2011.
11. In the case study, organizations, names, and other specific details have been altered to respect the confidentiality of participants and organizations.
12. This conclusion rests upon the premise that activists of all stripes typically approach the Internet as an information resource or a toolbox that may be used to enhance the effectiveness of more traditional mobilization practices (Marmura 2008; Margolis, Michael, and Resnick 2000).
13. This has become standard practice in emergency communications studies. See Vieweg et al. 2010.
14. I borrow this metric from Zheng and Wu 2005 and Java et al. 2007.
15. I must emphasize strongly here, in an attempt to avoid accusations of cultural essentialism, that classifying "obstacles" is a very context-specific and arbitrary process that involved follow-up interviews, fact checking, and a lot of subtleties, guesswork, and faith.
16. Interview, May 15, 2012, Salwa, Kuwait.
17. Interview, May 3, 2012, Salmiya, Kuwait.
18. Activists O and P were the only glaring examples of activists who were highly connected to others on Twitter. Their dense connections are contrasted with the fact that the SMOs they are part of are the smallest.
19. Interview, March 10, 2012, Bneid al Gar, Kuwait.
20. Interview, May 3, 2012, Rumaithiya, Kuwait.
21. Interview, May 3, 2012, Rumaithiya, Kuwait.

Chapter 20

1. In the debate on research ethics, the term "research subject" is being replaced more and more frequently by "research participant," a term that is perceived as more politically correct. For field research, however, it seems to be misleading, as researchers strive to participate in the world of the actors being studied (cf. Yanow and Schwartz-Shea 2008). "Subject" is of course also problematic since it implies the researcher has more power, something that is also not so clear-cut in field research (Schwartz-Shea and Yanow 2012, 73–74). Until a better term is suggested in the discourse of research ethics, I will use the term "subject" but stress the agency of the person under study in the research process.
2. More critical points concerning the form of consent are discussed in Fujii 2012. In contrast, Kenney argues in favor of these forms, as they helped him de-escalate conflicts in the field because they created transparency and trust among the people being interviewed (2013, 41).
3. A good example of a checklist on how to ensure the confidentiality of interview data is Knights (2013, 120). To my knowledge, securing emails still relies on end-to-end encryption. This means that the recipient also needs to install and use the relevant software (which is not very user-friendly in the cases I know. but I am open to being convinced otherwise). For communicating with people in the field, I therefore still rely on regular email provider but avoid sensitive issues in my messages.

Chapter 21

1. The purpose of this visit was to decide whether I would accept a transfer to the local Lebanese UNDP office as part of a decision by the headquarters in New York to resend international staff to the country in the wake of the release of the last Western hostage (Terry Anderson) in the fall of 1991. For my weeklong visit, I was essentially given a car and a driver and spent the majority of my time being a "tourist" of the civil war, visiting much of still unreconstructed Beirut and its surrounding areas. While I did not accept the transfer, the experience remained with me as a motivator for a potential future focus of study.

2. The two Lebanese NGO coalitions were named respectively the NGO Forum and Le Collectif—the former representing many of the large communal welfare organizations in the country and the latter representing a mix of communal and secular-oriented ones.

3. Canada's foreign policy in the Middle East—historically associated with peacekeeping and development assistance—carries little of the "imperial" and "great power" political baggage associated with that of the United States.

4. For a discussion of the debates surrounding the role of the nondisabled in the lives of the disabled, including that of nondisabled researchers, see Shakespeare 2006, 185–199.

5. Rafik Hariri had been the prime minister in Lebanon for significant periods in Lebanon's early postwar period and had been a driving force behind the country's reconstruction program. His assassination sparked waves of popular mobilization in the country—some blaming the Syrians for his assassination and demanding an end to the overt Syrian presence in the country, others supporting the Syrians for their contribution to the end of the civil war.

Chapter 22

1. My work to date has focused on four groups: the Jewish settlers in the West Bank, the ultra-Orthodox Shas movement, the Islamic Movement in Israel, and the Palestinian Hamas.

2. "Arab-Jew" and "Israeli-Arab" are in parentheses here because they are imposed names and do not reflect how people falling in these categories refer to themselves.

3. The abbreviation "KKV" refers to the book *Designing Social Inquiry: Scientific Inference in Qualitative Research* by Gary King, Robert O. Keohane, and Sidney Verba. It is in a sense the introductory standard that first-year political science graduate students are presented with, and it offers positivist prescriptions for designing qualitative research in a manner that would make it intelligible and acceptable to mainstream, quantitative political scientists.

4. Ginat Gitit, "The Palestinian Who Infiltrated Shas," *Walla News*, June 5, 2014, http://news.walla.co.il/item/2752895 (accessed March 28, 2016).

5. I should mention, though, that I was not able to do fieldwork with Hamas because my Israeli-Jewish identity was a barrier to trust among potential research interlocutors, and for both ethical and practical reasons I did not want to disguise my identity in the field.

6. See Schwedler and Clark's chapter in this volume, "Encountering the Mukhabarat State."

7. I use pseudonyms to protect the privacy of research participants.

8. I am using these adjectives here uncomfortably, as none individually or collectively accurately capture my political commitments, but for the sake of space, and in order not to belabor the reader, these will do.

9. For others, who were not direct research interlocutors but have come across me casually at a research site, though, the lines at times were blurrier. I did experience people assuming that the presence of someone like me who was clearly an outsider entailed some sort of conversion process—*hitkhazkut* or strengthening of Jewish religiosity, or possible conversion to Islam, depending on the context. My approach was to correct people, explaining that I am doing research.

BIBLIOGRAPHY

Chapter 1

King, Gary, Robert Keohane, and Sidney Verba. 1994. *Designing Social Inquiry.* Princeton, NJ: Princeton University Press.

Kolman, Iris. 2016. "Gender Activism in Salafism: A Case-Study of Salafi Women in Tunis." In *Salafism after the Awakening,* ed. Francesco Cavatorta and Fabio Merone. London: Hurst, 187–204.

Mosley, Layna. 2015. *Interview Research in Political Science.* Ithaca, NY: Cornell University Press.

Parkinson, Sarah Elizabeth. 2014. "Practical Ethics: How U.S. Law and the 'War on Terror' Affect Research in the Middle East." In *The Ethics of Research in the Middle East.* POMEPS Studies 8, July 2. Washington, DC: Project on Middle East Political Science, George Washington University, 24–26.

Schwedler, Jillian, 2006. "The Third Gender: Western Female Researchers in the Middle East." *PS: Political Science & Politics* 39 (3): 425–428.

Volpi, Frédéric. 2017. *Revolution and Authoritarianism in North Africa.* London: Hurst.

Chapter 3

Anderson, Lisa. 1999. "Politics in the Middle East: Opportunities and Limits in the Quest for Theory." In *Area Studies and Social Science,* ed. Mark Tessler, Jodi Nachtwey, and Anne Banda, 1–10. Bloomington: Indiana University Press.

Banakar, Reza. 2016. *Driving Culture in Iran: Law and Society on the Roads of the Islamic Republic.* London: I.B. Tauris.

Bayat, Asef. 2010. *Life as Politics: How Ordinary People Change the Middle East.* Amsterdam: University of Amsterdam Press.

Berry, Jeffrey. 2002. "Validity and Reliability Issues in Elite Interviewing." *PS: Political Science & Politics* 35 (4): 679–682.

Dabène, Olivier, Vincent Geisser, and Gilles Massardier, eds. 2008. *Autoritarismes démocratiques et démocraties autoritaires au XXIe siècle.* Paris: La Découverte.

Fitzgerald, James. 2015. "Why Me? An Autoethnographic Account of the Bizarre Logic of Counterterrorism." *Critical Studies of Terrorism* 8 (1): 163–180.

Keshavarzian, Arang. 2015. "Mutual Comprehension and Hybrid Identities in the Bazaar: Reflections on Interviews and Interlocutors in Tehran." In *Persian Language, Literature and Culture,* ed. Kamran Talattof, 239–257. London: Routledge.

Maxey, Ian. 1999. "Beyond Boundaries? Activism, Academia, Reflexivity and Research." *Area* 31: 199–208.

Mir-Hosseini, Ziba. 1993. *Marriage on Trial: A Study of Islamic Family Law*. London: I. B. Tauris.

Mitchell, Timothy. 2004. "The Middle East in the Past and Future of Social Science." In *The Politics of Knowledge: Area Studies and the Disciplines*, ed. David Szanton, 50–73. Berkeley: University of California Press.

Nilan, Pamela. 2002. "'Dangerous Fieldwork' Re-examined: The Question of Researcher Subject Position." *Qualitative Research* 2 (3): 363–386.

Osanloo, Arzoo. 2009. *The Politics of Women's Rights in Iran*. Princeton, NJ: Princeton University Press.

Razazan, Malihe. 2016. "Uncivil Rites: An Interview with Steven Salaita." *Jadaliyya*, 7 January. Accessed March 11, 2016.

Rezai-Rashti, Goli. 2013. "Conducting Field Research on Gender Relations in a Gender Repressive State: A Case Study of Gender Research in Iran." *International Journal of Qualitative Research in Education* 26 (4): 489–502.

Saeidi, Shirin. 2010. "Creating the Islamic Republic of Iran: Wives and Daughters of Martyrs, and Acts of Citizenship." *Citizenship Studies* 14 (2): 113–126.

Salih, Ruba. 2015. "Academic Freedom, Ethics, and Responsibility: The Silencing and Censoring of Palestine in Western Liberal Academia." *Jadaliyya*, May 19. Accessed March 11, 2016.

Starr, Amory, Luis A. Fernandez, and Christian Scholl. 2011. *Shutting Down the Streets: Political Violence and Social Control in the Global Era*. New York: New York University Press.

Therme, Clément. 2012. "La diplomatie française à l'épreuve de l'Iran." *Revue internationale et stratégique* 85 (1): 28–38.

Wagley, Charles. 1948. *Area Studies and Training: A Conference Report on the Study of World Areas*. New York: Columbia University and Social Science Research Council.

Woliver, Laura. 2002. "Ethical Dilemmas in Personal Interviewing." *PS: Political Science & Politics* 35 (4): 677–678.

Chapter 4

Al Arebi, Saddeka. 1994. *Women and Words: The Politics of Literary Discourse in Saudi Arabia*. New York: Columbia University Press.

Altorki, Soraya. 1986. *Women in Saudi Arabia: Ideology and Behavior among the Elite*. New York: Columbia University Press.

Chauhdry, Kiren Aziz. 1997. *The Price of Wealth: Economies and Institutions in the Middle East*. Ithaca, NY: Cornell University Press.

Hertog, Steffen. 2010. *Princes, Brokers and Bureaucrats: Oil and the State in Saudi Arabia*. Ithaca, NY: Cornell University Press.

Jones, Toby. 2010. *Desert Kingdom: How Oil and Water Forged Modern Saudi Arabia*. Cambridge, MA: Harvard University Press.

Katakura, Matoko. 1977. *Bedouin Village: A Study of People in Transition*. Tokyo: University of Tokyo Press.

Le Renard, Amelie. 2014. *A Society of Young Women: Opportunities of Place, Power and Reform in Saudi Arabia*. Stanford, CA: Stanford University Press.

Menoret, Pascal. 2014. *Joyriding in Riyadh: Oil, Urbanism, and Road Revolt*. Cambridge: Cambridge University Press.

Okruhlik, Gwenn. 1992. "Debating Profits and Political Power: Private Business and Government in Saudi Arabia." PhD diss., University of Texas at Austin.

———. 1999a. "From Imagined Scholarship to Gendered Discourse: Bringing the Peninsula in from the Periphery." *Middle East Report*, July–September: 36–37.

———. 1999b. "Rentier Wealth, Unruly Law and the Rise of Opposition: The Political Economy of Oil States." *Comparative Politics* 31 (3): 295–315.

———. 1999c. "The Politics of Ethnicity in Saudi Arabia." In *The Global Color Line: Racial and Ethnic Inequality and Struggle from a Global Perspective*, ed. Pinar Batur Vander-Lippe and Joe Feagin, 215–236. Stamford, CT: JAI Press.

——. 2002. "Networks of Dissent: Islamism and Reform in Saudi Arabia." *Current History* 101 (651): 22–28.

——. 2004a. "Making Conversation Permissible: Islamism in Saudi Arabia." In *Islamic Activism: A Social Movement Theory Approach*, ed. Quintan Wiktorowicz, 354–384. Bloomington: Indiana University Press.

——. 2004b. "Struggles over History and Identity: 'Opening the Gates' of the Kingdom to Tourism." In *Counter-narratives: History, Contemporary Society and Politics in Saudi Arabia and Yemen*, ed. Madawi Al-Rasheed and Robert Vitalis, 201–228. New York: Palgrave Macmillan.

——. 2005. "The Irony of *Al Islah* (Reform)." *Washington Quarterly* 28 (4): 153–170.

——. 2009. "State Power, Religious Privilege and the Myths about Political Reform." In *Religion and Politics in Saudi Arabia: Wahhabism and the State*, ed. Mohammed Ayoob and Hasan Koselbalaban, 91–108. Boulder, CO: Lynne Rienner.

——. 2010. "Dependence, Disdain and Distance: State, Labor and Citizenship in the Arab Gulf States," In *Industrialization in the Arab Gulf: A Socioeconomic Revolution*, ed. Jean-François Seznec and Mimi Kirk, 125–142. New York: Routledge.

Silverstein, Ken. 2001. "Saudis and Americans: Friends in Need." *The Nation*, November 15.

Thiollet, Helene. 2015. "Migration and (Counter)revolution: Migration Policies and Labour Market Policies in Saudi Arabia." *Revue europeene de migrations internationales* 31 (3–4): 121–143.

Chapter 5

Bamyeh, Mohamed. 2015. *Social Sciences in the Arab World: Forms of Presence*. Beirut: Arab Council for the Social Sciences.

Challand, Benoit. 2009. *Palestinian Civil Society: Foreign Donors and the Power to Promote and Exclude*. London: Routledge.

——. 2011. "Coming Too Late? The EU's Mixed Approaches in Transforming the Israeli-Palestinian Conflict." In *The Nexus between the EU, Civil Society and Conflict in the European Neighbourhood*, ed. Nathalie Tocci, 96–125. London: Routledge.

Doumani, Beshara. 1996. *Rediscovering Palestine: Merchants and Peasants in Jabal Nablus, 1700–1900*. Berkeley: California University Press.

Hanafi, Sari. 2012. "Explaining Spacio-cide in the Palestinian Territory: Colonization, Separation, and State of Exception." *Current Sociology* 61 (2): 190–205.

Hanieh, Adam. 2013. *Lineages of Revolt: Issues of Contemporary Capitalism in the Middle East*. London: Haymarket Books.

Hilal, Jamil, ed. 2007. *Where Now for Palestine? The Demise of the Two-State Solution*. London: Zed Books.

Jamal, Amaney. 2007. *Barriers to Democracy: The Other Side of Social Capital in Palestine and the Arab World*. Princeton, NJ: Princeton University Press.

Judt, Tony. 1985. "The Spreading Notion of the Town: Some Recent Writings on French and Italian Communism." *Historical Journal* 28 (4): 1011–1021.

Le More, Anne. 2008. *International Assistance to the Palestinians after Oslo: Political Guilt, Wasted Money*. London: Routledge.

Malki, Majdi al-. 2011. "Researching in an Unsuitable Environment: The Palestinian Case." In *Critical Research in the Social Sciences: A Transdisciplinary East-West Handbook*, ed. Roger Heacock and Edouard Conte, 191–212. Birzeit: Birzeit University.

Pappe, Illan. 2011. *The Forgotten Palestinians: A History of the Palestinians in Israel*. New Haven, CT: Yale University Press.

Schaeublin, Emanuel. 2012. "Role and Governance of Islamic Charitable Institutions: Gaza Zakat Organizations (1973–2011) in the Local Context." Working Paper 9, Graduate Institute for International and Development Studies, Geneva.

Tamari, Salim. 1994. "Problems of Social Research in Palestine: An Overview." *Current Sociology* 42 (2): 65–86

Tartir, Alaa. 2015. "Securitised Development and Palestinian Authoritarianism under Fayyadism." *Conflict, Security & Development* 15 (5): 479–502.

Tartir, Alaa, and Benoit Challand. 2016. "Palestine." In *The Middle East*, ed. Ellen Lust, 603–631. Washington, DC: CQ Press.

Weizman, Eyal. 2007. *Hollow Land: Israel's Architecture of Occupation.* London: Verso.

Chapter 6

Buford, Bill. 1993. *Among the Thugs.* New York: Vintage.

Campbell, Susanna P. 2017. "Ethics of Research in Conflict Environments." *Journal of Global Security Studies* 2 (1): 89–101.

Clark, Janine A. 2006. "Field Research Methods in the Middle East." *PS: Political Science & Politics* 39 (3): 417–424.

Fisk, Robert. 2002. *Pity the Nation: The Abduction of Lebanon.* 4th ed. New York: Thunder's Mouth Press / Nation Books.

Fujii, Lee Ann. 2012. "Research Ethics 101: Dilemmas and Responsibilities." *PS: Political Science & Politics* 45 (4): 717–723.

Hubbard, Ben, and Anne Barnard. 2014. "Deadly Bombing in Beirut Suburb, a Hezbollah Stronghold, Raises Tensions." *New York Times*, January 2. http://www.nytimes.com/2014/01/03/world/middleeast/Beirut-Hezbollah-explosion.html.

Khalili, Laleh. 2013. "Thinking about Violence." *International Journal of Middle East Studies* 45 (4): 791–794.

Lake, Milli, and Sarah E. Parkinson. 2017. "The Ethics of Fieldwork Preparedness." *Political Violence @ a Glance*, June 5. http://politicalviolenceataglance.org/2017/06/05/the-ethics-of-fieldwork-preparedness/.

Loyle, Cyanne E., and Alicia Simoni. 2017. "Researching under Fire: Political Science and Researcher Trauma." *PS: Political Science & Politics* 50 (1): 141–145.

Mazurana, Dyan, Karen Jacobsen, and Lacey Andrews Gale, eds. 2014. *Research Methods in Conflict Settings: A View from Below.* Cambridge: Cambridge University Press.

Moughnieh, Lamia. 2012. "The Social Exchange of Violence and Bodies in Lebanon: Bomb as Routine." *The Interrogations of Shamshouma*, October 20. https://theinterrogationsofshamshouma.wordpress.com/2012/10/20/the-social-exchange-of-violence-and-bodies-in-lebanon-bomb-as-routine/.

Nordstrom, Carolyn, and Antonius C. G. M. Robben. 1996. *Fieldwork under Fire: Contemporary Studies of Violence and Culture.* Berkeley: University of California Press.

Pachirat, Timothy. 2011. *Every Twelve Seconds: Industrialized Slaughter and the Politics of Sight.* New Haven: Yale University Press.

Parkinson, Sarah E. 2010. "IDRF Field Report." Progress Report 2. New York: Social Science Research Council.

———. 2015. "Towards an Ethics of Sight: Violence Scholarship and the Arab Uprisings." *LSE Middle East Centre Blog*, August 26. http://blogs.lse.ac.uk/mec/2015/08/26/towards-an-ethics-of-sight-violence-scholarship-and-the-arab-uprisings/.

———. 2016. "Money Talks: Discourse, Networks, and Structure in Militant Organizations." *Perspectives on Politics* 14 (4): 976–994.

Said, Edward W. 1979. *Orientalism.* New York: Vintage.

Schwedler, Jillian. 2006. "The Third Gender: Western Female Researchers in the Middle East." *PS: Political Science & Politics* 39 (3): 425–428.

"UNIFIL Background." 2016. *UNIFIL: The United Nations Interim Force in Lebanon.* Accessed January 3, 2018. http://unifil.unmissions.org/Default.aspx?tabid=11554&language=en-US.

Wood, Elisabeth Jean. 2006. "The Ethical Challenges of Field Research in Conflict Zones." *Qualitative Sociology* 29 (June): 373–386.

Chapter 7

Abaza, Mona. 2011. "Academic Tourists Sight-seeing the Arab Spring." *Ahram Online*, September 26. http://english.ahram.org.eg/News/22373.aspx.

Al Sayad, Usama. 2016. "On Its Fifth Anniversary, Who Writes the History of the Egyptian Revolution." *Noon Post*, January 25. https://www.noonpost.net/%D8%A7%D9%84%D8%AB%D9%88%D8%B1%D8%A9-%D8%A7%D9%84%D9%85%D8%B5%D8%B1%D9%8A%D8%A9/%D9%81%D9%8A-%D8%B0%D9%83%D8%B1%D8%A7%D9%87%D8%A7-%D8%A7%D9%84%D8%AE%D8%A7%D9%85%D8%B3%D8%A9-%D9%85%D9%86-%D9%8A%D9%83%D8%AA%D8%A8-%D8%AA%D8%A7%D8%B1%D9%8A%D8%AE-%D8%A7%D9%84%D8%AB%D9%88%D8%B1%D8%A9-%D8%A7%D9%84%D9%85%D8%B5%D8%B1%D9%8A%D8%A9%D9%9F.

Amnesty International. 2015. "Egypt: Release Ismail Alexandrani (UA 275/15)." December 3. http://www.amnestyusa.org/get-involved/take-action-now/egypt-release-ismail-alexandrani-ua-27515.

Egyptian Initiative For Personal Rights and Selected Organizations. 2016. "Rights Organizations and Public Figures: The Case Lays the Groundwork for the Confiscation of the Right of Academic Research and Freedom of Information and Infringes Freedom of Association and Freedom of Opinion and Expression." https://eipr.org/en/press/2016/01/100-days-detention-hisham-gaafar-and-homeland-security-prosecution-renews-remand

El-Mahdy, Rabab. 2011. "Orientalising the Egyptian Uprising." *Jadaliyya*, April 11. http://www.jadaliyya.com/pages/index/1214/orientalising-the-egyptian-uprising.

Fahmy, Khaled. 2016. "The Death of Giulio Regeni and the Tragic State of Academic Research in Egypt." *Huffington Post*, February 9. http://www.huffingtonpost.com/khaledfahmy/the-death-of-giulio-regen_b_9196124.html.

Middle Eastern Studies Association (MESA). 2016. "Security Alert for Study and Research in Egypt." February 10. http://mesana.org/about/board-letters-statements.html#Egypt-Security-Alert.

Pyper, Neil. 2016. "The Murder of My Friend Giulio Regeni in Egypt Was An Attack on Academic Freedom." *The Guardian*, February 6. http://www.theguardian.com/commentisfree/2016/feb/06/murder-giulio-regeni-egypt-academic-freedom-students.

Raghavan, Sudarsan. 2016. "In New Egyptian Textbooks, 'It's Like the Revolution Didn't Happen.'" *Washington Post*, April 23. https://www.washingtonpost.com/world/middle_east/in-new-egyptian-textbooks-its-like-the-revolution-didnt-happen/2016/04/23/846ab2f0-f82e-11e5-958d-d038dac6e718_story.html.

Said, Atef. Forthcoming. Political Public Space in Counterrevolutionary Egypt. Paper supported by the Arab Research Support Program II. Arab Reform Initiative.

Chapter 8

Akesbi, Najib. 2014. "Which Agricultural Policy for Which Food Security in Morocco?" In *Seasonal Workers in Mediterranean Agriculture: The Social Costs of Eating Fresh*, ed. Jörg Getel and Sarah Ruth Sippel. London: Routledge.

Akl, Ziad A. 2016. "The Death of Giulio Regeni, a Fellow Researcher." *Daily News: Egypt*, February 16. www.dailynewsegypt.com/2016/02/16/the-death-of-giulio-regeni-a-fellow-researcher/.

Anderson, Lisa. 2016. "How to Respond to a Graduate Student's Death in Egypt." *Chronicle of Higher Education*, February 19. www.chronicle.com/article/How-to-Respond-to-a-Graduate/235537/.

Ayeb, Habib. 2012. "The Marginalization of the Small Peasantry: Egypt and Tunisia." In *Marginality and Exclusion in Egypt*, ed. Ray Bush and Habib Ayeb. London: Zed Books.

Ayeb, Habib, and Ray Bush. 2014. "Small Farmer Uprisings and Rural Neglect in Egypt and Tunisia." *Middle East Report* 272: 2–11.

Bernstein, Henry. 2010. *Class Dynamics of Agrarian Change*. Halifax: Fernwood Publications.

Breisinger, Clemens, Olivier Ecker, Perrihan Al-Riffai, and Bingxin Yu. 2012. *Beyond the Arab Awakening: Policies and Investments for Poverty Reduction and Food Security*. Food Policy Report. Washington, DC: International Food Policy Research Institute.

Bush, Ray. 1999. *Economic Crisis and the Politics of Reform in Egypt*. Boulder, CO: Westview Press.

———. 2001. "Time to Go." *Al Ahram Weekly's. Focus on USAID in Egypt: 25 Years*, June 21–27.

———. 2002. "Land Reform and Counter Revolution." In *Counter Revolution in Egypt's Countryside: Land and Farmers in the Era of Economic Reform*, ed. Ray Bush. London: Zed Books.

———. 2014a. "Food Security in Egypt." In *Food Security in the Middle East*, ed. Zahra Babar and Suzi Mirgani. London: Hurst.

———. 2014b. "Near East and North Africa." In *Deep Roots*, ed. Jacqui Griffiths. Rome: Food and Agriculture Organization of the United Nations.

———. 2016. "Agrarian Transformation in Near East and North Africa: Influences for the Work of Lionel Cliffe." *Review of African Political Economy* 43, issue supplement 1: 69–85.

Cliffe, Lionel. 2012. "Introduction: Neoliberal Accumulation and Class: A Tribute to Gavin Williams." *Review of African Political Economy* 39 (132): 213–223.

Collini, Stefan. 2016. "Who Are the Spongers Now?" *London Review of Books* (January 21): 33–37.

Cramer, Christopher, Deborah Johnston, Carlos Oya, and John Sender. 2015. "Research Note: Mistakes, Crises and Research Independence: The Perils of Fieldwork as a Form of Evidence." *African Affairs* 115 (458): 145–160.

de Sarden, Jean Pierre Olivier. 2008. *La rigueur du qualitif: Les contraintes empiriques de l'interprétation socio-anthropoligique*. Louvain-La-Neuve: Adaemia-Bruylant.

Duffield, Mark. 2014. "From Immersion to Simulation: Remote Methodologies and the Decline of Area Studies." *Review of African Political Economy* 41 (1): 75–94.

Evans, Brad, and Julian Reid. 2014. *Resilient Life: The Art of Living Dangerously*. Oxford: Polity.

Food and Agriculture Organization of the United Nations (FAO). 2009. "The Humanitarian Situation in Gaza and FAO's Response." Emergency Operations and Rehabilitation Division, January 23.

Houdret, Annabelle. 2012. "The Water Connection: Irrigation, Water Grabbing and Politics in Southern Morocco." *Water Alternatives* 5 (2): 284–303.

Human Rights Watch. 2011. "Work on Him until He Confesses." https://www.hrw.org/report/ 2011/01/30/work-him-until-he-confesses/impunity-torture-egypt.

Land Centre for Human Rights, Cairo. 2002. "Farmer Struggles Against Law 96 of 1992." In *Counter-revolution in Egypt's Countryside: Land and Farmers in the Era of Economic Reform*, ed. Ray Bush. London: Zed Books

Lowder, S. K., J. Skoet, and S. Singh. 2014. "What Do We Really Know about the Number and Distribution of Farms and Family Farms Worldwide?" Background Paper for the State of Food and Agriculture 2014. ESA Working Paper No. 14-02. Rome: FAO. http://www.fao. org/docrep/019/i3729e/i3729e.pdf.

McMichael, Philip. 2013. *Food Regimes and Agrarian Questions*. Halifax: Fernwood Publishing.

Mills, C. Wright 1959. *The Sociological Imagination*. Oxford: Oxford University Press.

Mosse, David. 2015. "Misunderstood, Misrepresented, Contested? Anthropological Knowledge Production in Question." *Focaal* 72 (10): 128–137.

Projects of Rural Egypt, Social Research Centre, American University in Cairo. No date. http:// schools.aucegypt.edu/research/src/Documents/Thematic%20Directions/Agriculture%20 and%20Rural%20Development/Projects%20on%20Agriculture.pdf.

Pyper, Neil. 2016. "The Murder of My Friend Giulio Regeni in Egypt Was an Attack on Academic Freedom." *The Guardian*, February 6. http://www.theguardian.com/commentisfree/2016/ feb/06/murder-giulio-regeni-egypt-academic-freedom-students.

Saad, Reem. 1999. "State, Landlord, Parliament and Peasant: The Story of the 1992 Tenancy Law in Egypt." In *Agriculture in Egypt from Pharaonic to Modern Times*, ed. Alan Bowman and Eugene Rogan. Oxford: Oxford University Press.

————. 2002. "Egyptian Politics and the Tenancy Law." In *Counter-revolution in Egypt's Countryside: Land and Farmers in the Era of Economic Reform*, ed. Ray Bush. London: Zed Books.

Sowers, Jeannie. 2014. "Water, Energy and Human Insecurity in the Middle East." *Middle East Research and Information Project* 271: 1–5 and 48.

Stevenson, Tom. 2015. "Sisi's Way." *London Review of Books* 37 (4) (February 19): 3–7.

van der Ploeg, Jan Douwe. 2010. "The Peasantries of the Twenty First Century: The Commoditisation Debate Revisited." *Journal of Peasant Studies* 37 (1): 1–30.

————. 2013. *Peasants and the Art of Farming: A Chayanovian Manifesto*. Halifax: Fernwood Publishing.

Van Onselen, Charles. 1993. "The Reconstruction of a Rural Life from Oral Testimony: Critical Notes on the Methodology Employed in the Study of a Black South African Sharecropper." *Journal of Peasant Studies* 20 (3): 494–514.

World Bank. 2007. *Making the Most of Scarcity: Accountability for Better Water Management Results in the Middle East and North Africa*, Washington, DC: World Bank.

————. 2010. *Egypt's Food Subsidies: Benefit Incidence and Leakages*. Washington, DC: Arab Republic of Egypt and the World Bank.

Zurayk, Rami, Anne Gough, Ahmad Sourani, and Mariam Al Jaajaa. 2012. *Food Security Challenges and Innovation: The Case of Gaza*. Rome: High Level Expert Forum.

Chapter 9

Aberbach, Joel D., and Bert A. Rockman. 2002. "Conducting and Coding Elite Interviews." *PS: Political Science & Politics* 35 (4): 673–676.

Berry, Jeffrey M. 2002. "Validity and Reliability Issues in Elite Interviewing." *PS: Political Science & Politics* 35 (4): 679–682.

Cammett, Melani. 2015. "Using Proxy Interviewing to Address Sensitive Topics." In *Interview Research in Political Science*, ed. Layna Mosley. Ithaca, NY: Cornell University Press.

Goldstein, Kenneth. 2002. "Getting in the Door." *PS: Political Science & Politics* 35 (4): 669–672.

Kapiszewski, Diana, Lauren M. MacLean, and Benjamin L. Read. 2015. *Field Research in Political Science*. Cambridge: Cambridge University Press.

Leech, Beth L. 2002. "Asking Questions." *PS: Political Science & Politics* 35 (4): 665–668.

Likkeker, Darren G. 2003. "Interviewing the Political Elite." *Politics* 23 (3): 207–214.

Mosley, Layna. 2015. "Introduction. 'Just Talk to People?': Interviews in Contemporary Political Science." In *Interview Research in Political Science*, ed. Layna Mosley, 1–28. Ithaca, NY: Cornell University Press.

Peabody, Robert L., et al. 1990. "Interviewing Political Elites." *PS: Political Science & Politics* 23 (3): 451–455.

Rivera, Sharon Werning, Paulina Kozyreva, and Eduard Sarovskii. 2002. "Interviewing Political Elites." *PS: Political Science & Politics* 35 (4): 683–688.

Scoggins, Suzanne. 2014. "Navigating Fieldwork as an Outsider." *PS: Political Science & Politics* 47 (2): 394–397.

Chapter 10

Clark, Janine A. 2006. "Field Research Methods in the Middle East." *PS: Political Science & Politics* 39 (3): 417–424.

Hsueh, Roselyn, Francesca Refsum Jensenius, and Akasemi Newsome. 2014. "Symposium: Fieldwork in Political Science: Encountering Challenges and Crafting Solutions." *PS: Political Science & Politics* 47 (2): 391–417.

Kurzman, Charles. 2004. "Conclusion: Social Movement Theory and Islamic Studies." In *Islamic Activism: A Social Movement Theory Approach*, ed. Quintan Wiktorowicz, 289–304. Bloomington: Indiana University Press.

Lieberman, Evan, Marc Howard, and Julie Lynch. 2004. "Symposium: Field Research." *Qualitative Methods Newsletter* 2 (1): 2–15.

Ling, L. H. M. 2015. "Orientalism Refashioned: 'Eastern Moon' in 'Western Waters': Reflecting Back on the East China Sea." Unpublished manuscript.

Mahmood, Saba. 2011. *Politics of Piety: The Islamic Revival and the Feminist Subject.* Princeton, NJ: Princeton University Press.

Mosley, Layna. 2013. "Introduction: Just Talk to People? Interviews in Contemporary Political Science." In *Interview Research in Political Science*, ed. Layna Mosley, 1–30. Ithaca, NY: Cornell University Press.

Said, Edward W. 1978. *Orientalism.* New York: Pantheon Books.

Schaffer, Frederic Charles. 2000. *Democracy in Translation: Understanding Politics in an Unfamiliar Culture.* Ithaca, NY: Cornell University Press.

Varisco, Daniel Martin. 2012. *Reading Orientalism: Said and the Unsaid.* Seattle: University of Washington Press.

Vikør, Knut. 2005. *Between God and the Sultan: A History of Islamic Law.* Oxford: Oxford University Press.

Wagemakers, Joas. 2009. "A Purist Jihadi-Salafi: The ideology of Abu Muhammad al-Maqdisi." *British Journal of Middle Eastern Studies* 36 (2): 281–297.

———. 2012. *A Quietist Jihadi: The Ideology and Influence of Abu Muhammad al-Maqdisi.* Cambridge: Cambridge University Press.

Wiktorowicz, Quintan. 2000. "The Salafi Movement in Jordan." *International Journal Middle East Studies* 32 (2): 219–240.

———. 2006. "Anatomy of the Salafi movement." *Studies in Conflict & Terrorism* 29 (3): 207–239.

Chapter 11

Wiktorowicz, Quintan. 2000. "The Salafi Movement in Jordan." *International Journal Middle East Studies* 32 (2): 219–240.

———. 2006. "Anatomy of the Salafi Movement." *Studies in Conflict and Terrorism* 29 (3): 207–239.

Chapter 12

Al-Ali, Nadje. 2010. "Women and War in the Middle East." Speech given at San Diego State University, San Diego, CA, November 17. https://www.youtube.com/watch?v=PesOOpeuo4I.

Baker, Alison. 1998. *Voices of Resistance: Oral Histories of Moroccan Women.* Albany: State University of New York Press.

Bartky, Sandra Lee. 1990. *Femininity and Domination: Studies in the Phenomenology of Oppression.* New York: Routledge.

Benz, Terressa. 2014. "Flanking Gestures: Gender and Emotion in Fieldwork." *Sociological Research Online* 19. http://www.socresonline.org.uk/19/2/15.html.

Butler, Judith. 1990. *Gender Trouble: Feminism and the Subversion of Identity.* New York: Routledge.

Cook, Chris. 2012. "Little Qatar Goes Big in Education." *Financial Times*, November 15. http://blogs.ft.com/the-world/2012/11/little-qatar-goes-big-on-education/.

Dalmasso, Emanuela, and Francesco Cavatorta. 2014. "Islamist Women's Leadership in Morocco." In *Gender, Conservatism and Political Representation*, ed. Karen Celis and Sarah Childs. Colchester: ECPR Press.

Henderson, B. Frances. 2009. "We Thought You Would Be White: Race and Gender in Fieldwork." *PS: Political Science & Politics* 42 (2): 291–294.

Henry, Marsha Giselle. 2003. "Where Are You Really From? Representation, Identity and Power in the Fieldwork Experiences of a South Asian Diasporic." *Qualitative Research* 3: 229–242.

Kerr, Simeon, and Roula Khalaf. 2013. "Sheikha Moza, Matriarch of the Modern Gulf." *Financial Times*, June 28. http://www.ft.com/cms/s/0/1fa6da02-de77-11e2-b990-00144feab7de.html.

Mihai, Mihaela, 2012. "Introdução." "E-cadernos CES 16: A manipulação xenófoba e política dos direitos das mulheres." http://www.edisoportal.org/noticias/publicaciones/276-e-cadernos-ces-16-a-manipula%C3%A7%C3%A3o-xen%C3%B3foba-e-pol%C3%ADtica-dos-direitos-das-mulheres.

Mügge, M. Liza. 2013. "Sexually Harassed by Gatekeepers: Reflections on Fieldwork in Turkey and Surinam." *International Journal of Social Science Research Methodology* 16 (6): 541–546.

Nencel, Lorraine. 2005. "Feeling Gender Speak, Intersubjectivity and Fieldwork Practice with Women Who Prostitute in Lima, Peru." *European Journal of Women's Studies* 12 (3): 345–361.

Ortbals, D. Candice, and Meg E. Rincker. 2009. "Fieldwork, Identities, and Intersectionality: Negotiating Gender, Race, Class, Religion, Nationality, and Age in the Research Field Abroad: Editors' Introduction." *PS: Political Science & Politics* 42 (2): 287–290.

Preciado, B. Paul. 2014. "Las subjetividades como ficciones políticas." Speech given at Hay Festival, Cartagena, Colombia, February 2. https://www.youtube.com/watch?v=4o13sesqsJo.

Preciado, Beatriz. 2008. "Pharmaco-pornographic Politics: Towards a New Gender Ecology." *Parallax* 14 (1): 105–117.

Ramírez, Ángeles. 2006. "Other Feminism? Muslim Associations and Women's Participation in Morocco." *Etnográfica* 10 (1): 107–119.

———. 2007. "Paradoxes et consensus: Le long processus de changement de la Moudawwana au Maroc." In *Femmes, famille et droit au Maghreb*, ed. Karima Dirèche-Slimani. Paris: CNRS Editions.

Schwedler, Jillian. 2006. "The Third Gender: Western Female Researchers in the Middle East." *PS: Political Science & Politics* 39 (3): 425–428.

Tabet, Paola. 2004. *La grande arnaque: Sexualité des femmes et échange économico-sexuel.* Paris: L'Harmattan.

Townsend-Bell, Erica. 2009. "Being True and Being You: Race, Gender, Class and the Fieldwork Experience." *PS: Political Science & Politics* 42(2): 311–314.

Chapter 13

Cammett, Melani. 2017. "Development and Underdevelopment in the Middle East." In *Oxford Handbook of the Politics of Development*, ed. Carol Lancaster and Nicolas van de Walle. Oxford: Oxford University Press. Available at doi: 10.1093/oxfordhb/9780199845156.013.25.

Checkel, Jeffrey T., and Andrew Bennett. 2015. "Beyond Metaphors: Standards, Theory, and the 'Where Next' for Process Tracing." In *Process Tracing: From Metaphor to Analytic Tool*, ed. Andrew Bennett and Jeffrey T. Checkel, 260–275. Cambridge: Cambridge University Press.

Collier, David, and Ruth Berins Collier. 1991. *Shaping the Political Arena: Critical Junctures, the Labor Movement, and Regime Dynamics in Latin America.* Princeton, NJ: Princeton University Press.

George, Alexander, and Timothy J. McKeown. 1985. "Case Studies of Organizational Decision Making." *Advances in Information Processing in Organizations* 2: 21–28.

Haggard, Stephan. 2015. "The Developmental State Is Dead: Long Live the Developmental State." In *Advances in Comparative-Historical Analysis*, ed. James Mahoney and Kathleen Thelen, 29–66. Cambridge: Cambridge University Press.

Holland, Paul. 1986. "Statistics and Causal Inference." *Journal of the American Statistical Association* 81 (396): 945–960.

Johnson, Chalmers. 1982. *MITI and the Japanese Miracle: The Growth of Industrial Policy, 1925–1975.* Stanford, CA: Stanford University Press.

Lieberson, Stanley. 1992. "Small N's and Big Conclusions: An Examination of the Reasoning in Comparative Studies Based on a Small Number of Cases." In *What Is a Case? Exploring the Foundations of Social Inquiry*, ed. Charles C. Ragin and Howard Becker, 105–118. Cambridge: Cambridge University Press.

Lijphart, Arend. 1971. "Comparative Politics and the Comparative Method." *American Political Science Review* 65 (3): 682–693.

Mahoney, James. 1999. "Nominal, Ordinal, and Narrative Appraisal in Macrocausal Analysis." *American Journal of Sociology* 104 (4): 1154–1196.

Nielsen, Richard. 2016. "Case Selection via Matching." *Sociological Methods & Research* 45 (3): 569–597.

Przeworski, Adam, and Henry J. Teune. 1970. *The Logic of Comparative Social Inquiry.* New York: John Wiley & Sons.

Skocpol, Theda. 1979. *States and Social Revolutions: A Comparative Analysis of France, Russia, and China.* Cambridge: Cambridge University Press.

Sunar, Ilkay. 1974. *State and Society in the Politics of Turkey's Development.* Ankara, Turkey: Ankara University Faculty of Political Science.

Waldner, David. 1999. *State Building and Late Development.* Ithaca, NY: Cornell University Press.

———. 2002. "Anti Anti-Determinism: Or What Happens When Schrodinger's Cat and Lorenz's Butterfly Meet Laplace's Demon in the Study of Political and Economic Development." Paper presented at the Annual Meeting of the American Political Science Association, Boston, September.

———. 2012. "Process Tracing and Causal Mechanisms." In *The Oxford Handbook of the Philosophy of Social Science,* ed. Harold Kincaid, 65–84. Oxford: Oxford University Press.

———. 2015a. "What Makes Process Tracing Good: Causal Mechanisms, Causal Inference, and the Completeness Standard in Comparative Politics." In *Process Tracing: From Metaphor to Analytic Tool,* ed. Andrew Bennett and Jeffrey T. Checkel, 126–152. Cambridge: Cambridge University Press.

———. 2015b. "Process Tracing and Qualitative Causal Inference." *Security Studies* 24 (2): 239–250.

———. 2015c. "Aspirin, Aeschylus, and the Foundations of Qualitative Causal Inference." Working paper, University of Virginia.

Chapter 14

Ahmed, Amel, and Rudra Sil. 2009. "Is Multi-method Research Really 'Better'?" *Qualitative and Multi-Method Research* (Newsletter of the American Political Science Association Organized Section for Qualitative and Multi-Method Research) 7 (2): 2–6.

Bates, Robert. 1996. "The Replication Debate: Introduction." *APSA-CP* (Newsletter of the APSA Organized Section in Comparative Politics) 7 (1): 5.

Carapico, Sheila. 1998. *Civil Society in Yemen: The Political Economy of Activism in Southern Arabia.* Cambridge: Cambridge University Press.

Dresch, Paul. 2000. "Wilderness of Mirrors: Truth and Vulnerability in Middle Eastern Fieldwork." In *Anthropologists in a Wider World: Essays on Field Research,* ed. Paul Dresch, Wendy James, and David J. Parkin, 109–127. London: Berghahn Books.

Elman, Colin, and Diana Kapiszewski. 2014. "Data Access and Research Transparency in Qualitative Research." *PS: Political Science & Politics* 47 (1): 43–47.

Fenno, Richard. 1986. "Observation, Context, and Sequence in the Study of Politics." *American Political Science Review* 80 (1): 3–15.

Jackson, Patrick Thaddeus. 2011. *The Conduct of Inquiry in International Relations.* London: Routledge.

King, Gary. 1995. "Replication, Replication." *PS: Political Science & Politics* 28 (3): 443–449.

Lustick, Ian. 1996. "Read My Footnotes." *APSA-CP* (Newsletter of the APSA Organized Section in Comparative Politics) 7 (1): 6–10.

Moravcsik, Andrew. 2009. "Active Citation: A Precondition for Replicable Qualitative Research." *PS: Political Science & Politics* 43 (1): 29–35.

———. 2015. "One Norm, Two Standards: Realizing Transparency in Qualitative Political Science." *Political Methodologist,* January 1. http://thepoliticalmethodologist.com/2015/01/01/one-norm-two-standards-realizing-transparency-in-qualitative-political-science/.

Owton, Helen, and Jacqueline Allen-Collinson. 2014. "Close but Not Too Close: Friendship as Method(ology) in Ethnographic Research Encounters." *Journal of Contemporary Ethnography* 43 (3): 283–305.

Rathbun, Brian. 2011. "Stuff Political Scientists Like #6: Soaking and Poking." *Duck of Minerva*, July 12. http://duckofminerva.com/2011/07/stuff-political-scientists-like-6.html.

Schatz, Edward, ed. 2009. *Political Ethnography: What Immersion Contributes to the Study of Politics.* Chicago: University of Chicago Press.

Schwartz-Shea, Peregrine, and Dvora Yanow. 2012. *Interpretive Research Design: Concepts and Processes.* London: Routledge.

Schwedler, Jillian. 2006. "The Third Gender: Western Female Researchers in the Middle East." *PS: Political Science & Politics* 39 (3): 425–428.

Tillman-Healy, Lisa. 2003. "Friendship as Method." *Qualitative Inquiry* 9 (5): 729–749.

Varisco, Daniel Martin. 1986. "On the Meaning of Chewing: Qat (*Catha edulis*) in the Yemen Arab Republic." *International Journal of Middle East Studies* 18 (1): 1–13.

Wedeen, Lisa. 2004. "Concepts and Commitments in the Study of Democracy." In *Problems and Methods in the Study of Politics*, ed. Ian Shapiro, Rogers M. Smith, and Tarek Masoud, 274–306. Cambridge: Cambridge University Press.

———. 2008. *Peripheral Visions: Publics, Power, and Performance in Yemen.* Chicago: University of Chicago Press.

Yadav, Stacey Philbrick. 2011. "Antecedents of the Revolution: Intersectoral Networks and Post-partisanship in Yemen." *Studies in Ethnicity and Nationalism* 11 (3): 550–563.

———. 2013. *Islamists and the State: Legitimacy and Institutions in Yemen and Lebanon.* London: I. B. Tauris.

Chapter 15

Charmaz, Kathy. 2006. *Constructing Grounded Theory: A Practical Guide through Qualitative Analysis.* Introducing Qualitative Methods Series. London: Sage.

Flick, Uwe. 2009. *An Introduction to Qualitative Research.* London: Sage.

Glaser, Barney G. 1978. *Theoretical Sensitivity: Advances in the Methodology of Grounded Theory.* Mill Valley, CA: Sociology Press.

Guest, Greg, Arwen Bunce, and Laura Johnson. 2006. "How Many Interviews Are Enough? An Experiment with Data Saturation and Variability." *Field Methods* 18 (1): 59–82.

Hammami, Hama. 2010. "The Position of the Worker Party from the Protests in Sidid Bouzid." *YouTube*, December 26. https://www.facebook.com/photo.php?v=143619465693817&set=vb.117241681622132&type=2&theater.

Higher Committee for the Coordination of National Opposition Parties (HCCNOP). 2011. "The Higher Committee for the Coordination of National Opposition Parties Proposes an Alternative National Program." *Amman Net*, January 16. http://ar.ammannet.net/news/89240.

Iskander, Elizabeth. 2012. *Sectarian Conflict in Egypt: Coptic Media, Identity and Representation.* London: Routledge.

Jebnoun, Noureddine. 2013. "Ben Ali's Tunisia: The Authoritarian Path of Dystopian State." In *Authoritarianism: Roots, Ramifications, and Crisis*, ed. Noureddine Jebnoun, Mehrdad Kia, and Mimi Kirk, 101–123. London: Routledge.

Massad, Joseph Andoni. 2013. *Colonial Effects: The Making of National Identity in Jordan.* New York: Columbia University Press.

O'Reilly, Michelle, and Nicola Parker. 2012. "'Unsatisfactory Saturation': A Critical Exploration of the Notion of Saturated Sample Sizes in Qualitative Research." *Qualitative Research* 13 (2): 190–197.

Snow, David A., and Robert A Benford. 1992. "Master Frames and Cycles of Protest." In *Frontiers in Social Movement Theory*, ed. Aldon D. Morris and Carol McClurg Mueller, 133–155. New Haven: Yale University Press.

Strauss, Anselm. 1987. *Qualitative Analysis for Social Scientists.* Cambridge: Cambridge University Press.

Strauss, Anselm, and Juliet M. Corbin. 1990. *Basics of Qualitative Research.* Newbury Park, CA: Sage.

Chapter 16

Benstead, Lindsay J., Amaney Jamal, and Ellen Lust. 2015. "Is It Gender, Religion or Both? A Survey Experiment on Electability in Transitional Tunisia." *Perspectives on Politics* 13 (1): 74–94.

Bush, Sarah Sunn, and Amaney A. Jamal. 2015. "Anti-Americanism, Authoritarian Politics, and Attitudes about Women's Representation: Evidence from a Survey Experiment in Jordan." *International Studies Quarterly* 59 (1): 34–45.

Buttorff, Gail. 2015. "Coordination Failure and the Politics of Tribes: Jordanian Elections under SNTV." *Electoral Studies* 40: 45–55.

Clark, Janine A. 2004. "Social Movement Theory and Patron-Clientelism: Islamic Social Institutions and the Middle Class in Egypt, Jordan, and Yemen." *Comparative Political Studies* 37 (8): 941–968.

Corstange, Daniel. 2010. "Vote Buying under Competition and Monopsony: Evidence from a List Experiment in Lebanon." Paper presented at the Annual Meeting of the American Political Science Association, Washington, DC.

Elsayyad, May, and Shima 'a Hanafy. 2014. "Voting Islamist or Voting Secular? An Empirical Analysis of Voting Outcomes in Egypt's 'Arab Spring.'" *Public Choice* 160 (1–2): 109–130.

Gana, Alia, Gilles Van Hamme, and Maher Ben Rebah. 2012. "Géographie électorale et disparités socio-territoriales: Les enseignements des élections pour L'assemblée Constituante en Tunisie." *L'espace politique: Revue en ligne de géographie politique et de géopolitique* 18.

Garcia-Rivero, Carlos, and Hennie Kotze. 2007. "Electoral Support for Islamic Parties in the Middle East and North Africa." *Party Politics* 13 (5): 611–636.

Jamal, Amaney A. 2006. "Reassessing Support for Islam and Democracy in the Arab World? Evidence from Egypt and Jordan." *World Affairs* 169 (2): 51–63.

Jamal, Amaney A., and Mark A. Tessler. 2008. "Attitudes in the Arab World." *Journal of Democracy* 19 (1): 97–110.

Jamal, Amaney A., Robert O. Keohane, David Romney, and Dustin Tingley. 2015. "Anti-Americanism or Anti-interventionism? Evidence from the Arabic Twitter Universe." *Perspectives on Politics* 13 (1): 55–73.

Marinov, Nikolay. 2013. "Voter Attitudes When Democracy Promotion Turns Partisan: Evidence from a Survey-Experiment in Lebanon." *Democratization* 20 (7): 1297–1321.

Nielsen, Richard. 2014. "Networks, Careers, and the Jihadi Radicalization of Muslim Clerics." Available at: https://pdfs.semanticscholar.org/091b/c167f38254f8c942af1b6864ba79823b43cf.pdf.

Pellicer, Miquel, and Eva Wegner. 2013. "Electoral Rules and Clientelistic Parties: A Regression Discontinuity Approach." *Quarterly Journal of Political Science* 8 (4): 339–371.

———. 2014a. "Socio-economic Voter Profile and Motives for Islamist Support in Morocco." *Party Politics* 20 (1): 116–133.

———. 2014b. "The Mechanical and Psychological Effects of Legal Thresholds." *Electoral Studies* 33: 258–266.

———. 2015. "The Moroccan Party of Justice and Development in Local Politics." *Middle East Journal* 69 (1): 32–50.

Pellicer, Miquel, Eva Wegner, and Francesco Cavatorta. 2015. "Is There Strength in Numbers?" *Middle East Law and Governance* 7 (1): 153–168.

Robbins, Michael D. 2010. "What Accounts for the Success of Islamist Parties in the Arab World?" Dubai School of Government Working Paper No. 10-01.

Tessler, Mark. 2002. "Islam and Democracy in the Middle East: The Impact of Religious Orientations on Attitudes toward Democracy in Four Arab Countries." *Comparative Politics* 34 (3): 337–354.

Tessler, Mark, and Eleanor Gao. 2005. "Gauging Arab Support for Democracy." *Journal of Democracy* 16 (3): 83–97.

Tessler, Mark, and Amaney A. Jamal. 2006. "Political Attitude Research in the Arab World: Emerging Opportunities." *PS: Political Science & Politics* 39 (3): 433–437.

Tessler, Mark, Amaney A. Jamal, and Michael Robbins. 2012. "New Findings on Arabs and Democracy." *Journal of Democracy* 23 (4): 89–103.

Wegner, Eva. 2011. *Islamist Opposition in Authoritarian Regimes.* Syracuse, NY: Syracuse University Press.

Wegner, Eva, and Francesco Cavatorta. 2016. "Are Party-Voter Linkages in the Middle East and North Africa Only Clientelistic?" Paper presented at the Annual Meeting of the Midwest Political Science Association, Chicago, April 7–10.

Chapter 17

Benstead, Lindsay J. 2014a. "Does Interviewer Religious Dress Affect Survey Responses? Evidence from Morocco." *Politics and Religion* 7 (4): 734–760.

———. 2014b. "Effects of Interviewer-Respondent Gender Interaction on Attitudes toward Women and Politics: Findings from Morocco." *International Journal of Public Opinion Research* 26 (3): 369–383.

Benstead, Lindsay J., Amaney A. Jamal, and Ellen Lust. 2015. "Is It Gender, Religiosity or Both? A Role Congruity Theory of Candidate Electability in Transitional Tunisia." *Perspectives on Politics* 13 (1): 74–94.

Blaydes, Lisa, and Rachel M. Gillum. 2013. "Religiosity-of-Interviewer Effects: Assessing the Impact of Veiled Enumerators on Survey Response in Egypt." *Politics and Religion* 6 (3): 459–482.

Brooke, Steven. 2017a. "Sectarianism and Social Conformity: Evidence from Egypt." *Political Research Quarterly* 70 (4): 848–860.

Brooke, Steven. 2017b. "From Medicine to Mobilization: Social Service Provision and the Islamist Political Advantage." *Perspectives on Politics* 15 (1): 42–61.

Bush, Sarah, and Amaney A. Jamal. 2015. "Anti-Americanism, Authoritarian Politics, and Attitudes about Women's Representation: Evidence from a Survey Experiment in Jordan." *International Studies Quarterly* 59 (1): 34–45.

Cammett, Melani. 2014. *Compassionate Communalism: Welfare and Sectarianism in Lebanon.* Ithaca, NY: Cornell University Press.

Cilliers, Jacobus, Oeindrila Dube, and Bilal Siddiqi. 2015. "The White Man Effect: How Foreigner Presence Affects Behavior in Experiments." *Journal of Economic Behavior and Organization* 118: 397–414.

Corstange, Daniel. 2016. *The Price of a Vote in the Middle East: Ethnicity and Clientelism.* New York: Cambridge University Press.

Druckman, James N., Donald P. Green, James H. Kuklinski, and Arthur Lupia, eds. 2011a. *Cambridge Handbook of Experimental Political Science.* New York: Cambridge University Press.

———. 2011b. "Experimentation in Political Science." In *Cambridge Handbook of Experimental Political Science,* ed. James N. Druckman, Donald P. Green, James H. Kuklinski, and Arthur Lupia, 3–14. New York: Cambridge University Press.

———. 2011c. "Experiments: An Introduction to Core Concepts." In *Cambridge Handbook of Experimental Political Science,* ed. James N. Druckman, Donald P. Green, James H. Kuklinski, and Arthur Lupia, 15–26. New York: Cambridge University Press.

Gaines, Brian J., James H. Kuklinski, and Paul J. Kirk. 2007. "The Logic of the Survey Experiment Reexamined." *Political Analysis* 15 (1): 1–20.

Glynn, Adam N. 2013. "What Can We Learn with Statistical Truth Serum? Design and Analysis of the List Experiment." *Public Opinion Quarterly* 80 (2): 159–172.

Holbrook, Allyson L., Melanie C. Green, and John A. Crosnick. 2003. "Telephone versus Face-to-Face Interviewing of National Probability Samples with Long Questionnaires: Comparisons of Respondent Satisficing and Social Desirability Response Bias." *Public Opinion Quarterly* 80 (3): 79–125.

Kane, James G., Stephen C. Craig, and Kenneth D. Wald. 2004. "Religion and Presidential Politics in Florida: A List Experiment." *Social Science Quarterly* 85 (2): 281–293.

Kramon, Eric, and Keith R. Weghorst. 2012. "Measuring Sensitive Attitudes in Developing Countries: Lessons from Implementing the List Experiment." *The Experimental Political Scientist* (Newsletter of the APSA Experimental Section) 3 (2): 14–24.

Kuklinski, James H., Michael D. Cobb, and Martin Gilens. 1997. "Racial Attitudes and the 'New South.'" *Journal of Politics* 59 (2): 323–349.

Kuklinski, James H., Paul M. Sniderman, Kathleen Knight, Thomas Piazza, Philip E. Tetlock, Gordon R. Lawrence, and Barbara Mellers. 1997. "Racial Prejudice and Attitudes toward Affirmative Action." *American Journal of Political Science* 41 (2): 402–419.

Kosinski, Michal, Sandra C. Matz, Samuel D. Gosling, Vesselin Popov, and David Stillwell. 2015. "Facebook as a Research Tool for the Social Sciences." *American Psychologist* 70 (6): 543–556.

Lawrence, Adria. 2017. "Repression and Activism among the Arab Spring's First Movers: Evidence from Morocco's February 20th Movement." *British Journal of Political Science* 47 (3): 699–718.

Lijphart, Arend. 1971. "Comparative Politics and the Comparative Method." *American Political Science Review* 65 (3): 682–693.

Lyall, Jason, Yuki Shiraito, and Kosuke Imai. 2015. "Coethnic Bias and Wartime Informing." *Journal of Politics* 77 (3): 833–848.

Masoud, Tarek, Amaney A. Jamal, and Elizabeth Nugent. 2016. "Arab Responses to Western Hegemony: Experimental Evidence from Egypt." *Journal of Conflict Resolution.* https://doi.org/10.1177%2F0022002716648738.

Morton, Rebecca B., and Kenneth C. Williams. 2010. *Experimental Political Science and the Study of Causality: From Nature to the Lab.* New York: Cambridge University Press.

Mutz, Diana C. 2011. *Population-Based Survey Experiments.* Princeton, NJ: Princeton University Press.

Robbins, Michael B., and Noble Kuriakose. 2016. "Don't Get Duped: Fraud through Duplication in Public Opinion Surveys." *Statistical Journal of the IAOS* 32 (3): 283–291.

Rosenfeld, Bryn, Kosuke Imai, and Jacob N. Shapiro. 2016. "An Empirical Validation Study of Popular Survey Methodologies for Sensitive Questions." *American Journal of Political Science* 60 (3): 783–802.

Shadish, William R., Thomas D. Cook, and Donald T. Campbell. 2002. *Experimental and Quasi-Experimental Designs for Generalized Causal Inference.* Boston: Houghton-Mifflin.

Chapter 18

Alterman, Jon. 1998. "New Media New Politics? From Satellite Television to the Internet in the Arab World." Policy Paper No. 48, Washington Institute for Near East Policy.

Boyd, Douglas. 1999. *Broadcasting in the Arab World: A Survey of Electronic Media in the Middle East.* Ames: Iowa State University Press.

Hine, Christine. 2000. *Virtual Ethnography.* London: Sage.

Howard, Philip, and Muzzamil Hussain. 2013. *Democracy's Fourth Wave? Digital Media and the Arab Spring.* Oxford: Oxford University Press.

Iskander, Elizabeth. 2009. "Coptic Media Spaces." Paper presented at workshop of Middle Eastern Christians Network, February 9, University of Stirling, UK.

———. 2011. "Connecting the National and the Virtual: Can Facebook Activism remain Relevant after Egypt's January 25 Uprising?" *International Journal of Communications* 5: 1225–1237.

———. 2012a. *Sectarian Conflict in Egypt: Coptic Media, Discourse and Representation.* London: Routledge.

———. 2012b. "The 'Mediation' of Muslim-Christian Relations in Egypt: The Strategies and Discourses of the Official Press during Mubarak's Presidency." *Journal of Islam and Christian-Muslim Relations* 23 (1): 31–44.

Jones, Steve, ed. 1999. *Doing Internet Research.* London: Sage.

Kaplowitz, Michael, Timothy Hadlock, and Ralph Levine. 2004. "A Comparison of Web and Mail Survey Response Rates." *Public Opinion Quarterly* 68 (1): 94–101.

Kendall, Lori. 1999. "Recontextualising Cyberspace: Methodological Considerations for Online Researchers." In *Doing Internet Research*, ed. Steve Jones, 55–75. London: Sage.

Khamis, Sahar, and Katherine Vaughn. 2012. "We Are All Khaled Said': The Potentials and Limitations of Cyberactivism in Triggering Public Mobilization and Promoting Political Change." *Journal of Arab & Muslim Media Research* 4 (2–3): 145–163.

King, Storm. 1996. "Researching Internet Communities: Proposed Ethical Guidelines for the Reporting of Results." *Information Society* 12 (2): 119–128.

Mann, Chris, and Fiona Stewart. 2000. *Internet Communication and Qualitative Research*. London: Sage.

Mann, Stewart, 2000. *Internet Communication and Qualitative Research*. London: Sage.

McCallum, Fiona. 2010. *Christian Religious Leadership in the Middle East*. Lewiston, NY: Edwin Mellen Press.

Miller, Daniel, and Don Slater, 2000. *The Internet: An Ethnographic Approach*. Oxford: Berg.

Monier, Elizabeth. 2012. "The Arab Spring and Coptic-Muslim Relations: From Mubarak to the Muslim Brotherhood." *European Yearbook of Minority Issues* 11: 169–186.

Phillips, D. 1996. "Defending the Boundaries: Identifying and Countering Threats in a Usenet group." The Information Society 21 (1): 39–62.

Reid, Elizabeth. 1996. "Informal Consent in the Study of On-line Communities: A Reflection on the Effects of Computer-Mediated Social Research." *Information Society* 12 (2): 169–174.

Silverman, David. 2001. *Interpreting Qualitative Data*. 2nd ed. London: Sage.

Tadros, Mariz. 2013. *Copts at the Crossroads: The Challenges of Building Inclusive Democracy in Egypt*. Cairo: American University in Cairo Press.

Talbot, Mary. 2007. *Media Discourse: Representation and Interaction*. Edinburgh: Edinburgh University Press.

Wallace, Patricia. 1999. *The Psychology of the Internet*. New York: Cambridge University Press.

Chapter 19

Al Najjar, Ghanim. 2000. "The Challenges Facing Kuwaiti Democracy." *Middle East Journal* 54 (2): 242–258.

Al-Nakib, Farah. 2014. "Revisiting Hadar and Badu in Kuwait: Citizenship, Housing, and the Construction of a Dichotomy." *International Journal of Middle East Studies* 46 (1): 5–30.

Beinin, Joel, and Frederic Vairel. 2013. *Social Movements, Mobilization, and Contestation in the Middle East and North Africa*. Stanford, CA: Stanford University Press.

Borgatti, Steve, and Daniel Halgin. 2011. "On Network Theory." *Organization Science* 22 (5): 1168–1181.

Burt, Ronald. 1995. *Structural Holes: The Social Structure of Competition*. Cambridge, MA: Harvard University Press.

Crystal, Jill. 1989. "Coalitions in Oil Monarchies: Kuwait and Qatar." *Comparative Politics* 21 (4): 427–443.

Dahlberg, Lincoln. 2007. "Rethinking the Fragmentation of the Cyberpublic: From Consensus to Contestation." *New Media & Society* 9 (5): 827–847.

Diamond, Larry 2010. "Liberation Technologies." *Journal of Democracy* 21(3): 69–83.

Della Porta, Donatella. 2012. "Communication in Movement: Social Movements as Agents of Participatory Democracy." In *Social Media and Democracy Innovations in Participatory Politics*, ed. Brian D. Loader and Dan Mercea, 800–819. New York: Routledge.

Eltantawy, Nahed, and Julie Wiest. 2011. "Social Media in the Egyptian Revolution: Reconsidering Resource Mobilization Theory." *International Journal of Communication* 5: 1207–1224.

Everett, A. 2006. "The Revolution Will Be digitized." *Visual Culture* 3 (244): 129–130.

Gamson, William. 2004. "Bystanders, Public Opinion and the Media." In *The Blackwell Companion to Social Movements*, ed. David Snow, Sarah Soule, and Hanspeter Kriesi, 242–261. Malden, MA: Blackwell.

Ghabra, Shafeeq. 1997. "Balancing State and Society: The Islamic Movement in Kuwait." *Middle East Policy* 5 (2): 58–72.

Granovetter, Mark. 1973. "The Strength of Weak Ties." *American Journal of Sociology* 78 (6): 1360–1380.

Hagagy, Ahmed. 2012. "Police in Kuwait Teargas Opposition Protesters." Reuters, October 21. http://www.reuters.com/article/us-kuwait-politics-protest-idUSBRE89K0FJ20121021.

Honari, Ali. 2013. "From Virtual to Tangible Social Movements in Iran." In *Civil Society in Syria and Iran: Activism in Authoritarian Contexts*, ed. Paul Aarts and Francesco Cavatorta, 143–167. Boulder, CO: Lynne Rienner.

Java, Akshay, Xiaodan Song, Tim Finin, and Belle Tseng. 2007. "Why We Twitter: Understanding Microblogging Usage and Communities." In *Proceedings of the 9th WebKDD and 1st SNA-KDD 2007 Workshop on Web Mining and Social Network Analysis, Baltimore, MD, August 12*, 55–65. New York: Springer.

Kareem, Mona. 2013a. "Kuwait Cracks Down on Dissent, Twitter." *Al Monitor*, January 25. http://www.al-monitor.com/pulse/originals/2013/01/kuwait-war-twitter.html# ixz z2JDoKp6oh.

———. 2013b. "Kuwait: Between Sectarianism and Revolution." In "What Does the Gulf Think about the Arab Awakening?" European Council on Foreign Relations, April. http://www.ecfr. eu/page/-/ECFR75_GULF_ANALYSIS_AW.pdf.

Lim, Chaeyoon. 2008. "Social Networks and Political Participation: How Do Networks Matter?" *Social Forces* 87 (2): 961–982.

Longva, Anh Nga 2006. "Nationalism in Pre-modern Guise: The Discourse on Hadhar and Bedu in Kuwait." *International Journal of Middle East Studies* 38 (2): 171–187.

Margolis, Michael, and David Resnick. 2000. *Politics as Usual: The Cyberspace Revolution*. London: Sage.

Marmura, Stephen. 2008. "A Net Advantage? The Internet, Grassroots Activism and American Middle-Eastern Policy." *New Media & Society* 10 (2): 247–271.

Martin, Geoffrey. 2013. "Instrument or Structure? Investigating the Potential Uses of Twitter in Kuwait." MA thesis, Department of Political Science, University of Guelph. https://atrium2. lib.uoguelph.ca/xmlui/bitstream/handle/10214/6676/Martin_Geoff_201305_MA.pdf?se quence=1&isAllowed=y.

McAdam, Doug. 1995. "'Initiator' and 'Spin-off' Movements: Diffusion Processes in Protest Cycles." In *Repertoires and Cycles of Collective Action*, ed. Mark Traugott, 217–239. Durham, NC: Duke University Press.

McAdam, Doug, John McCarthy, and Mayer Zald. 1996. *Comparative Perspectives on Social Movements: Political Opportunities*. New York: Cambridge University Press.

McCarthy, John, and Mayer Zald. 1977. "Resource Mobilization and Social Movements: A Partial Theory." *American Journal of Sociology* 82 (6): 1212–1241.

McFaul, Michael. 2007. "Ukraine Imports Democracy: External Influences on the Orange Revolution." *International Security* 32 (2): 45–83.

Morozov, Euvgeny. 2011. *The Net Delusion: The Dark Side of Internet Freedom*. New York: Public Affairs.

Oliver, Pamela, Jorge Cadena-Roa, and Kelley Strawn. 2003. "Emerging Trends in the Study of Protest and Social Movements." *Research in Political Sociology* 12: 213–244.

Plattner, Mark. 2012. "Media and Democracy: The Long View." *Journal of Democracy* 23 (4): 62–73.

Rheingold, Howard. 2003. *Smart Mobs: The Next Social Revolution*. New York: Basic Books.

Salem, Fadi, and Racha Mourtada. 2011. "Arab Social Media Report." Dubai: Dubai School of Government. http://www.dsg.ae/en/asmr3/index.aspx? AspxAuto Detect CookieSupport=1.

Shuai, X., S. Chen, Y. Ding, Y. Sun, J. Busemeyer, and J. Tang, J. 2012. "There Is More than Complex Contagion: An Indirect Influence Analysis on Twitter." In *Proceedings of the ACM Workshop on Mining Data Semantics*, August, 4. ACM: New York.

Snow, David. 2004. "Framing Processes, Ideology and Discursive Fields." In *The Blackwell Companion to Social Movements*, ed. David Snow, Sarah Soule, and Hanspeter Kriesi, 380–412. Malden, MA: Blackwell.

Snow, David, and Robert D. Benford. 1988. "Ideology, Frame Resonance, and Participant Mobilization." *International Social Movement Research* 1 (1): 197–217.

Soule, Sarah. 2004. "Diffusion Processes within and across Movements." In *The Blackwell Companion to Social Movements*, ed. David Snow, Sarah Soule, and Hanspeter Kriesi, 94–310. Malden, MA: Blackwell.

Takhteyev, Y., A. Gruzd, and B. Wellman. 2012. Geography of Twitter Networks." *Social Networks* 34 (1): 73–81.

Tarrow, Sidney. 1998. *Power in Movement: Social Movements, Collective Action and Politics*. Cambridge: Cambridge University Press.

Tilly, Charles. 2004. "Observations of Social Processes and Their Formal Representations." *Sociological Theory* 22 (4): 595–602.

Van Laer, Jeroen. 2010. "Activists Online and Offline: The Internet as an Information Channel for Protest Demonstrations." *Mobilization* 15 (3): 347–366.

Vieweg, Sarah, Amanda Hughes, Kate Starbird, and Leysia Palen. 2010. "Microblogging during Two Natural Hazards Events: What Twitter May Contribute to Situational Awareness." In *Proceedings of the 28th International Conference on Human Factors in Computing Systems, Boulder, CO, April 10*, 1079–1088. New York: ACM.

Wiktorowicz, Quintan. 2004. *Islamic Activism: A Social Movement Theory Approach*. Bloomington: Indiana University Press.

Yom, Sean, and F. Gregory Gause III. 2012. "Resilient Royals: How Arab Monarchies Hang On." *Journal of Democracy* 23 (4): 74–88.

Zheng, Yongnian, and Guoguang Wu. 2005. "Information Technology, Public Space, and Collective Action in China." *Comparative Political Studies* 38 (5): 507–536.

Chapter 20

Brown, Nathan. 2014. "No Bureaucratic Pain, No Ethical Gain." In *The Ethics of Research in the Middle East*, POMEPS Studies 8, July 2, 13–14. Washington, DC: Project on Middle East Political Science, George Washington University.

Carapico, Sheila. 2006. "No Easy Answers: The Ethics of Field Research in the Arab World." *PS: Political Science & Politics* 39 (3): 429–431.

Clark, Janine. 2006. "Field Research Methods in the Middle East." *PS: Political Science & Politics* 39 (3): 417–424.

Dolnik, Adam. 2013. "Up Close and Personal: Conducting Field Research on Terrorism in Conflict Zones." In *Conducting Terrorism Field Research: A Guide*, ed. Adam Dolnik, 224–250. New York: Routledge.

Friedrichs, Jörg, and Friedrich Kratochwil. 2009. "On Acting and Knowing: How Pragmatism Can Advance International Relations Research and Methodology." *International Organization* 63 (4): 701–730.

Fujii, Le. 2012. "Research Ethics 101: Dilemmas and Responsibilities." *PS: Political Science & Politics* 45 (4): 717–723.

Guillemin, Marilys, and Lynn Gillam. 2004. "Ethics, Reflexivity, and 'Ethically Important Moments' in Research." *Qualitative Inquiry* 10 (2): 261–280.

Kenney, Michael. 2013. "Learning from the "Dark Side": Identifying, Accessing and Interviewing Illicit Non-state Actors." In *Conducting Terrorism Field Research: A Guide*, ed. Adam Dolnik, 26–45. New York: Routledge.

Knights, Michael. 2013. "Conducting Field Research on Terrorism in Iraq." In *Conducting Terrorism Field Research: A Guide*, ed. Adam Dolnik, 103–123. New York: Routledge.

Maier, Shana L., and Brian A. Monahan. 2010. "How Close Is Too Close? Balancing Closeness and Detachment in Qualitative Research." *Deviant Behavior* 31 (1): 1–32.

Project on Middle East Political Science. 2014. *The Ethics of Research in the Middle East*. POMEPS Studies 8. Washington, DC: Project on Middle East Political Science, George Washington University.

Schwartz-Shea, Peregrine, and Dvora Yanow. 2012. *Interpretive Research Design: Concepts and Processes*. New York: Routledge.

Schwedler, Jillian. 2014. "Towards Transparency in the Ethics of Knowledge Production." In *The Ethics of Research in the Middle East*, POMEPS Studies 8, July 2, 21–24. Washington, DC: Project on Middle East Political Science, George Washington University.

Tetlock, Philip. 2005. *Expert Political Judgment: How Good Is It? How Can We Know?* Princeton, NJ: Princeton University Press.

Yanow, Dvora, and Peregrine Schwartz-Shea. 2008. "Reforming Institutional Review Board Policy: Issues in Implementation and Field Research." *PS: Political Science & Politics* 41 (3): 483–494.

———. 2014. "Encountering Your IRB: What Political Scientists Need to Know." *Qualitative & Multi-method Research* 12 (2): 34–40.

Chapter 21

Allina-Pisano, Jessica. 2009. "How to Tell an Axe Murderer: An Essay on Ethnography, Truth, and Lies." In *Political Ethnography: What Immersion Contributes to the Study of Power*, ed. Edward Schatz. Chicago: University of Chicago Press.

Carapico, Sheila. 2006. "No Easy Answers: The Ethics of Field Research in the Arab World." *PS: Political Science & Politics* 39 (3): 429–431.

Geertz, Clifford. 1983. "'From the Native's Perspective': On the Nature of Anthropological Understanding." In *Local Knowledge: Further Essays on Interpretive Anthropology*. New York: Basic Books.

Herod, Andrew. 1999. "Reflections on Interviewing Foreign Elites: Praxis, Positionality, Validity, and the Cult of the Insider." *Geoforum* 30: 313–327.

Katz, Cindi. 1994. "Playing the Field: Questions of Fieldwork in Geography." *Professional Geographer* 41 (1): 67–72.

Kingston, Paul. 2001. "Patrons, Clients and Civil Society: A Case Study of Environmental Politics in Postwar Lebanon." *Arab Studies Quarterly* 23 (1): 552–572.

———. 2013. *Reproducing Sectarianism: Advocacy Networks and the Politics of Civil Society in Postwar Lebanon*. Albany: State University of New York Press.

Leenders, Reinoud. 2012. *Spoils of Truce: Corruption and Politics in Postwar Lebanon*. Ithaca, NY: Cornell University Press.

Mullings, Beverley. 1999. "Insider or Outsider, Both or Neither? Some Dilemmas of Interviewing in a Cross-Cultural Setting." *Geoforum* 30: 337–350.

Schatz, Edward. 2009. "Introduction." In *Political Ethnography: What Immersion Contributes to the Study of Power*, ed. Edward Schatz. Chicago: University of Chicago Press, 2009.

Shakespeare, Tom. 2006. *Disability Rights and Wrongs*. New York: Routledge.

Chapter 22

Ben Shitrit, Lihi. 2015. *Righteous Transgressions: Women's Activism on the Israeli and Palestinian Religious Right*. Princeton, NJ: Princeton University Press.

Cho, Sumi, Kimberlé Williams Crenshaw, and Leslie McCall. 2013. "Toward a Field of Intersectionality Studies: Theory, Applications, and Praxis." *Signs* 38 (4): 785–810.

Dahan-Kalev, Henriette. 2001. "Tensions in Israeli Feminism: The Mizrahi Ashkenazi Rift." *Women's Studies International Forum* 24 (6): 1–16.

Hancock, Ange-Marie. 2007. "When Multiplication Doesn't Equal Quick Addition: Examining Intersectionality as a Research Paradigm." *Perspectives on Politics* 5 (1): 63–79.

———. 2016. *Intersectionality: An Intellectual History*. Oxford: Oxford University Press.

Hassan, Manar. 2005. "Growing Up Female and Palestinian in Israel." In *Israeli Women's Studies: A Reader*, ed. Esther Fuchs. New Brunswick, NJ: Rutgers University Press.

Kanaaneh, Rhoda. 2002. *Birthing the Nation: Strategies of Palestinian Women in Israel*. Berkeley: University of California Press.

King, Gary, Robert O. Keohane, and Sidney Verba. 1994. *Designing Social Inquiry: Scientific Inference in Qualitative Research*. Princeton, NJ: Princeton University Press.

Motzafi-Haller, Pnina. 2001. "Scholarship, Identity, and Power: Mizrahi Women in Israel." *Signs* 26 (3): 697–734.

Omer, Atalia. 2017. "*Hitmazrehut* or Becoming of the East: Re-orienting Israeli Social Mapping." *Critical Sociology* 43 (6): 949–976.

Robinson, Shira. 2013. *Citizen Strangers: Palestinians and the Birth of Israel's Liberal Settler State*. Stanford, CA: Stanford University Press.

Sa'ar, Amalia. 2007. "Contradictory Location: Assessing the Position of Palestinian Women Citizens of Israel." *Journal of Middle East Women's Studies* 3 (3): 45–74.

Shalhoub-Kevorkian, Nadera. 2012. "The Grammar of Rights in Colonial Contexts: The Case of Palestinian Women in Israel." *Middle East Law and Governance* 4 (1): 106–151.

Shenhav, Yehouda A. 2006. *The Arab Jews: A Postcolonial Reading of Nationalism, Religion, and Ethnicity*. Stanford, CA: Stanford University Press.

Shohat, Ella. 1988. "Sephardim in Israel: Zionism from the Standpoint of Its Jewish Victims." *Social Text* 19–20: 39–68.

Chapter 23

Abels, Gabriele. 1993. "Zur Bedeutung des Female-Stream für die Methodendiskussion in den Sozialwissenschaften." *Soziologie* 1: 6–17.

Abu-Lughod, Lila. 1998. "Fieldwork of a Dutiful Daughter." In *Arab Women in the Field: Studying Your Own Society*, ed. Soraya Altorki and Camillia El-Solh, 139–161. Syracuse, NY: Syracuse University Press.

Al-Ali, Nadje, and Heba El-Kholy. 1999. "Inside/Out: The 'Native' and the 'Halfie' Unsettled." *Cairo Papers in Social Science* 22 (2): 14–38.

Alcadipani, Rafael, and Damia Hodgson. 2009. "By Any Means Necessary? Ethnographic Access, Ethics and the Critical Researcher." *TAMARA: Journal of Critical Postmodern Organization Science* 7 (3/4): 127–146.

Altorki, Soraya. 1988. "At Home in the Field." In *Arab Women in the Field: Studying Your Own Society*, ed. Soraya Altorki and Camillia El-Solh, 49–68. Syracuse, NY: Syracuse University Press.

Altorki, Soraya, and Camillia El-Solh. 1988. "Introduction." In *Arab Women in the Field. Studying Your Own Society*, ed. Soraya Altorki and Camillia El-Solh, 1–23. Syracuse, NY: Syracuse University Press.

Bayard de Volo, Lorraine, and Edward Schatz. 2004. "From the Inside Out: Ethnographic Methods in Political Research." *PS: Political Science & Politics* 37 (2): 267–271.

Cerwonka, Allaine. 2007. "Nervous Conditions: The Stakes in Interdisciplinary Research." In *Improvising Theory: Process and Temporality in Ethnographic Fieldwork*, ed. Allaine Cerwonka and Liisa Malkki, 1–40. Chicago: University of Chicago Press.

Clifford, James, and Marcus George. 1986. *Writing Culture: The Poetics and Politics of Ethnography*. Berkeley: University of California Press.

Coffey, Amanda. 1999. *The Ethnographic Self: Fieldwork and the Representation of Identity*. London: Sage.

Floyd, Alan, and Linet Arthur. 2012. "Researching from Within: External and Internal Ethical Engagement." *International Journal of Research & Method in Education* 35 (2): 171–180.

Harders, Cilja. *Staatsanalyse von unten: Urbane Armut und politische Partizipation in Kairo*. Hamburg: Deutsches Orient Institut, 2002.

Harding, Sandra. 1991. *Whose Science? Whose Knowledge? Thinking from Women's Life*. Ithaca, NY: Cornell University Press.

Hartsock, Nancy. 1999. *The Feminist Standpoint Revisited and Other Essays.* Boulder, CO: Basic Books.

Joseph, Suad. 1988. "Feminization, Familism, Self, and Politics." In *Arab Women in the Field: Studying Your Own Society*, ed. Soraya Altorki and Camillia El-Solh, 25–47. Syracuse, NY: Syracuse University Press.

Kanaaneh, Moslih. 1997. "Indigenous Anthropology: Theory and Praxis." *Dialectical Anthopology* 22 (1): 1–21.

Karim, Wazir Jahan. 1993. "Epilogue: The 'Nativised' Self and the 'Native.'" In *Gendered Fields: Women, Men and Ethnography*, ed. Pat Bell, Karim Caplan, and Wazir Jahan, 248–251. London: Routledge.

Kempny, Marta. 2012. "Rethinking Native Anthropology: Migration and Auto-Ethnography in the Post-accession Europe." *International Review of Social Research* 2 (2): 39–52.

Lenner, Katharina. 2014: "Policy-Shaping and Its Limits: The Politics of Poverty Alleviation and Local Development in Jordan." PhD diss., Freie University Berlin.

Merton, Robert. 1972. "Insiders and Outsiders: A Chapter in the Sociology of Knowledge." *American Journal of Sociology* 7 (1): 9–47.

Narayan, Kirin. 1993. "How Native Is a 'Native'Anthropologist?" *American Anthropologist*, new series 95 (3): 671–686.

Okely, Judith. 1996. *Own or Other Cultures.* London: Routledge.

Rabinow, Paul. 1977. *Reflections on Fieldwork in Morocco.* Berkeley: University of California Press.

Robbins, Joel, and Sandra Bamford. 1997. "Fieldwork Revisited: Changing Contexts of Ethnographic Practice in the Era of Globalization." *Anthropology and Humanism* 22 (1): 3–5.

Shami, Seteny. 1988. "The Complexities of a Shared Culture." In *Arab Women in the Field: Studying Your Own Society*, ed. Soraya Altorki and Camillia El-Solh, 115–138. Syracuse, NY: Syracuse University Press.

Sherif, Bahira. 2001. "The Ambiguity of Boundaries in the Fieldwork Experience: Establishing Rapport and Negotiating Insider/Outsider Status." *Qualitative Inquiry* 7 (4): 436–447.

Van Ginkel, Rob. 1998. "The Repatriation of Anthropology: Some Observation on Endo-Ethnography." *Anthropology & Medicine* 5 (3): 251–267.

Wedeen, Lisa. 2010. "Reflections on Ethnographic Work in Political Science." *Annual Review of Political Science* 13: 255–272.

INDEX

abductive reasoning, 13, 169, 170
activists, 6, 7, 12, 13, 26, 28, 37, 40, 42, 43, 85–93,
    101, 118, 125, 128, 136, 138, 139, 143, 173,
    176–181, 183–185, 189, 218–230, 233, 236,
    238, 239, 254–259, 261, 263
administrative data, 10, 187, 188, 191, 192, 195
Algeria, 136, 138, 188, 195
al-Banna, Hassan, 193
Al-Qaeda, 133
Amal, 77, 78
Arab Spring (uprisings/revolts), 2, 7, 66, 188, 195,
    207, 208, 209, 218, 219, 239
authoritarianism, 6, 7, 9, 36, 37, 46, 47, 49, 55, 60,
    61, 175, 195, 206, 207
automated text analysis, 187, 188, 192

Bahrain, 219, 220
Boko Haram, 133

Cairo, 31, 66, 83, 87, 88, 97, 99, 101, 113, 154,
    161, 171, 172, 191, 199, 236
case selection, 158, 222
categorization, 38, 175, 178–180
causal graphs, 162, 163
causal inference, 19, 129, 154, 159–163, 198,
    202, 206
causality, 159, 187, 218, 230, 251
class (social), 25, 49, 57, 61, 78, 95, 98, 131, 160,
    161, 182, 189, 192, 199, 244, 249, 254–257,
    259, 260, 266
coding, 10, 85, 87, 175, 178, 180–186, 192, 193,
    196, 212, 218
confidentiality, 3, 18, 49, 110, 119, 212, 214, 216,
    235, 237, 272
content analysis, 218, 224

control variable, 156, 257
Copts, 176–178, 211–214
counterrevolution, 84, 85, 90, 91, 94
cross case comparisons, 19, 155, 159

data collection, 27, 100, 103, 216, 265
data protection, 3, 69
democracy, 157, 158, 188, 189
    sectarian democracy, 244
dependent variable, 129, 151, 160
development (economic), 66, 70, 98, 103, 104,
    154, 155, 157, 158, 191

economic liberalization, 104
Egypt, 2–4, 12, 13, 16, 18, 63, 67, 69, 83–99,
    101–105, 109, 116, 145, 149, 154, 171,
    175–179, 181, 185, 188, 190–192, 195,
    197, 202–204, 209, 210, 213, 214, 220,
    235–238, 255
elections, 8, 176, 190, 192, 195, 197, 205, 239,
    269, 271, 272
elites, 7, 102, 109, 111, 112, 118, 157, 160,
    161, 187
empirical research, 139
ethics, 6, 17–19, 25, 40, 41, 75, 81, 96, 101, 102,
    109, 122–125, 130, 171, 233, 234, 237, 240,
    241, 266
ethnography (ethnographic research), 8, 26, 27,
    85, 87, 96, 97, 165, 169, 171–174, 216, 249,
    251, 263–266, 272, 273

Facebook, 11, 27, 68, 73, 74, 87, 90, 198, 208, 209,
    211, 213–217, 220, 221, 238, 239
Fatah, 75, 76, 78, 79